PLOTS AND PARANOIA

PLOTS
AND PARANOIA

*A history of political espionage
in Britain
1790–1988*

Bernard Porter

London
UNWIN HYMAN
Boston   Sydney   Wellington

Published by the Academic Division of
Unwin Hyman Ltd
15/17 Broadwick Street, London W1V 1FP, UK

Unwin Hyman Inc.,
8 Winchester Place, Winchester, Mass. 01890, USA

Allen & Unwin (Australia) Ltd,
8 Napier Street, North Sydney, NSW 2060, Australia

Allen & Unwin (New Zealand) Ltd in association with the
Port Nicholson Press Ltd,
Compusales Building, 75 Ghuznee Street, Wellington 1, New Zealand

First published in 1989

British Library Cataloguing in Publication Data

Porter, Bernard
    Plots and paranoia: a history of political
    espionage in Britain, 1790–1988.
    1. Great Britain. Politics. Role, history of
    espionage
    I. Title
    320.941

    ISBN 0-04-445258-6

Library of Congress Cataloging-in-Publication Data

Porter, Bernard.
    Plots and paranoia : a history of political espionage in Britain,
    1790–1988 / Bernard Porter.
        p.   cm.
    Bibliography: p.
    Includes index.
    ISBN 0-04-445258-6
    1. Police–Great Britain–Political activity–History
2. Political crimes and offenses–Great Britain–History
3. Intelligence service–Political aspects–Great Britain–History
4. Secret service–Political aspects–Great Britain–History
I. Title.

HV8195.A3P67 1989   89-34953
364.1'31–dc20   CIP

Typeset in 10 on 12 point Garamond and printed in Great Britain by
The University Press, Cambridge

Contents

For Deirdre,
Zoë, Ben and Kate

Preface

Domestic espionage is the hidden underside of political history. It may be immensely important. It is possible that without it we would be a very different country from what we are today. We might have a different religion, a different queen, or a different political system. We might be a satellite of a French or German or Russian empire. We could even have a Labour government. All these happy escapes have been credited to Britain's security services at one time or another. Yet historians – who are supposed to tell why things have happened in history – have had almost nothing to say about this side of it at all.

Non-historians have noticed this. 'Secret services', claims Ladislas Farago, a novelist, 'have exerted far greater influence on history than on the historians.' In his opinion, 'Behind every great event, and behind the statesmen who shaped them, stood the spies.'[1] Many historians would dispute the 'statesmen who shaped them' bit too. This may give a clue as to why the secret services have been so neglected. Of course it may all be a plot. History, after all, is usually written by its winners. They may just be being very careful not to let on how they have won. As one of the fraternity of historians myself, however, I am not conscious of this as a motive. What I am conscious of is a reluctance among historians nowadays to believe that important events could have been caused by individual great men and women, rather than by underlying factors: broad impersonal historical forces and the like. If they do not like the idea of great men and women being decisive, they are hardly likely to take kindly to unknown ones determining the way things have turned out. To take an example: one secret service explanation for the outbreak of the First World War shortly afterwards was that it was all due to a plot, which would have been prevented if the Austrian secret service had been more on its toes.[2] This is clearly not good enough, for a profession that has been trained to think that big events must have rather bigger causes than this.

The other main reason for neglect, of course, is the problem of evidence. There are two difficulties here. The first is that there is not enough of it. In many cases there probably never was enough of it, simply because secret agencies do not always write things down. In other instances it has been destroyed, possibly in order to hide things; or is still kept locked away. This applies to most twentieth-century material on MI5 and the Special Branch, which makes the historian's job a particularly frustrating one. The stuff is there, but he cannot get at it. So he cannot come to informed judgements; only guesses, which can be overturned. That is a strong temptation to ignore this area entirely, and concentrate on what seem at any rate to be the much more open faces of history.

The other difficulty compounds this one, but also eases it in a way. The fact is that all evidence in this area is undependable. That means that even if we were able to see the official record, it might not help. It also means that we cannot rely on the evidence we are able to see. The reason for this is that all spies and secret agents are liars, trained in techniques of deception and dissimulation, who are just as likely to fake the historical record as anything else. This is why the first rule for the reader of any book about secret services, including this one, is *not to trust a word of it*. It could all be lies and disinformation; not on the part of the writer necessarily, but on the part of the sources he is gullible enough to believe. That is another deterrent to historians who might be tempted to venture into this area. No one likes to risk being taken for a ride.

But what if it *is* important? What if our present state of national good health (or whatever) really can be attributed to the work of our security services? We may not *want* to believe in the treatment, or trust the doctors administering it; but we cannot ignore entirely the possibility that it could have worked. Besides, if we do we might miss some other significant things. Treatments have side-effects. Sometimes they turn out to be more drastic than the original diseases. That has been true of domestic espionage in Britain at certain times. Secondly, treatments can tell us a great deal about the doctors who prescribe them, and the assumptions and general ethoses of their times. That is also manifestly true in this case. Even if the history of British counter-intelligence were not important in a practical, causal sense – and it may have been that too – it is certainly highly revealing about the societies and polities that relied on it, or did not, as the case might be.

These are my excuses for writing this book. I believe that the subject of it is important in one way or another, and probably both. Britain's counter-intelligence agencies have sometimes been effective: in fighting subversion in a few cases, and assisting it in at least one other (the 'Wilson plot'). They have also done their fair share of 'dirty tricks' throughout their history, and of undermining what today are usually called 'civil liberties'. Most importantly, they mirror their country and their times. They may not mirror them very accurately; indeed, we would get a dreadfully distorted picture of some periods of British history if we judged them only by their reflections in the secret services' glass. On the other hand, you cannot understand anything properly without knowing something of what goes on underneath it. I think I understand nineteenth- and twentieth-century Britain far better now than I did before I embarked on this study. I believe it tells me an awful lot about the mid-Victorians, for example, to know that they had virtually no domestic secret service organization at all; and as much about present-day Britain, and the fundamental difference between her values and the Victorians', to know that she now has easily the largest and probably the most intrusive domestic secret service in the whole of her peacetime history. Those are the serious reasons for reading about this topic. A less serious reason is that it is also – if you do not allow yourself to spoil it by getting too cross – enormous fun.

This book does not pretend to offer authoritative answers to all or even most of the questions raised in it. That is too much to expect in this field. What it tries to do is to review the available evidence in its context, and discuss the possibilities. By 'available evidence' I mean mainly secondary and primary printed sources, except for the Victorian and Edwardian periods, where I have myself done much of the documentary research. By 'context' I mean many things: the situation of the country at various times, the perceptions of people in power, popular attitudes towards 'subversion' and how to counter it generally, the backgrounds of the men who engaged in secret service activities, the likely effect of those activities themselves on their perceptions and attitudes, the degree of their 'accountability' and how *that* is likely to have affected them: and so on. Some of this will be speculative. All of it will be highly sceptical of everyone's claims in this field, and their motives for making them: those of the agencies themselves, and of their critics. Nothing will be taken on trust. All judgements – and there will be some – will be hedged around with caveats. If any do not seem to be, perhaps a general overriding caveat could be taken as read here. It should apply in particular to the final couple of chapters of the book, on very recent times, which are built on foundations which are inherently unstable in any case, and shifting all the time. Some of what I say in them is likely to be superseded by the events which are planned for the nine months that this book will be in the press, including two major Acts of Parliament and a flood of books by other writers, some of them former spies. If there turn out to be mistakes and omissions in the earlier parts of the book – as is highly likely – they will be due to the nature of the subject, carelessness, and perhaps in some cases, though hopefully not too many, prejudice.

I certainly had a number of prejudices when I first approached this field (which was, incidentally, long before the present bandwagon came along). Most of those prejudices were of the conventional liberal sort. Some of them have not changed at all in the course of my studies, but have rather been borne out by them, which I hope means that they should no longer be regarded as prejudices – *pre*-judgments – in the strict sense. I still, for example, deplore the excessive official secrecy which makes research in this area so very difficult, and which as everyone must know by now contrasts unfavourably with nearly every other country in the Western world. If that is a prejudice, then it is a natural and indeed a necessary one for an academic, whose job is to discover the truth about things, in the teeth of officials whose purpose sometimes appears to be the precise opposite. I also still cannot, I am afraid, bring myself to regard spies and informers as honourable people, and could never make friends with one knowingly. That prejudice was boosted slightly recently by a report I read in a newspaper – it may have been mistaken – that an organization calling itself the Campaign for Student Freedom (*sic*) was asking its members to inform secretly on subversive leanings among their lecturers.[3] That chilled me a little. On the other hand I no longer have quite the same feelings about espionage in the abstract that I used to. I do not believe that it always does harm. It can be used to allay panic, and so pre-empt over-reaction, as well as to stoke it up. There are examples of that in the following pages. Francis Bacon, as we shall see, put it best.[4] The more people know, in most circumstances, the less they will fear. That is a good argument for espionage. By the same token, of course, it is an even better argument for the kind of openness in most areas of life that would render espionage less necessary. Another change in my outlook is that I no longer disbelieve in the potency of 'conspiracy' in political affairs quite as much as I once did, perhaps naïvely. Again, openness might be the antidote to that. These are the biases which inform this book: or the ones that I am aware of. I have tried not to let them get too much in the way.

This is not the first book in this general field, or even the first by an academic historian. There are dozens by non-academic writers, most of them with very different prejudices from mine, and some with close secret service connections themselves. (I have no such connections; though of course I might not let on if I did.) One way of telling these is that they often for some odd reason (because it is easy enough to find out who they are) use *noms de plume*. They include 'Richard Deacon' (Donald McCormick), 'Nigel West' (Rupert Allason) and Chapman Pincher, who is one of the few to use a version, at any rate, of his real name. A second group of spy writers who have dabbled in history comprises radical critics, like Tony Bunyan, whose *History and Practice of the Political Police in Britain* (1976) was a real trail-blazer, and Phillip Knightley, whose *Second Oldest Profession* (1986) is one of the two best general histories of the British secret service (foreign as well as domestic) in the twentieth century. The other is the first by an academic historian: Christopher Andrew's *Secret Service: The Making of the British Intelligence Community* (1985), which is masterly and highly entertaining. The debt I owe to it will be evident from the endnotes.

This present book differs from all the others in concentrating on the domestic – British and Irish – side of British domestic secret service history;

having more on earlier periods; and devoting proportionately more space to analysis and speculation – the whys and wherefores – as against narrative description. It starts ages back, as some of the others do as well, with the objects of putting more recent events into some sort of perspective, and correcting some common general misconceptions; but this very early ground is covered (in Chapter 1) at a bit of a gallop, and the book really only gets going seriously in Napoleonic times. It then ploughs steadily forward, faster for some periods than for others, depending on how much domestic secret service activity there was at the time, though never skipping periods entirely for this reason, because the *lack* of such activity is just as interesting and important to account for, I think, as the presence of it; and it comes to a halt as late as I can possibly make it: which is the day on which I finished this Preface, at the very end of 1988.

I have only a few 'Acknowledgements', but they are all important and heartfelt. Christopher Andrew has been a great help, not only through his *Secret Service*, but also with documents (especially the Dancy and Isham material) and in other ways. Professor John Dancy has kindly allowed me to use his father's memoirs. Robin Ramsay has educated me into the 'Wilson plot', and nearly convinced me about it; put me on to an amazing number of sources I would have missed otherwise; and in general been far more generous with his time than one would have imagined my 'naturally conservative breeding' (his phrase, in a review of an earlier book of mine) deserves. I teach an optional course on this sort of thing as part of the final year of the History degree course at my university; the first two batches of students on it have been the best and most enthusiastic I have ever taught, which has been a great encouragement, and have also found out things for me that I did not know. I am sure that none of them belongs to the Campaign for Student Freedom; they are far too nice. The staff of the Brynmor Jones Library at Hull have been enormously helpful, as always, despite the Library's own financial difficulties; as have in smaller ways – because I have not demanded so much of them – the staffs of the British Library, the University Library Cambridge, the National Library of Scotland and the Scottish Record Office. I owe a great deal to my academic collegues at the University of Hull. My publisher, Jane Harris-Matthews at Unwin Hyman, has been a tremendous stimulus and encouragement all through, from the moment I first proposed this project to her nine months ago. Lastly, my wife Deirdre and children Zoë, Ben and Kate have been marvellous. This book is the end-product of a comparatively short and intense bout of writing, which has inevitably had effects on them. I do not want to give the impression that I have been self-indulgently dreadful all the time, but I may have been a little distracted or crabby occasionally, and they have handled it more tolerantly than I probably deserved. Their greatest sacrifice was when they all agreed to fly off to Crete for a fortnight without me, while I wrote Chapter 7. A lot of credit for this book must go to them. On the other hand, if it is not as good as I hoped it might be, they are not to blame.

BERNARD PORTER
Cottingham, East Yorkshire
December 1988

Chapter 1

Sly and subtil fellowes
(4000 BC to AD 1790)

Most histories of espionage begin by describing it as 'the second oldest profession'. One even takes that as its title.[1] It is a clever phrase. By linking espionage with the oldest profession of all – prostitution – it tars it, albeit lightly, with some of the latter's disrepute. It also, of course, makes a point about its age. That point is crucial to many views of secret service work. Most of its defenders insist that it goes back to the earliest beginnings of history. They also maintain that it has been continuous. Every state and every government has resorted to it, since the dawn of time. The implication of this is that espionage is both necessary and 'natural', despite its disreputability. This can be seen both to excuse and to explain it, in a way.

All this may be true. It is important to understand at the outset, however, that there is no *historical* evidence for it. There may be other kinds of evidence. It may for example be possible to argue that espionage *must* have been ancient and continuous, because men and women are made that way. They are naturally curious, distrustful and prone to conspiracy, and so it is fair to assume that they have always indulged in curious, distrustful and conspiratorial acts. This is a somewhat cynical view of human nature, but it may be justified. It is not a view, however, which is derived from history.

History itself – the surviving record of the past – is inconclusive. In fact the earliest reference of all to espionage was a false alarm. This may indicate that imagining or inventing spies is older than the 'profession' itself. The Book of Genesis, chapter 42, describes how Joseph, who was working for the Pharaoh in Egypt at the time, *pretended* to suspect that his brothers had been sent there by the Israelites as spies 'to see the nakedness of the land'

1

when in fact, as he knew full well, they had come to beg for corn. The first reference to espionage proper comes a little later, in the Book of Numbers, where we are told that Moses sent twelve men 'to spy out the land of Canaan', and return with intelligence about its people, products and fortifications. He did this on the direct orders of God, who thus becomes the first spymaster in recorded history. In fact the mission was not entirely successful, with the Israelites divided over how to interpret the intelligence thus obtained. A little later one of Moses' twelve spies, Joshua the son of Nun, sent two of his own men from Shittim to spy in Jericho, where they were soon suspected, however, and spent all their time sheltering in an attic. The attic belonged to Rahab the prostitute, who clearly had a heart of gold when it came to fellow professionals.[2]

The ancient Egyptians may have been better at this sort of thing. But we are unlikely ever to know for sure. They do provide us with one of the first ever accounts of what today would be called a 'covert operation', when a provincial governor called T'hutiy captured the town of Jaffa (then Joppa) by sending in his best warriors concealed in panniers carried by donkeys. This may have been the origin of Ali Baba's Forty Thieves. A man who was clever enough to think that up might well have used spies too. But there is little direct proof of it; and a certain amount of evidence that the Egyptians were, in fact, somewhat naïve in this regard. Around 1400 BC, for example, Amenhotep III was completely gulled by a Hittite double agent, Aziru of Amor, whose brief was to spread disinformation, as well as to spy.[3] The Hittites came from Cappadocia in Asia Minor; and it is from around that area and further east that the first convincing accounts of ancient espionage and intelligence networks come. The masters of these arts were the Babylonians, the Assyrians and the Persians. Around 490 BC Sun Tzü of the Kingdom of Wu in China wrote his celebrated *The Art of War*, which carries a chapter on the importance of military espionage. One of Sun Tzü's training methods was to cut young girls' heads off when they did not do what he told them to.[4] Early espionage was generally associated with this kind of regime.

That may be why it does not feature so prominently in Europe's own slightly gentler ancient traditions. Classical Greek literature features it at one or two points. Book 4 of the *Odyssey*, for example, has Odysseus stealing in and out of Troy disguised as a beggar at the height of the siege. That same siege was also the occasion for the most celebrated covert operation in all history, when Odysseus took Troy by persuading its citizens to wheel in his wooden horse filled with fifth columnists. Later, on his way back from Troy, his skill – or luck – seems to have deserted him. Book 10 of the *Odyssey*, for example, carries an account of a scouting expedition by some of his men in Telepylus, which was aborted when a local chieftain's wife, 'a creature of mountainous proportions', rumbled them and threatened to serve them up to her husband for his supper.[5] That one went badly wrong.

All this evidence is ambivalent, not least because it is entirely mythical. When we come on to less mythical times, however, there is scarcely more to go on. For Greece there is almost nothing. We know that military commanders used scouts to survey the terrain ahead of them, and extracted information from turncoats and prisoners. They also often got help from disloyal factions in enemy cities, who might be described as 'fifth columnists'. Their ambassadors, or *proxenoi*, sometimes doubled as spies.[6] All this was in the realm of foreign intelligence. There may have been some domestic espionage too. One would expect this in Sparta, which was continuously threatened by helot revolts, some of which were nipped in the bud on the basis of 'information received'; but there is no evidence – and it does not necessarily follow – that this information came from spies. Sparta's *krypteia* have been described as a 'secret police' force, but they had no *intelligence* function, and so do not count. (The *krypteia* were young upwardly mobile Spartans sent to hide in the country areas and sally out at night to slaughter any helots they found indiscriminately, in order to terrify them into submission.) A better example may be the Athenian 'sycophants', translated in Brewer's *Dictionary of Phrase and Fable* as 'fig-blabbers', who began by informing on people whom they found exporting figs illegally, and then broadened their operations. Alexander the Great employed agents among his officers and men to sniff out plots against him.[7] So there are some crumbs of evidence. But it does not amount to very much.

The Romans seem to have neglected intelligence almost entirely at first, under the republic. This was apparently because 'the simple, straightforward, unspoiled Roman peasant stock, the basis of the proud Roman race, looked with supreme disdain upon anything which appeared artificial and disingenuous'.[8] (Very much later on English Whig opponents of espionage, with their solid grounding in the classics, made a great deal of this.)[9] It seems to have done the Romans no great harm until the time of the Punic Wars, in which the Carthaginians outwitted them more than once. The Carthaginians had probably learned *their* intelligence skills from their trading links with the East. Those skills included espionage, secret signs and codes, and disinformation. They were nearly Rome's undoing. Some Romans drew the inevitable lesson. Around 200 BC Scipio Africanus, for example, who helped turn the tables on Carthage, used to dress up his soldiers as slaves to spy on the enemy. Once he was nearly found out when a Numidian general thought he recognized one of the 'slaves' as an old boy of his school in Greece. A century later Quintus Sertorius, serving in Roman Gaul which was under threat from neighbouring Teutons, offered to spy on them by 'putting on Celtic dress and acquiring the commonest expressions of that language for such conversation as might be necessary'. Thus prepared, 'he mingled with the barbarians, and after seeing or hearing what was necessary, came back'. But these were unusual enterprises at that time.[10]

Later on, as Rome became more imperial and more corrupt, such practices became less unusual. They also became turned inwards more. Earlier intelligence agencies had been designed mainly for external military purposes: to discover what was being planned among enemies or potential enemies abroad. Sometimes, when those enemies abroad were defeated and incorporated into great empires, they remained potentially subversive, and so needed to be carefully watched. So did the men sent out to govern them, who might – and often did – cultivate provincial power-bases to challenge the central authority from. The favourite counter to this was a corps of loyal functionaries, serving overtly as messengers or inspectors, whose real job was to report back on signs of disloyalty. In many ancient societies they were known as the 'Eyes and Ears of the King'.[11] In some ways they were the equivalents of today's secret or political police.

The Roman Empire used its fire brigade for this purpose, manned by *vigilantes*, as they were called, and charged with looking out for signs of rebellion as well as for fires. It may have got this idea from Egypt.[12] Later on a class of men known as *frumentarii*, because of their origins as grain dealers (*frumentum* = corn), was organized into a wide-ranging imperial intelligence network both in the provinces and in Italy. Epictetus described how they sometimes worked.

> A soldier, dressed like a civilian, sits down by your side, and begins to speak ill of Caesar, and then you too, just as though you had received from him some guarantee of good faith in the fact he began the abuse, tell likewise everything you think, and the next thing is – you are led off to prison in chains.[13]

Later on he would have been called an *agent provocateur*. The *frumentarii* were also used for covert operations, like the spreading of 'black' propaganda, and even assassinations. Apparently Nero employed them to make sure that all his courtiers came to his lyre recitals, and kept awake.[14] They became so unpopular in the third century AD that the Emperor Diocletian abolished them; but then found he missed them too much, and started up another intelligence cadre – the *agentes in rebus* – to take their place. They survived into the Byzantine period, changing their name to *curiosi*, very aptly, around AD 380.[15]

The early Arab and Muslim empires also employed networks of secret police. They were often headed by eunuchs. In early ninth century Baghdad, for example, the Caliph's domestic intelligence agency included 1,700 old women, watching and reporting back to him. In sixteenth-century India the Emperor Akbar used state scavengers, or dustbin men, for the same purpose.[16] They also employed merchants and pedlars. The practice appears to have been widely accepted amongst the Muslims, and even justified. 'Sending out police agents and spies', wrote the eleventh-century Persian Nizam al-Mulk, 'shows that the ruler is just, vigilant, and sagacious.'[17] That was a point of view which finds echoes in some modern societies.

So what does all this tell us? At first glance, not a lot. There is absolutely no proof that espionage is the 'second oldest profession', or anything near it; or that it had an uninterrupted history even in ancient times. Examples can be found of ancient rulers and generals using intelligence-gathering techniques of various kinds, and covert tricks to gain advantages in battles, but only sporadically. A 'profession' is a full-time occupation, which is officially remunerated; and it is surely unlikely that espionage as a 'profession' in this sense predated – for example – flint-knapping, or witch-doctoring, or sooth-saying, or a dozen other vital specialist jobs in the ancient world.

Some classical societies appear to have done without it entirely. Certainly contemporaries looking back from later to earlier periods thought so. Pericles in his Funeral Oration, for example, boasted proudly of how 'open' his city – Athens – had been 'to all the world' in the fifth century BC, so that nothing there was kept hidden even from foreigners. Later on the second century BC historian Polybius wrote of a time in the past when 'states neither used secret weapons nor sought to mislead their foes about time and place of battle', which sounds more like cricket than war. Republican Rome had the special reputation of being free from this kind of thing. 'Rome of old explored the limits of freedom,' wrote Tacitus around AD 100; 'we have plumbed the depths of slavery, robbed even of the interchange of ideas by the secret police.'[18] Such statements *may* indicate that there were gaps in the tradition. They certainly indicate that there was also a *counter*-tradition in ancient times: of opposition to domestic and even military espionage, on moral and civil libertarian grounds.

We do not have to believe Pericles and Polybius and Tacitus. Some present-day historians do not. This is not because they have contrary evidence, but because they simply cannot credit their accounts.[19] One such is the American Francis Dvornik, who published a pioneering general survey of ancient intelligence systems in 1974. His starting-point was the belief that successful ancient polities *must* have had extensive intelligence networks, because it was inconceivable that they could have been successful otherwise. This applied especially, he thought, to regimes which 'neglected the social and economic welfare of their subjects', who would surely have found ways of throwing off their oppressors if the latter had not employed covert means to keep them down. (One might add that Dvornik was originally commissioned to write his book by an ex-head of American intelligence, General 'Wild Bill' Donovan, with the object of demonstrating historically 'the importance of a good intelligence service for the security of our country': but we can let that pass.)[20] Clearly such an interpretation goes beyond what the surviving evidence on its own will bear. But that is not to say that it is inherently unreasonable.

The problem is, of course, that paucity of evidence in this field does not prove a thing. It may well be that intelligence activities in ancient times *were* far more extensive than we can know. The point is that one would expect the evidence to be scanty in any case. Secret agents have to be adept at covering their tracks, which usually means covering them from the eyes of posterity too. Because we cannot find evidence of covert activities at certain periods, it does not mean that those activities did not go on. It *might* mean, on the contrary, that they went on far more cleverly at those times than at others, when they did leave traces for us to find. Alternatively, it might mean that they had thoroughly scared everyone into keeping quiet about them, even in what they wrote. After all, writes one historian, 'to what extent would novelists or historians living in the police states of today discuss their surveillants?'[21] If you believe that espionage is 'natural', or essential to the success of a state, then that is what you will prefer to think. This is a problem that dogs the historian of later days too.

Bearing this in mind, the lessons we can draw from these ancient times must be tentative. Here are some of them. It is likely that some societies abjured covert activities almost entirely – even Dvornik exempts the Roman Republic – and did not suffer unduly from it. That does not necessarily point any moral; they may merely have been lucky in their friends and enemies, or stronger in other ways. Such activities were more common in wartime, as one might expect, and more acceptable then than in peace. Full-time professional espionage agencies were comparatively rare. Intelligence, whether military, foreign, or domestic, was far more often gleaned through other channels entirely – captured prisoners, defectors, occasional informers, gossips, government officials, merchants, diplomats – than from genuine agents or spies. One of the reasons for this may have been the difficulty of passing oneself off as a member of a community which in the ancient world was bound to be far smaller than today, and where consequently strangers stood out more.

The first genuine espionage agencies did not emerge fully fledged, but evolved from organizations which initially had other functions – delivering mails, fighting fires, collecting taxes, distributing grain – which placed them in positions where they could perform this other duty too. For some of these organizations espionage remained a sideline, whereas others (like the *frumentarii*) were entirely taken over by it. So far as foreign espionage is concerned, it seems that expansionist, imperialist states indulged in it oftener than static and pacific ones. Domestic espionage was more likely to be directed against rivals to a ruling faction among the political élite of a state, obviously because that was where most realistic threats came from, than against the lower classes of society. There is scattered evidence of rulers abusing their secret services, and of complaints against this (like

Tacitus's); and a general impression in the late imperial Roman literature, especially, that regimes resorted more to secret agents and policemen the more corrupt and tyrannical they became. There are also hints that some people felt that such activities were unhealthy and corrupting in themselves. 'States', warned Euripides in the fifth century BC, 'whose policy is dark and cautious, have their sight darkened by their carefulness.'[22]

After the fall of the Roman Empire in the West, the best evidence we have of espionage activities comes from its Eastern successor states and their rivals. The Byzantine Empire, for example, posted agents on its borders with both espionage and counter-espionage duties, one of whom (probably a tenth-century character called Basil Pantherios) became the first secret agent super-hero in literature, under the name of 'Digenes Akritas'.[23] The great Asian military empires of Europe's Middle Ages invariably employed spies, to glean information both about the lands they were next intending to conquer, and then – when they had settled down – among their own subjects.[24] We have seen already that the latter was not always regarded as a mark of tyranny in Asia, as it often was in Europe. To some observers, spies were simply a sign that a ruler was taking a proper paternalistic interest in his people, and looking after them thoroughly.

Contemporary western Europe was probably a little behind the East in this regard. In the thirteenth century we find one Italian writer advising Christian rulers to take a lesson from Islam, and use spies more to avoid 'trouble and anxiety', especially in time of war. One barrier to that was the code of chivalry. According to one chivalric treatise, for example, if a herald discovered some enemy plan and then revealed it to his own side, he also had to tell the enemy what he had done, so that no unfair advantage would be gained. By the fourteenth century, however, most such qualms had been overcome. During the Hundred Years War between England and France, military and diplomatic espionage was fully accepted, and indeed common practice.[25]

What we have less evidence of is *domestic* espionage; which may indicate that the evidence has simply not survived, which is likely for this period; or that domestic espionage was not carried on then in any systematic way. The latter is a strong possibility. Proper espionage systems require developed bureaucratic structures to implement them. Feudal Europe, by and large, did not employ bureaucrats, or servants of the state. (The church was an exception, and may therefore be the likeliest place to find an embryo secret service in medieval times.) Secular rulers governed through networks of mutual obligations, and not through an apparatus which could have supported an effective spy system at home. No doubt every emperor and king had his informants and agents among the people, attached to him (he hoped) by bonds of personal loyalty. But that was what they remained: a personal retinue, and not in any sense an apparatus of the state. Before that could come about, the state itself had to be invented; which did not happen in most places until the sixteenth century, or after. Even then, it was some time before anything like an espionage system on the later Roman pattern was seen in Europe again.

It was not seen, for example, in Machiavelli's time. If espionage had been an important activity then, we should surely have heard about it from him. *The Prince* (1513) and the *Discourses* (1512–17) offer practical advice to rulers on how to stay in power, and to rebels on how to topple them; but in neither work is there a single mention of espionage or even counter-espionage as a means. *The Prince*'s advice is that rulers can best protect themselves against conspiracies by being popular. The *Discourses* are pretty scathing on the value of covert operations generally, even in a military context; most conspiracies, claims Machiavelli, fail or are betrayed of their own accord, from which it follows that counter-measures are unnecessary. In *The Art of War* (1521) he suggests that a military commander could take advantage of someone suspected of betraying secrets by supplying him with false information, in order to 'lead the enemy into an error that may possibly end in its destruction'; but there is no suggestion that commanders should take initiatives in this field, and no other mention of military intelligence, apart from the obvious point that it is advisable to send scouts out before marching an army through terrain where there is a danger of ambush.[26] In a way it is surprising that Machiavelli has no more help to offer the intelligence community than this. Unless he was giving his advice on these matters *secretly*, which might be in character, this can only be because the culture of Renaissance Italy was not one in which that particular form of deception was widely known.

Machiavelli missed it, however, by only a few years. The second half of the sixteenth century saw European espionage flourish, both abroad and domestically. We shall meet some English examples later. At the other side of Europe, one of the measures which made Ivan IV seem so Terrible was his creation in 1565 of a new secret political police force, in order to repress any hints of dissent. That body is often taken to mark the origin of the nineteenth-century Okhrana, and of today's KGB.[27] At the same time western Europe's first recognisable proper police force was being founded in France, under Francis I, though it seems to have had no significant political function as yet.[28] During the next century, in other parts of Europe, this was to evolve into a genuine political police.

A political police is a body of men and women whose duty is to keep tabs on the political opinions, activities and intentions of the subjects of a state. In Anglo-Saxon eyes it is usually associated with state tyranny. That may be justified in many cases; but it is also important to be aware that in early modern times there was another possible view of it. In a way it was reminiscent of Nizam al-Mulk's way of looking at the Persian secret police. It arose out of divergent French and English notions of the relationship between liberty and the state. For the English, liberty was something that had to be protected *against* the state. For the French, it should be guaranteed *by* the state. The state had a crucial positive role to play in securing the welfare of everyone within its bounds. This was the purpose of its laws, its regulations and the people who enforced the regulations: including the police. Regulations were essential. The more of them there were, and consequently the more policemen, the more it showed that the government cared.

Louis XIV was, in this sense, the most 'caring' of France's kings. His Paris police, under a new post of *lieutenant-général* created in 1667, took almost the whole city in hand. Among the *lieutenant*'s functions were supervising the street lighting, controlling the traffic, cleaning the streets, regulating the food supplies, collecting refuse, administering the *bourse* and monitoring the brothels. On top of all this he ran an extensive espionage system, which was supposed to penetrate 'all levels of society'. Whether it can be called a *political* espionage system is doubtful. Apparently it concerned itself primarily with personal matters, in order to 'suppress private disorders, lest they should spread and give rise to scandal'. Political dissent did not come into it. That was why 1789 caught the French police so badly prepared.[29] Later on, as we shall see, they made amends. But in the meantime the Paris system (or something like it) spread to Prussia, where the name 'police state' (*Polizeistaat*) was coined for it; and to the Austrian Empire of Joseph II (1741–90), where for the first time it took on an unambiguously political role.

Joseph's secret police was directly administered by him, and generously funded. It worked through carefully selected police agents who in their turn recruited informers from every walk of life, especially servants. The object was to keep the closest possible watch on anyone who might conceivably pose a political threat: government officials, army officers, clergy, secret societies, political clubs, and so on. It was far more intrusive than the French system, and remained so – apart from during the revolutionary years – well into the nineteenth century. It was probably well meaning. Joseph's object was not to 'tyrannize his people', but to protect them. He wished, as one historian has put it,

> to free them, by supervision, of the danger of falling prey to agitators, demagogues and revolutionaries. He wished to free them from their slavery of ignorance, ingenuousness and immaturity; and to do so he put them under the tutelage of an all-pervasive police.[30]

That was the system's rationale. It was a deeply paternalistic one, and consequently only likely to be appreciated by men and women of a paternalistic bent. By others, it was liable to be misunderstood.

The people who misunderstood it most of all – or perhaps understood it only too well – were the British. They equated the Hapsburg system and others like it with sheer tyranny. In the eighteenth and nineteenth centuries the absence of a secret political police force in Britain was considered to be the main mark of her superiority over countries like Austria and France, and of her 'freedom', as Britons understood the word. Many of them thought it was embedded in the national character, and went back to earliest times. Traditionally, no 'true-born Englishman', or Welshman, or Scotsman (it has never been easy to include the Irish in this), would brook any form of domestic political espionage.

There is some truth in this, in that there have been times when Britons have not been aware that they were brooking espionage because they have not known – or have not wanted to know – that it was going on. It is also true that political policing in Britain never before the modern period reached the pitch of sophistication that it reached in France during the revolution, in the Austrian Empire under the Hapsburgs and in Russia at almost any period from Ivan the Terrible on. Nevertheless Britain has a tradition of domestic espionage which runs very thinly in certain periods, and may be actually broken at one or two points, but is strong and healthy (if that is the right word) at other times. One of its high points was the reign of Elizabeth, who was a contemporary of Ivan's; but there were one or two earlier precedents too.

In 1066 Harold apparently used military spies, and William did not. That dents the case of the pro-espionage lobby a little, but as one of them points out, the battle of Hastings *was* a close-run thing.[31] The earliest official record of espionage in England comes later, and concerns the interception of mails. This is appropriate, because postal (and later telephone) intercepts have formed the staple diet of Britain's secret services right through to the present day. The document in question is a royal writ of 18 December 1324 to officials in ports around the English coast, which berates them for not observing 'previous orders *de scrutinio faciendo*', and reminds them of their duty, therefore, 'to make diligent scrutiny of all persons passing from parts beyond the seas to England ... to stop all letters concerning which sinister suspicions might arise', and to send these to the king 'with the utmost speed'.[32] That method of intelligence-gathering is also referred to in Shakespeare's *Henry V*, during Scroop's plot, where Bedford announces that 'The king hath note of all that they intend,/By interception which they dream not of.'[33] That, of course, may reflect Shakespeare's knowledge of the practices of his own time, rather than of Henry V's.

Henry V's time, however, was certainly familiar with *military* espionage, from the wars with France in which his victories were almost his only claim to fame. The Scots, who were England's other main enemy in the fourteenth and fifteenth centuries, also employed what one of their churchmen called 'slycht' and 'sutelte'. Spies from both countries operated in England, as well as against the English armies abroad. Public opinion was constantly aware of them: even exaggeratedly so. Parliament repeatedly petitioned against the appointment of alien clergy to English benefices and monastic houses, on the grounds that they could be French agents in disguise. Foreign spies were spotted everywhere, in a manner reminiscent of the great spy scare of the years before the First World War. Hundreds of them were seized and hurled into gaols, on no better grounds than that they spoke in strange ways. This, in fact, was the government's main sanction against them: the vigilance of the king's patriotic subjects, backed up on occasion by special measures. These included stringent port controls, searches of ships, full-scale house-to-house searches, the forcible removal of aliens from coastal areas, orders to monasteries to refuse entry to foreign clergy, expulsions, arrests and imprisonment.[34] They do not seem to have included the formation of any distinct counter-espionage *agency*. Nor is there any evidence of organized secret counter-subversive activity of any other kind. In general, both kinds of subversion – alien and native – seem to have been dealt with in medieval times in more overt ways.

Much of the anti-spy reaction of the fourteenth century was over-done, and had elements in it of simple xenophobia, or paranoia. Anti-spy paranoia, in fact, has as long and impressive a history in Britain as espionage itself, and one which is sometimes entirely unrelated to the latter. One period in which they both flourished, but probably the paranoia more than the reality, was the sixteenth century. There were a number of reasons for this, most of which had their roots in the basic social and religious upheavals of the time. Basic upheavals never upheave everyone uniformly; which means that they engender conflict, which is likely to operate covertly as well as in the open.

It used to be thought that another effect of these upheavals in England was to set in motion a 'Tudor revolution in government' early in the sixteenth century, of just the kind to sustain – one would have imagined – a proper 'system' of domestic espionage, or political police. Today that 'Tudor revolution' looks less firmly established than it used to; but in any case the main protagonist of the idea, G. R. Elton, never claimed that Thomas Cromwell, the leading revolutionary, was quite as modern as this. Cromwell's contemporaries were not always so sure. He had the reputation of being a 'Machiavel', which simply meant that he was unscrupulous; it did not matter that Machiavelli himself had no specific advice to offer in this area, if Cromwell was capable of thinking it up on his own.[35] People certainly suspected him of having his informers among them; when for example one of the abbot of Peterborough's servants told him that he wished to take up a new job with Cromwell, the abbot's retort was: 'What will ye do with him? Be one of his spies?' There is firm evidence that Cromwell 'laid espials' on one occasion, in order to arrest a couple of Franciscan friars in 1533. That is unlikely to have been the only case. But it did not amount to something which could properly be called a 'spy system'; for which there is no unambiguous evidence (no record of payments, for example), and which in any case is unlikely, claims Elton, in view of the government's penury at that time.[36]

Tudor England, as another historian has put it, was full of 'imagined fears', of 'inner and hidden spasms that gripped the bowels', but were more often than not either baseless, or exaggerated, or at least misdirected.[37] This may account for some of its fear of spies. It was also natural, in view of the poor success rate among contemporary conspiracies. The fact was that if anyone hatched a plot against the sovereign in Thomas Cromwell's day, he was almost bound to be found out. It is possible that some innocent (or relatively innocent) men and women were 'found out' too: that is, framed. This was sometimes taken to point to the ubiquity of an organized spy system under Cromwell, but that is not the only possible explanation. Some Tudor plots failed because they were ludicrously inept. Others were betrayed, but not by formal spies. Co-conspirators got cold feet, and confessed; or people around them – especially servants – informed, out of simple loyalty, or to gain favour or gold. 'Except in foreign parts,' writes Lacey Baldwin Smith, 'there was no real need for a paid spy system.' 'This was not the way things worked,' confirms Elton; 'information came, and did not have to be sought for.'[38]

This may well have changed later on. In the reign of Elizabeth I intelligence-gathering seems to have become noticeably more systematic than it had ever been before, and more professional. The playwright Christopher Marlowe may have been one of its targets, on ideological grounds. 'This Marlow ...' claimed an informer, Richard Baines, 'persuadeth men to Atheism willing them not to be afeared of bugbeares and hobgoblines and utterly scorning both God and his ministers.' As if this were not enough, Baines claimed to have heard him saying that all Protestants were hypocritical asses, that he had as much right to coin as the queen, and that 'he counted all men who loved not tobacco as fools'. There is also a chance that Marlowe himself may have worked as a government spy, among the Scots. (The transition from victim to agent of espionage is not uncommon in history.) His violent death in an alehouse at Deptford Strand in May 1593 could have been connected with this: at least one of the witnesses was another spy, and may have been playing a double game.[39] Whatever the truth may be, it looks murky.

If Marlowe was spied on because of his atheism, that was not the government's prime concern. Atheists scarcely posed a threat. The Roman Catholics, however, did, especially when they could count on assistance from abroad. The combination of the two – an internal ideological threat, and an external military one – has been a potent spur to the development of domestic espionage systems more than once in Britain's history. In this case the man mainly responsible for the development was Francis Walsingham, Elizabeth's chief secretary of state from 1573 until his death in 1590. He, and not Thomas Cromwell, should be regarded as the true father of the British secret state.

Even in Walsingham's case it is easy to exaggerate his achievement. To create a secret service in Elizabethan times was not difficult. The flow of voluntary intelligence still ran as copiously as it had done earlier in the century, fed by men and women who required no prompting to sneak on people they suspected might be up to no good, without its needing to be ferreted out or organized. All that was required was to let such people know that their information was valued. Walsingham cultivated the reputation that he was insatiable for it. He also *paid* for it, initially out of his own purse, because the queen was too tight-fisted. She also clearly did not share his own philosophy, which was that 'knowledge is never too dear'.[40] That greased the channels. Informers were encouraged to come to him with their stories, and then to come again. This is the first thing that distinguishes Walsingham's 'system' from Cromwell's, very few of whose informers informed more than once.[41] A habitual informant is clearly in a different category from a one-off one. He is halfway, at least, to being a 'spy'.

Most of Walsingham's genuine spies – possibly all of them – were recruited via this route. Even before he became chief secretary he knew about genuine espionage, from the help he had given to William Cecil around 1570 in organizing his system abroad. In the 1580s he applied this experience closer to home, and in particular among the Catholics. We know the names of about fifty of his spies and regular informers, and there were probably many more. The most effective may have been 'Preists, Jesuits and Traitors' whom according to the testimony of his brother-in-law he 'corrupted with moneye ... to bewraye the practises against this Realm'.[42] Some of those were planted in gaols to gain the confidence of Catholic prisoners, or found jobs in the service of suspected high-born recusants, or sent to seminaries on the Continent to find out what was being plotted there. One lay spy who infiltrated the English College in Rome, Anthony Munday, came back with hair-raising accounts of treasonable talk amongst the inmates. These included the fervently expressed wish that 'ere long' Queen Elizabeth – 'that proude usurping Jezabell' – might have her flesh torn from her by dogs; and the observation that 'my Lord keeper, the Bacon hogge, the Butchers sonne, the great guts' (Sir Nicholas Bacon, presumably) would 'fry well with a Faggot': which was not only treacherous, but sounded like it. Munday's published reminiscences, from which these extracts are taken, may be the earliest example of what by now has become a popular literary genre: the spy memoir. Most of Cecil's and Walsingham's other agents were more reticent.

Munday's main success was to help get Edmund Campion and his fellows executed – and consequently half-hanged, castrated, disembowelled, beheaded and quartered – in 1581–2. (He watched the executions, and then wrote describing how cowardly his victims had behaved during them.)[43]

Other Elizabethan agents were equally successful. Walsingham's most spectacular achievement in this field came in 1585, when the Babington plot was
scuppered by a spy, Gilbert Gifford, who had managed to insinuate himself
into the confidence of the imprisoned Queen Mary, no less. It was he who
gave her the idea of smuggling letters out in secret watertight compartments
in beer barrels, which he had made for her. This way Walsingham got to read
everything that passed between her and her co-conspirators.[44]

There are some doubts about this particular success, which we shall come
on to later. There were also some outright failures. One rather pathetic one
was the case of Walter Williams, an experienced agent who was sent to spy
on Lord Stafford in 1586, but then got 'merry' in Stafford's company and blurted
it out. The most tragic failure was Dr William Parry, another established
agent who concocted a plot to murder the queen in order (he claimed)
to incriminate someone else, but was then arrested, tried and hanged (and
all the rest) for it himself in 1585. Some say that this was in order to stop
him spilling the beans about Walsingham's 'spy system'.[45] It was certainly
effective, if so.

How long this system lasted is difficult to say. Walsingham died in 1590.
Shortly afterwards his brother-in-law wrote an account of his duties for his
successor, which mentioned how he used to employ spies and informers,
but also remarked that 'seeinge how much his liberalitie was misliked, I
doe not thinke that you can followe the like example'.[46] Two years before
that, with the defeat of the Spanish Armada, the main combined foreign and
ideological threat to England came to an end. The domestic spy system may
have abated in intensity thereafter. There is, at any rate, less sign of it. If
James I and Charles I had a domestic secret service, then it has escaped
the attention of their historians, and seems to have done neither of them –
especially Charles – much good. The evidence starts warming up again, as
we might expect, at the time of the Civil War and Commonwealth. Oliver
Cromwell employed two 'Intelligencers', as they were called, who both left
accounts of their activities. One of them was notably more successful, in
every way, than the other.

The unsuccessful one was Thomas Scot, who wrote his 'Confession' in 1660,
in order to persuade the new regime to spare his life. It named names, which
presumably led to further arrests; but its main burden was to emphasize how
ineffective he really was. Perhaps the idea was to persuade his captors that he
was not worth executing. If so, it did not work, and in October he (literally)
lost his head. The other 'Intelligencer' was John Thurloe. He fared much
better, despite – or just possibly because of – a much more brazen testimony.
This describes a highly sophisticated Cromwellian counter-subversive system,
employing 'a great number of subtil and sly fellowes' as spies, and working to

some effect. Many of his spies were very highly placed: like Sir Richard Willis, who was a member of the London Royalist Council, and at the other end of the political spectrum John Wildman, a leading Leveller. Thurloe also made great use of the 'Generall Letter Office', to intercept suspicious mails. Henry Cromwell (one of Oliver's sons) once told him: 'it is a wonder you can pick as many locks into the hearts of wicked men as you do'. From such a quarter, that was quite a testimony.[47]

Thurloe's 'Discourse' also gave some useful tips. He advised, for example, that hostile factions should each be infiltrated by *two* spies, unknown to one another, so that 'they may be of checks to each other for the more sure discovery of the truth'. He also recommended that spies and informers did not report back to their spymasters' own offices or homes 'unlesse sometimes in a dark Winter night', because those places were likely to be 'constantly watchd almost by all parties to see who came out, or went in, and consequently to finde out who of their brethren probably betrayed them'. It may have been this sound and very practical advice which saved him from the noose.[48]

The later Stuarts carried on these practices, though not efficiently enough to save them in 1688. Men and women were sent to spy on dissenters, and among suspect political groups. A number of early conspiracies, including the Yorkshire or Derwentdale plot of 1663, were discovered by these means. The money to pay for this came out of a 'Secret Service' grant, which Parliament voted on the understanding that it would not pry into how it was spent. A published account of its expenditure in this period, however, reveals that only a small proportion of it was used for secret service work, the rest going to a host of other purposes the king wanted kept quiet, including buying fripperies for Nell Gwynn.[49]

When the Glorious Revolution came along, some people doubtless hoped that it would put an end to this kind of thing. But of course it did not. Revolutions may in fact be one of the strongest stimuli to domestic espionage, involving as they are almost bound to do the possibility of counter-revolution by supporters of the deposed regime. There were plenty of those between 1688 and 1745: Jacobites living in Britain or over the water in France, and looking forward eagerly to the resumption of the Stuart line. Again, there was that fearful combination of internal subversion and external threat which always seems to get the spies scurrying in Britain. It did after 1688. One of them – a rogue called Lunt – was instrumental in uncovering the Lancashire plot of 1690.[50] Another was the second (after Marlowe) in a long line of 'literary agents' in British secret service history: Daniel Defoe, the author of *Robinson Crusoe*, who for a time in the early 1700s, in the guise of a visiting merchant, ran a network of spies for Robert Harley in Scotland. 'I have my spies and my pensioners in every place,' he reported back on one occasion; 'and I confess 'tis the easiest thing in the world to hire people here to betray their friends'. That does not say much for the Scots. Nevertheless he claimed it was dangerous work. In 1707 he wrote to Harley, in an effort to persuade him to continue his fee, that he ran 'as much risk of my life as a grenadier storming a counterscarp'.[51]

Robert Walpole took a particular interest in this work, especially after the help his spies gave him in cracking the Atterbury plot in 1722. After Atterbury was exiled to France the following year, Walpole set another spy on to him: John Macky, one of the most resourceful and long-serving secret agents in British history, who was active for thirty-five years before he died (of natural causes) in 1726. After his death his son found a manuscript of his father's memoirs, which he published in 1733, but without an account of the Atterbury case, possibly on the grounds – as he explained in his preface – that '*Secret Services*, too recent, are not to be exposed'. The historian of all this, Paul Fritz, suggests that 'at no other period in English history, save during wartime, was so much time and energy devoted to the securing of intelligence'.[52] That may be an exaggeration: the problem with intelligence history in the past has been that historians of little bits of it have not generally been much aware of the histories of other little bits, and so could not make proper comparisons. On an overall view, Walpole has some strong rivals for the title of Britain's greatest spymaster: Walsingham, for example, and Thurloe, and Pitt, and Sidmouth, and whoever pulls the intelligence strings in our own day. Nevertheless he is in the top half-dozen. And the reason for that was clearly the Jacobite threat, whose recession after 1745 was probably followed (though we can never be certain) by a diminution of Britain's home secret service too.

Domestic secret service in Britain, then, has a long pedigree. But it is also a very uneven one. There was little continuity about it. This was because it was hardly ever formalized. One major exception, however, was the Post Office, which did develop a formal secret service agency of its own.

At first it was haphazard. In origin the Post Office was a means of transmitting the *king*'s letters: hence 'Royal Mail'. This gave him the right to scrutinize the mails, which also extended to private citizens' letters when they were allowed (probably in the later Middle Ages) to make use of it too. In the Civil War period this right passed from the king to Parliament, which initially (according to Thurloe) insisted on seeing the contents of every single letter 'without ceremony'; and then to Oliver Cromwell, who set up a special 'Secret Man' with his own private room at the Post Office to open, read and re-seal any letters he thought looked suspicious, between 11 and 4 every night. The first 'Secret Man' was one Isaac Dorislaus, who soon developed, said Thurloe, 'a very great perfection of knowing men's hands', but on the other hand 'was not at all dexterous in opening and closing up letters, which caused great mutterings and many complaints to be made'. Nevertheless the practice seems to have continued. In 1711 it was regularized further, with a warrant now being required, signed by one of the principal secretaries of state, before any letter could be opened. Shortly afterwards Dorislaus's old office was split into two, with a 'Secret Office' to deal with foreign correspondence, and a 'Private Office' for domestic letters.[53] There was also a deciphering branch, which is alluded to in Swift's *Gulliver's Travels* (1726): 'a set of artists, very dexterous in finding out the mysterious meanings of words'. For example, Swift went on,

> they can discover a close-stool, to signify a privy-council; a flock of geese, a senate; a lame dog, an invader; the plague, a standing army; a buzzard, a prime-minister; the gout, a high priest; a gibbet, a secretary of state; a chamber pot, a committee of grandees

and so on.[54] Apart from Swift, not many people were aware of the extent of the Post Office's secret activities in the eighteenth century. Foreigners, if ever they found out, seemed surprised that it should go on at all 'in England, the freest country in Europe'.[55]

Here, then, was a genuine espionage agency, with a structure and personnel of its own, recognized by statute, independent (in one sense) of governments, but there for any minister to use when he wanted: a precursor, in a way, of today's GCHQ. But it was unusual. Other spy systems – those which involved the use of *agents* – were far less organized. Thomas Scot tells us that there was a formal structure in his day, with all the secret service work of the Commonwealth being overseen by a committee of five men.[56] Aside from this, however, espionage was generally handled on a personal basis by individual ministers, who developed their networks and methods on their own initiatives, without guidelines, and consequently with little progression from one minister or regime to the next.

One effect of this may have been that the practice and techniques of intelligence never really advanced very much during these years. With no formal office to store its knowledge and accumulated experience, little being committed to writing and so many breaks in its history, each generation of 'intelligencers' started virtually from scratch, and repeated the same mistakes as the one before. So, for example, it is unlikely that Walpole's agents were any more sophisticated than Walsingham's, just because they came later. Espionage and counter-subversion were static arts between the sixteenth and eighteenth centuries, hampered – for reasons it is easy to understand – by the lack of that free flow of information on which progress in any field depends.

This may have had a bearing on their effectiveness. We shall see throughout this book that measuring the effectiveness of any secret service agency is a difficult and usually an impossible task. The best successes of espionage systems should be preventive, and there is no way in which anyone can ever say what might have happened in any situation if it had not been for this or that. That problem is compounded by the fact that it is invariably in the interests of people connected with the secret service to assume or even pretend that something would have happened, if it were not for their vigilance. Ideally this should not be so. A good secret service should allay unnecessary fears, as well as counter genuine threats. One of the best justifications for espionage, though he did not intend it as such, is Francis Bacon's dictum that 'There is Nothing makes a Man *Suspect* much, more than to Know little.'[57] Ignorance breeds paranoia, and consequently over-reaction. Spies can be a corrective to this. In later periods, as we shall see, they sometimes were. But most of the pressure on them was the other way. Ministers engaged them, and *paid* them, for uncovering plots. That, at any rate, was the common understanding. There was little profit to be made out of bland reassurances. Spymasters were often aware of this, but could do little about it. A rather pathetic little admission by Thomas Scot says it all. 'There were likewise', he recounted in his 'Confession', 'informacions brought mee of several persons designing the Carrying away of shipps and vessels, for which the Informants got money and wee lost no vessels, but whether they were really designed vpon I cannot say.'[58]

The years between 1500 and 1750 were full of revolutions of one kind or another, and putative revolutions and rebellions which failed. Whether the failures owed anything to the effectiveness of the sitting governments' espionage agencies, or the successes to their neglect, can be argued any way. Most of the plots that were discovered were pathetic affairs, which would certainly have collapsed even without secret service help. Some of them may even have been egged on in order to boost the credit of their betrayers: of which more in a while. In these cases, of course, it means that the secret service, far from preventing conspiracies, was actually the cause of them. On the other hand, it was arguable – in a cynical kind of way – that provoking a small plot in order to discover it might deter bigger ones. It was all part of what could become a very devious game.

The problem was, as it usually is, that the system was very easily abused. It could be abused, for example, by the ministers in charge of it for their own partisan or personal ends: though little sign of this has come to light. Charles II, as we know, misappropriated some of the secret service money in order to reward his mistress. Early eighteenth-century ministers may have used it to bribe electors. On one occasion Walpole was suspected of using Post Office interceptions to gain privileged commercial knowledge for himself.[59] These are examples of secret service facilities being used for wrongful purposes. They could also be used for their proper purposes, but in illegal ways. The 1711 rule on Post Office warrants, for example, was frequently bent. The official returns for letter-opening warrants sanctioned by principal secretaries from 1712 to the time of the French Revolution show a paltry number of interceptions: usually just one or two, and never more than seven, in each year. On the other hand it is known for certain that many more letters than these were in fact opened, usually merely on the informal suggestion of an under secretary. In this case, as the historian of the eighteenth-century Post Office puts it, 'secrecy made legality unimportant'.[60] That will have applied to other areas of secret service activity also. If questions were asked, in Parliament for example, they could be parried with appeals to 'public safety' – what today is called 'national security' – in order to justify ministers' ducking them.[61]

Lower down the hierarchy abuse was more likely, and even probable. One reason was the character of the people who engaged in this kind of work: the men and women who were chosen – or volunteered – as spies. A very large proportion of the ones we know about were sheer villains, the dregs of contemporary society. Some of them were full-time thieves, confidence tricksters, blackmailers, pimps, or murderers, with espionage merely as a profitable sideline. William Parry, for example, was an ex-convict, who narrowly escaped hanging in 1580 for robbery with violence. A spy called Maude, who was active in uncovering the Babington plot, had been gaoled in 1583 for attempting to blackmail the Archbishop of York. One Roger Walton was described in 1588 by Stafford, who did not know then that he was one of Walsingham's men, as 'a swearer without measure and tearer of God, a notable whoremaster'.[62] One of Charles II's spies, William Leving, was also a highwayman. The man Lunt who uncovered the Lancashire plot of 1690 was once tried for bigamy. One of the men who contributed towards Atterbury's arrest, James Plunket, was 'a broken-down Irish confidence trickster'.[63] These were by no means unrepresentative, at least of the lower ranks of the spy fraternity.

Some went into spying to save their liberties, or even their necks. Two Elizabethan examples are William Fowler, who helped keep an eye on Franco-Scottish goings-on in 1582–3, and Thomas Barnes, who was another of Walsingham's men involved in the Babington plot.[64] Most of the rest probably did it for money. Ministers were always complaining about their venality, but paid them well nevertheless. Our friend Lunt did so well that by the time of the trial of the plot he had uncovered he was employing a footman. This was a man who had started off as a labourer.[65] Some Elizabethan agents also made tidy little sums on the side, by agreeing to plead with Walsingham for the lives of apprehended Catholics, in return for, say, £20 or £30 a head. Walsingham seems to have connived in this practice, which had the advantage for him of bolstering his spies' credit among the Catholics.[66] But it was not a very honourable trade.

One or two may have gone into the work out of pure patriotism or religious principle. 'I profess myself a spy,' wrote Nicholas Berden, one of Walsingham's best agents, to the latter's secretary in 1584; 'but I am not one for gain but to serve my country'. Maliverny Catlyn, another top Elizabethan agent, also seems to have been a bit of a zealot, this time of the religious kind.[67] But purity of motive did not necessarily guarantee honesty on the job. It might not, for example, if their principles were the wrong ones. John Lefebure, who supervised the interception of foreign letters at the Post Office in the 1740s, was a secret Jacobite, and passed information to the Stuarts too. There is no suggestion that he did that for financial gain: though he no doubt had an eye to the security of his job, in case the Jacobites ever got in.[68] That was one danger. The other was of what today are called 'dirty tricks'. Secret agents were notorious, then as now, for framing suspects, planting evidence and provoking conspiracies. They were as likely to do this out of patriotism – if, for example, they genuinely believed that a suspect was a danger to his country, or perhaps an abomination to God – as out of avarice. This is usually the object of 'dirty tricks' in the intelligence field: not to entrap the innocent, but to be able to convict (and so disarm) men of whose guilt the entrappers are morally sure.

In any case, and whatever the motives, there can be no doubt that the system bred the occasional *agent provocateur*. We have come across one clear example – poor William Parry – already. There were others. Maude and a man called Dr William Gifford, for example, very likely helped 'provoke' the Babington plot in 1585. When incriminating documents were found in Francis Throgmorton's house in 1583, he claimed at first that they had been 'foisted' (or planted) there: but then retracted, with a little help from the rack.[69] (That is one of the problems which often arises when an intelligence agency gets a poor reputation: it can be accused of knaveries it might be innocent of.) There are some good examples of genuine knaveries from later Stuart times. One is a man called Edward Potter, one of Charles II's spies, who revealed that his orders were to infiltrate subversive groups, 'help them forward in any plot against the government', and then uncover them. One Peter Crabb was given £10 in 1661 for forging a letter purporting to implicate a leading Baptist in a plot.[70] Later on one of Walpole's agents induced Lord Mar to write a letter which would seem to incriminate Atterbury. There is little sign that ministers connived in any of this. In 1723 Walpole wrote to one of his spies, William Thomson, warning him *not* to try to 'amuse and deceive him', and 'upon no account [to] say anything that is not strictly true';[71] but that was easier said than done. Thurloe's advice – to engage several spies to corroborate each other independently – was sound, but might be difficult to follow in situations where it was hard enough to find *one* man prepared to betray his friends. Problems like this were intractable. And they in turn gave rise to others.

One was that spies were thoroughly disliked. This was both an effect and a cause of their villainy. They were disliked because they were villainous;

and they were villainous because no one but a villain would go into such an unpopular trade. It was always so. No one had ever had a good word for spies, except those who needed their services. Many of the latter probably despised them underneath. When Shakespeare wanted a really offensive phrase to describe the sin of jealousy for *Venus and Adonis*, he came up with 'This sour informer, this bate-bearing spy'.[72] 'Bate' means discord, which was supposed to be one of the malevolent effects of the practice. 'The evil', reported the Spanish ambassador from London in 1564, 'lies in the universal distrust, for a father dares not trust his own son.'[73] A very early dictionary defined the verb 'to spy' as 'to pry, sneake into corners, thrust his nose into every thing'. A seventeenth-century alias for the Devil was 'Black Spy'. It is difficult to find even a neutral use of the word in English, until Dr Johnson's *Dictionary* (1755), which defined it simply as 'One sent to watch the conduct or motions of others'.[74] Even that, as we shall see, did not imply that he or his countrymen approved of it.

How far espionage was nevertheless *tolerated* depended largely on how far it impinged on those who were called on to do the tolerating. While the secret service confined its activities to high-born papists or Jacobites, few people probably minded, except of course the high-born papists or Jacobites themselves. One of the former, the Catholic divine Humphrey Ely, ended an indignant account of *Jesuit* espionage amongst his co-religionists in Rome with the observation that 'Nothing is so contrary to an englishmans nature, as to be betrayed by him whom he trusted. If such spies were in Oxford ... they would be plucked in peeces.'[75] But of course they were not in Oxford, or anywhere else where they could violate the privacy of the average, solid, free-born Englishman. That free-born Englishman could be an awkward customer if he did ever sniff out a spy. We have seen already the murmurings and complaints that the interception of mail aroused, on the rare occasions when it was spotted.[76] In the 1660s, when the secret service began informing on ordinary dissenting worshippers, the reaction was furious. Then, writes the historian of the Restoration secret service, 'these parasites ... were often mobbed in the streets, denounced from the pulpit, and their mischievous practices exposed in tracts and popular ballads'.[77] There could be no mistaking the popular feeling on the subject of spies.

In the eighteenth century they became progressively more detested, as the practice of using spies and 'common informers' to detect ordinary, non-political crime spread. Around the beginning of the eighteenth century efforts were made to regularize it and try to make it respectable, especially in the field of morality. Middle-class 'Societies for the Reformation of Manners' tried to put over the idea that people had a civic duty to keep an eye on their neighbours and expose what was called 'Profaneness and Debauchery' among the lower orders; but it never properly caught on. The societies' agents were widely unpopular, and on one or two occasions were killed by angry mobs.[78] So far as crime was concerned, the practice was encouraged by laws granting immunity from prosecution for criminals who betrayed their accomplices, and by a complicated system of rewards. When a reward was given for the discovery of a capital offence, it was called 'blood money'. Some people took up this kind of work full-time. Because they were paid by results, they often notoriously invented and provoked crimes. There were several public scandals in the later eighteenth and early nineteenth centuries over cases in which it was found that men had been transported and even hanged for offences they had been 'decoyed' into by such people. In a less scrupulous age than ours, this might perhaps have been accepted if it had had the effect of deterring real crimes. But it clearly had not. Crime rates rose alarmingly, partly due, suggested *The Times* in 1816, to the sheer numbers of these contrived ones.[79] At the same time, it made genuine villains more difficult to put away. 'The perjuries of informers', wrote Lord Bathurst in 1743, 'are so flagrant and common, that the people think all informations malicious', with the effect that juries often refused to convict. They also, Bathurst went on, 'began to declare war against informers, many of whom they treated with great cruelty, and some they murdered in the streets'. The result of this was that 'the law ... has been now for some years totally disused'.[80] Spies were not only unpopular, therefore; they were counter-productive too.

Those who attach importance to tradition, and are impressed by the fact that Britain has a long history of domestic espionage, must take on board this very powerful rival tradition as well. So far as the following political generation was concerned, it was easily the more important of the two. Espionage was essentially 'un-English'. The word was even *pronounced* in an un-English way. If the thing it described had featured at all before the nineteenth century, then it was assumed that it had been foisted on the English by their foreign aristocratic tyrants (the 'Norman yoke'). The ordinary English themselves (the Saxons) had resisted it. By and large their resistance had been successful. The tangible proof of this success was the fact that Britain still did not have, at the beginning of the nineteenth century, and almost uniquely among the nations of Europe, a proper, formal 'police'.

There was something in this. There were a number of factors behind English anti-police feeling in the eighteenth century. One was the expense which it was believed a police system would involve. Another was the association of police with bureaucracy and over-regulation. In the eyes of the greatest anti-bureaucrat of them all, Adam Smith, a police force should not be *necessary* in any country which encouraged individual responsibility through free enterprise and minimal government, because crime itself was the result of what he called 'dependency'.[81] That rings curiously false today, at a time when free enterprise, crime and policing all seem to be marching forward together; but no doubt the modern disciples of Adam Smith have an explanation for it. The main eighteenth-century reason for disapproving of the police, however, was the fear that it could be 'perverted', as Lord Shelburne put it in the early 1780s, 'into an *espionage*, a word which he thanked God, would not *yet* admit to an English interpretation'. The danger was not just a theoretical one. On the other side of the Channel it had actually materialized: a dreadful warning to all free Englishmen. In France, claimed Shelburne, the government had turned their police into 'a system of spies, employed to watch the private dinners of individuals, to pry into their family concerns, to hunt out their secrets, and to render the life of every denomination of the subjects, a life of terror and a life of danger'. Shelburne thought that this danger could be avoided in England with proper municipal accountability. But the law reformer Sir Samuel Romilly disagreed. 'If the police of France is to be adopted,' he wrote in 1786, 'it must be adopted throughout. to leave out of such a system the employment of spies and of soldiers, is to omit that part of it on which the success of the whole depends.' Beyond this, police forces were fundamentally demoralising. 'A system, which betrays the greatest distrust of the people, must never look for public support; all that it can expect from the public is a constrained and reluctant obedience.'[82] That would never do. Governments must trust people. And that meant not spying on them.

That sounds all very noble. The trouble was, as we have seen, that it did not prevent governments from spying on people at all. Espionage flourished in eighteenth-century England, but even more clandestinely than would have been necessary if the public had taken a more tolerant attitude towards it, and undertaken by men who – in view of the public's *int*olerance – were almost bound to be rogues. This was ironic. English public opinion opposed espionage because it was intrusive, despotic and corrupt. The effect of this opposition was not to outlaw espionage, which still went on under both official and private patronage. It may have made it less intrusive and despotic than it would otherwise have been. But it undoubtedly made it *more* corrupt. It could hardly be otherwise, in a situation in which spies were considered to be the dregs of humanity, and so generally turned out to be so; and where profit was almost their only motive for being spies. But the irony did not stop there. The process was circular. As well as being corrupt because they were detested, they were also detested for being corrupt. This had two effects, which could rebound against ministers who employed them. First, it meant that people did not believe their testimony, which was important when ministers needed people – juries – to convict their victims. Secondly, some of the detestation rubbed off on those ministers. Governments which gained the reputation of instituting 'spy systems' became instantly unpopular, and consequently less secure. No doubt this was one reason why Machiavelli had not recommended them. It was a serious problem in Britain; and one faced by governments constantly, as we shall see, in the years following the outbreak of the French Revolution in 1789.

Chapter 2

The most powerful means of observation (1790–1805)

Jacobites were one thing. They ceased being a realistic threat in 1745, long before their last convincing Pretender, Charles Edward Stuart, no longer the 'bonny' Prince Charlie of all those years ago but a fat, dissolute drunkard, died in exile in Rome in January 1788. Jaco*bins*, however, were something else. They came on to the European scene just a few months after Charles's death. They were a more serious danger than he had been, because they represented a social revolution as well as a political one. Strictly speaking, 'Jacobins' were members of a particular French revolutionary club, which folded in 1794; but the name was taken to cover extreme republican and democratic views generally. Those views were found in Britain as well as in France, and consequently were feared there too. After 1792 such fears were compounded by a pledge given by the French Convention in November to help like-minded revolutionaries abroad. That created the dangerous situation – once again – in which a domestic subversive threat and a foreign military one were combined.

There could never be any real doubt about the genuineness of both threats, though some contemporaries tried to make light of the first of them. One who did was Richard Brinsley Sheridan, the playwright. He believed, in effect, that the danger of domestic subversion presented by Pitt's government as its justification for repressive legislation in 1795 was trumped up. The 'present alarm', he told the House of Commons in November, 'had been created solely by ministers, for the corrupt purpose of libelling the country'. They had done this through their spies and informers, who invented the worst atrocities, for gain. This, he claimed, was endemic in the system: 'when once a government encouraged spies and informers, it became a part of their business to commit such forgeries and create such terror'. He told the story of a man who was given a retainer of one guinea a week for information, then two guineas for a really alarming piece of news: with the result that he made sure thereafter that all his intelligence was of the two-guinea variety. That – a distrust of spies – was one reason for Sheridan's scepticism. The other was a whiggish belief, which many besides him shared, that the conditions simply did not exist in Britain for the kinds of events they had seen in France. 'The enormities committed by the French people were occasioned by the despotism under which they had so long groaned; their excesses, when they were free, were to be attributed to their former slavery'; whereas in Britain, under 'a well regulated and limited monarch', things were entirely different. 'The nature of the people of both countries was directly opposite; it was therefore impossible that similar enormities could ever happen in England.'[1] It followed from this that the government's counter-measures – both repressive legislation, and its use of spies – were unnecessary, and probably really intended as a sneaky way of discrediting reasonable political opposition by associating it with foreign atrocities.

Sheridan's case was strengthened by the fact that the material evidence for a serious subversive threat at that time in Britain was extremely thin. There had been one recent attempt uncovered to assassinate the king, with a poisoned dart shot from a 'pop-gun' disguised as a walking stick while he was at the theatre in September 1795; and a physical attack on his coach by a mob outside Parliament a month later. The former could be put down to *agents provocateurs*; the latter, perhaps, to high spirits. Apart from these events, there was little but rumour: of treasonable talk, blood-chilling oaths, pikes being stockpiled, men drilling, covert negotiations with French emissaries, and the like. The government took these as proofs that the danger was there, under the surface, and could have broken through if it had not been for its success in suppressing it. But this is always the problem with successes of this sort: that by snuffing out the threat, they also snuff out the justification for the snuffing. If the government had been less repressive, perhaps the threat would have been plainer, and consequently more people would have credited it.

On the other hand, it may have been the repression that *created* the threat, by driving moderate and non-violent opposition underground. Charles James Fox gave a prophetic warning of this during the same debate that Sheridan was speaking in, which was on the second reading of the Treasonable Practices bill in November 1795. 'You may prevent men from complaining,' he said; 'but you cannot prevent them from feeling . . . Depend upon it, if men speak less, they will feel more, and arms will be left them as the only resource to procure redress to themselves, or exercise vengeance upon their oppressors.'[2] This may have been the pattern both in the case of the English 'Corresponding Societies', which never looked like being really dangerous until they started being harried and eventually banned; and in that of the 'Society of United Irishmen', whose career as a subversive and truly revolutionary force started with its formal suppression in the autumn of 1795.

Whether or not these suppressions were wise, however, they were understandable in the climate of their time. There is no need to conjure up a Machiavellian motive for ministers, in order to account for their reaction – even if it was an over-reaction – to the social and political events of these revolutionary years. Whatever Sheridan might have believed – and he had no responsibility for the safety of the realm – there were genuinely ominous signs.

The most ominous were in Ireland, where if you were a man of property you had every reason to feel insecure. You were surrounded by a degree and extent of poverty and degradation found nowhere else in the British Isles. Because you were propertied, it almost certainly meant that you were a member of a race and religion, as well as of a class, which most other Irish regarded as alien. Your position was bolstered by privileges which by any rational way of looking at them were indefensible, and by an administrative system which was blatantly unjust and corrupt. You would be aware of Irish 'patriot' murmurings against this state of affairs, which threatened your situation in a very obvious way. You would be bound to notice the rejoicings and celebrations in the streets, when the Paris Bastille fell in May 1789. You might get to know of the French revolutionary propaganda which was flooding into the country, and being widely distributed there and (presumably) read. You would have heard of Wolfe Tone's new 'Society of United Irishmen', founded in 1791 to agitate for radical reforms in Ireland. If you had anything to do with Dublin Castle, you might have heard whispers of secret Irish rendezvous with French agents sent over to help them, like the one between Jean Benoist and an Irish 'Revolutionary Committee' in November 1792;[3] or, if not, you would almost certainly suspect such things. Of all the constituent parts of the Kingdom in the 1780s and 1790s, in fact, Ireland was unquestionably the ripest for a revolution on the French model. The only question seemed to be whether the Irish could carry one through successfully. Some years later Ludwig Feuerbach, a philosopher whose materialism was so basic that he once reduced it to the execrable German pun 'der Mensch ist was er isst' (man is what he eats), claimed that the cause of the Irishman's lack of success in this regard was that he was too filled with *traeges Kartoffelblut* (sluggish potato-blood) for him to rebel effectively. Feuerbach's solution to this, and to all Ireland's political problems, was a simple one: *Böhnen* (beans).[4] This had not occurred to the Irish patriots yet. But that was no comfort to the English, who were equally unaware at this time of the handicap the potato imposed on the Irish revolutionaries, in slowing them down.

In England itself the prospects were not much rosier. Eighteenth-century Britain also had its extremes of poverty and wealth, its blatant injustices, a history of mass violence and a revolutionary tradition of sorts. She did not have Ireland's national, patriotic component, or the particular grievances which had provoked that; but she did have special grievances of her own, especially in the manufacturing districts, arising out of the industrial and capitalist revolutions; and her putative rebels on the whole ate a better-balanced diet than the Irishmen's *Kartoffeln*, to stimulate their revolutionary blood. Her mobs were always rioting, for one cause or another: either for church and king, which was not particularly worrying in this context, or for Wilkes and liberty, which was. In 1789 the French Revolution had its open supporters in Britain, as well as in Ireland, though they may not have been quite so demonstrative; and (from the beginning of 1791) a new form of organization, the Corresponding Societies, to debate and promulgate its message. If nothing dreadful actually happened in Britain before 1795, the same could also be said of Ireland during the same period; and that, as it turned out, was no indication at all that nothing dreadful would happen there later on.

What did happen after 1795 was taken by the authorities to vindicate their tough line on sedition and subversion; though we have seen that there is a case for saying that that tough line merely added fuel to the flames. The most frightening events were in Ireland, where the French also took a hand. Between December 1796 and July 1803 there were two attempted French invasions, and two major Irish uprisings. The tragedy from the Irish point of view was that the invasions and the uprisings did not coincide. When General Lazare Hoche sailed his French fleet into Bantry Bay in a snowstorm on 21 December 1796, he found no one there to meet him, and so turned his ships around and sailed back again. The first serious United Irish rebellion did not break out until May 1798, when it was put down after heavy fighting: four months before the second French invasion force, under General Jean Humbert, landed in Killala Bay and managed to take control of a part of Connacht for a couple of weeks. The Irish continued hoping for French help – at the time, for example, of Thomas Emmet's abortive rebellion in Dublin in July 1803 – but it never again materialized. The French may well have given up on them by then.

There was a French 'invasion' of Britain too, which landed on the north Pembrokeshire coast in February 1797; but that turned into a drunken farce, and collapsed the following day.[5] So far as mainland Britain was concerned the most serious domestic crisis was that engendered by the naval mutinies which broke out later the same year at Portsmouth, Plymouth, Yarmouth and the Nore, though there are doubts about the degree to which they were politically inspired. If they were, then some of the 11,500 Irish sailors who were serving in the navy then will have been involved: in particular those Irish political suspects whom a new government policy of 1795 had decided to send to the Fleet rather than incarcerate in Ireland, in order to punish them and keep them out of trouble at home.[6] That was clearly a mistake. In fact the Irish and British revolutionary movements were connected in other ways too: inevitably, in view of the overlap of their populations. Irish immigrants joined the English Corresponding Societies in large numbers, and ran a branch of their own United Irishmen in London.[7] Then, in 1797, an ultra-militant section of that society started spreading its gospel in Britain through a sister organization called the United Britons, which by the following year had supporters as far apart as Edinburgh and Cornwall. One of its English-based members was an Anglo-Irish ex-army officer called Edward Marcus Despard, who was arrested at a pub in Lambeth in November 1802 on suspicion of plotting a bloody uprising, and later executed for high treason.[8] All these events (with the possible exception of the last) were genuine, and threatening. None of them was contrived. In all of them, however, spies were involved to a certain extent, and in one or two of them crucially.

However much spies were disliked in the eighteenth century, there was no real way to avoid their use after 1789. The government had to know what was going on. It may have been its ignorance of what was going on which was partly responsible for its over-reaction (if that is what it was) in 1794 and 1795; though it is likely that straight prejudice was also greatly to blame. Britain, it should be remembered, was very under-governed at this time. She had a tiny professional bureaucracy (only about twenty men at the Home Office, for example), and no proper police. To keep order she depended chiefly on unpaid magistrates, honorary local officials and their helpers, and the presence of an army – a crude weapon against most forms of disorder – in the background. The main deterrent to crime was not supposed to be the likelihood of detection, which would have required a detective police force, but the fear of the penalty if you ever were found out. Leon Radzinowicz calls this 'the principle of suspended terror'.[9] Hence the eighteenth century's extensive capital code, under which you could be hanged for 220 separate offences, including – as is well known – something as trivial as stealing a sheep.

In the case of the most serious political offence – high treason – the deterrent was more terrifying still. Technically an offender could still be put through the same repulsive rigmarole he was subjected to in Elizabethan times: drawn backwards to the gallows behind a horse, half-hanged, cut down alive, have his 'privities' cut off and burned before his eyes, be disembowelled, beheaded and quartered, and then have the bits of him stuck on the tops of pikes; but by the later eighteenth century this had been mercifully reduced to simple public hanging, beheading and quartering.[10]

That may still have deterred most people. But most people were not potential traitors anyway; and no penalty ever devised by even the most sadistic of legislators has ever been enough on its own to daunt every brave, desperate and maybe foolish revolutionary. Hence the need for covert surveillance, and possibly action too.

Some of the covert activity took place abroad. Obviously, the ideal place to staunch a revolution is at its source, which in this case was France. At the beginning of the revolution Britain was suspected by royalists of egging it on by covert means, in order to reduce her rival to weakness and penury.[11] If that was so – and it is highly unlikely – then she soon changed direction. Her main agent in all this was a young cosmopolitan called William Wickham, who made two undercover trips to the Continent between 1794 and 1801 in order to fund counter-revolutionary agencies many of which were corrupt, and none of which stood the proverbial snowball's chance of success.[12] In many ways his projects are reminiscent of CIA operations today, except that more of them failed. Richard Cobb attributes their failure to the fact that Wickham was blinkered by an ideological prejudice against the French lower orders.[13] But Wickham never seems to have been discouraged, and extended his secret service proclivities into other areas too.

It is possible, in fact, that Wickham was the most important and innovative intelligence figure throughout this period, and deserves a place in the top rank of the British secret service pantheon alongside men like Walsingham, Thurloe and some of its more recent heroes. If so it would not be for his escapades abroad, which we have seen were futile; but for his contribution to domestic counter-subversion while he worked for the Home Office between 1794 and 1799, and then in Dublin as Chief Secretary for Ireland between 1802 and 1804. His original position at the Home Office – conferred on him in September 1794, just a month before he left on his first foreign mission – was as one of three 'Superintendents of Aliens' attached to the Alien Office, which was created under the wing of the Home Office as a result of the Alien Act of 1793. The main task of the Alien Office was to look out for French spies who might try to sneak over to England in the guise of refugees. Wickham, however, claimed that he made much more of it than this. Shadowing foreign spies sometimes led them to suspicious Englishmen; and by this means a wider picture of subversive activities in Britain could be built up. In this way, he wrote in 1801, 'without bustle, noise or anything that can attract Public Attention, Government possess here the most powerful means of Observation & Information ... that was ever placed in the hands of a Free Government'; a sort of 'System of *Preventitive* Police'.[14]

Wickham's testimony may not be absolutely reliable. There was clearly a strong streak of wishful thinking in his character; and in 1801 he was endeavouring to make as powerful a case as he could for the continued funding of an agency which was then under threat. Very few papers survive to indicate the full range and nature of the Alien Office's activities during this period; but then we would not necessarily expect them to. It is plausible that it did fulfil an important espionage function in the 1790s, and even that it was – in Roger Wells's phrase – the 'nerve centre' of British counter-revolutionary intelligence at that time.[15] It was well placed to deal with Anglo-French conspiracies, in a period when they were believed to pose the most serious threat to Britain's internal stability. Another advantage of having the Alien Office as your 'nerve centre' was that no one would have yet caught on to the fact that it was engaged in this kind of work; unlike the Home Office and the Post Office, whose espionage functions were well known.

The Post Office's espionage functions may have been *so* well known, in fact, that it effectively neutralized them. In 1798 the Irish revolutionary Arthur O'Connor (Feargus's uncle) told the Home Office that he knew perfectly well that 'I have had my letters opened at the Post Office, which has made me frequently use other names'. Other ruses were to write in code, or to avoid the official post altogether and send letters by alternative means.[16] It is just possible, therefore, that Post Office espionage diminished in value and importance during the 1790s; which may explain the curious fact that its 'Private Office' (for domestic interceptions) actually lost its 'Clerk', or head, in these critical years between 1793 and 1798.[17]

In that case most of the responsibility for domestic intelligence will have devolved on the Home Office. In its Alien department it had, as we have seen, a means of keeping tabs on a certain category of suspects *systematically*. It is unlikely that it was ever as systematic in other ways. It could not hope to be. Its sources of information were still as 'fragmentary and varied'[18] as they had ever been. It depended a great deal on voluntary co-operation from provincial JPs, local constabulary forces, postal officials and ordinary patriotic members of the public who wrote in. This situation was no different from at any other time in the eighteenth century, and indeed was not to change significantly for at least fifty years. Some of these people got their information from spies and informers of their own. One of them, John Reeves, ran quite a little network of them, through his private 'Association for the Preservation of Liberty and Property against Republicans and Levellers', set up in 1792.[19] But the Home Office also sought covert intelligence first-hand. Some of it came from occasional informers; the rest from spies. Most of the latter began as the former: *volunteered* information in the first place, and then were employed regularly, until their covers were blown.

It was not yet anything that could be called a 'system'; but it seems to have had some systematic *elements*. The way the Home Office collected its intelligence, for example, was far from being entirely haphazard. Most of its knowledge will have come from informers who were already associated with radical organizations when they volunteered their help: perhaps for money, or because they were shocked by what they found. 'I wished for

Reform,' one of them told the Home Office, explaining why he had joined such an organization, but had now decided to betray it; 'I hate murders and Equality.'[20] Such informers were acquired randomly, and generally could not be moved around. Others, however, were deliberately planted by the Home Office in places where such spontaneous sources were not forthcoming; either men in its own employ, or – on several occasions – Bow Street Runners, through a magistrate at Bow Street (Richard Ford) who seems to have taken on – or been given – the job of keeping a watch on radicalism in the capital.[21] Besides these, the Home Office also seems to have had a number of men it could send out on short-term surveillance tasks. We shall come across one of them operating in the West country shortly, on the trail of a couple of suspected French spies.

The Home Office was also discriminating. Prospective informers were vetted in order to establish, as far as possible, that they were reliable. When George Lynam, who became one of the Home Office's leading agents in the London Corresponding Society, first offered to spy on it in 1792, an under secretary wrote first to the magistrate in Birmingham, where he came from, to check on him. Others were turned down, as being fundamentally untrustworthy or malicious.[22] Unsolicited information was always regarded critically, and apparently disregarded entirely if it was anonymous, or if it was not corroborated from another source. Sometimes we find under secretaries taking Thurloe's advice, and sending a second agent to check on the report of a first one. The best spies were aware, as one of them put it in December 1792, that 'Exaggerated communications are worse than no communications at all.'[23] Another explicitly promised in 1799 not 'to fabricate plots to have the merit of discovering them', but only to report what he saw. He – William Barlow – was paid a regular salary, rather than by results, in order to encourage this self-restraint. In the end he did not keep to his own good advice, and started embellishing; with the result that the Home Office hauled him in, came to the conclusion that he was 'a complete Alarmist' and gave him the sack.[24] That incident may say something about the inherent unreliability of the sort of men who became spies in the 1790s; but it also says much about the Home Office's concern to keep its channels of information as pure as possible. Most modern historians agree on this: that ministers were genuinely concerned to find out what was happening, and not merely to have their prejudices confirmed.

That is not to say, however, that this is what they wanted the *public* to know. It was one thing for the government to have pure and reliable information; whether the *hoi polloi* – or even MPs – could be trusted with it was an entirely different matter. At various times between 1794 and 1801 'Committees of Secrecy' of the House of Commons were set up to examine the evidence for sedition and treason in Britain and Ireland. That evidence was always carefully selected and edited by ministers, partly in order to protect sources, but chiefly, it seems, in order to put it in as alarming a light as possible. This, wrote our friend Wickham in March 1799, was the purpose of these committees: 'to explain the state of things, in a manner that must draw the attention of the public to a sense of the general danger and the means of preventing it': not, it is worth noting, 'to explain the state of things' *alone*.[25] To point these morals more directly the government also used secret service money to pay its agents to write for the press. One of them, John Taylor, actually edited the *Morning Post* from 1788 to 1790, and then continued writing for the newspapers while at the same time informing on the London Corresponding Society, for a secret salary of £161 a year. Another media infiltrator was a minor dramatist (author of *The Distress'd Baronet*) called Charles Stuart. He received £200 a year, which was about the usual rate.[26]

In Ireland the pattern was similar. Secret service money was used for propaganda purposes, just as in England: publishing pamphlets, for example, and issuing doctored accounts of treason trials.[27] It was also used – massively – for intelligence. There was never any shortage of this. Most of it came from magistrates, officials and other people in authority in most of the thirty-two counties. Some of it came from the editor of the conservative *Freeman's Journal*, who ran a private espionage network of his own.[28] The problem initially, however, was that the information thus obtained was of uneven quality, and random. The authorities did not always find it easy to *direct* inquiries. On one occasion during the 1780s, for example, they had to send to London for informers, because they had no one of their own capable of observing 'the daily history of a man's motions' without giving himself away.[29]

Later they did better. Their first 'systematic informer' was a man called Thomas Collins, who was recruited in 1792.[30] In January 1794 they got their luckiest break, when a French agent called William Jackson arrived in England with an offer of military help for an Irish uprising, but made the mistake of first calling on an old friend, John Cockayne, who told Pitt. Pitt suggested that Cockayne accompany Jackson to Dublin, where he (Jackson) failed to win over the United Irishmen, who suspected *him* of being the British spy, but soon incriminated himself. He was arrested, tried for high treason and convicted. Then came an unusual drama. As he stood in the dock awaiting the death sentence, 'The spectators were struck with his ghastly pallor, with the convulsive twitches of his countenance, and with the perspiration that rose from him almost like a steam.' A few moments later he died painfully, poisoned with arsenic administered (it was said) by his wife.[31]

That case led the government to another valuable informer, Leonard McNally, a founder member of the United Irishmen, who may have been frightened into turning traitor by his association with Jackson. 'There is so much evidence against this person,' wrote the Irish lord-lieutenant in 1794, 'that he is – I am informed – completely in the power of the Government.' McNally was another dramatist, quite a celebrated one in his own time, with 'a certain faculty for sprightly dialogue and smooth versification', as the *Dictionary of National Biography* puts it, who also wrote the song 'Sweet Lass of Richmond Hill'. But his main trade was as a barrister. In 1803 he helped defend Emmet at his treason trial, but at the same time secretly passed information over to the prosecution. (Emmet, not surprisingly, lost and was hanged.) McNally was never suspected in his own lifetime. Jackson trusted him sufficiently to charge him with taking care of his widow and unborn child before he died. Thereafter – for a few years at least – informers flooded in. Most of them appear to have volunteered; including their best one, Samuel Turner, a member of the Ulster Revolutionary Committee, who simply turned up at the house of Lord Downshire in London one night in October 1797 offering to tell him – for a consideration – everything he knew. In his case the consideration may have run to several thousand pounds a year.[32]

This was not unusual. In general Irish informers seem to have been paid more than English ones. Thomas Reynolds, who was the most notorious of them, but only because he was suspected from the start, may have netted more than £45,000 in all: though he claimed that his losses far exceeded that.[33] Some of them were also given comfortable sinecures in the colonies when they had finished.[34] This was probably partly because the government considered the situation to be more dangerous in Ireland than in England (which it was), and partly because of the greater risks the Irish informers ran. Those risks could be chilling. Reynolds, for example, survived several brutal attempts on his life, and was eventually driven to live abroad. He lived another thirty-eight years and then, we are told, 'fell asleep in Jesus without a struggle or even a sigh';[35] but that was unusual. Others met far less peaceful ends. Edward Newell, whom we shall be meeting later, was assassinated on the eve of his flight to America in June 1798, though there is disagreement over where and how.[36] Turner was challenged to a duel and shot dead on the Isle of Man in 1807. Another spy called Phillips – a priest – had lead weights put in his pockets and was then drowned above a dam near Belfast in 1795.[37] In November 1797 a Youghal farmer was found with his bowels torn out, his wife, servant, pigs, dogs and poultry all slaughtered with him, and a label attached to him warning others that this was the reward for treachery. Others, apparently, 'sought refuge in self-destruction'.[38] English informers ran nothing like the same risks. The worst they had to fear, if they were discovered, was ostracism and loss of trade. In 1803 Francis Lynam wrote to the Home Office retailing how his brother George had suffered after he had given evidence against the democrat Hardy in 1794. His 'reputation and character', he claimed, had been destroyed; 'his business then in the East India line which netted him seven hundred per annum' had been 'annihilated'; and he had been 'deserted by his friends and relations and frequently insulted in the streets which so preyed upon his mind that both he and his wife's days were thereby shortened'. (They had died just two years after the Hardy trial.)[39] That was sad, but it was better than having your bowels torn out. Hence the higher market price for an Irish informer.

It was, however, enough. Dozens of Irishmen took the money and turned traitor in the 1790s; as they continued to do for a century or more. Michael Collins believed that this had been a prime reason for the failure of Irish nationalism before his time, when – as we shall see – he decided to tackle the problem head on.[40] Some Englishmen rather gloated over it. The nineteenth-century historian J. A. Froude, for example, thought it arose out of defects in the Celtic character. It was only to be expected, he wrote, from men who were too cowardly to fight for their cause in 'the open field of courage and honour', but preferred instead 'the assassin's dagger and the incendiary's torch'. W. J. Fitzpatrick, another Victorian (this time an Irishman) who spent his life unmasking old traitors, questioned this, and went back to Philip of Macedon to show that there had always been men willing to sell their countrymen for gold.[41] Whether treachery figures larger in Irish history than in other national histories is a moot point. But it undoubtedly helped the British to hold on.

It was particularly helpful between 1794 and 1798. Those were the years when British intelligence in Ireland was at its most effective. It anticipated the 1798 rising, and even egged it on a little in order to get it to peak prematurely: which worked. This was thanks largely to the help of Thomas Reynolds, whose own motive, he claimed, was to prevent what had started off as a respectable and moderate nationalist movement destroying itself.[42] The suppression of that rebellion, therefore, can be counted a great intelligence triumph. But then the going got a little harder. This was inevitable in a way. One effect of the 1798 failure was that most of the old United Irish leaders were imprisoned or hanged, which meant that new ones took over, who were less well known to Dublin Castle's spies. Another effect was to make the United Irishmen far more careful about whom they let in. New members were only admitted if they were recommended by trusted patriots, and after vetting. That excluded many government agents, some of whom were suspected already. The government also found Irish society at large more resistant to it, less willing to co-operate, perhaps out of resentment against its repression of the United Irishmen. The result was that when the next big explosion took place, with Emmet's rising in 1803, it came as a surprise. It was put down with little bother; but that was no thanks to British intelligence.[43]

It was at this late stage that Wickham took a hand. He came to Dublin as Irish chief secretary in March 1802. Immediately afterwards the Irish chancellor wrote of what a 'great relief' his appointment was to all of them there. 'We are now', he went on, 'getting into the established routine' which Wickham had learned or instituted (he was not sure which) at the Home Office. Before long all would be 'in a state of regularity', and they would have 'an alphabetical list of all persons against whom informations have been made, when given, [and] by whom'.[44] They clearly had nothing of the kind then. The implication of this is that Wickham was trying to inject some 'system' into the Irish counter-subversive set-up, as well as the English. What we do not know is how far he succeeded. He clearly had not done enough to allow the Castle to forestall Emmet's uprising in July 1803. That event is said to have 'astonished' him: 'that such a preparation for revolution could be carried on in the very bosom of the seat of Government, without discovery, for so long a time, when any of the party could have made their fortunes by a disclosure of the plot'. He put it down to the fact that 'they were mostly all mechanics, or working people . . . and said that if the higher orders of society had been connected, they would divulge the plot for the sake of gain'.[45] That suggests an interesting sociology of treachery. Wickham left very shortly afterwards, at the beginning of 1804, apparently because he found his position in Dublin 'distasteful'.[46] It would be nice to know how far he had managed to reform the system in the meantime; if only to be able to decide whether he really does merit his niche in our pantheon.

It is just possible that Wickham's 'distaste' for his job arose out of its repugnance in most people's eyes. This was always an enormous handicap. The depth and extent of the repugnance are unquestionable. George Lynam's experiences, and even more the Youghal farmer's, are testimony to it. The journalist Charles Teeling called spies and informers 'hired monsters', 'traffickers in human blood', 'reckless ruffians who rioted on the unhallowed hire of perjury and blood, fabricated plots, feigned conspiracies, and in the hour of Ireland's distress perpetrated more misery than was ever inflicted by the sword'. Teeling however was a United Irishman, and so not an objective witness.[47] More telling is the testimony of some of the informers themselves. When Robert Holden agreed to furnish the government with information from Rotherham in 1794, for example, he refused to accept payment for his services, and asked that they be kept secret, 'as I should not like to risque the odium which would necessarily attend a Discovery; to say nothing of the unpleasantness of such a Task'. Another reluctant spy was John Pigot, who in 1792 only agreed 'to undertake an employment looked upon by the world as a most degrading [one] for a gentleman' out of patriotism.[48] Even their employers could feel contaminated. 'My occupation now', wrote Lord Cornwallis, the new Irish viceroy, in 1799,

is of the most unpleasant nature, negotiating and jobbing with the most corrupt people under heaven. I despise myself every hour for engaging in such dirty work . . . How I long to kick those whom my public duty obliges me to court.[49]

Cornwallis was a professional soldier, in the days when soldiers had strong views about what was 'honourable'. Whether his politician colleagues felt quite as deeply is doubtful. But they were aware that the general public did.

The effects of this were as they had always been in the past. Because spies were regarded as scoundrels, it was mainly scoundrels who became spies. Despite all the precautions taken by those supposedly in charge of them, the spy class of 1792–on had its share of these. The very worst was probably the Ulsterman Edward Newell, who in 1798 published an autobiography which openly proclaimed (and maybe exaggerated) his villainies. This, for example, was how he described himself giving evidence to the 1797 Secret Committee on Irish sedition.

> I went through the subject of the examinations, improving largely on the hints and instructions Cooke had given me; propagating circumstances which never had, nor, I suppose, ever will happen; increased the number of United Irishmen, their quantity of arms and ammunition; fabricated stories which helped to terrify them, and raised me high in their estimation as a man whose perfect knowledge of this business made his information of the highest importance. I told them of laws framed to govern the republic, when they had overthrown the present Government; many of which they approved of highly, though they had no foundation but the effusions of my own brain.

As well as this he was employed to ride around Belfast at night with his face blackened and a guard of soldiers to protect him, telling them whom to arrest. He boasted that this way he got £2,000 in just ten months out of the government, and caused the imprisonment of 227 and the flight of 300 entirely innocent men. Then he claimed he tired of the woman he was living with and betrayed her to her husband; and ended up wallowing in 'wine and debauchery', contracting 'the fashionable disorder, acquired by improper connections' as a result. One of his editors called him 'mercenary vermin', which in the circumstances does not sound too strong.[50]

Newell was in a class of his own; but there were many other unsavoury characters besides. Some were *agents provocateurs*. The radical Francis Place once described the excesses of a member of the London Corresponding Society, James Powell (another minor playwright), in the 1790s. 'There was no absurdity, no sort of proceeding among them that Powell did not eagerly go into, nothing which any villainous spy could suggest that he would not adopt, and he was therefore the most dangerous among them.'[51] Place did not know then that Powell was himself a spy, and clearly out to push his fellow democrats to excess. We have already seen how the 1798 Irish rising was 'pushed' from the inside in this way. Back in England, considerable suspicion attaches to the 'pop-gun plot' of 1795, which was probably provoked or contrived by an informer called Thomas Upton, who had a shady past.[52] In April 1798 an anonymous agent 'planted' some pike-heads on a meeting of the Society of United Britons in the George Tavern, Compton Street, London, to be used in evidence against the members when they were arrested by Bow Street officers minutes afterwards.[53] In 1794 there was a case in Edinburgh reminiscent of William Parry's two hundred years before: when a wretch called Robert Watt was convicted and executed for a plot which he claimed he had joined as a government agent, and in order to betray it. This was the view too of one of his accomplices, who was pardoned: that 'this wild and ridiculous plan was never even seriously thought of by Watt himself; and that he was merely trying to draw weak and ignorant men into a seeming adoption of it, and then to make a sacrifice of them to his own sordid and avaricious views'.[54] If so, it was clearly a perilous strategy.

The excuse for this kind of ruse was that it was necessary in order to produce *evidence* of wrong-doing, in situations when spies could not be called as witnesses. There were several reasons why spies could not be called as witnesses. One was that it might endanger them; and in fact many spies only agreed to work for the government on condition they were not asked to give evidence in open court, on these grounds. Another was that giving evidence immediately blew their cover and finished them as spies. This was why no spy evidence was brought against Despard in 1803: in order that these 'sources of useful intelligence' should remain 'unsuspected and unimpaired for the *future security of the State*'.[55] A third reason for not calling spies as witnesses was the public odium that attached to them, and consequently to their evidence. The government learned this the hard way, in 1794 when the treason trial of Thomas Hardy, Horne Tooke and others failed, largely because Erskine, their counsel, decided to go for the spies. One of the latter retorted at one stage that 'I do not think, upon such an occasion, being a spy is any disgrace'; but it clearly did not wash.[56]

After 1794 governments were much more careful about this. It could be frustrating. 'The intelligence with which we are furnished', wrote the Irish viceroy in December 1797, 'would, if certain persons could be brought forward, be sufficient to bring the conspiracy to light.' But this could not be done. In Ireland the first two problems were more serious than the third. If an informer could be induced to give evidence, the authorities were halfway there. Juries were clearly less repelled by spies than their English counterparts. Thomas Reynolds, for example, gave evidence against the 1798 conspirators, and was attacked by the defence in much the same way as the English informers had been by Erskine: but to less effect.[57] The main difficulty in Ireland was getting informers into the witness box in the first place. The result of that, as J. A. Froude commented, was that 'The Government was in the absurd position of being driven to prove, by imperfect and inferential testimony, what they knew to be beyond the shadow of doubt.'[58]

There were only two ways out. One was to accept that some guilty men would escape. In February 1798, for example, Father James Coigley (or O'Coigley), the founder of the United Britons, was arrested with four others at Margate on his way to France to ask for French help. The main reason for suspecting them was the testimony of spies and Bow Street officers, who had been shadowing them for weeks. All of them were tried, but only Coigley was convicted and hanged, because he was found with an incriminating document in his pocket. Any documents which would incriminate the others had been flushed down a toilet in the King's Head in Margate, when one of them had been allowed by the Bow Street Runner guarding them to leave the room. The government was reluctant to bring out its informers to give evidence against them, and so they got off. The inconvenience of this was mitigated a little by the suspension of habeas corpus, which allowed one of them – John Binns – to be kept in prison for two years without trial.[59]

The other solution was to 'plant' evidence, and the like. The trouble with that was that it was counter-productive in the long run. No doubt the British distrust of spies was irrational and prejudiced in origin; but it was enormously bolstered by any revelations of 'dirty tricks' that came along. They bred distrust. 'Innocence itself', wrote John Binns in his *Recollections*, 'was but a slender safeguard against the arts and influence of such a government' and its spies.[60] Whether or not he really believed this, others were willing to. Charles James Fox went so far as to claim in 1800 that such 'insurrections and rebellions ... *never did exist* but in the imagination of *a set of men who raise such reports* that they may the more easily depress the cause of freedom'. They were saying that in Ireland too.[61] If spies could manufacture evidence, the argument went, why could they not manufacture entire plots?

That was the dilemma. Spies were a terribly flawed weapon, however necessary they might have been. They could detect plots, but they could not prove them in open court. They were driven to contrive other ways of proving them, therefore; which only discredited them the more. The more discredited they were, the more discreditable they became. It was a vicious circle; or rather, a pattern of interlocking ones. There was no way out, in the climate of opinion as it was then.

The public feeling against spies is indisputable; but that is not to say that it was justified. No spy, of course, can ever be an entirely honest man or woman; but some of these spies may at least have been straight in what they reported and did. Many were reliable informants: George Lynam in England, for example, and Samuel Turner in Ireland, who so far as we can make out sent back accurate information, and did not embroider or exaggerate. That secret agents could be moderately intelligent, balanced and open-minded is evidenced by a little incident that took place in August 1797 regarding the sighting of two ominous-looking foreigners in the Quantock Hills in Somerset. The incident also exemplifies some of the real difficulties the authorities were up against in this kind of field.

The men were first spotted by a Thomas Jones of Alfoxton. He then told Charles Mogg, who told Dr Lysons of Bath, who wrote on their behalf to the Home Secretary: that 'some French people had got possession of the Mansion House', and were acting highly suspiciously. One of them, for example, had come up to Christopher Trickie and asked him whether a certain brook was navigable to the sea. Every day and night they were seen walking around with maps, and 'a Portfolio in which they enter their observations, which they have been heard to say were almost finished', and that 'they should be rewarded for them'. They had also been observed 'washing and Mending their cloathes all Sunday'. One of them had 'no wife with him, but only a woman who passes for his sister'. It all looked very odd. So the Home Office sent one of its spies, a 'G. Walsh', down to scout around. 'You will narrowly watch their proceedings,' ran his instructions; making sure that his conduct gave 'no cause of suspicion to the Inhabitants of the Mansion house'. If they moved house, he was to 'follow their track'. He was given £20 for his expenses.

When Walsh got to Alfoxton, he soon found that the pair were not spies, but something even more exciting. Thelwall, the famous agitator, had been in the area recently, and was bound to have paid a call. So, reported Walsh on the 15th, 'I think this will turn out no French affair, but a mischievous gang of disaffected Englishmen.' The next day he had more news. One of the men had a servant, 'who is very Chatty', and had told Thomas Jones 'that her Master was a Phylosopher'. He had also, he wrote, 'just procured the Name of the person who took the House. His name is *Wordsworth*.' He had with him 'a Mr Coldridge and his wife . . . This Coldridge came last from Bristol and is reckoned a Man of superior Ability.' He was also suspected of writing a book. All this could only mean one thing. 'The inhabitants of Alfoxton House are a Sett of violent Democrats.'

All this comes from government documents. Unfortunately the official reports end there. Many years later Samuel Taylor Coleridge – who had been on holiday with his wife and his friends William and Dorothy Wordsworth, writing and talking and sketching Nature – gave his version of the affair. He described how the 'detective' came up and insinuated himself into conversation with him, pretending to be a Jacobin to draw him out. Before long he was reassured by what Coleridge had to say, and revealed himself as a spy. He told how he had listened to their talk from behind a bank near the beach, and on one occasion thought he had been discovered: 'for he often heard me talk of one *Spy Nozy*, which he was inclined to interpret of himself and of a remarkable feature belonging to him'. Presumably after that the operation was called off, leaving the poets to discuss their Spinoza in private. But no confirmation of that is extant.[62]

If Walsh was as wise in the outcome as Coleridge paints him, then we can forgive his original error. It was not, after all, such a gross one. It was not unreasonable to fear a French invasion on the Somerset coast, just six months after the Pembrokeshire landing. Walsh had seen almost straight away that these two strangers were not necessarily French, just because their speech seemed 'foreign' to some Somerset yokels, and because they did their washing on the Lord's day. Both the poets could be classed as political radicals, so he was not far wrong there. Coleridge had indeed corresponded with Thelwall, though nothing had come of it. Walsh had allowed himself to be persuaded of the men's 'innocence', which is not the mark of a paranoiac. All in all, the incident – or what we know of it – does not reflect too discreditably either on 'Spy Nozy' Walsh, or on the men who employed him. It is something to put on the other side of the balance, against the rather more oppressive bulk of Edward John Newell.

Chapter 3

Spies and bloodites!
(1805–25)

French agents or British democrats: in the 1790s it came to very much the same thing. This was what helped justify setting spies on home-grown subversives: the belief that however home-grown they claimed to be, they were in effect acting as fifth columnists for a putative invader. That was Pitt's government's main reason, or excuse, for its domestic secret service. It was an extension of the main military effort against France.

That rationale worked for a while. It did not silence all the critics of Pitt's 'spy system', but it isolated and disarmed them, so that there was no serious challenge to that system, for example, in Parliament. Government spies – so long as they kept clear of law courts – could get on with their work relatively unhampered by a hostile public opinion, or a minister nervous of the same. They appear to have been effective. After 1803 subversion and sedition receded both in Britain and in Ireland. A spy called Joseph Thomas claimed that this was as a result of the discovery of the Despard plot, since when, he said, people had become 'sick of Politicks', because they knew now that they could do nothing 'without exposure'.[1] If this was true, then it was one up to the spies. Another explanation is that English Jacobins had become thoroughly disillusioned – as well they might – with the progress of the revolution in France. That halved the French threat, so far as the government was concerned. Napoleon remained to be defeated; but after he made himself emperor in December 1804 he could never again be an English or a Scottish or even an Irish democrat's great white hope. The potent link between domestic subversion and foreign menace was broken, and remained broken, as it turned out, for more than a hundred years.

That was good for the government in one way; but a side-effect was to weaken its justification for employing spies. Subversion was at a low ebb after 1803, but that did not mean it was gone for good. It could easily rear its head again, and this time without any foreign gleam in its eye. That would make a difference. How would the authorities cope with it? Could they still resort to domestic espionage in a situation where there was no longer any convincing threat of foreign invasion, and against dissident movements which were clearly and unambiguously British? *Would* they? And if they did, how would the public respond?

In fact the relative domestic peace which followed the failure of Despard's conspiracy was never likely to last. There are three possible reasons for the absence of dissent and sedition in any society. One is that people are contented; the second is that they are cowed; and the third is that they believe protest is pointless. The quiet of the seven or eight years after 1803 owed much to the second and third reasons, and very little to the first. A vast number of people were cowed and discouraged, but by no means contented with their lot. This was because that lot was, objectively, awful.

Two things combined to make it awful. One was the effects of the war against France, which hit employment by taxing and also interrupting trade, and then – when it was over – hit it again by cutting off the demand for war materials while at the same time disgorging thousands of ex-soldiers on to the labour market. The second was the Industrial Revolution: the process by which Britain was currently being transformed from an agrarian feudal society into an industrial capitalist one. That, of course, was a much longer-term event, which started way back, and may not be fully completed yet; but it has never been an even, steady transformation, and happened to be in one of its least steady phases in the 1810s. Traditional domestic manufacturing methods were being displaced by mass production in many areas, especially textiles. Hand-loom weavers, forced to compete with the new system, found themselves impoverished or ruined. Factory workers were subjected to market disciplines they had been largely sheltered from before. In times of trade depression those disciplines could be very harsh indeed, producing what Earl Grey in 1817 called 'severe and intolerable distress'.[2]

Grey believed that it was this distress which was causing the 'irritations' of that time. It also to a large extent determined the forms those irritations took. Many of them were straightforwardly economic. Strikes – like the one which at one stage in 1808 stopped 60,000 Manchester cotton looms – were an obvious form of economic protest. Luddism was even more so. That started up in Nottinghamshire in the winter of 1811–12, spread rapidly and widely thereafter, and eventually died away in 1816. The Luddites' main targets were the factories and machines which they saw as the direct cause of their sufferings, with occasionally a millowner or overseer who got in the way of their mobs. It was a desperate cause, and doomed to failure. One reason for that was supposed to be Parliament's intransigence, which consequently turned many working people to the question of parliamentary reform. In Scotland, for example, impoverished weavers first struck for higher wages, then petitioned for a minimum wage and then, when their petitions fell on stony ground, began agitating for the wider franchise which would – they hoped – spread a more fertile humanitarian topsoil over the stones. 'Hampden Clubs' sprang up from 1812 onwards, mainly composed of artisans, to press for 'Reform'. (By that time the adjective had become superfluous: everyone knew what needed to be reformed.) In 1816 came the first of a series of mass demonstrations to this end: in Thrushgrove near Glasgow at the end of October, when an estimated 40,000 people attended, and then at Spa Fields in south London in December. The latter turned into a riot, which gave rise to a celebrated trial. One of the reasons it was celebrated was that it was a trial not merely for rioting, but for high treason. The government was back on that old track again.

With it returned all the associated paraphernalia of the French revolutionary years. 'Committees of Secrecy' met once more, examined witnesses, deliberated, and reported ominously to Parliament. Habeas corpus was suspended. Dreadful conspiracies were uncovered. One involved a handful of men who set out to march on London from Manchester in March 1817, and were called the 'Blanketeers' because they carried blankets to keep them warm at night. That was broken up by troops. In June 1817 came the 'Pentrich rebellion', which was apparently designed to be just part of a nationwide uprising embracing hundreds of thousands of men and women converging on London to seize the government, but in fact in the end involved just two or three hundred, who scarcely got any distance at all before a troop of Hussars put them down. In August 1819 came the 'Peterloo massacre', when the local yeomanry lashed out at men, women and children attending a monster meeting on St Peter's Fields in Manchester, killing eleven and wounding around four hundred, because they feared that a revolution might be in the air. Later that year the Glasgow magistrates called out the army to prevent a revolution that was said to be about to break out there; in the event nothing happened, which means either that nothing was about to happen, or that the magistrates' precaution was effective. Soon afterwards something did happen – or was meant to – in London, when on 23 February 1820 a group of conspirators in a room in a house in Cato Street in Marylebone was surprised while plotting to assassinate the entire Cabinet at a dinner, and most of them captured. Two months after that, in April 1820, there was a general strike in western Scotland, and a mass meeting which led to yet another attempt at a revolution: this time by a pathetic group of a couple of dozen men who set out on a march to Stirling, but were caught by a platoon of soldiers as they stopped off for a rest on Bonnymuir just outside Glasgow. The soldiers expected them either to surrender or to try to flee, which would have been sensible in the circumstances; and were surprised when the rebels instead decided to stand their ground and fight. (They were Glaswegians, after all.) That was the 'Battle of Bonnymuir'. It marked the end of this particular revolutionary phase of Britain's history: if, that is, any of these incidents really was important enough to merit the description 'revolutionary'.

Lord Liverpool's government either believed so, or affected to. Hence the spate of treason trials that followed that of the Spa Fields rioters in June 1817, and in the end accounted for the deaths (by public execution) of around a dozen 'traitors', not to mention the imprisonment and transportation of several scores more. Enormous controversy surrounded those trials at the time, and surrounds them still. They were certainly not fair in many ways, partly because the contemporary atmosphere was not right for fairness in this field. They seemed to make revolutionary mountains out of molehills, either deliberately, or because the perceptions of judges and jurors were genuinely distorted by their fears. 'These men', said Earl Grey, incredulously, referring to Spa Fields, 'were without means, without influence, support, or plan; yet it was said, they meant to barricade Oxford-road, to block up the streets leading to the Bank, to seize the shipping in the river, and to attack the Tower without cannon.'[3] Who on earth could really credit that?

Yet some apparently did. For proof, they pointed to the conclusions of their Committees of Secrecy, which in this particular case, for example, insisted that 'however improbable the success' of such a plot might seem, it was real enough. The country was riddled with subversion. Some of it went under the guise of 'Reform' societies – Hampden Clubs and the like – which were rarely as moderate and innocent as they liked to pretend. This was especially so in the manufacturing districts of the north of England, where the clubs were 'composed of the lower orders of artizans' whose real, secret object was 'nothing short of a revolution'. There was widespread talk of rebellion; of 'overturning what they call "the privileged class"'; of seizing and redistributing property; of undermining the 'habits of decent and regular subordination' among ordinary people; and even of abolishing God. Revolutionary plans were being co-ordinated nationally, so that when one town rose, all the others in Britain would too. Orders had been placed with pike manufacturers. 'The facility of converting implements of husbandry into offensive weapons has been suggested.' Drawings had been discovered of a projected machine 'for clearing the streets of cavalry'. Soldiers and sailors had been suborned. 'Black books' were being compiled of men who stayed loyal. And most terrifying of all, for those who had not yet forgotten the events of the 1790s: 'tricoloured' ribbons, cockades and standards – 'the symbols of the French revolution' – had been definitely spotted among the crowds in Thrushgrove and Spa Fields and elsewhere.

These were some of the 1817 committee's conclusions. Its members were adamant that they were not exaggerating. They found the evidence that had been presented to them convincing. Unfortunately they could not reproduce any of it there, 'without hazarding the personal safety of many useful and many respectable individuals'.[4] Some of those individuals were government spies. That was where the problem lay. By 1817 spies were a subject of controversy in themselves. The next few years saw the entire breed discredited in the eyes of probably a majority of the public, due to the alleged and well-publicized villainies of three or four of them. This led to the widespread suspicion that all this Secret Committee 'evidence' – or at least, much of it – could have been invented, manufactured, or 'provoked' by them.

Although the main furore about spies broke out in 1817, this was not the first time since 1804 that the authorities had used them. In fact they had never stopped using them; but without anyone being greatly aware of it, partly because the remainder of that decade was – from a subversive point of view – so dull.[5] They came back into the public eye when the Luddites started up: though initially the government had problems here. The early Luddites proved highly resistant to infiltration and treachery, even when large rewards were offered them. This exasperated but also quite impressed many of their betters, one of whom, for example, felt that such loyalty was 'worthy of a better cause'.[6]

It may have had something to do with their class. Most seditious movements in the past had been at any rate *led* by men of 'substance' and education. The Secret Committee of 1812 seemed surprised that this one was not. It had been told on good authority, it reported, that the Luddites' leaders, 'although they may possess considerable influence, are still of the lowest orders', however unlikely that might seem.[7] (Some people would never credit this, and maintained that if intelligent Englishmen were not at the centre of the conspiracy, then intelligent Frenchmen must be.)[8] The Luddites also clearly had the sympathy of the general populace, though that could have been accounted for (suggested the committee) by the terror tactics they used against informers.[9] This stumped the authorities. None of the inducements which had traditionally succeeded with other classes of subversive seemed to work at all here. They could not worm their own men into the movement, which was the method they preferred, because they would stand out so. (They may not have had any genuinely working-class spies on their books; and they certainly did not have any who could pass as Nottinghamshire stocking-makers.) When they tried to fall back on local material, they often found it was unsuitable. The men of the West country, apparently, were the worst. 'The Inhabitants of these parts', wrote General Maitland, who was the officer commanding the troops there in 1812, 'have not the sharpness of understanding nor the determination of Character which belong to those of the North, and it is therefore very difficult to find amongst them Persons fit for the purpose': which the men of the North, if they had been able to read this, might not have taken as an unambiguous compliment to them.

The root of the problem, however, went deeper. Clearly what deterred many competent men from acting as spies was their moral scruples. The sort of people they could rely on, wrote Maitland again, felt 'extreme difficulty in going to the lengths they must necessarily do to be of any real utility', which he acknowledged was 'very much to their credit', but meant that government had to do instead with men 'of a Character whose information must be received with extreme caution'.[10] That was bound to lead to trouble.

It did. Except in one regard, government espionage among the Luddites was never satisfactory. The one satisfactory aspect to it was that it helped bring Luddism to an end. One of the advantages of any domestic spy system (from the authorities' point of view) is that it can inflict enormous damage on its target, even if it is relatively inefficient in other ways. It does this mainly by undermining morale. If a secret society is persuaded that it is infiltrated by spies, then it is very soon paralysed. It cannot function if it is constantly fearing exposure, or manipulation by *agents provocateurs*. If the spy system is efficient, then it helps, because the conspirators can see their genuine plans being betrayed or sabotaged. But it does not need to be. Mistrust is something that can be nurtured and cultivated even when there is no real ground for it. Whisper the word 'spy' urgently enough in a gathering of conspirators, and some of them, at least, will believe that even their most revered leaders are in the pay of the police. The early nineteenth-century radical Samuel Bamford described one period, around 1817, when 'A cloud of gloom and mistrust hung over the whole country', because of the informers and *provocateurs* who were supposed to be rife.

> Our Society . . . became divided and dismayed; hundreds slunk home to their looms, nor dared to come out, save like owls at nightfall, when they would perhaps steal through bye-paths or behind hedges, or down some clough, to hear the news at the next cottage . . .

and all through *fear* of espionage.[11] This, according to F. O. Darvall, was one of the main reasons for the defeat of Luddism in Yorkshire. 'Once the Luddites lost confidence in their security, and began to fear detection, as they did soon after spies began to be employed, the movement came rapidly to an end.'[12]

This success, however, says nothing for the intrinsic merits of the government's spy network in the early 1810s. A glance at either of the Committee of Secrecy reports which were put before Parliament in the summer of 1812, for example, suggests that they were constructed on an extremely threadbare basis of solid intelligence. Much of their information – about riots which had already taken place – could have been gathered from any newspaper. On the secret side of the Luddite 'conspiracy', most of their conclusions were based simply on inference ('Their proceedings manifest a degree of caution and organization which *appears* to flow from the direction of some persons under whose influence they act'), or gossip. Little appeared to come from the *inside*.[13] Samuel Whitbread, who was a member of one of the committees, revealed that a number of anonymous reports *had* been placed before them, but without their being given the opportunity to examine their veracity or even their sources. Some of the reports, he claimed, were self-evidently 'violent and contradictory'; and all in all he felt that 'no reliance whatever' should be placed on them. He was also influenced in this by the testimony of an adjutant of one of the local militias, to the effect that ten of his men had gone among the Luddites in Bolton with their faces blacked up as a disguise, in order to persuade them to burn down the local workhouse. So far as he was concerned that sullied the evidence of them all.[14]

He was almost certainly right to be sceptical. The tale of the black-faced Bolton militiamen was true. One of those militiamen was half of a father-and-son spy team, Simeon and John Stones, whom the surviving records show to have been persistent *agents provocateurs*. One of the most celebrated Luddite attacks, the firing of Wray & Duncroff's mill at Westhoughton on 24 April 1812, had been plotted by them weeks before. That does not mean quite what it seems. The Stoneses had urged the Luddites to burn the mill, so that the authorities could come in and arrest them while they were at it; but had seemed to get nowhere with them. When the mill was eventually attacked, it was independently of the spies, and at a moment when the authorities were not expecting it.[15] Whether or not the incident can be attributed to *agents provocateurs*, therefore, is a moot point. Nevertheless, the proof of *agent provocateur* activities is there. And this was not an isolated case. The Stoneses may have been the shadiest of the anti-Luddite spies, but they were not the only suspicious ones. A man called MacDonald, who helped convict some Halifax men for taking illegal oaths in 1812, was so disreputable that even the prosecution lawyer was surprised that the jury had accepted his word. Later on the testimony of another spy, Samuel Fleming, was thrown out when a defence witness who had overheard the meeting at which Fleming claimed oaths had been administered deposed that nothing of the sort had gone on there at all. One historian claims that *all* the cases involving this particular offence were either trumped up or else provoked by spies.[16] If so, then the intention was clearly deliberate. In other cases spies may have exaggerated or imagined things out of sheer stupidity. One example is the leading Bolton informer Bent, who swallowed the most lurid rumours that came to him, and was always predicting dreadful revolutionary events that never transpired.[17] Bent was typical of a large number of men the government relied on for its intelligence, to the scorn of Samuel Whitbread and his ilk.

The main reason for this clearly lay in the Luddites' sense of solidarity, which meant that in very few cases were spies able to penetrate their higher echelons. Another reason may be that there were no higher echelons – no real hierarchy – to penetrate. It left the spies with two alternatives. One was to report from the edges of the movement only, and hope that accurate information filtered through: which it rarely did. The other was to *create* some hierarchies on their own account. That seems to have been the policy in Lancashire, where a number of 'secret committees' were formed, supposedly to direct and co-ordinate the conspiracy, in which spies were prominent from the start.[18] This ensured that the intelligence getting through was accurate: but in some instances only because it was contrived. The problem with that was that genuine radicals often got wise to it. Samuel Bamford, for example, kept well clear of the 'Manchester Committee' after he learned that it was 'reported to be under the influence of spies from the police'.[19] Such committees could usually find one or two men with less sense than Bamford to go along with them, and take their bait; but they could never land the really big fishes, who were more wary. As well as that, the suspicion that this sort of thing might be going on had another important counter-effect. It allowed radicals to claim, and possibly to believe, that *all* the most violent incidents were contrived in this way. This became a powerful argument later on.

Bamford, for example, took this line. 'It was not until we became infested by spies, incendiaries and dupes,' he later wrote in his memoirs, ' ... that physical force was mentioned amongst us.'[20] That put the main responsibility for all the worst atrocities firmly at the authorities' front door. Another radical went further, and claimed that the entire Luddite phenomenon was a plot on the part of the government to justify turning Britain into a tyranny.[21] The latter charge can be rejected out of hand, because there is not a sliver of evidence for it. More moderate versions of it, however, have featured in the debate about early nineteenth-century protest ever since.

For the radicals of the time the idea had obvious attractions. It brought the government into disrepute; and it might – if they could get enough people to accept it, especially jurors – save some other radicals' necks. Whigs were also attracted to it, because they were predisposed to doubt the reality of the revolutionary threat anyway. They may have been mistaken. Just because spies invented and provoked conspiracies, it does not follow that every conspiracy was invented or provoked by them. The circumstances of the time, after all, were dire enough to push desperate men to all kinds of 'excesses', without government agents needing to be involved. Secret oaths and committees, and drilling and arming, and all the rest of the revolutionary trappings that were reported by spies in the early 1810s, were not *unlikely* products of a period of history when so much was changing so fundamentally, and so many men and women were suffering as a result of that change.[22] It may be that the testimony of the spies – even the 'sensationalist' ones –

was sometimes accurate in essence, even if it was not in hard fact. In the long term, however, this did not matter, because so many of their hard facts became discredited. This was the line the radicals plugged then; and it had momentous results.

For the second most significant effect of the use of spies by Lord Liverpool's government against the Luddites, after helping to destroy *them*, was to help destroy the spy system itself. In this regard it resembled a bee, which in stinging its adversary in order to repel it also brings an end to its own life. The process took longer than it does with a bee; but there was one climactic moment, when the sting entered the alien body, so to speak, just before becoming separated. That was between 1817 and 1820, when the government (to switch metaphors) decided to wield its spy weapon against a dragon which it called 'high treason', and the weapon shattered in its hand.

Why it should have risked this in the *first* instance, in the trial of Dr James Watson arising out of the Spa Fields meeting of 2 December 1816, is not easy to understand. Watson was a wild revolutionary who was clearly responsible, with others, for inciting part of the Spa Fields crowd to riot. He could have been convicted and hanged for that with very little trouble at all. But the authorities were not content with that. They wanted to get him and his cronies for high treason. This may have been because they were genuinely persuaded of it by the intelligence that came to them; or because they had an ulterior motive, such as catching important radical leaders like Hunt and Cobbett in their net, or persuading Parliament of the need for firmer measures. To prove high treason, they had to show that the riot in which Watson and company had participated had been deliberately plotted beforehand. The man to do that, they hoped, was John Castle (or Castles), a maker of paper dolls for children, who gave evidence.

Making paper dolls for children probably went in his favour. But it was the only thing about him that did. When he was called to give his evidence, as a witness for the prosecution, he was soon seen to labour under two disadvantages. One was that he had been actively implicated in Watson's 'plot' himself, and by his own admission had been vital to various stages of it. Other witnesses testified that he had tried to egg on more moderate (or cautious) radicals to violence, on one occasion by proposing the fine old Jacobin toast: 'May the last of the kings be strangled with the guts of the last priest.' The second thing against him was his character. This, again, was revealed by his own testimony, cleverly winkled out of him by a gleeful defence attorney. It transpired from this that he had already acted as an 'approver' – that is, someone who participates in a crime and then turns king's evidence – on two occasions before. On one of them (a forgery case) his victim had been hanged. He had a wife (*née* Prickett) who had been in a position to corroborate some of his charges, if they had been true, but had been mysteriously spirited away into Yorkshire before the trial, and could not be found. At the same time as he had been married to her, he had also cohabited with a Mrs Thoms, who kept a boarding house for young ladies in Soho which he now admitted to have been a brothel, though he claimed that it had not occurred to him at the time. A *Times* reporter who had known him from childhood stated that he was 'a person not to be believed at any time on his oath'. Much of his evidence was directly contradicted by others. Watson's defence lawyer, Sergeant Copley, thanked the Crown warmly for calling Castle as a witness: as well he might. The jury did not credit a word this 'bawdy-house bully' had to say. It may also have found his account of Watson's plot simply too ludicrous; as we have seen, Earl Grey did too, when that selfsame account (clearly from the same source) appeared as the basis of the Committee of Secrecy report in February. Watson was acquitted; and the charges against his co-conspirators, which had been intended to follow, were dropped.[23] The judge – the prejudiced old reactionary who had succeeded in getting Despard condemned fourteen years before, and had hoped to do the same again – was mortified.[24] It was a famous anti-spy victory: one of the very few there have ever been.

Castle now became the most notorious spy villain in British memory, entirely displacing Reynolds, who had held that honour until then. But Castle was not to carry it for long. His humiliating cross-examination in the Watson case came on 11 June. Just three days later the *Leeds Mercury* announced that it had found a card to trump him. He was known as William Oliver, though his real name is supposed to have been Richards. Accounts of him describe him as a builder or a builder's clerk, nearly six feet tall, 'inclined to be corpulent', with fair hair and red whiskers, and smartly dressed. He was originally Welsh, but had lived in London for thirty years.[25] According to the *Mercury* Lord Sidmouth, the Home Secretary who took most of the stick for these goings-on, had sent him up to the north and Midlands on a mission to provoke radicals into a treasonable rebellion, which could then be broken by the government. His technique was to travel from place to place pretending to be a delegate from a radical committee in London, and telling the men in each town he visited that those in the town he had just come from would rise if they did.[26] The outcome of this was the Pentrich rebellion in Derbyshire, after which three men – the leader, Jeremiah Brandreth, and two others – were hanged and decapitated for high treason in November, and twenty-three transported.

This may have been why 'Oliver the Spy' always thereafter retained his pre-eminent place in radical demonology, even though on the surface Castle looks a likelier candidate. There have always been doubts surrounding Oliver, and even defenders: from the Tory MP Henry Bathurst, who insisted in February 1818 that Oliver's 'private character' was 'to that hour unimpeached',[27] to at least a couple of modern historians, who assert that there is no convincing proof that he was ever anything more than an ordinary spy.[28] Castle has never had any defenders. But then he failed, whereas Oliver (if his detractors are right about the link between him and Brandreth) succeeded: which made him the more effective villain, and therefore, by extension, a more craven one. There was another thing. Oliver succeeded because he was never exposed in front of a defence lawyer and a jury like Castle had been, so that he could not (from the prosecution's point of view) prejudice the result of any trial. This meant that less was known about him. And it is always easier to make demons out of men of mystery, than out of people whose every little vice and weakness has been prodded and laid bare.

In a way it was odd that Oliver never did – at least in this role – see the inside of a court room. Apparently the prosecution in the Pentrich case had him at the ready, signed in to an inn nearby under an alias, in case he was needed there. But it was not going to introduce him itself. Afterwards there was much discussion over why the *defence* did not call him, when all the newspapers were shouting that he was the one who had egged the Pentrich rebels on. Lord Denman, who appeared for them, had planned to make this the main plank of his defence originally, but then changed his mind. He afterwards explained the reasoning behind this: which was that if Oliver had been *his* witness, he would not have been allowed to cross-examine him, which would have meant that the weight of his evidence would have gone against his clients. Alternatively, Denman may have been 'bought' by the government; or attracted by a plea bargain; or genuinely persuaded that Oliver was not in fact the *provocateur* his enemies claimed.[29] In any event the latter was unlikely to have had the same effect on this case as Castle had done earlier on. Castle's undoing had been his immoral life-style; there was far less dirt available on Oliver, though rumour had it that he had been a fraudster, a prisoner in the Fleet, a bigamist (like Castle) and a Freemason.[30] Then again, the evidence against Brandreth without Oliver was far more convincing than the evidence against Watson without Castle had been: which was another reason why the Crown did not call Oliver – it did not need to. Lastly, the jury was packed. Local solicitors had been hard at work in Derby in the days before the trial opened there, collecting 'intelligence ... as to every Juror', to ensure that they were all 'respectable'.[31] Such a jury might not have been over-impressed by an 'anti-spy' defence even if a convincing one could have been got up. So Oliver was kept from the court, and then – apparently – smuggled out of the country under yet another *nom de guerre*. One assumes it was to a nice little living at the Cape. In any event, nothing was ever seen or heard of him again.

The result of this, as one of his more recent champions fairly points out, was that 'he has never had the right of reply'.[32] If he had stayed around, it is unlikely that he would have been given one even then. A contemporary pamphlet vividly illustrates why. It described how a poor innocent butler

called J. McCullen was once walking along Oxford Street in London, when
suddenly

> a hackney-coachman who had conceived some ill-will towards him called
> out, '*There goes Oliver the spy*'. A mob immediately surrounded the unfor-
> tunate butler, and he was first hustled and jostled about, then pelted with
> mud and filth, and finally dragged towards the nearest pump.

When he was eventually rescued, by a concerned passer-by, he was 'more
dead than alive'. That demonstrated, concluded the pamphleteer, 'what sort
of reception Mr. Oliver is likely to meet with, should he ever be discovered'.[33]
Popular feeling was in no mood to be reasoned with.

It was on the basis of this initial prejudice, and the mystery surrounding
Oliver, that the truth of his role and activities in the summer of 1817 – whatever that may have been – became encrusted with myths. He started appearing
everywhere in retrospect. Samuel Bamford, looking back, remembered once
meeting 'a well-dressed, and apparently affluent stranger', who was trying
to push the Lancashire men to all kinds of desperate deeds, and who he
now realized must have been 'Oliver the Spy'.[34] He popped up again three
years later, in connection with an illegal proclamation planted on a Scottish
schoolmaster, John Fraser, which Fraser himself claimed in his autobiography
was 'proved ... some years afterwards' to have been 'concocted under the
auspices of Government by two spies, Oliver and Richmond'.[35] In that case
he cannot have gone to South Africa after all. He was also traced further *back*.
'A Correspondent' reported in 1817 that 'Oliver is by no means a novice in
matters of treason, but that he was closely and deeply implicated in the mad
schemes of Colonel Despard and his associates' in 1802.[36] No doubt if he had
been old enough his hand would have been seen in the Gunpowder Plot too.
In this way a figure of no great intrinsic historical importance, one of a large
number of government spies in the 1810s, who seems to have worked in that
capacity for only a few months, and was probably not the wickedest of them,
was transformed into a monster, an ogre, a byword for treachery and deceit.

That may have been more than the real Oliver strictly deserved. But then
the mythical Oliver was not supposed to be true to the man. Rather, he was
symbolic of a system: a system which countered unrest born of genuine
material distress by seducing the restless into desperate excesses, and then
hanging and decapitating them before crowds of other distressed people in
order to deter them from voicing similar dissent. This, at any rate, was how
it appeared to the critics.

Those critics really started to make their voices heard in the summer of
1817. They were not very effective at first. So far as Parliament was concerned,
the main result of the events of that time was to frighten the government's

supporters to persist with repression. Habeas corpus was suspended in February 1817, and then again just after the Pentrich rising in June. The measure was carried comfortably on both occasions. On the second one, however, it also aroused vociferous minority opposition, most of which turned on the practice of using spies.

The onslaught began on 16 June. In the Lords Earl Grosvenor compared the likes of Oliver to 'Satan himself' and claimed that only 'tyrannies' employed them. Earl Grey – another Whig – called Oliver 'the foulest of traitors, and the most atrocious of criminals; a person setting at defiance the laws of God and man'. As for the system under which he had operated, Grey went on, he understood that it had been

> condemned by orators and statesmen, by writers and great men of every age and nation; that it was a practice sanctioned only by the most despotic governments; that it poisoned the sources of confidence between man and man; that it was destructive of domestic happiness and individual security, and altogether inconsistent with the existence of public freedom.

Other peers followed suit. In the Commons the attack was led by Sir Francis Burdett, on the basis of the *Leeds Mercury* report.[37] The row went on through the summer, and then was resumed the following February. In both the Lords and the Commons there were calls for an official inquiry into the use of spies.[38] They came to nothing; but the feeling exhibited in them was intense.

It was the same in the country at large. Attacks on the 'spy system' appeared everywhere. Leigh Hunt's *Examiner* for 6 July 1817 carried a lengthy diatribe against what he called 'those jackals of despotism, those dastardly beasts of prey'. William Hazlitt devoted two articles in the *Morning Chronicle* to attacking this 'new French pattern' of keeping order in the state. Other newspapers followed suit. Broadsheets and pamphlets were published devoted just to this issue. One of them took the form of a popular account of Watson's trial.[39] Another, called *Spies and Bloodites!*, was sub-titled *The Lives and Political History of those Arch-Fiends Oliver, Reynolds, & Co., Treason-Hatchers, Green-Bag-Makers, Blood-Hunters, Spies, Tempters, and Informers-General to His Majesty's Ministers*: which can have left no one in much doubt as to the line it would take. ('Green-Bag-Makers' referred to the evidence presented to the 1817 Committee of Secrecy, which was packed in a green bag.) The question aroused the strongest of feelings, on a broad political front. This was because it touched two particular nerves.

The first was to do with 'blood money', about which there had been considerable controversy in the past.[40] Hence the neologism 'bloodite', which was clearly coined (by Sir Francis Burdett) with this in mind. 'Blood money' was the payment made over to people who detected or informed the authorities of capital crimes. Some men were supposed to make a regular living from it, by entrapping the people they betrayed. Everyone deplored it in the case of 'ordinary' crimes. With political offences it was supposed to be worse, because it could be perverted by despotic governments, and because of the nature of its victims. Generally those victims were not criminals, or the criminally inclined, but men driven by desperation and idealism into foolishness. This was the theme of countless condemnations of the 'spy system' around 1817. The young Irish peer Lord Nugent, for example, waxed indignant about 'wretches whose trade it is to create disaffection in order to betray it . . . associating with traitors, encouraging and abetting and fortifying their treasons, in order to sell their blood at a better price!' Another MP spoke of them 'selling the blood of the people' – poor people, earning just six or seven shillings a week for working fifteen hours a day – for a salary twice that size, or more. Nothing, claimed Burdett, could be 'more atrocious, especially in these times of wretchedness and distress, than for a government to hire and pay people to *excite* sedition . . . Could anything be more odious and detestable . . .?'[41] 'The spy', wrote the anonymous author of *Spies and Bloodites!*, 'obtains gold for blood, and the more blood he can spill the more gold does he obtain.'[42] The very idea conjured up the most revolting of images.

The second nerve which critics of the spy system could expect to get a tweak from was the patriotic one. Patriotism implied something different then from what it implies today. Now it is generally linked to reactionary causes, but in Regency times and for many years afterwards it was more often associated with radical ones. What patriots took most pride in was their British *liberties*: which at this time were seen to be directly under threat from the government. This made that government – a Tory one – appear un-British, as well as reactionary. Its 'spy system' was a case in point. For a long time there had been thought to be something peculiarly foreign about spies. The Napoleonic years associated them firmly with the French. That was mainly the doing of Joseph Fouché, Duke of Otranto, who between 1799 and 1815 (with interruptions) perfected the nineteenth century's most ubiquitous, powerful, ruthless, efficient and consequently notorious 'police state'. It was that, more than anything else, which made Bonaparte's championing of *liberté* seem hollow, and highlighted the superiority of the British kind. Nearly every critic made something of this. Here is the Duke of Bedford, speaking in the House of Lords:

> Such a system of *espionage* (he used the French word, because, and he rejoiced in it, there was no adequate word in the English language to express the same meaning) was utterly inconsistent with the free constitution of Britain.

If it were to be adopted there, he suggested, then the secretary of state 'had better go over to Paris and take lessons from M. de Cazes, or some other superintendent of police'.[43] ('Police', of course, were foreign too.) The same point was made – again – in *Spies and Bloodites!*. Spying was part of a plot against 'the liberty of Britons'; a threat to the British constitution; a device borrowed from 'our enslaved neighbours'; 'a system which is of foreign, of *French* origin'.[44] In this sense, it was worse than the disease it was meant to prevent. Some were prepared to follow the implications of this all the way through. One of these was Lord Nugent, who told the House of Commons in June 1817, apropos of espionage, that 'I had rather see my country revolutionized, than see it enslaved'.[45]

Most critics, however, did not accept that this was the real choice before them. That was because the alternative to espionage was not revolution at all. The main evidence for revolutionary tendencies, Lord Archibald Hamilton pointed out, came from the spies themselves, who in his view created 'a total misconception of the real feelings of the population' either on purpose, or through ignorance. They also *provoked* rebellions; from which it followed, obviously, that there would be less chance of rebellions without them. One MP claimed that by employing them, the government had simply 'thrown firebrands into the heap of combustible matter'. Another likened the system to applying 'a blister ... to a sore place', and remarked on how as soon as Oliver had been 'withdrawn' from his mission, 'tranquillity was restored as by a charm, and all was peace'. Of course there was distress, and consequently unrest in the manufacturing districts; but it had been 'loose, scattered, undefined, unregulated' before he had come along.[46] It was the spies themselves, therefore, who contrived the very dangers they pretended to counter and prevent. This was the *practical* argument against them.

The whole case against domestic espionage in 1817–18, though flawed in some respects, was mighty powerful. Eventually, as we shall see, it was to win through. But it did not win against Lord Liverpool's government at the time. That government had its answers ready: both on the particular question of Oliver, who they simply denied was a *provocateur*; and on the broader one. On the latter, the use of spies generally, everything rested on the assumption that there was a genuine threat to order in 1817. Tories were convinced of this. 'We had plots,' said a junior minister, the future Lord Glenelg;

> we had secret oaths; we had organized societies, committees, sub-committees, and delegates; blasphemous and seditious songs; and, above all, the prostitution of the press to the most infamous purpose of destroying all loyalty to the throne and all reverence towards religion; thus making the people immoral, impious, and turbulent upon system.

That being so, it was only sound sense to take counter-measures. Those counter-measures were well tried, and perfectly reasonable and legitimate. Of course they were not confined to 'tyrannies'. Lord Liverpool claimed that they were found 'in all the free states of antiquity', and in Britain for many years. He was, he said, prepared to go further, and 'to assert, that spies and informers had been at all times employed by all governments, and ever must be'. That was because there was no other means 'to secure the information necessary for public tranquillity'.[47]

Of course it was a dirty business. But then many other essential functions of society were too. Some of these spies were not nice people. George Canning admitted that among them might even be some with more than the regulation number of wives. In that case, he asked, what was the government to say to them? '"Be off, you infamous scoundrel; how dare you, a bigamist, presume to give information as to any treasons or plots. You are not worthy of becoming an informer"'? That raised a laugh. But the point was a serious one. 'Were they to make it a rule to accept no intelligence but from persons of the purest virtue? ... In this degenerate age so faultless a monster could hardly be found.' They had no choice but to accept the information that came to them, whatever its source. They could doubt it, question it, try to check it; and of course they ought to take any precautions they could against the danger of agents inciting crimes. In the last resort, however, spies were indispensable. The question boiled down to this: 'whether they would employ the only means which offered themselves, or suffer the state to go to wreck'. Canning's was an eloquent defence of espionage, and went down well. *Hansard* tells us that when he resumed his seat after it, it was 'amidst the loud cheering of the House, which lasted for a considerable time'.[48]

It lasted – figuratively speaking – for another two or three years, during which time Sidmouth's spies continued to be out in force. It was not quite the same game as it had been. Their victims, for example, were on the look-out for them more. When they caught them, they could be very rough. We have already seen how rough they were with poor innocent McCullen, the man who was supposed to be Oliver the Spy. In Manchester on 15 August 1819 they were even rougher with a couple of genuine spies. One of them, a gingerbread maker called James Murrey, later recounted what happened. He and a companion, Shawcross, were keeping watch on some radicals who were drilling on White Moss, when someone shouted out, 'Spy!'

It ran along the lines, and I heard the words, 'Mill them!' 'd--n them!' 'mill them!' and then I heard a cry of 'They are constables;' and the answer to that was 'D--n them! kill them!' I moved off, and so did Shawcross, and we were followed by eighty or ninety men. They overtook Shawcross, and knocked him into the ditch. From twenty to thirty followed, and overtook me. They began to beat me with sticks, and kicked me most violently with their clogs ... They continued beating me; and one said, 'Shall we kill him out and out, and put him in the pit, or let him go?' . . . They then desisted, and held a consultation, after which one of them asked me if I would go down on my knees and never be a king's man again, and never name the king any more. I said 'yes', as I considered my life in danger. I fell on my knees; the words I now mention were proposed to me, and I repeated them, and they let me go.

But the humiliation was not yet through. The next day, confined to bed with his injuries, he heard a crowd marching outside in the road. When it reached his door it stopped, 'and began to hiss very loud'. No further harm came to him, but that was probably enough. Murrey's adventure was retailed in all the local papers afterwards, and may have deterred others from taking employment as spies. On the other hand, according to Samuel Bamford (who was in no real position to know), it was this event which provoked the Manchester authorities to unleash the military on the crowd at 'Peterloo', just four days afterwards.[49]

Events like this, however, were unusual. Generally the radicals' new-found vigilance just meant that they were careful whom they talked to and what they did. Most of them took immense care to avoid the risk of being compromised. In Glasgow, for example, they kept studiously clear of gunpowder and bundles of pikes that were apparently put out for them as bait. Strangers who came along with bold revolutionary plans were immediately sent packing.[50] The Scottish spy Alexander Richmond described how he suddenly came under suspicion in the wake of the Oliver affair. His name, he recalled,

> was immediately associated with a Reynolds, a Castles, and an Oliver . . . If I condemned any measure adopted by government, it was for the purpose of entrapping. If I approved of any, it was to call forth an opposition that some one might commit himself. If I remained silent, I was an eavesdropper, against whom every one ought to be on his guard.[51]

This was bound to make things difficult; and for Richmond it ended his career as a spy. (He was offered the customary passage to the Cape, but turned it down, claimed he had been promised a pension, and then when he was refused it wrote this *exposé*: a pattern we shall see closely repeated on two occasions later on.)

From the government's point of view, however, this was a very minor inconvenience. Its spies were less effective now because the radicals were more wary; but they were only more wary because they thought the spies were *more* effective: which had a tremendous deterrent effect. This was Samuel Bamford's reason for counselling moderation in 1818, for example: that 'ministers had eyes to see and ears to hear, and tongues to whisper whatever occurred', to such an extent that no one was now able to 'take one step beyond the pale of the law, without being instantly in the gripe of the executive'.[52] But it was worse for them than this. Even if they kept within the law, the executive could still get them. This was thanks to the suspension of habeas corpus, which enabled it to detain people without trial. That took care of the other main repercussion of the 1817 spy controversy: which was the harm it had done to the reputation of spies who appeared as witnesses. If there was no trial, there was no need for witnesses; which meant that the government's agents were not exposed. It was all quite neatly done. Spies, it appeared, could convince members of Parliament, but not members of juries. So evidence from spies had been used to persuade members of Parliament to enact a measure to bypass juries. This produced almost the best of all possible worlds. Radicals were deterred from lawbreaking, but imprisoned all the same, and without putting at risk the cover or the reputation of any government spy.

It was not quite the best of all worlds, because men could not be executed in it. Many ministers, and probably more judges, believed that there was nothing quite like a good hanging to make a putative subversive think twice. If spies were finding it more difficult to detect subversive plots, and juries were less likely to trust them anyway, it might still pose a problem. Samuel Bamford was aware of this, and while he was in detention in 1817 organized a system whereby he and his fellow prisoners coached themselves in a single, agreed version of their evidence. Then, as he pointed out, 'if government brought them to trial, it would have to unmask its spies and informers, instead of making them fall by their mutual contradictions, mistrusts, and jealousies, which as it seemed to me, the government would prefer doing'.[53] On this occasion it worked. If every radical had been as wise as Bamford, the effect might have been to frustrate those who hankered after deterrent sentences. But of course some radicals were less wise. In 1820 eight men came forward and (in effect) stuck their own heads into the noose. In each case there was a powerful suspicion that *agents provocateurs* had been at work. But the eight swung nevertheless. This was because the authorities were clever enough to cover their provokers' tracks.

Five of the victims were the ringleaders of the 'Cato Street conspiracy' of February 1820. One of them, Arthur Thistlewood, had also been one of the men arrested after the Spa Fields affray, charged with high treason, and then acquitted when the case against Watson collapsed. Now the government could have a second bite at him. This time it made sure its teeth did not slip. As in the previous case, a government spy was involved. He was called George Edwards, a plaster modeller, who had a small shop in Eton High Street. Apparently his best-selling line was a little image of Dr Keate, the headmaster of Eton, which the boys used to buy in order to throw things at it.[54] He was also employed by the Bow Street magistrates to infiltrate the conspiracy, and may have egged it on. That is what the other conspirators claimed. He was present at the meeting in Cato Street at which the arrests were made, but avoided arrest himself. He also avoided appearing at the trial. The defence – not wishing to repeat Denman's mistake in 1817 – tried to get hold of him. They had depositions from witnesses indicating his guilt. (One of them also claimed that he had plotted – Guy Fawkes-like – to blow up Parliament with a bomb made up to look like a book).[55] They sent these to Sidmouth, to back up a warrant for his arrest. Sidmouth refused to issue one. Edwards escaped secretly, probably with government assistance, first of all to the Channel Islands, and then possibly to the Cape. The trial went on without him. The defence made as much of his disappearance as they could. What were they to infer from it, they asked, 'but that the plot has no foundation in reality; and if all could be investigated, it would prove that the treasonable part is altogether the brewing of a spy and an informer'? But it was not the same as having the man there before them, in the witness box. The prosecution did not need him, because they had another inside informant: Robert Adams, who was not a spy but had agreed to turn king's evidence in return for his life. The five were convicted on 28 April, and executed – with what seems like less than decent haste – on 1 May.[56] The following day Alderman Wood, MP for the City of London, raised the question of Edwards in the House of Commons, as a matter of parliamentary privilege; but by then it was, for practical purposes, a little late.[57]

The other three men to be hanged for high treason in 1820 – the last for very many years – were all implicated in the Scottish rising of that year. Two of them, Andrew Hardie and John Baird, had been caught in the 'Battle of Bonnymuir'; the third, an old 1790s radical called James Wilson, had led a rebellion at Strathaven in Lanarkshire a few days afterwards. Spies were certainly involved in this whole affair, and consequently the same questions arose as in previous cases: how far were they responsible for it? A letter from the Glasgow police chief, Captain James Mitchell, to Lord Sidmouth in March 1820 suggests that he was at any rate contemplating giving it a push. The situation, he reported, was this. They knew that a treasonable plot was afoot, and the names of 'many of the vipers' involved in it. But there was a problem: which was that

> the disaffected are too weak and unorganized at this date to carry out their wicked intent. Thus, my lord, if some plan were conceived by which the disaffected could be lured out of their lairs – being made to think that the day of 'liberty' had come – we would catch them abroad and undefended.[58]

On the surface that looks like a clear statement of intention to provoke. It is also consistent with the known activities of a number of Mitchell's agents – John King, Duncan Turner, John Craig, Robert (or Thomas) Lees – in the weeks prior to Bonnymuir. Their technique was very similar to the one associated with Oliver: encouraging radicals in one town to rise by persuading them that radicals in other towns in Britain were due to rise simultaneously. The result was the series of fiascos which put an end to the Scottish rebellion prematurely, and led to the executions of Wilson in Glasgow on 30 August, and of Hardie and Baird in Stirling on 8 September, for their part in it.[59]

These, together with the Cato Street executions, formed the climax of the Liverpool government's campaign against treason in the years 1817–20. It was followed, however, by a little coda. In October 1820 a young boy was sentenced to three months in a house of correction for posting up seditious handbills, headed 'Bread or Blood!', in the London streets. He was illiterate, so it was unlikely that he realized what the handbills said. The man who had employed him to post them was a Mr Franklin; who turned out to have connections with the government. A warrant was put out for him, but he fled to France. That came to be called the 'Placard plot'.[60] The word 'plot', of course, referred to the government's suspected part in it; not to any genuine radical conspiracy.

At the execution of James Wilson, who was a popular old man, there were hisses and cries of 'Murder!' from the watching crowd. Hardie's and Baird's hanging elicited the same response. At the execution of the Cato Street conspirators, cavalry had to be deployed to hold a potentially hostile mob back, and there were more cries of 'Murder!', directed at the authorities. One of the victims, the Cato Street conspirator John Brunt, was forcibly prevented from addressing the audience in case he stirred them up. All of them were reported by independent witnesses to have died with fortitude, though James Ings, clearly demented with terror, spoiled the dignity of the Cato Street occasion a little by shouting, laughing and doing a little jig. This contrasted with the coolness displayed by James Wilson, who was heard to say to his executioner as he mounted the scaffold: 'Did y'ever see sic a crowd, Tammas?' The last words of most of the rest of them were about liberty and tyranny, and their letters from prison, printed and widely distributed afterwards, were full of sweet and noble sentiments. Other circumstances attending the executions also went against the government: like the gruesome difficulties experienced by some of the masked headsmen (often medical students supplementing their incomes) in severing the heads of the traitors from their bodies cleanly. Even some of the soldiers on guard were reported to have fainted at the sight. After the Scottish executions crowds of men roamed the streets of Glasgow and Stirling, attacking the houses of prosecution witnesses at the trials.[61] If the object of these occasions was to instil terror, it probably succeeded. They also, however, succeeded in instilling a widespread sense of resentment, which smouldered for many years afterwards.

That was the lasting legacy of these events. After 1820, nothing quite like them ever happened again. Men continued to be charged with high treason, and spies still roamed the land, as we shall see; but none of the latter was quite so provocative – in every sense of the word – as Oliver and Edwards had been. Neither were they championed so vigorously by governments. 'I hope, Sir, we have heard spies defended for the last time in this House,' said John Cam Hobhouse in a maiden speech in the debate on Edwards in May 1820;[62] he was disappointed in the short term, when Canning got up a few minutes afterwards and did that very thing: but defences of spydom became very rare indeed in the years ahead. The whole system was discredited. Why had this come about?

It was clearly not the fault of these events alone. One of the reasons why they aroused such high passions was that people were set against spies in any case. They always had been. In earlier years that feeling had been slightly muted, by the foreign danger spies were supposed to be a defence against; but that no longer applied in the 1810s. Some Tories pretended it did, by trying to tar native radicalism with a Jacobin brush – all that talk of Frenchmen masterminding the Luddites, for example, and tricolours in Spa Fields – but none of this was convincing any more. Even the Marquis of Wellesley, who was the older brother of the Duke of Wellington and a Tory, acknowledged in 1817 that things were different then, with 'no circumstances to excite alarm; no foreign enemy to encourage; no secret intriguers to ferment; no persons of rank, education, or talents, to lead and to support'.[63] That took away much of the justification for using spies. Using them against Frenchmen was one thing. Free-born Britons – even low-born free-born Britons – were something else.

This lay at the root of the prejudice that manifested itself against Oliver and his ilk in the 1810s. Now that the foreign threat had receded, everything had changed. Without a French revolutionary monster lurking behind them, Brandreth, Thistlewood and *their* ilk did not look half so menacing. They were portrayed (perhaps unfairly) as pathetic, desperate simpletons, the products of genuine distress, who had no realistic chance at all of setting fire to the country, and probably knew it in their heart of hearts. If any monsters at all came into their picture, manipulating and 'subverting' them, then it was the government's own spies: who were consequently far more convincing villains than they could ever be. That was one of the problems ministers were faced with. It was difficult for them to persuade people that Brandreth and Thistlewood constituted serious threats. Consequently they were easily projected as victims, of a class of men which was widely detested anyway.

The French boot was now on the other foot. One of the reasons why spies were detested was that they were associated with French methods: with what today we might like to characterize as state paternalism, but Britons then preferred to call simply 'tyranny'. Critics were always harping on this. George Tierney, for example, maintained in 1818 that Britain now had 'as many spies as France herself', and 'ministers as minutely inquisitorial as their prefect of police': which was exactly what your average free-born Briton had spent centuries struggling to avoid. Sir Richard Wilson, just back from soldiering in France, railed against the 'organized spy system' he saw appearing in Britain in 1820, in imitation of the Continent.[64] That really stung. It made the government appear (as we have seen) unpatriotic. But it may also have been not entirely fair.

In fact there is a case for saying that many of the problems of Sidmouth's 'spy system' arose from the fact that it was not systematic *enough*. The benefit of a real spy system – a closely organized and centralized one – is that you can choose your own men for it, train them how you like, send them where you like, and – so long as you can get them accepted by your 'subversives' – be pretty sure of getting reliable information back. Sidmouth's 'system' was not like this at all. It was different in two ways. First, it was highly *de*centralized. Most of the spies we have met with in this chapter were not directly employed by the Home Office, but by local law men – magistrates and the like – on whom the Home Secretary depended almost entirely for his provincial intelligence. He had little control over them, and consequently no means of monitoring the men and methods they used for this work, which may in some cases have been less scrupulous than he would have preferred. The second difference was that Sidmouth's system was a volunteer one. It did not set out to recruit spies. Instead, they more or less recruited themselves. There were some exceptions: constables sent by magistrates to keep a watch on radical meetings, for example, like poor James Murrey of Manchester in 1819; but most of the really deep-seated government agents of the 1810s, the ones who betrayed the most secret conspiracies, were men who had approached the authorities off their own bat.

The advantage of this method was that it enabled the government to mount a plausible defence, whenever it was accused of 'employing spies'. Its point was that it did not employ men to *become* spies, but only men who had decided to be spies in any case. That, apparently, made all the difference morally (the difference, perhaps, between seducing a virgin and going with a prostitute). But it may also have made a difference practically. The trouble with ready-made spies is that you cannot vet or control them. Because you have not chosen them, they are unlikely to be the sorts of people you would have chosen if you had. You will not know whether their information is accurate, or complete. If they exaggerate, it may cause you to over-react; if they do not, it is not likely to calm you like one of your own trained agents, if you had any, could. This explains many of Sidmouth's problems with his 'spy system'. It was inherently untrustworthy, because he had to take it as he found it, instead of organizing his own.

If governments could not trust it, ordinary folk could even less. This was scarcely surprising, in view of the evidence. There can be no doubt at all, for example, that Castle really was a villain, and very little doubt (surely) that Oliver and Edwards were too. The *Examiner* believed that villainy was an essential attribute for a spy.

> His business is to betray, and he must of necessity be a liar; he must of necessity also be a hypocrite; he must of necessity, if he prefers this business to any other upon earth, and takes a sixpence for it, be a mercenary and a cold-blooded scoundrel.[65]

That was probably broadly true for that time. Indeed, in a literal sense, parts of it are self-evidently true for any time.

It may not be absolutely true. Not all Regency spies were corrupt. The surviving records from this period contain a number of apparently objective spy reports, as well as alarmist ones.[66] It may even be possible, theoretically, to imagine a whole spy system which is (relatively) pure. In 1824 one of the government's own agents, Alexander Richmond, described one such, which he claimed to have operated among the Glasgow weavers in 1817. It involved infiltrating radical groups in order, first, to dissuade them from taking foolish actions, and then to reassure his employer (the Lord Provost of Glasgow) that no plots were afoot. Another purpose was to inform the authorities of the true state of distress amongst the working classes, 'in a state of society, where the greatest evils have resulted from their knowing too little'.[67] The effect of this should have been beneficial all round: not only to the government, but to the working classes too. Sadly, it did not work. Richmond was rumbled, and no one had any time for these excuses of his. For a while he became Scotland's very own 'Oliver', as notorious there as the latter was further south. (According to one account the government was so embarrassed by his published revelations that it bought up all the copies it could lay its hands on, in order to suppress them.)[68] If he was lying, then it backs up the *Examiner*'s point about intrinsic villainy. If he was not, then it shows how far the villainy of others had poisoned the reputation of such as he.

All this undermined the reputation and consequently the effectiveness of Sidmouth's 'spy system' in many ways. Of course it had some successes. It probably uncovered a few genuine plots, deterred many more and sowed fear and distrust amongst radicals of all political hues. We have the radicals' own words for some of that. But these achievements were only won at a price. The main price was that no one could possibly know how great the achievements really were. By the 1820s, people had grown highly sceptical of government accounts of the revolutionary plots it had foiled. Radicals were wise to this, and started attributing every single political excess, as the Solicitor-General put it, 'to a conspiracy of government'.[69] If *Marianne* herself, the personification of the French Revolution, had suddenly appeared on the ramparts of the Tower of London with a tricolour in one hand and a musket in the other, most people would probably have assumed it was Lord Sidmouth in drag. That was the measure of the latter's achievement. The system had become counter-productive. This is one of the reasons why so little was seen of it after this time.

Chapter 4

Mild and paternal government
(1825–50)

The year 1820 saw the end of one phase of serious popular discontent in Britain. That may have been due to Sidmouth's firm measures against it, including his 'spy system'; but it probably had more to do with an upturn in the economy at that time. By the time the next phase of protest came around, at the beginning of the 1830s, a great deal had changed. Three of the four main architects of the earlier government's counter-subversive policy had come to sticky ends, all comparatively young: Castlereagh, in a fit of depression, by his own hand. Henry Hunt called this the judgement of God. To round it off, he would have liked to see the sole survivor, Lord Sidmouth, brought before the judgement of his fellow men.[1] That was not to be; but there was a sort of comfort to be derived even from this. It meant that Sidmouth, unlike Liverpool, Canning and Castlereagh, lived to experience his own discomfiture, when the measure he had so strenuously opposed in the 1810s actually passed into law, on 7 June 1832. 'The tables are now fairly turned,' wrote Peter Mackenzie in the 'exposure' of the Glasgow spy system he published in the following year.

> The men who in 1819-20 wielded an iron rod against the friends of Freedom, are now ... , we trust, for ever humbled! Blessings on the French Revolution! – Blessings on that mild and paternal government which now exists, and may it long continue to exist in England![2]

That was written in the immediate aftermath of the passage of the great parliamentary Reform Bill, which in the outcome turned out to be far less 'paternal' than radicals like Mackenzie had hoped. For example: the

65

depressed weavers of Glasgow had turned to 'Reform' in the 1810s in the
hope of bringing into Parliament men who would ease their sufferings under
the operation of market conditions.[3] In fact the outcome turned out to be
the very reverse. Almost the first major measure enacted by the reformed
House of Commons was a law which was widely regarded, probably fairly, as
punishing the victims of the market by denying them relief except in prison
conditions: an act which showed quite clearly which side of the economic
fence the new Parliament stood. By the part they had played in agitating
for this Parliament – sometimes at the cost of their liberties and lives –
working-class reformists (it seemed) had done themselves no lasting good.
They had drawn the teeth of one class enemy, but only to fashion a set for
another. It was not long before this dawned on them, with Chartism – the
new and more democratic reform movement of the later 1830s and 1840s
– as the result.

There was a crucial difference, however, between this class enemy, and
the last. That difference can be expressed in the single word 'whiggery'.
Whiggery (in this context) is a belief in the inevitability and beneficence
of liberal 'progress', from which it follows that it is unnatural to try to stop
it, and also undesirable. Because things are getting better, there is no need
to fear change. It is also unwise to obstruct it, because that only has the
effect of turning it into dangerous channels. If men with reasonable and
moderate demands are thwarted, it provokes them to become unreasonable
and extreme. That, in fact, is the likeliest explanation for most political
extremism: like the build-up of pressure in a boiler with no safety-valve.
The implication of this for national security is clear. To avoid disaffection
you do not try to repress it: you appease. Rebellion is much more likely to
be killed by kindness than by the headsman and his provider, the spy.

It would take a good deal of political confidence, even bravado, for any
government to embrace that implication to the full, and no government
before 1850 was ready for it yet. The time was clearly nowhere near ripe.
The 1820s were relatively peaceful in Britain, but the 1830s and 1840s were
not, and indeed some of those years – 1830–1, for example, and 1837–40
– were as disorderly as any in Lord Sidmouth's time. The underlying cause
of the trouble was the same: the current transformation of Britain into a
capitalist and predominantly industrial society, which, whatever its ultimate
benefits may have been, was a source of deep and widespread material
distress in the short term. The early parliamentary reform riots, for example,
during which Bristol's Mansion House and Nottingham's castle were both
destroyed by mobs, were an indirect offshoot of that process. The 'Captain
Swing' agricultural riots of 1830–2 in the south of England were provoked
by the introduction of machinery there. A strike wave in the early 1830s,
which led to the transportation of the famous 'Tolpuddle martyrs' for trade
union activities in 1834, was anti-capitalist in essence. In 1842–4 there were

more riotous strikes in the Durham coalfield, and in Lancashire, where strikers pulled the plugs out of the boilers powering the steam engines in factories in order to close them down. Some of the worst riots in the north of England were directed against workhouses, which were the most widely hated of all the symbols of the new capitalist ethos, and the police, who were often regarded as that ethos's guardians. Then, of course, there was Chartism, which after 1838 gathered many of these protesting energies together, and gave them for the first time an overtly political edge. It was then that many non-protesters began to fear that revolution was imminent, and possibly with better reason than when they had feared it before. On the surface this does not seem to have been a promising time for governments to lower their guard. We shall see that they never did, completely. Nevertheless, they did make a start.

The first step was the Reform Bill. Its whiggish rationale was clearly spelled out by the ultra-whig historian and MP Thomas Babington Macaulay, in a famous speech in March 1831. 'We have tried anodynes,' he told the House of Commons; 'we have tried cruel operations.' They had had coercion, new laws, new treasons; 'we have had blood'. (He will have had Peterloo and the 1820 executions in mind.) None of this had worked to remove the danger of rebellion in Britain. 'The event has proved that these were mere palliatives. You are at the end of your palliatives. The evil remains.' If it was not dealt with then, 'great and terrible calamities' would befall. The only way left was concession. But not *outright* concessions, to all the revolutionaries' demands. Macaulay's idea was to concede just enough to detach 'reasonable men' – the propertied middle classes – from the revolutionaries, to isolate the latter and so diminish the threat. The working classes could not be enfranchised yet, because they could not be trusted to behave. That was because they were 'occasionally in a state of great distress', and distress tended to make men unreasonable in their demands. Later, when distress had been eradicated, that would change. (The catalyst here would be free market capitalism: but more of that anon.) Then the labouring classes could be given the vote too, and no one would have any cause to rebel. There would thus be no more threat, and no need for repression. Until then, however, it was clearly implicit in Macaulay's train of argument that there *would* be such a need. Reform was no substitute for policing; or, at any rate, not yet.[4]

The point was, however, that the policing could now be gentler, more restrained, and consequently less provocative. This was partly because the Whigs' philosophy was gentler, as we have just seen; and partly because it could afford to be. Without its middle-class allies, working-class protest was not half the menace it had been in the past. It was not just a question of numbers, but of leadership too. This was supposed to be the middle classes' main role. The workers could provide the revolutionary energy; but to be effective that energy needed to be driven by superior brains. Otherwise it resembled a headless chicken: capable of causing a certain amount of mayhem in the chicken run, but no serious damage to the regime. That was why Brandreth and Thistlewood and the rest, who were widely depicted as rude mechanicals, had failed. This was one of the main priorities of every early nineteenth-century domestic spy: to establish the extent to which 'the higher orders or ... the middle class of society' were involved in plots.[5] With the passage of the Reform Act such involvement became far less likely. This made the government's counter-subversive task after 1832 both easier, and different.

It was easier because it was more acceptable. One major problem with counter-subversion in Sidmouth's time had been that it provoked widespread resentment. This was because its targets were political offenders; and because it operated through terror – spies, treason trials and the hangman's noose. 'However injurious political crimes may be to the interest of society,' wrote Alexander Richmond, who was wiser than his many enemies gave him credit for, ' ... the bulk of the people are always disposed to consider the sufferers as martyrs.'[6] After 1832 governments, if they were sensible, could avoid all this. The type of popular protest that characterized the next two decades was, with some rare (Chartist) exceptions, blunter than previously. Generally it took the form of riots, strikes and machine-breaking: activities which were less overtly political, and posed problems of public order rather than of subversion, properly so called. Because they were less overtly political, there was a much smaller pool of public sympathy for them. There was also less need, or temptation, for governments to hang the perpetrators, which meant less martyrdom.

Consequently the most hated items in Sidmouth's counter-subversive weaponry could now be dismantled, or at least wheeled back into the armoury for dismantling at a later date. Treason trials could be dispensed with, to be replaced by the ordinary criminal law, which was perfectly adequate. Government spies could be pensioned off, as surplus to the requirements of the new age. The hangman could be redeployed against more conventional criminals, and the headsman sent back to his medical studies. That was the intention. It was not, as we shall see, realized in its entirety yet. But it was the way things seemed to be inexorably moving, in the reign of William IV and the first dozen years of Victoria's.

It was not all done out of blind whiggish faith. It could not have been done at all without another crucial development of these years: which was the formation in Ireland and London and then the extension into the British provinces of an effective system of police. That underpinned the faith in a very practical way.

Such a thing had been mooted, of course, but never implemented, for very many years. The case against it then had been that it would threaten British liberties. A much-quoted statement by the future Earl Dudley in 1811 put it in a nutshell. 'They have an admirable police at Paris,' he said, 'but they pay for it dear enough. I had rather half-a-dozen people's throats should be cut in Ratcliffe Highway every three or four years than be subject to domiciliary visits, spies, and all the rest of Fouché's contrivances.'[7] Ratcliffe Road in Wapping in east London had been the scene of some particularly ghastly and notorious murders recently. What the anti-police propagandists were saying was that you could not prevent that kind of thing without drifting into the worst excesses of what today is called the 'police state'. They had other arguments against policing too. One powerful one was the expense. Another was its implications for local autonomy. Traditionally police powers had been under the control of magistrates, who were supposed to be independent of governments. One champion of the old system regarded this as tantamount to a 'people's' police. Now the proposal was for Whitehall to take over. That raised a new and even more horrifying spectre. Policemen, asserted our old-school champion, were inherently corruptible. They were cut off by their occupation from ordinary, decent society. They were paid so little – in order to meet the criticism about cost – that they were bound to be tempted by offers of illicit reward. They were also likely to stoop to illicit methods: like spying, provoking crimes and manufacturing evidence. Magistrates could monitor and moderate these tendencies. Governments might not *wish* to. This was the ultimate danger: that when he became 'the menial of the Ministry' the policeman would be made into 'a political spy', and employed on 'the worst kinds of espionage'.[8]

These fears were not enough to prevent the formation of new police forces eventually, in Ireland in 1822 and in London seven years later. The London pattern was then repeated piecemeal in the provinces, until 1856 when a law was passed requiring every local authority to set up a police system. All these forces came under local and not central control, in order to prevent their being turned into a French-style state police. The only British exception was London, and then only because no London-wide local government existed yet. In Ireland (outside Dublin) the system was entirely different, with a militia-style police force, quartered in barracks and answerable after 1835 to the lord lieutenant of the province. This difference was to widen and become more significant as time went on.

Both these initiatives were very largely the doing of Sir Robert Peel. 'I want to teach people', he wrote, 'that liberty does not consist in having their houses robbed by organized gangs of thieves'; which met the traditional libertarian argument head-on.[9] So far as the middle classes were concerned, in a period of rising crime, it was probably this sort of reasoning which won the day. There was also a whiggish rationale behind it. Before 1829 the means of preserving public order in Britain were, to say the least, crude. Chiefly they relied on three agencies: the military, to disperse riots;

spies, to detect crimes and conspiracies; and the hangman, to punish them. These methods were inherently cruel, arbitrary and consequently in many cases counter-productive. They were necessary – so the argument went – because there were no more moderate means to hand of controlling crime and disorder. The London Metropolitan Police was presented as just such a means. The idea was that its very presence in the streets of London would deter men from committing the offences which, if they were detected, might lead them to the scaffold. The corollary of *that* – a highly whiggish one – was to make scaffolds less necessary, for all but the most serious of crimes.

On this, the Whigs were as good as their word. One of the first measures taken by Earl Grey's government after the formation of the Metropolitan Police was the abolition of capital punishment for horse, sheep and cattle stealing and for forgery in 1832, and then for scores of other crimes in the years after that. By the end of the 1830s murder was effectively the only crime for which a person could be hanged; though technically there were a few others, like rape, treason and sodomy. (Sodomy was not called that in the Act, but simply 'a nameless offence of great enormity', and may have been missed out simply because no one liked to ask what it was.) Consequently the number of executions carried out each year also dwindled: from an average of seventy-three in the 1820s to an average between 1837 and 1846 of only ten.[10] Most people agreed that this marked an advance in civilization, even though they might still differ over whether or not it made them more 'free'.

A similar transformation – albeit not quite so dramatic – took place on the public order front. One of the most useful skills the Metropolitan Police developed in its early years was the ability to control public demonstrations with minimal force. It took a little time. There was a notorious occasion in May 1833, for example, when the police were accused of brutality against a crowd of protesters in Cold Bath Fields, and the jury at the inquest into the death of a police constable who was stabbed there arrived at the somewhat perverse verdict of 'justifiable homicide' to make their feelings against them plain. Later there were several occasions when police methods failed to control riots, and the military had to be called in just like in the bad old days. Nevertheless there was a general improvement, and never, for example, any repeat of Peterloo. By 1834, when the new system was scrutinized by a parliamentary Select Committee, it had come to be widely accepted by the middle classes, if not by the classes it was mainly designed to control. A Hackney magistrate called it 'the most efficient and least offensive system for the protection of person and property that was ever devised'.[11] That form of words is significant. The lack of offensiveness was at least as important as the efficiency. The prime virtue of Peel's new police, in most people's eyes, was not just that it kept a lid on popular anarchy, but that it was a more humane and hence less provocative lid than hitherto.

Theoretically, the development of such methods should also have spelled the end for the 'spy system'. That was certainly the intention. It was implicit, for example, in the Metropolitan Police's very first set of *General Instructions*, issued in 1829, in which it was stated that their chief object was the prevention – not the detection – of crime.[12] Of course it can be argued (and often was later) that the best way of preventing crimes is to detect enough of them to deter others; but that is not what the founding fathers of the British police had in mind. Their original idea was for the police to adopt as high a profile as possible, so that their visible presence in the streets would put putative offenders off. To this end every man jack of them, including the commissioners, was put into a distinctive uniform, which for the lower ranks included tall, stove-pipe helmets. Outside a very tiny detective branch set up in 1842, scarcely any policing was done in plain clothes. That was considered to be an underhand way of getting your man. It was also another of the things associated with Fouché's secret police. Officers who were found to have disregarded this convention were reprimanded severely: like one constable in 1845 who pretended to be a cobbler in order to arrest a counterfeiter, and another in 1851 who hid behind a tree in a London park to observe an 'indecent offence'.[13] This indicates a considerable degree of prejudice against espionage. It also, of course, indicates that this prejudice was flouted, at least occasionally.

In the realm of politics it was flouted continuously, throughout the 1830s and 1840s. No government of that time, Whig or Tory, abjured the use of spies amongst radical groups which seemed to pose a threat to the state. Some of those spies were engaged by the various police authorities; others by magistrates, or by the military. At least one, as we shall see, was a London Metropolitan policeman himself. Sir Robert Peel saw nothing amiss in this. Of course the use of *agents provocateurs*, he told the House of Commons in March 1832, was totally wrong; but 'he could not, as an honest man, having some experience of Government, assent to the doctrine that Government were not justified under any circumstances in availing themselves of the assistance of spies'.[14] So far, there looks to be little change from the 1790s and 1810s. In fact, however, there were important differences.

The main one was that spies appear to have been kept on a tighter rein than before. There are far fewer examples of alleged *agent provocateur* activities, for example, than in 1817–20. The only notorious one is the case of William Steward Popay, the Metropolitan Police sergeant who infiltrated the Walworth and Camberwell 'class' of the National Political Union between 1831 and 1833 by masquerading as an out-of-work coal merchant, in order to spy on them. Early in 1833 he was rumbled, and a parliamentary petition was got up against him by some of his erstwhile comrades. That alleged

that he used to urge the members of the Union to use stronger language
than they did in their resolutions and other papers, which he sometimes
altered with his own pen, in order to introduce such stronger language;
that in his conversation with one of your Petitioners particularly, he railed
against the Government, damned the Ministers for villains, and said he
would expel them from the earth; that he told one of your Petitioners
that he should like to establish a shooting-gallery, and wanted some of
them to learn the use of the broad-sword, and did give one lesson of the
broad-sword to one of your Petitioners;

and so on: all of which was standard *provocateur* procedure. A House of
Commons Select Committee was appointed to look into these accusations,
which was a significant new departure in itself. Its report was unequivocal. It
censured Popay's conduct, as 'highly reprehensible'. It criticized his superior
officers in the police for not keeping a better eye on him. Lastly, although
it accepted the need for plain-clothes activities in some circumstances, it
also deprecated 'any approach to the Employment of Spies, in the ordinary
acceptance of the term, as a practice most abhorrent to the feelings of the
People, and most alien to the spirit of the Constitution'.[15] Conclusions like
these would have been inconceivable fifteen years before.

So would Popay's own personal fate; which was not, this time, to be spirited
away to a nice comfortable farmstead somewhere in Cape Colony at the
taxpayer's expense, but simply – according to the Solicitor-General of the day
– to be dismissed ignominiously from the police.[16] The question remains,
of course: was he alone in this work, or was he simply the only one to be
found out? The 1833 petitioners asserted that they had spotted others, 'whom
they knew to be policemen, disguised in clothing of various descriptions,
sometimes in the garb of gentlemen, sometimes in that of tradesmen or
artisans, sometimes in sailors' jackets, and sometimes in ploughmen's frocks':
which suggested that Popay was simply the tip of an intelligence iceberg.[17]
For their part Popay's superiors claimed that no one at all had ever been
instructed to go as far as he had gone. Other policemen were sent to observe
meetings, but were forbidden to take an active part in them, or to conceal
the fact of who they were. A few years later, in 1839, a Metropolitan Police
Order categorically prohibited officers from attending private meetings of
any sort.[18] All this was done out of deference to public opinion, which
was highly sensitive on this matter of a 'secret' or 'political' police. The
Metropolitan force was still controversial and consequently vulnerable for
many years after its inception in 1829. It had to be careful. This was one
reason why it steered as clear as it could of this type of activity, which, if
it provoked a scandal, could bring the whole edifice tumbling down.

The Popay affair did not put an end to political espionage in Britain. What it
did do, however, was subject it to a certain discipline. How firm that discipline

was in practice varied from agency to agency. At the Home Office, despite frequent Chartist allegations of a new 'spy system' to rival Sidmouth's in the 1840s, it seems to have been firmest of all. All the Home Secretaries of Chartist times – Lord John Russell, Lord Normanby, Sir James Graham, Sir George Grey – expressed their distaste for espionage, and probably genuinely meant it. Normanby told the Birmingham chief constable on one occasion in 1839 that in his opinion it was 'the most difficult and dangerous thing to manage', and usually ended in 'nothing but disappointment'. One fairly reliable guide to the amount of domestic espionage undertaken by any government is the amount of money the Home Office spends under the 'Secret Service' vote, which in this period was only a fraction of Sidmouth's. This was in spite of the fact that there was never any shortage of volunteers. The Home Office's post-bag bulged with letters from people offering information about plots, or their services as government spies. So far as we can tell, however, no Home Secretary ever took any of them up on it. Instead the usual practice was to pass them over to the Metropolitan Police.[19]

For their part the police checked them out, and accepted their information if it seemed reliable. This was considered different from espionage, and not covered, therefore, by the strictures of the Select Committee on the Popay case. Part of the difference lay in who took the initiative: if a Chartist (for example) offered off his own bat to betray his colleagues to the police, that was one thing; but if a policeman recruited a man to penetrate the Chartists, that was another. The distinction was supposed to be crucial. It could become blurred: if, for example, the authorities employed an informant on a regular basis, which must at some point transform him from a mere informer into a fully fledged police spy. When informers gave evidence against Chartists in court (which did not happen very often), defence lawyers closely questioned them on this. For example Thomas Powell (alias Johnson), who testified against several Chartists in 1848, was repeatedly asked 'At whose suggestion' he had joined them, and how much money he received from the police, simply in order to try to prove that he had stepped over this particular line. His replies – that joining had been his own idea, and that he was not getting a farthing for his testimony – were designed to put both him and the police in the clear; though in fact they were almost certainly lies. Powell may also have been an *agent provocateur*.[20] He and his colleague George Davis are the worst of the known post-Popay cases. It is tempting to assume that this is only because they were rumbled, and that there were many others like them working for the police, but on balance this seems unlikely. The Metropolitan force, as we have seen, had good reason to remain pure in these matters, and little official encouragement to be otherwise.

Some of Britain's other police forces may have rated this particular form of purity less highly. This was despite the fact that they were more independent of central government than the 'Met' was, and consequently theoretically less likely to be corrupted for political ends. That would have surprised some of the early critics of the new police. The reason may simply have been that provincial police forces felt themselves to be less under those critics' scrutiny. In certain circumstances – with liberally inclined ministers and a vigilant public opinion – government control over domestic espionage can be a moderating, or inhibiting, influence. It is only outside London, for example, that we hear of policemen acting as spies themselves after 1833. One example was a PC Barnett of the Birmingham City Police, who infiltrated the Chartists there in 1840, but was not helped by his superiors' insistence that when he was not infiltrating them he go back to his normal duties as a uniformed officer. (One of the reasons for this was that the Home Secretary refused to grant secret service money to the Birmingham force to allow it to employ him as a spy full-time.) Inevitably, he was once spotted in uniform in a theatre by some of his Chartist comrades, who may not have been entirely convinced by the explanation he gave: which was that he was working in a *private* capacity for the theatre manager. We know of others like him, especially in Birmingham and Liverpool.[21]

There was probably a much larger number of spies who were not members of the police, but reported either to them or to other government agencies. One, called John Donnellan Balfe, furnished the Dublin authorities with valuable information about the plans of the Irish Confederates in 1848, and seems to have been rewarded for this with a job in the prison service in Tasmania.[22] Other Irish police spies were uncovered during the trial of the Confederate leader Smith O'Brien for treason in 1848. One, called James Stevenson Dobbyn, was embarrassed towards the end of the trial when a late witness called Dalton burst into the court and gave evidence that Dobbyn had tried to recruit him as a spy. Worse followed.

> He said that if I joined a distinct club from him, and both our statements of information agreed, credit would be attached to it, and the more the better. And he likewise said this could be well managed by my drawing out ... propositions for my club ... and getting signatures to them, and communicating with him, and that he would communicate this to the detectives.

Dalton claimed that his response to this was to call him 'a rascal and a blackguard'.[23] It made no difference to the outcome of the trial.

There are English examples too. Some of the most reliable spies may have been employed by the military. General Napier, who commanded the troops in the north of England during the turbulent years 1839–41, and who incidentally was more sympathetic towards the Chartists than many of his politician contemporaries, liked to use enrolled pensioners, who by chatting with locals in pubs were made into spies – as he reported

– 'despite themselves'. Magistrates also retained them. One agent we know of, one Michael Flynn, became secretary – no less – to the Executive Council of the Chartist Association in Bradford in 1848, reporting to a magistrate called Ferrand.[24] He may have been one of the men uncovered in a pamphlet called *The Spy-System Exposed* published by ex-Chief Constable Briggs of Bradford in 1850, no copies of which appear to have survived. A review of it in a radical newspaper in that year found the 'revolting details' contained in it, of 'how spies are employed and evidence is cooked up', too painful to repeat. Consequently the Bradford spy system is now less exposed than it used to be.[25]

This is just one frustrating instance of the difficulties the historian is faced with in trying to measure the incidence of domestic espionage in Chartist times. There is no doubt at all that a significant amount of it went on. On a few occasions this intelligence was clearly crucial: most notably in the foiling of the violent conspiracy of Ritchie, Lacey, Cuffay and others in London in the summer of 1848, through the agency of Powell and Davis.[26] Espionage also had other, less tangible effects. It was immensely damaging to Chartist morale, even when – often because – the Chartists exaggerated its incidence. Most Chartist leaders came under the suspicion of their fellows at one time or another; either because they were too moderate, or because they seemed too violent. Spies could cause rifts in the movement even without trying: as our PC Barnett of Birmingham did on one occasion, for example, when one of the local leaders there turned on the rest for accusing him for being what in fact he was.[27] One way or another, espionage was one of the factors which contributed to the defeat of Chartism. But it was probably not a major one.

The strong impression that comes through from most of the books and documents relating to Chartism is that this was a very much paler version of a 'spy system' than hitherto. It certainly was not so apparent. There may have been other reasons for this. One is the fact that there were fewer treason trials in the 1830s and 1840s, and none at all involving capital sentences, which is what had done most to arouse popular feeling against spies – their association with 'blood money' – in earlier years. Another may simply have been that spies were cleverer now, and careful not to antagonize, so that they were less likely to be noticed. They were certainly, as we have seen, better disciplined, mainly by the knowledge that the men at the top – Home Secretaries, Metropolitan Police Commissioners – and at the bottom – public opinion – were highly jealous of what they regarded as 'abuses' of ministerial and police powers. This is also likely to have had the effect, however, of reducing recruitment into the profession: both on the side of the authorities, who were not especially keen to recruit, and among potential agents, who will not have wanted to risk the odium. The predominantly working-class character of political protest at this time will not have helped, in view of that class's greater resistance – which we have noticed before – to treachery.

(That may have had something to do with the weakness among them of the individualist ethic.) In any case, for whatever reason, the Home Office in the 1830s and 1840s preferred to get the bulk of its information from other sources. Some of those sources will have employed spies themselves, but not invariably. They included magistrates, lords lieutenant, military commanders, local postmasters, factory inspectors, newspaper reporters and (as we shall see shortly) the General Post Office.[28] None of these could have been as intimate with the Chartists as a good 'mole' would have been, but they were considered to be more reliable. This is probably the main reason for the relative paucity (relative, that is, to earlier periods) of evidence of covert domestic intelligence-gathering in early Victorian times. There was simply less of it.

There was one notable exception. This was the interception of mails via the Post Office's 'Private' branch. We last came across this in the 1790s, when it seemed to be slightly on the wane; but it had never ceased its operations completely, and indeed – if we can judge by the record kept of official warrants issued for opening letters – was more active in certain years after 1800 than it had ever been before. Altogether 372 warrants were granted between 1799 and 1844, affecting the correspondence – for varying lengths of time – of 724 named individuals, plus an unknown number whose letters were opened under warrants couched in very vague and general terms. Of these 372, just 77 were concerned with political crimes, including the treasons of 1817–20 and the strikes and riots of 1842–3.[29] All this first came to light through the efforts of a Commons Secret Committee set up to investigate the practice in 1844, after a row broke out in Parliament concerning the interception of the correspondence not of native British radicals, but of an Italian refugee.

This introduced a fresh factor into the controversy, which requires some explanation. The 1830s and 1840s were a time when a new liberal tradition was being forged in Britain. That was the tradition of 'asylum' for the victims of political persecution abroad. Hundreds of fugitives from failed revolutions on the Continent were seeking sanctuary there, and finding a warm welcome in whiggish circles: like Holland House in Kensington, where Lord and Lady Holland, the nephew and niece-in-law of Charles James Fox, put on lavish entertainments for the posher ones. In 1834 the House of Commons made a grant of £10,000 a year to relieve some of the less posh Poles, who after years of fruitless struggle against Russian tyranny now found themselves destitute.[30] As well as this, measures were taken to make it easier for them to come in. In 1826 the old Napoleonic Alien Act was amended, to make it statutorily impossible for the British authorities to keep any foreigner out of the country for any reason at all. That guaranteed an *absolute* right of asylum, which lasted (with just a short break in 1848–50) for eighty years. In 1844 another Act was passed to facilitate their naturalization.[31]

Some of this liberality stemmed from genuine admiration for the refugees, or hatred for their (usually Russian or Austrian) oppressors. Another reason for it was that very few Britons now felt threatened by foreign revolutionaries, as they had, for example, in the 1790s. Some, like Lord Auckland, put their trust in the Englishman's legendary xenophobia: 'The first word that a foreigner would have to utter, in which the letters *th* or the letter *w* occurred, would overthrow any attempt he might be disposed to make inimical to the public peace.'[32] For others, the key safeguard was Britain's liberal government. Whigs in particular tended to believe that only autocratic states needed to have anything to fear from revolutionaries, who would get insufficient backing from the subjects of a more benevolent regime to be able to do any harm. Consequently it was a matter of pride to most Britons that they could afford to receive these trouble-makers, and a mark of their national superiority over the Continent.

It was this feeling that fuelled the indignation that was felt when, in June 1844, the Radical MP Thomas Duncombe revealed to the House of Commons that letters addressed to the Italian patriot leader Giuseppe Mazzini in his London exile had been tampered with at the Post Office. It had been done at the request of the Austrian ambassador in London, who suspected Mazzini of fomenting rebellions in Italy. (Italy at this time, of course, was partly in Austria's hands.) The deception was discovered when Mazzini asked some of his correspondents to put poppy-seeds in the envelopes with their letters, which were then found to have disappeared when the letters reached him.[33] This raised again the whole wider question of espionage; for as Macaulay asked when he weighed in on the controversy a few days after Duncombe, 'what difference was there . . . between a government breaking the seal of his letter in the Post Office, and the government employing a spy to poke his ear to the keyhole'? Both practices were common enough on the Continent, he pointed out, but 'singularly abhorrent to the genius of the English people', and so should be stopped.[34] Others followed the same line of attack.

Most of the flak fell on the Home Secretary, Sir James Graham. That was ironic in view of the pride he took in being the least spendthrift of all Home Secretaries in the money he claimed – just £232 over five years – from the Secret Service fund.[35] In July he was forced to concede a Committee of Inquiry, from whose report (published the following month) most of our knowledge of Post Office espionage comes. It confirmed that Mazzini's letters had been opened, and also those of the Polish leader Stanislaus Worcell: the latter 'on grounds connected with the personal safety of a Foreign Sovereign, entrusted to the protection of England'. So far as British radicals were concerned, it gave details of interceptions right up to the year before, which it defended on the grounds that thereby ministers were alerted as to the 'real strength' of any conspiracy, and consequently prevented 'from taking exaggerated views of the force arrayed against the State'. (What it did not reveal, significantly, was that another victim of Post Office espionage in 1842 was Richard Cobden, the Corn Law reformer and MP; perhaps in order to avoid even more of a fuss.)[36] The committee's final recommendation was curious. It did not advise that the practice be either stopped, or overtly continued. The best thing, it felt, would be 'to leave it a mystery whether or no this power is ever exercised', so as to 'deter the evil-minded from applying the Post to improper use'.[37] For the mid-nineteenth century, that was uncharacteristically devious.

The upshot of all this was to leave the law as it stood, but change the practice. In April 1845 the government successfully resisted a move by Duncombe to make it illegal for the Post Office to open letters.[38] Behind the scenes, however, it had already taken steps in this direction. In August 1844 the 'Secret' branch of the Post Office (dealing with foreign letters) was abolished, together with its deciphering office. That left only the 'Private' branch. In February 1845 Graham made a misleading statement to the House of Commons which implied – probably deliberately – that no such office had ever existed.[39] That must have satisfied most MPs. In fact the Private branch seems to have continued, but at a much lower level of activity. Sir Rowland Hill, the inventor of the penny post, who served as chief secretary to the Post Office from 1846 to 1864, claimed that it never thereafter used its letter-opening powers 'except in a very few cases relating, so far as I can recollect, exclusively to burglars, and others of that stamp'.[40] If this was so – and there is no evidence to contradict it – it is highly significant. It means that Britain's most continuous and systematic domestic espionage agency for probably two hundred years had ceased operating entirely in the political field. It was rather as if – in our own day – GCHQ were to be suddenly closed down.

People still complained about government espionage in the 1830s and 1840s, often as though nothing had changed since the 1810s. In 1840, for example, Feargus O'Connor referred to what he called a 'complete and systematic plan adopted by the Government to goad the working classes into resistance' through the use of *provocateurs*.[41] That is a common accusation in history, especially by radical leaders whose supporters seem to be getting out of control. Sometimes it may be justified. In the 1840s it almost certainly was not.

There are two reasons for thinking so, neither of them conclusive. One is negative: the sheer lack of evidence of any such scheme as O'Connor described. That has been considered already. The other is of a different kind. It is that espionage on this scale and of this nature does not fit in with the prevailing ethos of the time. Of course it is always possible that things can happen behind the scenes of British public life which do not fit in with a prevailing ethos; but that does not seem to be significantly so in this case. In the 1830s and 1840s there can be no doubt at all that the prevailing ethos was antagonistic to espionage of all kinds, and becoming more so as time went on. Public opinion was against it. So was the bulk of the press, and the House of Commons, and one of the two commissioners – Charles Rowan – of the Metropolitan Police. (The other, Richard Mayne, was slightly more flexible.)[42] Home Secretaries said they were against it, and probably really were when they could afford to be. Peel was an exception, as were most High Court judges: like Sir William Maule, who presided over the trial of the Chartist Mullins in 1848, and launched into quite an eloquent defence of the profession of spying in his summing up. It included the ruling that, even if a spy was acting as a *provocateur*, it should in no way excuse the person he had entrapped in this fashion; for 'If a man is to be exempted from responsibility because an offence has been suggested to him, there would be very little responsibility for crime in the world.'[43] That was a perfectly sound and rational point of view; but it was lost on most of Maule's contemporaries. By 1848 espionage and entrapment were no longer widely acceptable means of counter-subversion. Soon, as we shall see, they were to become absolute anathema.

The reasons for this lay both in the past, and in the early Victorians' expectation of their future. The recollection of the events of 1817–20 was a powerful factor: a bed of embers which never quite dimmed but glowed ruddily all through these later years, to be raked over every now and then into a flickering flame. One such occasion was the time of the Great Reform Bill, which revived vivid memories of those earlier and bloodier battles for the same cause, and of the part played in them by government spies. In March 1832, for example, Henry Hunt presented a petition to Parliament praying for an inquiry into the Peterloo affray, and suggesting (though this possibility had never been seriously raised before) that 'Oliver' or his friends had played a part in that.[44] At the end of that same year, when the Bill was safely through, an imposing monument was erected at Thrushgrove in Glasgow to commemorate two other victims of Sidmouth's 'spy system': Andrew Hardie and John Baird, who (in the words of the inscription carved into its base) '*Were betrayed by infamous Spies & Informers*, And Suffered Death at Stirling, 8th September, 1820, For the cause of REFORM now triumphant'.[45] That juxtaposition of 'Spies' and 'Reform' was important, in associating the system of domestic espionage with rank reaction, and setting it in a darker age than the early Victorians considered themselves to be in. That told against it terribly, in a self-consciously 'progressive' period and place.

That really was the nub of it. Spying declined in Britain mainly because it did not square with people's view of the way things would be. That went back to whiggery. Whiggery taught that liberal regimes were safe from revolutionary threats, and so should have no need for counter-revolutionary precautions, like spies. The events of 1848, which may have been the last time for thirty years that a British government made substantial use of spies, gave an enormous boost to that idea. While the tyrannies of continental Europe became convulsed with rebellion and anarchy, liberal Britain, despite a few scares, remained calm and secure throughout the year. It was, objectively, a quite remarkable contrast; and for Whigs (less objectively) it just went to show how wise their whiggery had been. Even *The Times*, which did not have the reputation of being a whiggish paper, took this line. 'We avoid revolution,' it declaimed in April, 'and render sedition abortive, not by temporizing and putting off the evil day, but by a continual and ordinary compliance with the just demands of the age.'[46] That was the answer. The best antidote to revolution was not repression, but progress. Progress would eventually reconcile everyone. It had already reconciled enough Britons by 1848 to ensure that, even at a time of revolutionary upheaval abroad, far more people were on the government's side than against. Go on like this – as the Victorians intended to – and soon there would be no more opposition at all. When there was no opposition, there would be no one left to keep a watch on. Britain could then become spyless. That was the way things were tending before 1848. 1848 was the final test of the theory, which the latter passed triumphantly. After it, spylessness could be finally achieved.

Chapter 5

No police over opinion
(1850–80)

To most intents and purposes, domestic political espionage in Britain stopped shortly after 1848. That should mean that there is nothing much to write about at this stage, until the story picks up again in the early 1880s. This is not so, however, for two reasons. First, the fact that domestic political espionage virtually stopped after 1848 is so remarkable – certainly will be regarded as such by the 'second oldest profession' school of spy writers – as to require some explanation. Secondly, there are some exceptions, including one British secret policeman and one Irish spymaster in this period, who are arguably more interesting and important than anyone we have come across so far in this field since Wickham. That should be enough to fill a fair-sized chapter, and to provide a narrow bridge across this vast mid-Victorian chasm of spylessness, on to the firmer ground that looms later on.

Neither our secret policeman nor our spymaster had anything at all to do with ordinary domestic subversion in mainland Britain in the period after 1848; which is why we are still justified, despite them, in regarding these years as essentially spyless. The evidence for this is almost overwhelming. It is not absolutely overwhelming, because it is theoretically possible at any time for a secret service to remain so secret as to leave no historical trace at all; but it would be remarkable for a secret service (especially a British one) ever to be as *efficient* as this. One would expect a few clues. For the mid-Victorian period there are none. There are no surviving official records of spies being employed against native British subversives, and no indications that such records have ever existed in the past. No convincing complaints have come through from the sort of people who might have been imagined to be the targets of espionage that any such thing was going on. No political spies were spotted in the streets, or caught going through anyone's belongings, or cross-examined in courts of law. Espionage was never a subject of controversy or debate, except – mildly – in other connections we shall come on to soon. It seemed to have no place at all in the political culture of the time. That constitutes a prima facie case – albeit a negative one – that it simply did not exist.

This applies, incidentally, to all forms of espionage, not just the government kind. That is worth emphasizing, because it is possible for private enterprises to create their own spy systems, in the power vacuums left by some forms of liberal capitalist state. Pinkerton's detective agency in America, which could be hired by employers to spy on labour, is an example; as is Britain's Economic League today. The mid-Victorians had nothing like that. The nearest they came to it was with their 'Trade Protection Societies', which regarded themselves as 'a sort of moral police', but only seem to have bothered with bad – that is, fraudulent or non-paying – customers.[1] Britain's free entrepreneurs would not have dreamt of spying on anyone, including workers; or at least not systematically. It was against their principles too.

This also fits in with what is known in the diplomatic and military fields. The closure of the Secret and Deciphering departments of the Post Office in 1844 meant that Britain had no means of intercepting foreign messages after that time: no 'Sigint', in modern parlance. She also had no human intelligence network abroad in these years ('Humint'), beyond taking on the occasional freelance to wander around Europe and find out what he could. Even then Christopher Andrew has shown how essentially uncovert these 'agents' were, with one of them – Laurence Oliphant – dressing in 'coloured trousers and a distinctive hat' in Poland in the early 1860s to avoid being taken for a native.[2] One 'covert operation' has come to light: an attempt by the Italian refugee Antonio Panizzi to rescue some patriots from King 'Bomba's' gaols in Naples in 1855, subsidized clandestinely from the secret service fund with the private blessing of government ministers; but the motive behind that was liberal humanitarianism rather than national interest, and in any case it failed.[3] Military intelligence was, if anything, even thinner on the ground. In 1803 a 'Depot of Military Knowledge' had been established for the army, mainly to collect maps. After 1815 that was run down, with just 'one or two clerks' being kept on 'to dust the shelves'. No new maps were acquired or drawn, with the result that when the British army embarked on its next major war, in the Crimea in 1854, it had little idea of the terrain it was supposed to be fighting on.[4] This may be one reason why the military history of Britain during these years is more renowned for its glorious fiascos (like the Charge of the Light Brigade) than for any victories.

In the colonies, where Britain has been known to adopt breathtakingly double standards on occasions, the situation was very little different. Even

India was largely spyless. Though Britain got some of her ideas about ruling India from her Mogul predecessors, a recent authority points out, 'the systematic use of espionage was not one of them. In fact a strong aversion to the use of spies was one of the alien traditions of government which the British brought to India in the nineteenth century.' The only exceptions to this before the 1900s were either ineffective, or short-lived. The 'Thuggee and Dacoity Department' took on a mild political role after it had eliminated the Thugs in 1863. The assassination of the Indian viceroy Lord Mayo in 1872 led to the creation of a new political detective branch within that department under Edward Bradford (who later became head of the London Metropolitan Police); but that faded out after he left India in 1876. The government of India's nervousness of this kind of thing mirrored its political masters' in Britain. 'It would not do for the native press', wrote Lord Dufferin in 1887, 'to get it into their heads that we were about to establish a Third Section after the Russian pattern.'[5] That was a consideration in Britain too.

It is important to understand that this lack of intelligence-gathering activity in the mid-nineteenth century was not simply a matter of neglect. The Victorians were not just forgetful of intelligence, or ignorant of its value, or unwilling to pay for it; they deliberately and positively renounced it, as something that was unnecessary, counter-productive and wrong. There were a number of reasons for this. Contemporary notions of honour and decency had something to do with it: the chivalric ethos that was nurtured among the upper classes and in the public schools then, possibly as a reaction against the new entrepreneurial spirit of the time,[6] and which lay behind statements such as this one (from just after the Crimean War), that 'the gathering of knowledge by clandestine means [is] repulsive to the feelings of English Gentlemen'.[7] We shall see these sentiments – almost those very words – repeated again and again over the next few years. Espionage was underhand, unsporting, unworthy, degrading. The fact that foreigners indulged in it made no difference. It was one of the things that made them foreign. As in cricket, it was better to lose a battle than to win by such methods. No honourable Englishman would stoop to them.

Always when ideas have become outmoded in history, it is the sillier justifications of them which are emphasized, in order to rub home just how outmoded they are. That espionage should have been abjured in the nineteenth century because it was 'simply not cricket' now appears almost ludicrous, in an age when, arguably, even cricket is not 'cricket' any more. But that was not the full story. The whole point about the Victorians' distaste for espionage is that it was consistent with practical considerations too. Before anyone criticizes them for naïvety, he should consider this fact: that Britain never seriously *suffered* from her lack of covert intelligence between 1850 and 1880; was never defeated, or subverted, or thwarted in anything important either at home or abroad, simply because she did not like to use spies. That is a crucial point. It helps to explain why Britain was so self-denying in this area, and may also be felt to justify it. Of course luck came into it too. Poor intelligence might have lost her the Crimean War, for example, if it had not been for her alliance with the militarily superior French. In general, however, she survived her spyless phase because she did not need spies. We might consider that to be another stroke of good fortune. This, however, is not how contemporaries regarded it.

They saw it as a sign of national virtue: which it may indeed have been. In very broad terms the argument went like this. You set spies on people you fear. You can fear people either reasonably, or not. If there is no reasonable basis for your fear, then spies are likely to make things worse. If they are discovered, either abroad or at home, they will be resented, and consequently undermine trust. That creates tensions either between governments and other governments, or between governments and governed. Consequently it should be avoided. If on the other hand your fear does have a reasonable basis, espionage may be justified. But there are two important caveats here. The first is that it is *still* likely to undermine trust and create tensions, however justified it may be. So it is a dangerous necessity, at best. The second caveat is that the threat you fear may ultimately be your own fault. If you fear that another country might attack you, for example, it could be because you have done something to provoke it. Similarly, domestic subversion is very often a reaction against unjust government. If this is so – or in so far as it is so – you have the means in your own hands to alter or remove the circumstances that have given rise to the threat. You have, in other words, the power to create the conditions in which spies are unnecessary. And this, in turn, will enable you to avoid the damage that spies can do.

That is what mid-Victorian Britain did, or tried to. In foreign affairs, for example, her whole policy was geared to avoiding war in Europe, and indeed avoiding any kind of European involvement which might make continental intelligence important to her. In this she was broadly successful, especially on the war-avoidance front; though there was one serious aberration (Crimea), and a couple of possible near misses later on. It was called 'isolation'; though it was not simply a matter of Britain's withdrawing into her shell and letting the rest of the world go hang. For a start she did not let the rest of the world go hang, but annexed a good part of it, in Africa, Asia and elsewhere. That was supposed to be a first step towards the creation of a great free world market, in which national territorial frontiers would become less and less significant (because they would not be allowed to hamper trade), and consequently wars over frontiers less likely.[8] If wars were less likely, it followed that spies would be too. On the domestic scene much the same was meant to happen. Free internal trade, heralded by the abolition of the corn tax in 1846, would raise nearly everyone's prosperity, hence make nearly everyone contented, hence render revolution less likely and hence obviate the need for spies at home. It all hung together. Peace and security both rested on political freedom, underpinned by the free market economy. Espionage was a product of war and insecurity, and so fundamentally inimical to freedom in both usages of the word. This was whiggery infused with capitalism, and then stretched to its logical limit. It made anti-espionage into one of the central 'values' of Victorian times; though in the mythology of the twentieth century it has turned out to be one of the least enduring ones.

That is because the hopes of the early free marketeers for permanent peace and security through capitalism have not been realized in our century: of which more anon. In mid-Victorian times, however, they looked far more plausible, and especially in the domestic field, where quite suddenly and remarkably, after the furore of the 1840s, political peace reigned again. That is not to say that Britain was peaceful in every sense. There was a great deal of disorder in mid-Victorian times. The Victorian working man – and more especially the Victorian working youth – could always find a reason to demonstrate and riot if he or she wanted to. They were a turbulent lot. But turbulence does not necessary spell danger to the state.

In the 1850s the most common excuses for rioting were starvation, Sunday observance, the Catholic Church and the Irish. Starvation provoked 'bread riots', as they were called, in 1855 in Liverpool, the Midlands and London, with mobs ransacking and plundering bakers' shops, and terrorizing 'respectable' people in fashionable areas like London's Mayfair. The Sunday observance issue (government plans to close shops on Sundays) gave rise to a huge riot in Hyde Park in the summer of 1855, with a crowd of around 150,000 hurling clods of earth and stones at noblemen's houses, and then hunting, or 'chivvying', their footmen and beating them up. The Irish and Catholic issues, of course, were combined in some of the riots of the time, like a big one in Stockport in June 1852, when sixty-seven people were seriously wounded in battles between English and Irish, one man was killed, and a number of Catholic churches attacked. There were also anti-Catholic demonstrations which did not involve the Irish, like the 'Surplice riots' of 1858–9, directed against Church of England ministers who were considered to have adopted 'papist' ways. In the 1860s this sort of thing continued unabated, fired by an anti-Catholic tub-thumper called Patrick Murphy who used to inflame crowds with stories of monastic sodomy, young girls being seduced in the confessional and nuns being walled up alive in convents, so that they then went off and smashed up churches and convents. The worst of the 'Murphy riots' took place in Birmingham and Lancashire – both areas of heavy Irish immigration – in 1867–8. Murphy himself came to a bloody end when he was kicked to death by a mob of Irish Catholics in Whitehaven in April 1871. Two other pretexts for disorder in the 1860s were industrial disputes, and parliamentary reform. There was a whole series of 'outrages' connected with strikes during the 1860s, mainly in Lancashire and west Yorkshire, with widespread sabotage, attacks on employers, and blacklegs having their homes firebombed. The issue of parliamentary reform inspired a famous riot in Hyde Park on 23 July 1866, when despite a Home Office ban a huge crowd pushed over the park railings, trampled down the flower beds and then went on the rampage for several days, stoning the 'toffs' and their houses and clubs, and having to be put down eventually by troops. The 1860s also had their share of 'bread riots', including a serious one at Stalybridge in Lancashire in 1863, when the local relief committee cut grants to the unemployed and had its members' houses attacked and its stores plundered in return. This is only part of the picture.[9] It does not sound very peaceful. But there were important extenuating factors.

Very few of these riots, for example, had any political aim. The only real exception was the Reform League demonstrations of 1866, which did indeed put the fear of revolution into some poor Tories, but were very quickly bought off, in effect, when the Tories themselves conceded parliamentary reform in August the following year. Other disorder was far less worrying. Most riots were either sheer reactions against hunger, with no end in view beyond stealing a loaf or two of bread; or manifestations of religious prejudice similar to the 'church and king' riots of the eighteenth century, but this time aggravated by cheap Irish labour and Irish blacklegging; or else pure hooliganism, rather like soccer riots in our own day. Many of them were directed against 'scapegoats', like the Irish, which had the effect of diverting pressure away from the state. Most contemporary observers agreed that the participants in these events were the dregs of society: 'youths of the very lowest and dirtiest class, and dirty women and girls', as the *Annual Register* described the Sunday observance rioters of 1855, with merely 'a sprinkling of respectable persons who partook the views of the populace'.[10] That was significant, in view of the importance that we have seen was always attached (by the middle classes) to middle-class 'leadership'. If any of these disturbances and outrages and the rest were manifestations of social and political discontent, which they may have been, then they were wild, blind, fragmented ones, with no wiser leaders to guide them than Patrick Murphy, and no revolutionary programme beyond blacking the eyes of a few 'toffs'.

To the Victorians this made them not a political but a criminal problem, which was far more comfortable, and easier to cope with. It was no excuse for complacency. To some middle-class Victorians riots provided a salutary warning that there could be plenty of incendiary fuel still left in Britain, for any revolutionary engine that might come along. The point was, however, that there was no imminent danger of this. No revolutionary engine could be seen anywhere on the horizon. Between the collapse of Chartism around 1850 and the birth of the (Marxist) Social Democratic Federation in 1880, native British socialism was almost entirely defunct. Middle-class Victorians hoped and assumed it would remain defunct, while their new liberal capitalist system delivered – and filtered down – the economic goods. That was the way to draw any potential political sting that mid-Victorian riots might be thought to have. At the moment those riots posed no threat to the social or political fabric of the country. If capitalism lived up to its billing, as it was bound to, then they never would, because the riots would die out anyway.

Britain, therefore, was safe. More important: the governing classes knew she was safe. That was why they called their spy-hounds off. The realization seems to have come to them, almost in a flash, between 1848 and 1851. We have already seen the contribution made to this by the events – or myth – of 1848. 1851 put the final touches to it. That was the year when Prince Albert decided to put on a Great Exhibition of art and industry in Hyde Park, in which every country of the world could, if it wanted, display its wares. So far as industry was concerned Britain's wares were easily the most impressive; which gave another boost – as if it were needed – to her *amour propre*. (The fact that she was way behind in art was irrelevant, or even a matter of pride.) But her *amour propre* was also boosted in another way. The fact that she dared to hold the Exhibition at all, so soon after the turmoil of 1848, amazed some of her neighbours. Millions of people would be visiting it, many of them from abroad. Foreign ministers warned Britain of the dangers this might bring. Rumours abounded, of dastardly plots to overthrow her government under cover of the occasion. Revolutionaries were disguising themselves as trees, cunningly, so as not to be spotted in the park. Another report told of a conspiracy between continental socialists and American Catholics (!) to revolutionize the whole continent, starting with Britain, and then place Bishop Hughes of New York on the papal throne. An 'aeronaut' (or balloonist) wrote to the Home Secretary in April 1851 retailing a plot involving 90,000 foreign visitors and 200,000 Irishmen, co-ordinated by a cadre of Catholic priests disguised as match-sellers, who would then use their unsold matches to set London alight. Others would blow 'Balls of an inflammatory nature' from tubes made up to look like walking-sticks into shop doorways, which would all explode 'at a given time'; strategically placed agents would 'instantly stab' anyone running to fetch the fire-engines; and in the general confusion Buckingham Palace and the Bank of England would be seized. The Duke of Wellington, one of the Police Commissioners (Mayne) and the Chartist Feargus O'Connor all thought there might be something in this, but of course there was not. Our aeronaut was either being led on, or making it up. The Exhibition passed off peacefully, and successfully. Charles Dickens waxed quite sarcastic about the 'nervous old ladies, dyspeptic half-pay officers' and others who had ever feared anything else.[11] The foreign Cassandras had been shown up. Britain's fundamental solidity and stability had once again been demonstrated beyond dispute. Scarcely anyone in Britain did dispute it, for at least thirty years.

The sense of security rendered espionage redundant. The Victorians themselves, however, also put it the other way around. In August 1851 Lord Bloomfield, Britain's ambassador in Berlin, was asked by the Prussian Foreign Minister, Baron Manteuffel, why Britain's police were so exclusively concerned with 'Robbers and Murderers', and neglected 'political criminals', unlike in Prussia. Bloomfield replied thus: 'that it was the conviction of the people of England that the Police were solely employed in this manner which commanded respect for the Establishment throughout the Country'; in other words, that the absence of a political police helped create the conditions in which a political police was not needed. The reverse side of this coin, of course, was that political policemen provoked their own subversion. That was why when foreign governments complained of such subversion, Britain showed so little sympathy. More than once, especially in the 1850s, her Foreign Secretaries actually wrote and told them that if they found themselves being subverted, they only had themselves to blame. That did not go down too well.[12]

It was characteristic, however, of the high moral tone Britain adopted over the issue of espionage after 1848–51. She was not simply spyless, but assertively *anti*-spy. Espionage was seen as not merely unnecessary, but profoundly damaging, in all kinds of ways. 'Should the practice of spydom become universal,' said *The Times* in 1859, 'farewell to all domestic confidence and happiness.' That was in connection with a recent adultery case, in which a Mrs Sopwith of Tunbridge Wells had employed a private detective to spy on her husband's 'indecent familiarities' with their servant girl, Mary Prickett, 'among some furze bushes near Prickett's house'; but it applied more widely too.[13] (Whether it would have applied if it had been *Mrs* Sopwith's fidelity that had been under scrutiny cannot be known.) For the worst effects of espionage, the mid-Victorians usually looked abroad. An article published in Dickens's *Household Words* in September 1850, for example, painted a highly unsavoury picture of ordinary everyday life in southern Italy, where 'spydom' *was* universal, and with 'exceedingly demoralizing' results. Everyone was encouraged to spy on everyone else; no one knew whom to trust; no one dared speak his or her mind; everything was done covertly. Consequently there was 'no country in Europe where the low, secret vices' were so rife. For this, and for the southern Italians' 'low national character' generally, the 'Secret Police system' was largely to blame.[14] Such problems were endemic to espionage. Its effect was deeply corrosive: both on individual morality, and on the social virtues.

It was also fatal to 'freedom'. That was the mid-Victorians' chief objection to it. 'Political espionage', wrote the novelist Mayne Reid in 1853, 'is cuneiform. Give the vile system but the smallest insertion, and, wedge-like, it will help itself, until it has cleft the columns of our glory and sapped the foundations of our dear liberty.'[15] Erskine May, the historian and authority on Commons procedure, put it equally strongly (though less picturesquely) ten years later.

> Men may be without restraints upon their liberty: they may pass to and fro at pleasure: but if their steps are tracked by spies and informers, their words noted down for crimination, their associates watched as conspirators, – who shall say that they are free?

He went further. 'The freedom of a country', he asserted, 'may be measured by its immunity from this baleful agency.'[16] That was how important it was. Freedom *depended* on not having political spies.

If that was so, then it put Britain right at the top of the freedom league. This probably accounts for the immense satisfaction her people took in being (as they thought) entirely 'immune' from political espionage in mid-Victorian times. 'We have no political police,' *Household Words* proudly proclaimed, at the beginning of its article on the southern Italian scene;

> no police over opinion. The most rabid demagogue can *say* in this free country what he chooses, provided it does not tend to incite others to *do* what is annoying to the lieges. He speaks not under the terror of an organized spy system. He dreads not to discuss the affairs of the nation at a tavern, lest the waiter should be a policeman in disguise; he can converse familiarly with his guests at his own table without suspecting that the interior of his own liveries consists of a spy; when travelling, he has not the slightest fear of perpetual imprisonment for declaring himself freely on the conduct of the powers that be, because he knows that even if his fellow-passenger be a Sergeant Myth or an Inspector Wield, no harm will come to him.[17]

The upshot of this was that the British people were happier and nobler, their government more secure and their system better in every way than the Continent's. Spylessless was not an optional extra, or a fortunate accident. It was essential, no less, both to the material well-being and to the moral self-image of the mid-Victorian liberal capitalist state. That is another reason why it is difficult to believe that Britain could have been running a covert spy system behind the scenes. So much rested on her not doing so.

None of the exceptions to this general rule made any great inroads into it. All of them mainly (though not exclusively) involved the London Metropolitan Police. This had a great deal to do with it. Scotland Yard, as we have seen, had a strong anti-espionage tradition of its own. This is crucial to an understanding of its 'political' work. Its first plain-clothes detective branch was tiny, chiefly so as to avoid being taken for a 'secret police'. In 1850 it still only comprised eight men. There were one or two good ones amongst them – Jonathan Whicher, in particular, acquired quite a popular reputation – but throughout much of this period the constant complaint from within the force was that detective work never attracted the brightest men. That was partly because pay and promotion prospects were poor; but when that problem was met it merely gave rise to another, which was that the uniformed men now resented the preference they felt the detectives were getting.[18] There was also widespread suspicion of them outside. 'Men whose business it is to detect hidden and secret things', commented Anthony Trollope in 1869, 'are very apt to detect things that have never been done.'[19] They were subject to other temptations too. In 1877 the detective branch more or less collapsed, when three out of its four inspectors were convicted and imprisoned for fraud. (The fourth saved himself by turning queen's evidence.) Two years later one of the senior officers of the new 'Criminal Investigation Department' which had been set up to replace it in 1878 admitted that the best men still refused to join it, because of its reputation for being underhand; and the assistant commissioner in charge of it wrote of the 'enormous danger of moral contagion' those who did join were subject to.[20] Two things can be inferred from this. One is that plain-clothes ('spy') police were prone to corruption. The second, however, is that the *knowledge* that they were prone to corruption induced the hierarchy to keep them on a tight rein.

That hierarchy was scarcely likely to welcome the chance to send men like this into any area that was even remotely political. It only did it when it was ordered to, and then reluctantly. That happened in three different sets of circumstances. The first was when crimes had been committed, or were known to be contemplated, which happened to have a political connection. Then the detective branch could be sent in, just as it would be to any other crime. One example was our 'Aeronaut's' letter of 1851, giving notice of the plot to set London afire. In that case a policeman was sent to interview him, and came back with the news that he was anxious for his son to be employed by 'what he calls the Secret Service': which was a shame, in view of the fact that there was no such thing.[21] Another example came in 1861 when the Hungarian leader Louis Kossuth was found to be printing Hungarian banknotes, contrary to a whole sheaf of currency laws, as a way of raising capital for his nationalist cause.[22] These instances, and others like them, raised no problems. Crimes could not be ignored merely because the motivation behind them was political. Police who were put on to them did not thereby become 'political' police.

The second circumstance in which the Metropolitan Police could be asked to get involved in political work was under pressure from foreign governments. It was this, in fact, which gave rise to the closest equivalent to a British secret political police in these years: a kind of proto-'Special

Branch'. The pressure came about as a result of the continued presence in Britain of political refugees from the Continent, who after the failure of the 1848 revolutions and Louis Napoleon's 1851 *coup d'état* were reckoned to number around 7,000 politically active ones.[23] They represented no direct threat of any kind to Britain, though foreign governments sometimes tried to persuade her otherwise. (In 1850 Baron Manteuffel, for example, sent Palmerston a lurid report from his own police on the activities of Karl Marx, who was supposed to be plotting against the life of Queen Victoria from his lodgings in Soho: but Palmerston remained unconvinced.)[24] Nevertheless they did pose diplomatic problems. Though they had no designs on Britain, many of them still had hopes for their own countries, and some were active in schemes to put them to rights. When those schemes involved assassination plots hatched on British soil, or even lesser crimes (like Kossuth's), their targets were liable to feel that this was carrying hospitality too far. The most notorious case was in January 1858, when the ex-refugee Felice Orsini threw a bomb at the French emperor outside the Paris Opera, missed him, but slaughtered eight bystanders. The British Foreign Office was flooded with complaints, and on a couple of occasions in the 1850s was confronted with the possibility of a pan-continental alliance against Britain on this issue.[25] It could not simply ignore it. That was where Scotland Yard came in.

Initially it was nonplussed. When he was asked to look into Manteuffel's allegations about Marx, for example, Commissioner Mayne's first response was that this would be tricky, because he had 'no one connected with the police' – amongst all his 3,000-plus officers – 'who understands the German language'.[26] What he did have at that time was a number of presumably voluntary non-police informants, who sent in reports – some reliable, some not – of refugee goings-on. They included one who signed himself 'S', or 'JHS', and had been reporting on meetings of *French* refugees since October 1849 at the latest. His full name was John Hitchens Sanders. In 1850 or 1851 he was recruited on to the official strength of the force, as a detective constable attached to 'A' division, which took in Whitehall. It is highly likely, but cannot be proved, that he was taken on for the sole and specific purpose of keeping the refugees under surveillance, perhaps initially during the Great Exhibition. He had all the qualities for the job. He had lived in France for some years, was fluent in French and probably spoke English with a French accent. (Englishmen sometimes mistook him for a foreigner.) He was also clearly highly intelligent, and (as we shall see) discriminating. He was promoted to Sergeant in 1851, and Inspector in 1856, at the almost unprecedentedly young age of 31. He was Scotland Yard's, and hence the government's, only trustworthy source of intelligence about refugee affairs. He had one or two men working under him, including latterly a young constable called Adolphus Frederick Williamson, who will be cropping up later; and reported himself directly to the Chief Commissioner.

A radical newspaper which cottoned on to his activities fairly early on called his section of the police the 'foreign branch'. So far as is known, it had no formal title, so this will have to do. It lasted until August 1859, when Sanders died suddenly from 'apoplexy', still only in his mid-thirties, and his 'foreign branch' appears to have died with him.[27]

It was moderately significant while it lasted, because it appears to have been entirely unprecedented. It departed from previous Metropolitan Police orthodoxy in two ways. First, it existed to keep a continuous watch on a group of people who had not committed and were not believed to be about to commit any particular crime. That was new, and if it had been widely known about would have provoked widespread protest. Secondly, the only feature that was common to this group and distinguished it from others was a political one: its members were all foreign revolutionaries. That departed radically from two firmly established British police principles: not to 'spy' on people unless you had good and specific grounds to suspect them of criminal intent; and never to spy on people simply because of their politics. This cut right across the liberal ethos of the day, and justifies describing Sanders's 'foreign branch' as, in some senses, a 'political police'. We have seen why it was done: mainly to defuse foreign complaints about refugees abusing their asylum in Britain to plot bloody deeds on the Continent. But how did the police get away with it?

They did not, entirely. Sanders was occasionally spotted. One occasion was in the aftermath of the Orsini plot, when the government bent all its efforts to trying to winkle out any of Orsini's accomplices who remained in Britain, and in the process took greater risks. At midnight on 22 January 1858, for example, Sanders apparently searched Orsini's old lodgings without a warrant, and attracted some unwelcome publicity and criticism as a result.[28] That, however, was unusual. Generally both Sanders and his masters were far more cautious, careful not to seem to give substance to the popular suspicion that was always hovering above them, especially in 1858, that 'French' methods of policing were about to be sneaked in. This had the effect of considerably blunting the 'foreign branch's' political edge. For example, it confined its attentions to foreigners, and never – so far as can be ascertained – took any interest in native British radicals. There is not the slightest suspicion attaching to it of any *agent provocateur* tricks. Its methods of obtaining information are obscure – the Home Office, for example, had no idea what they were[29] – but they seem to have been discreet, and except for that one case in 1858 never aroused any controversy. It also never got publicly involved in court cases: partly because there were very few court cases involving refugees, and partly because Sanders was deliberately kept away from the only significant one, which was the trial of Simon Bernard in April 1858 for complicity in the Orsini plot.[30]

All this was chiefly made possible, however, because of certain fundamental precepts which informed Sanders's work. Some of them derived from ministers' perceptions of the requirements of the situation they found themselves in. They had set this watch on the refugees out of deference to foreign governments. Those foreign governments were greatly agitated by the activities of the refugees, on which they had their own sources of information: scores, possibly hundreds (certainly far more than Sanders had at his disposal) of their own police spies. British ministers distrusted those spies instinctively. 'The French government', wrote the Foreign Secretary in 1857, 'employ such a number of spies & pay them so absurdly high that they must furnish something for their wages & I am sure that all manner of absurdities are sent to Paris.'[31] The presumption was always that foreign police reports were exaggerated, invented, or 'provoked'. It suited Britain to believe this too, because it meant that the continentals had no real complaint against her. If the refugees were *not* misbehaving, then it took the pressure off her to legislate against them in some way. This was vital, in view of the enormous public hostility any such legislation was bound to provoke. (In February 1858 that public hostility was actually tested, and led to Palmerston's fall from power, when he tried to pilot through Parliament a really very mild and reasonable anti-refugee measure, in the shape of a Bill making it an offence to conspire to murder someone abroad.)[32] This was the exact opposite of what was supposed to have been the situation in the 1810s, when governments (it was claimed) had wanted excuses to legislate. In the 1850s and 1860s they did not. If the refugee community was indeed harmless, that was what they needed to be told. And that, in general, was what Sanders told them. This was the main reason why he made so few ripples, and why the significance of this early 'political' police branch, therefore, is as limited as it is.

Sanders was objective almost to a fault. Much of the information that came to him – either from his informants, or possibly from his own attendance at refugee meetings in disguise – would have terrified other men, even non-paranoiacs. Refugee rhetoric could be pretty bloodcurdling at times. No doubt the foreign police spies who heard it made as much of it as they could. Sanders did not. The general picture he painted was of a somewhat demoralized, impoverished and strictly law-abiding group of men and women, who occasionally uttered threats but without usually meaning them, and even if they did mean them were unlikely to be able to carry them out, because (on one occasion) 'they cannot find any of their party brave enough'. More often than not, he reported, the wildest talk came from *agents provocateurs*: men who pretended to be refugees, but 'are nothing else but spies, who excite the better class of Refugees to commit themselves'. Just occasionally even Sanders took fright. In Jersey, for example, where he was often sent on special missions, he found the French refugees particularly alarming – 'their excitement and violence has been beyond description', he once reported; 'They utter daily threats ... that they would not be satisfied until they had torn the flesh of Louis Napoleon and his *Valets* with their teeth' – and in

August 1855 he issued a rare warning that if something were not done there soon, things might become 'serious'.[33] When it heard that from the normally imperturbable Sanders, the government had to take notice; and so in October it expelled all the Jersey refugees, not from Britain, which was beyond its powers, but to other parts of the kingdom. That caused a bit of a public stir, but not very much, partly because the refugees were not really greatly put out. (Some of them merely decamped to Guernsey.)[34]

This was in line with Sanders's contribution generally. Usually 'police spies' are considered to be the enemies of the people they spy on. Sanders was, on the contrary, the mid-Victorian refugees' greatest friend. The effect of his intelligence was to protect them from the much more drastic actions the government might have felt impelled to take against them if it had not had him to reassure it. Is there the slight smell of a rat here? Sanders had French antecedents, was married to a French wife and had first been spotted by the Home Office as someone who was accepted as a revolutionary. Perhaps he *was* one all along, a secret ally of the men he was supposed to be policing; one of the first, and most successful, 'moles' in British intelligence?

If so, it did not really matter, to a government which, so far as the refugees were concerned, simply wanted an easy life. Sanders was very highly valued. He seemed to have an uncanny knowledge of everything the refugees did. (That, of course, would also figure, if he were one of them himself.) Lord Clarendon thought he was 'worth all the French police agents & spies put together'. Palmerston agreed; but also felt that it was 'absurd' that the police had no one else like him: that they were so dependent on one man.[35] The result of this was that when that man died in 1859 his system, such as it was, folded. This is another reason why Sanders's 'foreign branch' can only be said to be moderately significant: because there is almost no vestige of continuity between it and later political police branches, which would give it a longer-term import.

Even if Sanders had lived on, however, there would have been less need for his particular skills after 1859. The refugee problem eased: partly because many of the refugees returned home, and partly because foreign governments came to terms with the fact that Britain was not going to be able to help them with them. The British authorities, for their part, steered even clearer of 'political policing' than they had in the past, in view of the 'great animosity ... amongst a large class of the people' which, in the recollection of a new police commissioner in 1878, had been provoked by 'The Police action ... in the Orsini case' all those years before. That point was made to justify the police's refusal to accede to a request from the Russians to set a watch on *their* émigrés; which is one of a number of scattered pieces of evidence that for twenty-odd years after 1859 systematic surveillance of this kind was virtually unknown. Even the exceptions in this area really do seem to prove the rule. One such exception is a telling report from a policeman who was sent – again at the request of a foreign government – to find out about the activities of a group of foreign communists meeting over a public house in Islington in May 1872. He told how at the door he was asked whether he was a communist. His answer to that was 'No'; which one would have thought was a basic mistake for anyone who was really intending to be a spy. 'Upon that', he went on,

> a person (whom I can identify) caught hold of me and assisted by others carried me forcibly out of the room and intimated that if I returned they would break my head. I did not return in order that no breach of the peace should take place.

Three weeks later he tried again, at another venue, sat down, and refused to leave: at which the landlord instructed everyone else at the meeting to go. That seems to have been the best the police could do. Compared with Sanders's time, it was unimpressive. On the other hand the unsuccessful policeman's senior officers do not seem to have been too upset. They found another way to enlighten their masters about the communists, which was to write to 'Dr Charles Marx' direct. He turned out to be most helpful, sending a whole bundle of communist propaganda to them through the post. That was preferable in any case. It was the honest, open, *British* way of doing things.[36]

That series of little adventures happened during another peak in the graph of political immigration, when around 3,500 new French refugees (including spouses and children) entered Britain after the defeat of the Paris Commune in the summer of 1871.[37] The communards were accompanied, as invariably happened at these peaks, by foreign pressures on Britain either to expel them or, failing that, to keep them under control. There was no chance of her agreeing to the former, but she clearly co-operated with the French authorities short of that, in ways which took up a certain amount of detective time.[38] One of the detectives whose time was taken up in this way was Adolphus Williamson, now a superintendent, who counter-signed our Islington pub 'police spy's' report. He was also in charge of the inquiries that were made into Karl Marx's application for British naturalization in August 1874, and which concluded that, as a 'notorious German agitator' who had 'not been loyal to his own King and Country', he was probably not a very deserving case.[39] Police investigations of naturalization cases were routine. This one into Marx does not suggest that he was subjected to any police surveillance apart from this. Most of Williamson's other refugee work was similarly *ad hoc*, and unsystematic. He seems to have been Scotland Yard's political specialist throughout these years, and in this role forms a tenuous link between Sanders in the 1850s and the 'Special Irish Branch', which he headed, in 1883. But from the surviving evidence (which is incomplete) he does not appear to merit the description of a 'political policeman' in the full sense yet. He was concerned with crimes, or other normal police business, which *happened* to have political implications. Those political implications were never at the centre of his work.

In a sense this was true for the whole of this mid-Victorian period. Even when the surveillance of refugees was more thorough than it appears to have been under Williamson, it was not done for a British political end. In every single case it was done for the benefit of foreign governments, and in response to demands from them. Some ministers felt those demands were reasonable; others did not, but thought it would be impolitic to resist them. Very few indeed believed that Britain gained anything more directly from the watch she kept on the refugees. That was because the refugees – even the later communard ones – were not considered to be a threat. Other countries, of course, thought this was foolhardy, and tried to persuade Britain so. It was in response to a suggestion from one of them (Germany) that the Home Office conducted a brief survey of the native socialist scene in Britain just as the first communard refugees began arriving, in July 1871. But that did not change its mind. It was 'notorious', the survey reported, that most socialists in Britain were foreigners. Socialist ideas, 'though disseminated and sometimes discussed in England, have no root here'. Similarly, 'Ideas of revolution effected by force of arms, of destruction of public buildings, of "popular revenge on detested individuals", have taken no hold.' What you had were 'Vague notions of an enlarged co-operative system under which property and capital shall be peaceably absorbed for the benefit of all classes of society', which seemed to be catching on. 'But up to this time these notions are purely speculative, and no considerable section of Englishmen indulge the desire of propagating them otherwise than by peaceable discussion and the force of reason.'[40] So that was all right. If the Continent had reason to fear this kind of thing, Britain did not. That is why there were so very few genuine political policemen in Britain at this time, compared to foreign countries; and why she would have needed scarcely any at all if it had not been for them.

That, however, was to reckon without Ireland: which in modern British history it is always unwise to do. Ireland will be a recurring factor in our consideration of the history of British covert counter-subversion from this moment on. She first started impinging on the British domestic scene in 1866, when a group of Irish-American nationalists calling themselves 'Fenians' decided to take their fight against British oppression to Britain itself. Their two biggest coups were the rescue of two of their comrades from a Black Maria in the middle of Manchester in September 1867, in the course of which a police sergeant was shot dead; and a bomb they set off against the wall of Clerkenwell prison in London in December the same year which was intended to release one of the Manchester rescuers, failed, but killed several bystanders. That was the beginning, or resumption, of the

'Irish problem' so far as the Home Office and British police authorities were concerned.

It was not, of course, the beginning of it so far as the Irish Office and Dublin Castle were concerned. They had been used to this sort of thing for years, and on the whole coped pretty well. This was partly through the services of more of those informers who, as we have seen before, were always the bane of Irish nationalist life. 'Every considerable gathering of Fenians', wrote the contemporary Irish historian Justin McCarthy, 'had amongst its members at least one person who generally professed a yet fiercer devotion to the cause than any of the rest', and who was, of course, a spy. One of them, he claimed, pretended to be a Catholic when he was not, and took the sacrament in a Catholic church to preserve his cover, which in McCarthy's view was an 'outrage'.[41] From 1866 Britain's spies in America even included the president of the Council of the Irish Republican Brotherhood in New York, 'General' F. F. Millen. Most of this intelligence was gathered via the Irish Constabulary and the Dublin Metropolitan Police, the British ambassador in Washington, and an army lieutenant-colonel, W. H. A. Feilding, whose job it was to sniff out Fenianism among the troops. The Irish police also had their agents among the larger Irish communities in cities like Liverpool and Glasgow.[42] It has been suggested that it was because Ireland and Liverpool were so 'informer-riddled' in the 1860s that the Fenians thought of switching their attention to London.[43]

If so, it turned out to be not a bad idea. The London Metropolitan Police seemed to have no idea what to do in the face of this (for them) entirely unprecedented threat. 'They know as little how to discharge duty in connection with Fenianism as I do about translating Hebrew,' commented one Dublin policeman who worked alongside them in September 1867;[44] and even allowing for the jealousies which have always afflicted the relations between police forces in Britain, especially where the 'Met' is concerned, this was probably not unfair. The Home Office issued advice to all police chiefs to keep Fenian suspects under regular surveillance; put armed guards on railways lines the queen was due to travel along; and sent Williamson here, there and everywhere in pursuit of the malefactors. But then came the Clerkenwell bomb, which was particularly demoralizing because the London police had been given full and specific warning of it from Dublin, and yet still not managed to prevent it. The excuse they gave was that the intelligence from Dublin had stated that the prison was to be blown *up*, and not *down* or *across*: so they had naturally confined their search to the cellars and drains *underneath* Clerkenwell, and paid no attention to the barrel of gunpowder one poor PC on his beat had actually spotted standing against the wall before it went off. It was then that the government more or less gave up on them. 'Though for the most part they perform their ordinary duties efficiently,' the Prime Minister wrote to the queen, 'they are not equal to the present extraordinary demand. They are especially deficient . . . as a detective force.' Consequently, 'steps have . . . been taken to supply this deficiency by a separate and secret organization'. That separate organization was a new Home Office intelligence bureau, reporting directly to the minister, and headed by the army man, Feilding, assisted by another soldier, Captain Whelan, and a young Anglo-Irish lawyer, Robert Anderson.[45]

That could have been the start of a proper domestic intelligence-gathering bureau in Britain, had it lasted. It was disbanded, however, in April 1868. The main reason for that was that by then it had become clear that the Clerkenwell bomb had been a one-off operation, and not part of a wider conspiracy, which made a counter-conspiratorial agency unnecessary. Another reason may have been Feilding's moral distaste for the work, which he expressed when he was first asked to do it, on the grounds that 'spying' was incompatible with his status as an officer and a gentleman.[46] Perhaps nothing illustrates better the strength of prejudice in Britain at that time against espionage. What is most remarkable is the speed with which the authorities decided that the crisis was over after 1867, and dismantled their new machinery. A later Home Secretary, when confronted by a similar crisis in the 1880s, was critical of them for that.[47] But it was consistent with the spirit of the age; and it did them, as it happened, no great harm.

It may be that machinery like this cannot ever be completely dismantled, but always leaves some recognizable and serviceable fragments behind. The events of 1867 had two lasting effects. The first was to repair some of the deficiencies of the London police detective branch in this kind of area. In December 1867 the Home Office, as well as calling Feilding in, also told the Police Commissioner to look out for and recruit some men who could be employed on 'special and delicate services, which may be entrusted to them in other places'. 'Special and delicate' may have been a euphemism for 'political'.[48] Possibly as a result of this directive, a number of foreign-origin detectives were taken on shortly afterwards, including Sergeant Charles von Tornow, who was the officer sent to infiltrate the Islington communists in 1872, and Sergeant W. Reimers, who did the leg-work on the Karl Marx naturalization inquiry in 1874. They gave the detective branch greater variety; and ensured that it was a little better prepared than it had been in 1866-7 for the political problems and duties that descended on it later on.

The second and more significant legacy of the 1867 Fenian crisis was Robert Anderson. He stayed on at the Home Office after Feilding left, as what in later editions of *Who's Who* he called its 'adviser in matters relating to political crime'. The reason for this was almost certainly the relationship he had recently struck up with Thomas Beach, who under the *nom de guerre* of 'Henri le Caron' was to be the British government's major source of Fenian intelligence from the United States and Canada for twenty years. Beach became involved with the American Fenians in 1866, and wrote home about them to his father. He told his local MP, whose idea it was to alert the relevant authority, who at that time happened to be Anderson. Anderson interviewed Beach on a visit back to England in 1867, and took him on as a full-time, professional agent. He turned out to be an enormously valuable one. One of the conditions of their agreement was that Beach should report to Anderson alone, who would not divulge his name or show his letters to anyone else. Consequently Anderson was indispensable: which is undoubtedly what secured his job in Whitehall.[49]

In a way it was an enormous stroke of luck for him. Anderson was supposed to have other sources of Irish intelligence besides 'le Caron', and may have done initially. Later on in his career, however, they appear to have dried up, and when 'le Caron' stopped operating in 1889 there are suspicions, as we shall see, that he had no one at all. How really effective he was, therefore, is dubious. His own autobiography, published later, was typical of its genre in hinting that he had performed the most enormously vital services to his country but could not, of course, in the interests of national security, talk about them. Men who worked with him in the 1880s and 1890s, however, were more sceptical, and sometimes downright contemptuous. When his autobiography came out in 1910, consequently, it was greeted with a certain amount of derision.[50] In the 1860s and 1870s, however, he still had two advantages. One was 'le Caron', whose reports (many of which are still extant) made Anderson seem mysteriously omniscient, especially as he was pledged never to breathe a word about their source.[51] The second was the fact that he was alone, a one-man secret service band in Whitehall, with no one to challenge his own version of his role. It must have been gratifying, and not very hard work. It certainly gave him plenty of leisure for his other interests: which were writing books of fundamentalist Christian theology, and campaigning for harsher sentences for criminals.

That, then, was the state of Britain's covert counter-subversive agencies at the end of the 1870s. Ireland was well served, with police agencies which were skilled at espionage (especially the Dublin force), and informers in key posts. From America came information via the British ambassador and consuls, and from 'le Caron', deep at the heart of the Fenian conspiracy, via Anderson. So far as mainland Britain was concerned, however, the situation was very different. There was no surveillance of any kind over her own native radicals: a fact of which everyone was intensely proud. The only counter-subversive tools the authorities had there were some Irish policemen, reporting to Dublin on their own subversives; Robert Anderson, who despite being at the Home Office was mainly concerned with Fenianism in America, and whose effectiveness is questionable anyway; and some new members of the Metropolitan Police detective branch (now called the Criminal Investigation Department or CID), who were there to be employed on 'special and delicate' investigations if need be, under the command of Superintendent Frederick Adolphus Williamson, affectionately known as 'Dolly': who 'walked leisurely along Whitehall, balancing a hat that was a little too large for him loosely on his head, and often with a sprig of a leaf or a flower between his lips',[52] and was by all accounts an excellent and upright fellow, but was not exactly Sherlock Holmes. It was not an impressive defensive line-up. But it was what the mid-Victorians *wanted*; a matter – as we have seen – of deliberate choice.

Chapter 6

A permanent organization to detect and control (1880–1910)

Tracking spies in Britain before 1880 has not always been easy. Sometimes, especially in later years, the spoor has been very faint indeed, and even petered out. In most such cases we can be fairly confident – though never certain – that this is because the practice itself petered out, leaving no one to make any tracks. In the 1880s, however, we come for the first time on to a definite, strong, unbroken trail, leading us right up to the present day. That is the trail of what from 1887 onwards was called the 'Special Branch' of the London Metropolitan Police.

The Special Branch originated in response to two particular crises, neither of which was unprecedented. The first was a renewal – or rather, two renewals – of the Fenian bombing campaign in mainland Britain, in January 1881 and then two years later, at the beginning of 1883. The first renewal was a short-lived affair, whose only serious manifestations were some small explosions in the north-west of England. One of them, outside a barracks in Salford, killed a 7-year-old boy. A bomb was also found near the Mansion House in London in March, which was defused before it could go off. The 1883 campaign was more substantial. It began in Glasgow, with a gasworks, a coaling shed and a canal viaduct being damaged in January, but then passed on to London in the spring. From then until January 1885 there was a series of explosions all over the capital, which took in, for example, the offices of *The Times* newspaper, the Local Government Board in Whitehall, a gentlemen's club in St James's Square, the Tower of London, the Palace of Westminster, London Bridge, two underground trains, several London railway termini and (embarrassingly) the headquarters of the new police branch set up to counter all this activity at Scotland Yard. There were no more such incidents after 24 January 1885, though there was alleged to have been a plot to assassinate the queen during her golden jubilee celebrations in Westminster Abbey in the summer of 1887, which was foiled. Altogether about a hundred people were injured as a result of these 'outrages', though the only ones who died were three of the bombers themselves.[1]

The other crisis which contributed to the formation of the Special Branch was even more familiar from years gone by. It was to do with the old problem of political refugees in Britain, which flared up again after the assassination of Tsar Alexander II in St Petersburg on 13 March 1881. No refugees in England were involved in that crime, so far as anyone could tell; but the existence of Britain as a safe asylum for men and women of this stamp was widely regarded on the Continent as unhelpful to foreign governments in their efforts to counter political violence generally. Consequently the tsar's assassination led to pressure on Britain, direct and indirect, to modify her asylum policy in some way. That was out of the question, for the same reason it had been out of the question in earlier times. The Home Secretary, Sir William Vernon Harcourt, told the queen, who was very much in favour of booting them all out, that it would be 'politically impossible'. His Prime Minister, Gladstone, wrote that it would 'fly in the face' of all Britain's 'traditions'. Consequently they had to find other ways of placating continental opinion without betraying their liberal principles. One way was to institute criminal proceedings for libel against a German radical refugee called Johann Most, who edited a German-language anarchist newspaper in London called *Freiheit*, which on 19 March carried a bloodthirsty little piece celebrating the St Petersburg assassination and calling for other crowned heads to be dealt with in the same way. He was convicted, and sentenced to sixteen months' hard labour (oakum picking) in Cold Bath Fields prison. That, apparently, smoothed foreign governments' feathers a little.[2] But on its own it was not felt to be enough.

These events explain why the Special Branch came into being. Its early history is complicated, and sometimes a little blurred. Some of the complications matter, but others do not. It is clear that the Special Branch was not suddenly created out of nothing, either in 1883, which is the usual date given for its foundation, or in 1887, which is technically more correct. We have seen that the Metropolitan detective department had had at least one specialist in 'political' investigations for years, in the solid shape of Adolphus Williamson, who was still there in the 1880s. When the CID was formed in 1878 one of its duties was defined as 'Investigations for Governments', which were never spelled out, but were obviously intended to include, for example, cases like the *Freiheit* one. Its head was Assistant Commissioner Howard

Vincent, who had made a special study of foreign police forces, most of which had a political side.[3] In the first two or three years of its existence the CID took up a number of minor political cases, most of them involving foreigners whom continental governments regarded as a political danger to them. What happened after 1881 was that this situation was progressively regularized, with the result that eventually a separate sub-department of the CID – the 'Special Branch' – had evolved to deal with such matters full-time.

The process began on 23 January 1881, after the Salford bomb, when Harcourt ordered Vincent to put all his other work aside for the time being and concentrate entirely on trying to get intelligence about Fenians. The result of this was the creation of a special 'Fenian Office' at Scotland Yard, which also collaborated with Anderson at the Home Office, the Irish police and provincial police forces in Britain. For this Harcourt got some money from the 'Secret Service' fund, over and above the £500 per annum which had been the Home Office's limit for years. That was the Fenians dealt with. Next it was the turn of the refugees. Harcourt instructed the police to start keeping a regular watch on *them* on 26 March 1881, partly because until the *Daily Telegraph* had reported the original *Freiheit* libel they had no idea (quite properly) even of the existence of this particular little band of German socialists. Whether a separate 'office' was set up for that purpose we do not know; but whatever the formal arrangement, it was still working – and well – in the autumn of 1882.

By that time, however, it was clear that the counter-Fenian side was working less well. The earliest intimation of this came in Ireland, after the murder by 'Irish Invincibles' of the new chief secretary and under secretary, Lord Frederick Cavendish and Thomas Burke, in Dublin's Phoenix Park on 6 May 1882. That raised questions about Ireland's own counter-Fenian capacity under the Royal Irish Constabulary and the Dublin Metropolitan Police. The Irish viceroy, Lord Spencer, thought the former, especially, had 'got out of hand in late years'. The main problem, again, seemed to be intelligence, which at that time, he wrote, was generally too vague to be of any practical use. To put it right, he suggested that an army captain he had heard of called Henry Brackenbury, who had reorganized the Cyprus police after Britain's take-over of the island in 1878, be sent to help him. Brackenbury did not want to go, because he had heard that an invasion of Egypt was in the offing and wanted to join in the fun; but he was persuaded to go all the same, stayed long enough to set up a new independent Irish secret service department in Dublin Castle, and then resigned after two months. His successor was Spencer's own private secretary, an ex-Indian civil servant called Edward Jenkinson, who carried the work on. By March 1883 Spencer was highly pleased with the result, and told Harcourt so. The effect of this was that when the second wave of Fenian outrages in mainland Britain showed the 'Fenian Office' there up as something rather less effective than everybody had hoped, Harcourt asked

Spencer if he could borrow Jenkinson. That turned out to be rather like a pigeon-fancier asking to borrow a cat.[4]

By the time the cat arrived, shortly after 17 March, the pigeons were already in the process of reorganizing themselves. A new counter-Fenian bureau was being formed at Scotland Yard, presumably to supersede the 'Fenian Office', if that was still extant. It was headed by Williamson, with twelve other detectives under him. Williamson was to report directly to the Home Secretary, bypassing the commissioners; and to liaise daily with Anderson and the Irish police in London. The new agency was later called the 'Irish Branch', and is usually regarded as the earliest version of today's 'Special Branch'. It first met together at 10 a.m. on Wednesday 20 March 1883, and was given an office on the first floor of the Scotland Yard building, directly above a public urinal which was to play a part in its history a little later on.[5]

Jenkinson did not wait to see how it would turn out before he took a dislike to it. His task in England was to reorganize the collection and co-ordination of intelligence, in order to make them as effective as they were now supposed to be in Ireland. One of the ways to do this was through picked men of his own: like Major Nicholas Gosselin, an ex-Irish RM, whose main qualification for the job was that 'He understands these Irish scoundrels and can *talk* to them', and whom he consequently took on in the summer of 1883 to set up networks of informers in the English provinces and Scotland. But that was not enough. Jenkinson insisted that he would also need to use and therefore control the police. That was simply not on; but he could never understand why. 'Like many Indians,' Spencer had commented the previous year, 'he has not sufficient political instinct or regard for Parliamentary opinion.' The political objections were enormous. Jenkinson's status in England, both then and when he came over again for a more extended stay in March 1884, was highly irregular. It had to be kept secret, and Jenkinson paid out of Irish moneys, so as to avoid parliamentary scrutiny. (His official title was 'Assistant Under-Secretary for Police and Crime' in Dublin.) If he controlled the police, then it meant that Parliament did not. No one would brook that. 'I have pointed out to him over and over again', Harcourt wrote to Spencer in 1885, 'that the Commissioners of Police are the persons and the only persons constitutionally responsible for the protection of life and property in London, and that I have not the right even if I had the wish (which I have not) to over-ride their authority.' So Jenkinson was stuck with having to *co-operate*, with a force outside his control.[6] He turned out not to be very good at that.

The first pigeon he sent scurrying was Robert Anderson. The fact of Jenkinson's having been called over in the first place must have ruffled his feathers a bit. Since 1868 *he* was supposed to have been the Home Office's source of intelligence on Fenian matters; a position he held, as we have seen, mainly by virtue of his link with 'le Caron'. Jenkinson thought he and his sources, if he had any, were useless, and gradually edged him out. He finally left the Home Office in 1884, taking with him £2,000 as compensation for loss of earnings.[7] He returned later; but not while Jenkinson was there.

That left the Metropolitan Police's Irish Branch. They proved to be rather more resilient, despite the abuse Jenkinson heaped on them. The only man among them worth anything, he thought, was Williamson; and he was merely 'steady' and 'trustworthy', but without 'a trace of brilliancy or dash'. On a later occasion he described him as 'very slow and old-fashioned'. In March 1884 the branch's offices were blown up by a Fenian bomb placed in the lavatory underneath. The tone of Jenkinson's comments on that was predictable. 'There is not a man there with a head on his shoulders,' he wrote to Harcourt. 'They have no information and if anything happens they all lose their heads.' In fact they did *everything* wrong. When they found a clue, for example, they immediately trumpeted it to the press, so that the Fenians were put on their guard. Their surveillance of suspects was so clumsy that it generally drove them away. Sometimes they were found following RIC policemen around. They had no espionage sources of their own. When they were given information by others (such as Jenkinson himself), they either failed to act on it, as in January 1885, when they were warned about the Westminster bombs but did nothing to prevent them; or else they rushed in too quickly, before all the conspirators could be drawn into the net. All in all they were a bunch of blundering fools. Jenkinson found it impossible to suffer them gladly. 'I have had to give Mr Monro and Mr Williamson a bit of my mind today,' he wrote to Spencer in December 1884. (Monro was Vincent's successor as assistant commissioner in charge of the CID.) It had left them 'very much hurt just now', but he hoped that would pass. 'I could not possibly hold my tongue any longer ... It is dreadful having to work with such agents, & at the same time to have no official position.'[8] That, according to Jenkinson, was Scotland Yard's bright new Irish Branch.

It is difficult to know whether his strictures on it were fair. We do not have the Branch's own version, partly because all its records have been destroyed (or so they say).[9] There certainly was another side. James Monro, for example, had counter-complaints to make against Jenkinson: of which the most serious were that he acted behind his back, and deliberately kept valuable information affecting the safety of the Metropolis to himself. Jenkinson for his part did not deny any of this, but merely excused it on the grounds that it was not *safe* to tell the police anything. In his eyes it was a question of competence; in Monro's it was a matter of trust.[10] But it was not just this. Underneath all these rows there lay a fundamental and unbridgeable chasm, which had far more to do with Jenkinson's and Monro's respective *philosophies* of policing in this field. The battle between those philosophies was a vital one for the history of covert counter-subversion in Britain. In the short term the Irish Branch (the pigeons) won it; but not – as we shall see later – for good.

The fact was that if Scotland Yard was as incompetent as Jenkinson said it was, then it was not because it tried to be competent and failed, but because it did not try. It did not try because it did not believe in either the morality or, ultimately, the efficacy of the sorts of methods Jenkinson was trying to foist on it. The whole point was, as the Chief Police Commissioner told Jenkinson in 1885, that Monro 'objects to *all* Secret Agents'. This, of course, was a traditional Metropolitan Police prejudice. That Monro shared it is surprising, in view of the fact that he was not originally a Metropolitan policeman himself. (His previous post had been as chief of police in Bengal.) Nevertheless, just a few months in his new job made him into 'a real old Scotland Yardite', as Jenkinson put it, and consequently dead set against underhand methods like espionage. Williamson, of course, had been a genuine 'old Scotland Yardite' for more than thirty years. That explained why they made 'no attempt whatever ... to obtain information' of their own: because it was wrong. It also explained why their surveillance was so clumsy; and why they so often spoiled things for Jenkinson by stepping in and arresting suspects before their plots could properly come to the boil.

The root of it was that they still regarded themselves as a mainly *preventive* police. The best way to prevent a suspect committing a crime, they believed, was to let him know the police were on to him. Consequently if a 'shadow' was spotted, so much the better. Harcourt came up with a scheme in the summer of 1884 which worked precisely along these lines. He called it 'picketing'. The idea was that the Irish Branch should put watches or 'pickets' on all the Fenians Jenkinson told them about, to deter them from doing what they would have done otherwise. If they got up and left, they should be followed to wherever they went, even abroad. 'He says it is the easiest thing in the world to do,' reported Jenkinson; who for his own part, however, remained unconvinced. *His* approach was the exact opposite. If Fenians remained unaware of their surveillants they would be bolder, and so more likely to incriminate themselves. Likewise, if the police did not step in as soon as they heard of a plot, but bided their time, the plot would thicken, and come to involve more Fenians. That would mean more arrests, longer sentences and consequently (Jenkinson reasoned) less likelihood of further crimes. It was a seductive argument: but it went right against the old 'Scotland Yardite' ethos of Monro, Williamson and most of their men.[11]

They had other reasons for objecting to it too. One was that it was dangerous to allow this sort of crime to go too far in order to catch the criminals red-handed, when some of the red might be the blood of their victims, if the police cut it too fine. Another was that it could encourage the police, or their spies or informers, not only to wait for plots to develop, but also to egg them on. That may have happened under Jenkinson's aegis on a number of occasions. One possible one was the arrest of the Fenians John Daly and James Egan in the spring of 1884, which was celebrated as a great coup at the time, but which the Birmingham police chief, Farndale, claimed a couple of years later was largely the work of *agents provocateurs*. One of them, apparently, had 'planted' grenades on Daly just before he was arrested; another had buried nitroglycerine in Egan's back garden. Farndale thought the Home Secretary had had a hand in this; but it is more likely that if there was a plot here then it was Anderson, or Jenkinson, or Gosselin, or the RIC, or a corrupt section of the Birmingham police, or any combination of these who was responsible, without Harcourt's knowing a thing.[12] Another example was the 'jubilee plot' against the queen in 1887, which was probably cooked up by the British agent F. F. Millen, with Jenkinson's knowledge. Before that plot could come to fruition Jenkinson left, and Monro found out about it and put a stop to it. How much further Jenkinson would have allowed it to develop before *he* stepped in is anyone's guess.[13]

By the time he left the Home Office, in January 1887, the latter was in pretty bad odour all round. One of the things that told against him was that he did not appear to have been particularly effective. His greatest success was the Daly–Egan arrests, and they, as we have seen, were tainted. They also did nothing to stem the Fenian tide, with the Scotland Yard and St James's Square bombs following soon afterwards. He was spending what to a Liberal appeared to be an awful lot of money, to very little effect. (By 1885–6 the Home Office's 'Secret Service' expenditure had climbed to £11,300.)[14] Gosselin was also not coming up with very much. 'I have nothing but bad news to tell,' he reported in January 1884; 'all my plans have failed so far.' Jenkinson blamed as much of this as he could on the police, as we have seen; but Harcourt was not entirely persuaded. 'I have told you Jenkinson that your system of secret working is useless,' he said to him in December 1884. 'It comes to nothing.' Jenkinson found this 'disheartening', as well he might. He also resented the way Harcourt sided with Monro over the issue of the sharing of intelligence. 'It is all jealousy, nothing but jealousy,' Harcourt told him in 1885; 'you like to get information & keep it to yourself. You are like a dog with a bone who goes into a corner and growls at anyone who comes near him.' Harcourt may also have distrusted him. Later on, when they were both out of office, he would not rule out the possibility that Jenkinson had used dirty tricks against Daly and Egan. 'Jenkinson is such a rash and headlong fellow,' he wrote to Spencer, 'that one never knows what he may have done.'[15]

Whether he disapproved of such things on principle is difficult to know in Harcourt's case. He might have accepted them, or turned a blind eye to them, if they had brought Jenkinson (and consequently Harcourt) more success. The real point against them was that they could get the government into trouble. On one occasion one of Jenkinson's more venial dirty tricks apparently nearly did. He asked that the government trump up a charge against one of his spies, 'Red Jim' MacDermott, in order to divert Fenian suspicion away from him. Harcourt complied, because MacDermott seemed to be at real risk; but he did not like it one little bit. He told Spencer afterwards that 'It was very near being a great scrape.' If the trick had got out, the government would have been crucified, for perverting the law for political ends. That ought to serve, he went on, as 'a warning for the future': not to allow 'our friends in their zeal' to push them into compromising postures.[16] There were other ways it could happen. Someone might spot a 'shadow', for example; or discover that his letters were being opened at the Post Office. (That practice apparently started up again now.)[17] Or it might get out that a dynamite outrage had been 'provoked', or left to mature, which was almost as bad. Or people might find out that Jenkinson was not really in Ireland, where he was supposed to be, but in Room 56 on the first floor of the Home Office in Whitehall, unaccountable to Parliament, at the centre of a web of spies, and trying to give orders to the police. Public knowledge of any of these things would have been acutely embarrassing, because the public was not ready for them yet.

There were two reasons for this, one negative and the other positive. The negative reason was that the Fenian dynamite campaign, for all its ferocity, simply did not frighten enough people. Even in London, which was its main target, Sir Algernon West remarked in 1884 that 'It is very curious how calmly people take these outrages as matters of course!'[18] Most of the press ridiculed them. There had now been two years of this sort of thing, crowed the *Pall Mall Gazette* after the Westminster explosions of January 1885, and a dozen or more bombs; and yet what had the Fenians got to show for it all?

> Altogether they have not done more damage than £100,000 would easily make good. They have not killed a creature, blocked a railway, destroyed a building, or in any way checked for a moment the even flow of English life . . . A wretched twopenny halfpenny affair it is to be sure.[19]

Much of this may have been bravado; but that did not alter its effect. The point was that people were not going to allow these things to shake them out of their liberalism, whether or not they were as blasé about them as they appeared.

That last point was the positive reason for the public's resistance to 'underhand' counter-subversive methods: their continued adhesion to this particular little element of the Victorian liberal ethic. The prejudice against 'espionage', in particular, was as strong as ever, and showed no sign of weakening. It appeared everywhere. Harcourt spoke of it in a lecture he gave to some London policemen in 1881 – before the main Fenian assault – and with some pride. On that occasion he appeared to believe that the failure to detect a few crimes was a cheap price to pay for Britain's freedom from 'any organized system of espionage'. In 1883 the queen's secretary, writing to congratulate the police on the arrest of a dynamitard, said that he thought it was all the more splendid in view of their quite proper distaste for such methods: 'I doubt if Englishmen ever could take up the business as the French do.' Shortly after the Westminster bombs *The Times* carried a long leading article whose burden was to praise the police for *not* being clever detectives, which was the very thing, it claimed, that attached public opinion to them: unlike in France.[20] This may seem perverse, but it is true. The late Victorians preferred their policemen to be straightforward, and even a little stupid. If they could have met both Williamson and Jenkinson to compare them, they would have overwhelmingly plumped for the former. A few American-Irish bombs made no difference at all. A Fouché might well have got to the bottom of the conspiracy. But they felt safer living under PC Plod.

There are obvious parallels to be drawn between this Fenian crisis, and the previous one in 1867. In both cases the Metropolitan Police came out of them with egg on its face, and the apparently well-merited derision of its Irish counterparts. In both cases the government was consequently moved to call in an agent from outside, with Irish credentials and methods of working, to try to repair the damage: Feilding on the first occasion, Jenkinson on the second. Both these men left after the immediate crises were over, and were not replaced. But this may be where the similarity ends. After 1867, apart from Anderson at the Home Office, the authorities appeared to drop their mainland counter-Fenian defences entirely. Harcourt was adamant that this should not happen again. 'The great error of past years', he wrote to Gladstone in May 1883, was to regard Fenianism as 'a temporary emergency requiring a momentary remedy', and 'to relax precautions which are always essential even when overt danger seems to have passed away for the time'. In fact Fenianism was 'a permanent conspiracy against English rule which will last far beyond the term of my life and must be met by a permanent organization to detect and to control it'.[21] That probably goes some way to explaining the setting up in 1887 of the first agency calling itself the 'Special Branch'.

The immediate occasion for it was the resignation of Jenkinson at the beginning of 1887, when successive Home Secretaries – not just Harcourt – refused to give him the powers he hankered for. He apparently left in a huff, after destroying all his secret service records – for what reason we can only guess.[22] The immediate effect of this was for most of his functions to be taken over by the 'Scotland Yardites', which he will not have liked at all. His role of 'Secret Agent' passed to James Monro, the assistant commissioner in charge of the CID, who was a particular enemy of his. One of the first things Monro did in his new post was to recall Robert Anderson, whom Jenkinson had levered out in 1884. Later on Anderson succeeded Monro as head of the CID, and possibly as 'Secret Agent' too. Their main counter-subversive tool was the new 'Special Section' or 'Special Branch' which was formed in February in substitution 'for the private Anti-Fenian agents employed by Mr. Jenkinson'. (What happened to the original agents is a mystery; except for Gosselin, who stayed on.) This new branch comprised just four high-ranking officers, one of them transferred over from the Irish Branch. Originally, therefore, the Special Branch was separate from the Irish Branch, and had a different (Jenkinsonian) genesis. Before long, however, they were working together, and by the early 1890s had become a single 'Special Political Branch' in effect, except for accounting purposes. It seems to have combined the functions of the old Irish Branch with some of Jenkinson's, and to have added a couple more: protection duty (for royalty and visiting bigwigs), and keeping an eye on political refugees.[23] It comprised thirty-one officers altogether in London – twenty-seven Irish Branch and the four 'Special Section' men – plus a dozen or so attached to them but stationed at various ports around the British coast. At their head (under Monro) was a Scotsman, Chief Inspector John Littlechild, who was the man who was transferred from the Irish to the Special Branch at the start. He was also a founder member of the 'Metropolitan Police Minstrels'. Later he retired to go into private practice, where one of his first assignments was finding evidence for the Marquess of Queensberry to use against Oscar Wilde. He also published some memoirs, which however are disappointingly discreet on the Special Branch stage of his career.[24]

On the surface this appears to have been a pretty clean sweep for the 'Scotland Yardites' over the Jenkinsonians. The only casualty suffered by the former side was 'Dolly' Williamson, who now disappears from our view: sadly, because he has been a part of our story for a long time now. He first joined the police in 1852; served his apprenticeship under Sanders; arrested Simon Bernard for complicity in the Orsini plot in 1858; was the Metropolitan force's 'political specialist' throughout the 1870s; and led the Irish Branch from 1883 to 1887. That last spell of duty cannot have been a happy one. It took a toll on his family, and especially one of his children, who according to Monro suffered from 'weakness of intellect' as 'a direct consequence of Mr. Williamson's connection with Fenian inquiries' (though we do not know how). In 1887 he 'broke down', again apparently due to over-work and stress during the bombing crisis; he was absent ill for long periods afterwards; and he died, aged 58, in December 1889.[25] His death may possibly have marked the end of an era, but probably not, because Littlechild had the reputation, at any rate, of being just as honest and upright. While he and Monro were at the helm, the ship could be trusted to sail a straight course.

For a while it did; but possibly only because the seas were so relatively calm. The next few years were a kind of *inter-bellum* period, between the Fenian dynamite war, which ended in 1885, and violent anarchism, which first raised its ugly head in Britain in 1892. So far as the Fenians were concerned, they were probably waiting to see whether Gladstone could deliver on Home

110

Rule. There were plenty of other excitements in Britain: such as a newly vigorous socialism, strikes and some serious riots, including 'Black Monday' and 'Bloody Friday', which were the names given to two particularly violent clashes between workers and police in Trafalgar Square in 1886 and 1887; but none of these – so far as we can tell – involved Britain's covert counter-subversive agencies at all. Domestic political unrest was just not part of their job. Consequently they had little to do beyond keeping a general weather-eye open for Fenians, bodyguarding foreign dignitaries, and undertaking investigations for foreign governments.[26]

They will have had plenty of time, therefore, for another little task, which they were asked to help out with in 1888. That was in connection with the 'Parnell Commission', which was a special judicial inquiry set up to investigate allegations which had been made by *The Times* newspaper that the Irish nationalist leader Charles Stewart Parnell had been implicated in (among other things) the Phoenix Park murders of 1882. In the end the inquiry effectively collapsed when *The Times*'s key evidence – some letters purporting to be written by Parnell – was proved to be a forgery. (*The Times* has always been a sucker for forgeries.) Quite apart from this, however, powerful suspicions attached to the case.

It was supposed to be a matter entirely between Parnell and *The Times*, with the government of the day (a Unionist one) staying neutral and uninvolved. In fact, however, the government was very deeply involved. It may have offered to underwrite *The Times*'s expenses, and it certainly gave it facilities it was not entitled to in a private capacity.[27] Among those facilities was the use of British and Irish police forces and secret intelligence networks, in order to procure evidence against Parnell. In England that generally meant the Special Branch. So, for example, we find Littlechild being sent to Chatham gaol not only to interview a Fenian prisoner there, but also to make him an offer of a pardon and a job in the civil service if he testified against Parnell.[28] The person who sent him there was a man called William Joyce, who had been deputed to co-ordinate and direct all this police and secret service activity in support of *The Times*.

Later he wrote an account of all this, called *Sidelights on British Conspiracies*, which made even more serious allegations against the police and ministers. There are problems with it, as there always are with such exposés. Usually they are written by men with grievances, and often with character defects too. Joyce's grievance was that he had been denied promotion and proper remuneration after a particularly important job he had undertaken for the government in 1888, and his character defects (which may explain why he was not promoted) included alcoholism and paranoia. These would undoubtedly have been used against him if he had tried to embarrass the government with his revelations at the time, or shortly afterwards.[29] But they do not invalidate all his testimony, some of which is corroborated independently. It paints a picture of wholesale corruption among the Irish police at this time, especially in their use of *agents provocateurs*. It also, incidentally, confirms the general view of Anderson's ineptitude. His 'whole system as revealed to me', Joyce wrote, 'turned out, if not a huge fraud, most certainly a gigantic farce, although a very expensive one, and by no means free from traces of the *Agent Provocateur*'. This was after Anderson had been brought back to the Home Office, in 1888. Monro, according to Joyce, was far more scrupulous.[30] This also squares with the impression we have from other sources.

Joyce's most serious charges are unreliable, partly because they are not based on first-hand knowledge. One was that Fenian prisoners who spurned the inducements held out to them by such as Littlechild were victimized. One – Patrick Nally – was supposed to have been poisoned in prison, because he would not co-operate. There are hints in Joyce's account that the authorities or their agents went even further than this: that they tried to cover up the forgery when it was known, for example; that they spirited the forger (Pigott) out of England when he was rumbled, and then murdered him in Madrid to stop him blabbing (the usual story is that he committed suicide); and that after the failure of the commission they had a hand in the divorce case which eventually brought about Parnell's downfall, in November 1890.[31] This all looks very modern. But it is probably not true. All of it was retailed simply as *rumour* by Joyce; and there is no positive evidence for it.

Nevertheless, there is enough solid evidence to prove that the 'secret service' did help in other ways. 'Henri le Caron', for example, testified before the commission, with the drastic result that his cover was blown and his long career as a spy ended. (His life thereafter could serve as a cautionary tale for all prospective Irish informers: widely execrated by liberal opinion, abandoned by his patrons, guarded day and night by Special Branch men, terrified of being poisoned and eventually dying miserably only five years later, at the age of 53: *unless* his death was a deception, as some people suspected – it was supposed to have happened on All Fools' Day, 1894 – and he was really smuggled abroad to a new life in the colonies.)[32] More significantly: Robert Anderson also helped, in a much more underhand way. This was revealed in 1910, when he owned up to having been the anonymous author of some of the *Times* articles which had originally accused Parnell. That was clearly improper. Anderson was a public servant at the time (he was at Scotland Yard), and it was unorthodox – to say the least – for him to have used the intelligence coming to him in his official capacity in this freebooting way. Parliament was, very rightly, cross.[33]

The object of all this was not primarily to put down terrorism, but to try to discredit the cause of Home Rule and its supporters. The distinction is important. Home Rule, pursued through peaceful, parliamentary means, was a legitimate political policy, and the policy (as it happened) of two of the main parties in Parliament. Opposition to Home Rule was the policy of two others. Here, then, we have one of the earliest examples in modern British history of a phenomenon we shall see more of as our story progresses: secret agents with particular political viewpoints, probably in collusion with like-minded politicians, using the apparatus of the secret state for *partisan* ends. This is new. The rationale for it, as in later examples, was that those ends – the maintenance of the Union and the defeat of separatism – were not really partisan, but patriotic. That feeling may have been genuine. But it also, of course, raises some prickly issues: as we shall see later on.

That was Ireland, however, and to do with past events. It neither affected nor *re*flected the work of the mainland British security agencies in any significant way. Most of their work in these *inter-bellum* years was routine, undemanding and probably a little thin. That will be the main reason why they did not remain at the same strength as in 1887, but were scaled down. The Special Branch, for example, was reduced from thirty-one London-based officers in 1887 to twenty-five in 1891. The following spring Gosselin's spy networks at home and abroad were also cut drastically, at a saving of £1,200. Anderson thought all this was unwise, in view of a renewed 'outrage campaign' he had heard was imminent.[34] But then came a saviour; and the numerical decline of the Special Branch was checked.

The saviour was an anarchist from Walsall in Staffordshire called Joseph Deacon, who had been under police observation for some months, and was arrested in London's Tottenham Court Road with a parcel of chloroform on him on 6 January 1892. That was exactly a week after the last cut in the Special Branch's strength had been authorized. The following evening Inspector William Melville of the branch travelled to Walsall, found some fuses and casts for bombs in a house there, together with anarchist pamphlets which included directions for making bombs, and arrested two more men. Three others were apprehended later. Eventually four of these six were tried, convicted and imprisoned for between five and ten years each.[35] That seemed to prove Anderson's point, about a renewal of outrages.

In fact Anderson was wrong, as he usually was, because *his* intelligence had told him it was going to be a Fenian affair. Anarchism, however, would do just as well. The Walsall plot was providential; but it was also – partly for that reason – slightly fishy. Initial suspicions focused on the role played in it by one particular Walsall anarchist, Auguste Coulon, who was certainly a police spy and probably a *provocateur*. Later they were corroborated by the testimony of an ex-Special Branch sergeant, Patrick McIntyre, who published some 'revelations' of his time in the Branch in *Reynolds's Newspaper* in 1895. In them he claimed that not only the Walsall plot, but also most of those attributed to the Fenians in the 1880s, had been 'provoked' by various police agencies, including his own. That caused a bit of a stir.

There are problems with McIntyre's account, of much the same kind as there are with Joyce's. Like him, McIntyre had a grievance against the men he was now unmasking; indeed, a whole collection of them. They began with his demotion to the rank of uniformed constable in September 1893, for fiddling a time-sheet and also (he claimed) because Anderson suspected him of dallying dangerously with the pretty daughter of an anarchist. That was just the beginning of a succession of blows and humiliations he suffered at the hands of the authorities, which eventually led him to leave the force in October 1894. The Home Office believed that his grudges had also made him 'vindictive' towards the police, and so undermined his credibility.[36] That may be so; but the evidence for chicanery in this case is compelling even without him. If chicanery there was, then the likely culprits were Coulon, Melville and Anderson. The anarchists claimed that the order for the bombs they admitted they were were making had come via Coulon. Coulon was in Melville's pay. Melville was in cahoots with Anderson. If Coulon *was* a *provocateur*, it is impossible to know whether Melville and Anderson encouraged him in this, or knew about it. The balance of the evidence must be against them. But it is all circumstantial.

It made no difference in any case. Violent anarchism had made its appearance. Thereafter the Special Branch was kept going comfortably on a regular diet of it, right through the 1890s and into the next century. It was never as strong a diet as on the Continent or in America, where some of the crimes perpetrated by anarchists and other political extremists were horrendous. Their victims included Moscow's secret police chief, Solotouchine, in 1890; President Carnot of France in 1894; the Spanish Prime Minister Cánovas del Castillo in 1897; the Empress Elizabeth of Austria in 1898; King Humbert of Italy in 1900; and President McKinley of the United States in 1901. They also included scores of lesser mortals, some of them deliberately slaughtered – in theatres, for example, or pavement cafés, or religious processions – as part of a policy of 'terrorism' in the strict meaning of that often misused word.

These were a warning to Britain; but she never experienced anything as bad herself. The worst that happened to her was when a French anarchist called Martial Bourdin blew his own guts out with a bomb in Greenwich Park in February 1894, in an incident which Joseph Conrad later used for his novel *The Secret Agent*. In April the same year two Italian anarchists called Farnara and Polti were arrested on their way to plant a bomb at the Royal Exchange, in order to get their own back for the annual English tourist invasion of Italy. There were many other bomb scares, but most of them turned out to be false alarms. One of them involved a Swiss called Cavargna, who claimed his bombs were designed to exterminate rabbits in New South Wales. (They were made to look like eggs, to fool the rabbits, but with ribbons attached which would be tied round their necks, so that when they scuttled back to their warrens their entire families would be blown up. At first the police did not believe this story. Cavargna claimed they should have known that his bombs were not anarchist bombs, because all anarchist bombs were pear-shaped.) On another occasion an entire street was cleared when a new design of baby's feeding bottle was found on a bus, and mistaken for a bomb. MPs got a scare in December 1894 when they all received bomb shells through the post; which turned out to have copies of a magazine in them, devised by two contestants in a competition to find the most original way of advertising it.[37] That was how most of these 'anarchist bombs' turned out. But, of course, you could never be sure.

That was one good reason to act against the anarchists. Another was that Britain's neighbours – once again – insisted on it. The climax to this particular wave of demands came in 1898, when Britain was pressured into attending an international 'Anti-Anarchist Conference' of all the European powers in Rome, and then while she was there into promising new anti-anarchist legislation of her own, which in the end she found she could not deliver.[38] It was her old problem. She could not ban anarchism in Britain, or bar anarchists, without compromising her traditional freedoms of speech and asylum. The best she could do was to reassure her foreign critics that she had the anarchists living in Britain on a tight rein. That was where the Special Branch came in.

It may, however, have been a slightly different Special Branch from before. Changes had taken place in its leadership, which could have affected its methods and ethos too. Littlechild, for example, went early in 1893, leaving the day-to-day running of the Branch to the hero of Walsall: William Melville, now raised to chief inspector on the strength of his success. Shortly before that Williamson and Monro had also gone: both of them 'old Scotland Yardites', in Jenkinson's phrase. They were replaced by Anderson, whom we have met already, and Melville MacNaghten, an ex-Indian planter, who in his autobiography described Monro, significantly, as 'a fine old policeman of a type now obsolete'.[39] The new brooms were all of them either Irish, or from Anglo-Irish families (MacNaghten was actually born in Essex), as were most of the Special Branch men under them. This is important, because of Ireland's very different policing tradition from Britain's. That tradition had sanctioned espionage and its associated techniques for years. In British police circles those techniques were still widely regarded with distaste. That may account for the fact that when the authorities needed men to do this sort of work for them, it was to John Bull's Other Island that they turned.

Melville headed the branch for ten years, after which his further career is something of a mystery. The best guess is that he was assigned to 'more responsible and spectacular duties which entailed extensive travel on the Continent during which he played an active part in the suppression of Anarchism', before he went to work with the organization which later became

MI5 in 1910.[40] That would explain the impressive list of foreign decorations he had accumulated by 1914, which included the Légion d'Honneur, the Crown of Italy, the Order of Isabel la Catolica, the Order of Christ (no less) of Portugal and the Order of Dannebrøg of Denmark.[41] Before then, while he was still at Scotland Yard, his reputation was very different from Williamson's and Littlechild's, and he may have given the Special Branch a more effective and slightly less scrupulous stamp.

Effective it certainly appears to have been, by comparison, for example, with the 1880s. It made a few mistakes. The worst one was probably its failure to anticipate the Greenwich bomb.[42] Luckily, however, none of the mistakes turned out to have really serious repercussions, except on poor Martial Bourdin. The Special Branch exercised as close a surveillance over the anarchists as was possible with just a couple of dozen officers, which generally simply meant tailing them from where they embarked in England to where they were staying, and noting down their addresses.[43] It carried out raids on anarchist clubs and printing offices, one of which (in 1894) succeeded in closing down the main British anarchist journal, the *Commonweal*. (The raid is described in a contemporary novel called *A Girl among the Anarchists*, written by the daughters of the painter Dante Gabriel Rossetti, who went through an anarchist phase themselves.)[44] It arrested and successfully prosecuted revolutionaries for seditious libel, including a well-known Russian, Vladimir Burtsev; and even managed to get a couple of notorious French anarchists, Jean-Pierre François and Théodule Meunier, extradited back to France. This was a particular achievement, because all Britain's extradition treaties had a clause in them specifically exempting political crimes; but that little difficulty was overcome by a clever judge who ruled that because anarchism was against all politics, it could not in logic be called a political creed.[45]

The Special Branch also sometimes broke the rules. The anarchists themselves accused it of all kinds of roguery, ranging from planting bombs in order to incriminate innocent men, to paying street urchins to heckle at anarchist meetings.[46] Most of these charges were nonsense, but some were not. The best reason for believing this is that its top officers admitted as much. Anderson even insisted on it. 'I would say emphatically', he wrote in 1898, 'that in recent years the Police have succeeded only by straining the law, or, in plain English, by doing utterly unlawful things, at intervals, to check this conspiracy.'[47] His successor in 1901, Edward Henry, corroborated this. That referred to officially sanctioned illegalities. There were probably many more unofficial ones. The temptations for ordinary detectives to 'strain the law' must have been virtually irresistible in the 1890s, in situations where they were highly unlikely to be found out, and where so much 'kudos', as Anderson again put it, attached to the detection rather than the prevention of crimes. Anderson believed that this could encourage officers to leave plots to grow, so as to have more to detect, or even to egg them on.[48] The widespread use of informers compounded this. 'I have to confess', wrote Littlechild in his *Reminiscences*, 'that the "nark" is very apt to drift into an *agent provocateur* in his anxiety to secure a conviction.' That may well be what happened in the Walsall case in 1892. The moral Littlechild drew from this was that 'narks' should be carefully watched.[49] But then Littlechild, according to McIntyre, had very little to do with Walsall; which as we have seen was Anderson's and Melville's affair.

Anderson may have had Walsall in mind when he referred to 'utterly unlawful things' in 1898. On the other hand there are no other serious cases after Walsall in which the hand of British police *provocateurs* can be seen. (Greenwich may have been the work of a foreign police agent: but that does not count.) Most of Anderson's 'unlawful things' were probably measures which would be regarded as relatively mild today: searching houses without warrants, intercepting letters, adopting disguises to enter premises, and so on. (A favourite disguise of Melville's was as a sanitary inspector, doubtless because all anarchist premises were presumed to be *in*sanitary.) The police may also have harassed anarchists by sneaking on them to their landlords and employers, and generally by means of warnings and threats. It was all a case of petty 'illegalities', not major ones; and yet no less effective for that.

There was a celebrated instance in 1898, which involved a society called the Legitimation League. The league had begun with the simple aim of removing the disabilities which attached to bastardy – hence the name – but had become much wider ranging since. It also published a journal, called *The Adult*, which preached sexual liberation, by which was usually meant easier divorce. The Special Branch found that some anarchists were attending its meetings, and sent Detective Sergeant John Sweeney along there. He quickly became convinced that it was all an anarchist plot to undermine the very fabric of society, by destroying all respect for morality and law. So he infiltrated it. Unfortunately neither their meetings nor *The Adult* were doing anything illegal. He decided, therefore, to attack them indirectly. He got friendly with the secretary, George Bedborough, who also sold 'advanced' books on the side. From him he bought a copy of Havelock Ellis's *Sexual Inversion*, which was about homosexuality, and then arrested him for selling it to him. Bedborough was charged with seeking to 'debauch and corrupt the morals of the liege subjects of our Lady the Queen' by means of a 'lewd, wicked, bawdy, scandalous and obscene libel', for which the penalty could be several years in prison. He was terrified, as Sweeney knew he would be. So he went along to him, and promised that he would get him off lightly, if he would not only plead guilty, but also close down both the League and his magazine. Bedborough agreed, the League collapsed, and *The Adult* ceased publication. Sweeney was immensely proud of this achievement, which he believed had saved civilization from 'a Frankenstein monster', no less.[50]

Sweeney's exalted notion of the importance of the activities of the Special Branch is typical. Around a dozen pre-war members of the Branch published memoirs afterwards, and all shared – or pretended to share – this kind of view. One of them, called Herbert Fitch, wrote of bloody revolutions and world wars averted by the branch before 1914; all through what he described as 'the merciless activity of brains keener than Sherlock Holmes's'. One example he gave featured himself disguised as a waiter in a restaurant where Lenin – 'a smooth-haired, oval-faced, narrow-eyed, typical Jew' – was dining around 1905. He was with a secret society called the 'Foreign Barbers of London', who were working out the agenda for the Russian revolution they had planned for that year. Fitch pretended to drop his napkin accidentally, and while Lenin swore at him for his clumsiness picked it up with some of his papers concealed underneath. Later the Special Branch sent those papers to the tsar; with the result that a successful revolution was staved off for another twelve years.[51] That sort of thing, apparently, happened frequently. Unfortunately most of it could never be revealed, because it was too sensitive. So Fitch's readers just had to take his word for it. Most of this was obvious rubbish. Winston Churchill described it well in 1910, with particular reference to Robert Anderson's reminiscences, which were published in *Blackwood's Magazine* that year. They seemed to him, he said,

> to be written in a spirit of gross boastfulness. They are written, if I may say so, in the style of 'How Bill Adams Won the Battle of Waterloo.' The writer has been so anxious to show how important he was, how invariably he was right, and how much more he could tell if only his mouth was not what he was pleased to call closed.[52]

That just about sums this *genre* up.

But it does not alter the fact that the security services in the 1890s and 1900s, despite the ridiculous Anderson, were as effective as they *needed* to be. That is to say, they did enough to enable the government to persuade other governments that they were doing their best; which was the important thing. The main role of the Special Branch at this time, after all, was not so much to safeguard Britain, as to help safeguard neighbours who might be less fortunate – more vulnerable to anarchist crime – than herself. Melville MacNaghten claimed in this connection that 'In anarchist circles our information was always so good that, had a plot been in the hatching, I think the Yard would have got wind of it within twenty-four hours.' Government ministers made similar claims. They seemed generally impressed. So were foreign governments; like that of King Louis of Portugal, for example, who was reported to have wished on one occasion that his police 'were more like them'. Occasionally foreign police forces recruited men from Scotland Yard to head their own political sections: which was probably the best kind of tribute to them.[53] So they must have improved, first of all under Melville and then, after 1903, under his successor: another Irishman, Patrick Quinn.

That was the situation at the beginning of 1910. Things had come a long way in thirty years. In 1880 no permanent police agency to deal with 'special' or political crimes had existed at all. Now there was the Special Branch, with a complement of thirty-eight officers in the summer of 1909; plus Gosselin's little outfit (headed now by C. A. Wilkins, who is an even more shadowy figure than Gosselin);[54] and with Melville possibly at loose as a secret anti-anarchist agent on the Continent. Means and methods had changed too, as prejudice within the British police hierarchy against what had used to be regarded as 'underhand' methods had melted away, and as the Irish gradually took over around 1890. In 1910, therefore, Britain *almost* had what could be described as a 'secret political police'. But she did not quite have one yet.

There was one key ingredient missing. A political police, properly so called, is one that is concerned with people's political opinions for their own sake: because they are considered to be in some way 'subversive' in themselves, rather than because they are likely to result in crimes. Before 1910 the Special Branch was not like that at all. There may have been some exceptions: the affair of the Legitimation League points to an obvious one; but usually the Branch took no interest in 'extremist' political opinions except when it had reason to believe that those opinions might give rise to violent crimes. This was why it left domestic British radical politics alone too, except on its wilder anarchist edges; which is another thing that distinguishes the pre-1910 Special Branch from political police agencies in other places and times.

These differences really are crucial. Merely because we have picked up a trail in the 1880s which leads to the present, it does not follow that the animal which made those tracks was the same creature then as it is now. It was not. In many ways it was far closer to some of the mid-Victorian creatures we examined in the last chapter, than to today's far more oppressive (in Victorian terms) secret state. The changes that took place between 1880 and 1910 were important steps towards the latter, but they were not the really vital ones. Those were to come, with a rush, during the course of the next decade; for a variety of reasons we shall need to spend a little time analysing, before we come on to the changes themselves.

Chapter 7

A holy alliance against this midnight terror (1910–20)

Historians of the British welfare state often date its origins back to the half-dozen or so years before the First World War. It may or may not be a coincidence that the same period also witnessed the beginnings of the '*secret* state' as we know it today. Most of the key developments, in fact, took place over a much narrower span of time, between the summer of 1909 and the autumn of 1911. It was in those years that MI5 and MI6 were both born; the modern Official Secrets Act was passed; the 'D-Notice' system for vetting newspaper stories bearing on 'national security' was devised; a register of aliens living in Britain was set up; blanket interceptions of certain categories of mail at the Post Office began; and the Special Branch was brought close to being a proper domestic counter-subversive agency on modern lines. These developments marked a crucial stage in the transformation of Britain from a relatively open liberal democracy into the far more restrictive one we have today. They were the opening shots of something akin to a revolution: but a revolution accomplished covertly, with scarcely anyone outside a narrow circle of men even being aware that it had happened.

Why did it happen? As with all developments of this kind, there were particular reasons, and general ones. Some of the particular reasons – the incidents which triggered things off – were so trivial, or even imaginary, that we need the general reasons to make sense of them. Those general reasons *did* make sense. Underlying everything was a prevailing sense of apprehension in Edwardian times, which was justified. At the beginning of those times Britain had won a war, her biggest war for nearly half a century; but in such an unconvincing manner as to give no cause for rejoicing at all. The truth was that for two and a half years a British army of 200,000 highly trained men had been held at bay, had rings run around it, by a force of South African peasants just a fraction of its size, before sheer weight of numbers, not military ability, had won through. This was worrying. Britain's next enemy might not be so small a nation as the Boers. If it was France or Russia or Germany, for example, it would be a bold man who would give her any odds at all; and France, Russia and Germany all looked likely antagonists at different times. Many people in the 1900s worried that Britain would not be able to avoid a European war for ever; in which case she would be hard pressed even to survive. This was the chief threat that loomed over her, and coloured her perception of all the other threats that arose.

Not everyone, of course, acknowledged it; which for those who *did* was another cause for concern. Some people were fooled by the superficial appearance of things – a victorious army, the world's largest navy and all those imperial red patches splattered over the map of the world – into thinking that Britain was still supreme and secure; others were naïve enough to believe that international co-operation could remove any dangers to her, if she was not. This made things worse. The first requirement for a society which wants to resist an external threat is for all its members to accept the existence of that threat; and from their actions it was clear that millions of Britons at that time did not. How else could one explain, for example, the divisive politics of the prewar years, the industrial strikes, the appeals to class loyalty, and the self-indulgent exploits of the militant suffragettes: when all truly patriotic people should have been concentrating their energies against the common enemy without?

To the worriers, the ones who had identified the enemy, this seemed to be nothing short of treachery, albeit of the passive, unwitting kind. Some wondered whether it might not go further than that. Suspicions were voiced during the 'great labour unrest' of 1911–14, for example, that some of that unrest might be being deliberately fomented from abroad. A Methodist minister claimed in February 1911 that the 'ringleaders' of the Ton-y-pandy riots were 'a foreign gang of socialists'; though he did not know any of their names. One name that was identified after the outbreak of the war was that of the Baron von Horst, a German-born American, who had apparently been stumping the country in 1912 providing free meals for strikers' children, subsidizing the *Daily Herald*, supporting the suffragettes and ordering rifles for the nationalists in Ireland.[1] The curious things about him are that he was not spotted earlier, and that he seems to have been the only foreign industrial saboteur to be identified at all. For some this might have seemed reassuring; but to contemporary worriers it was far from that. Either it meant that most enemy agents were clever enough to escape detection. Or – even worse – it meant that enemy agents were *not* involved in British industrial unrest at all.

This was worse, because it meant that there must have been other, deeper reasons for that unrest. In a way it was a comfort to believe that strikes were the results of enemy plots, because the implication of that was that British workers would still be working happily if it were not for them. That is what many on the right of British politics wanted to think. The workers were fundamentally sensible, patriotic people, who were easily led astray, however, by what one Special Branch man of the time called 'communist tommy-rot'.[2] In fact it may have been less simple than that. Britain's economy and society were experiencing real structural problems in the 1900s, which were likely to cause dissension of their own accord. British manufacturing industry was in relative decline. Average wages had stopped rising, and if anything were falling back, for the first time for decades. The gap between rich and poor was widening, and being rubbed in by the tasteless extravagance of many of the *nouveaux riches*. (Mr Toad in *The Wind in the Willows* is a good example of that.) All this was a considerable set-back for those who were still able to remember the confident hopes of liberal capitalism's high Victorian noon. It was not how things had been supposed to work out.

There were a number of competing explanations for it, each resting on a different political ideology. For socialists the problem was intrinsic to capitalism, which was bound to spawn contradictions like these as it passed into its later developmental stages. For the 'new' Liberals who ran the country after 1905 it showed what could happen if capitalism was not controlled and disciplined, so as to spread its benefits fairly. Extreme free marketeers blamed socialism, by which they generally meant the social reforms Disraeli had first put in train in the 1860s, and which had now reached their apogee with Lloyd George's welfare package of 1906–10 (national insurance, old age pensions, free school meals and the rest). In their view these were sapping the self-reliance of the ordinary Briton. 'By trade unions, workhouses, doles, free schooling, charities which demand no effort on the part of those aided', wrote the eminent and highly self-reliant Egyptologist Flinders Petrie in 1907, 'there has been set up a "compulsory glorification of sloth" more deadly than all the wars of Napoleon.' Another writer blamed socialism for keeping alive people of 'feeble physique and low intelligence' who in older, better days 'would never have survived infancy'.[3] According to this sort of analysis, which was a common one, the solution to Britain's problems was simple: let the runts die, and make the rest work. It was never, of course, put quite like this; probably partly because of its lack of electoral appeal.

That was the other difficulty. It had been anticipated years before, by (among others) Walter Bagehot in the introduction to the second edition of his *English Constitution*. That was written just after Disraeli's 1867 Reform Act, which had doubled the electorate, and which Bagehot warned was likely to lead to disaster by forcing political parties to pander to the demands of working-class voters against their own better judgement. Since then the electorate had been nearly doubled once again (in 1884), and the working classes (or at least, working-class men) were now a power in the land. The trouble with the working classes – stout fellows that they undoubtedly were otherwise – was that they did not always know what was good for them, especially, as we have seen, when they were 'led astray'. This compounded the rightists' gloom.

It was a gloom that earlier generations had not, by and large, shared. We have seen how in mid-Victorian times most liberals had thought that the working classes would get to know what was good for them in time. What was good for them, of course, was liberal capitalism, whose benefits to everyone would eventually filter through. As they did, the working classes could be progressively enfranchised, without putting the system on which those benefits depended at risk. Liberal capitalism, consequently, was fully compatible with liberal democracy; and indeed the two systems were inter-dependent, each bolstering the other and justifying it. That was what had underlain the mid-Victorians' resistance to illiberal expedients like espionage and secret political police forces, which were unnecessary then and would become even more so as the country (and then the world) became more liberal. This was because economic liberalism (free market capitalism) and political liberalism (self-government) were interlocked.

If they ever became *un*locked, the implications would be unsettling. If democracy could not be depended on to be capitalist, then capitalism might not be able to afford to be democratic. Liberals would need to make a choice. Bagehot (in professional life a banker) made his choice early on. In 1886 the Liberal Party as a whole split over which kind of liberalism it wished to give priority to, with the political liberals offering self-government to the Irish, accepting some interference in the market mechanism in both islands for social reasons and staying with Gladstone; while the economic liberals – the defectors – went for free market purity and what today would be called the 'strong' (or Unionist) state. (Coincidentally – but probably only coincidentally – this happened at almost exactly the same time as the creation of the Special Branch.) Over the next several years this prising apart of the two sorts of liberalism continued, with economic liberals drifting across to the political right, and political liberals taking on board some measure of socialism, in one of the most significant ideological shifts of the past hundred years.

This relates to the subject of our present inquiry in two ways. First, it removed, as we have seen, much of the liberal confidence that had sustained the anti-spy culture of mid-Victorian times. Secondly, the anti-(political) liberal reaction it represented was the main breeding ground for the twentieth-century British 'secret state'. Except in wartime, nearly everyone connected with covert counter-subversion in this century has been to the right, and often the extreme right, of British politics. This was true in the later nineteenth century too. One partial exception was Edward Jenkinson, who was a committed Irish home ruler;[4] but even he, as we saw, could be very illiberal in many things, and in particular in his contempt for Parliament. Lord Spencer attributed this to his Indian background; which was something else he shared with many others in his line of work. This connection – between the British Empire and the early British secret service – is another strong one, with nearly all the senior officers of the security services since 1880 having been recruited from colonial, and usually colonial military, backgrounds. Anderson and Gosselin are the only significant exceptions: unless we count an Anglo-Irish background as equivalent to a colonial one. Brackenbury had been a soldier in Cyprus, and private secretary to an Indian viceroy for a year. Monro came from the Bengal civil service. Sir Edward Bradford, the chief police commissioner throughout the 1890s, had served in the Madras army and with the 'Political and Secret Department' of the India Office, and at one stage, as we saw, organized a sort of Special Branch for the Indian police.[5] His successor, Edward Henry, came from the Bengal police. And the line, as we shall see, continues almost down to the present day.

There are good reasons for this. Whatever else the British Empire was (and it was many things), no one could accuse it of being either liberal or democratic. (The exceptions were its self-governing provinces: Australia, Canada and the rest; which significantly did *not* provide any of Britain's secret police or espionage chiefs.) It was rather like Anglo-Ireland in this respect: protected from the 'progressive' viruses which had so enervated the mother country, and consequently a rich source of alternative values and principles to the ones that were prevalent there. We can see the influence of it in the leadership of most of the burgeoning reactionary causes of the 1900s and 1910s: the National League for Opposing Women's Suffrage, for example, where ex-colonial governors were highly prominent; the movement for military conscription, headed by Lord Roberts, the leading imperial warrior of his day; and the Boy Scouts, whose founder, Robert Baden Powell, spent most of his military career in Africa, and was one of Britain's earliest imperial spies. All these movements were partly designed to counter the corrosive effect of democracy and socialism on the British working classes (the first version of Baden Powell's Scout Promise had boys swearing to do their duty not only to God and the king, but to their employers too);[6] as was the wider campaign to make the empire itself more popular, in order to furnish an alternative focus of working-class loyalty to rival socialism.

None of these antidotes worked to the entire satisfaction of the British political Right before the First World War. Many feared that in spite of them Britain was coming very close to disaster then: with suffragism, a constitutional crisis in 1910, conflicts over Irish Home Rule, and – most frightening of all – the biggest and longest and best co-ordinated industrial strike wave in her history, fired in certain areas (like the railways) by 'syndicalism', which was a new socialist variant. Basil Thomson, who became assistant commissioner in charge of the Metropolitan CID in June 1913, was heard to remark at around that time that Britain was headed straight for revolution, 'unless there was a European war to divert the current'.[7] That was a measure of *his* desperation. But European war was a somewhat drastic – and, as we shall see, not altogether reliable – prophylactic. Consequently other measures might also need to be taken, in order to meet the challenge of the enemy within.

In Kenneth Grahame's *The Wind in the Willows*, which was published at around this time, the nightmare becomes a reality. While Mr Toad is flaunting his vulgar wealth up and down England, and neglecting his duties back home, Toad Hall is taken over by the stoats and the weasels – the 'Wild Wooders' – who clearly represent the workers, misled by communist tommy-rot. In the end (for this is supposed to be a children's story), everything ends happily. Toad and his more solid upper middle-class friends (Mole, Ratty, Badger) return and turf the Wild Wooders out. The interesting aspect of this for our purpose, however, is the way they effect this counter-revolution: by means of a *secret underground passage* into the hall where the stoats and weasels are revelling. Coming as it does from a secretary of the Bank of England (which was Grahame's job at the time), could this be a cleverly disguised agenda for the twentieth-century Right?

As yet, in 1910, none of the British state's secret underground passages led anywhere near the Wild Wooders. Over the next ten years, however, this was to change. The biggest changes, as one would expect, came during the course of the 1914–18 war, which may have had a greater impact on the composition and scope of the domestic secret service in Britain than any other event for a hundred years. Some of those changes, however, were anticipated before then. The main reason for this was that the war was widely anticipated too.

One of the fruits of that anticipation was Britain's other main modern covert counter-subversive organization, which is now usually known as MI5. As with the first one, the Special Branch, it began as a very different creature from the one it eventually became. At the start it was purely a counter-*espionage* agency, concerned to detect and neutralize German spies and saboteurs. It began in August 1909, when a 'Foreign Espionage' subcommittee of the powerful Committee of Imperial Defence set up a new 'Secret Service Bureau', which was initially intended to combine both British espionage abroad and domestic counter-espionage. The two aspects were separated later, with the counter-espionage side being put in the charge of Captain Vernon Kell. He eventually ran it for thirty years. But at the beginning it looked a much frailer plant than that.

Something like it had been in the minds of certain military personnel, including Kell, for many years. At first the Liberal government of the day took little notice of their suggestions, until it was forced to by a press campaign which started with a somewhat ludicrous story about suspected spies in the *Globe* in April 1907. One of the orchestrators of this campaign was a popular novelist and *Daily Mail* journalist called William Le Queux (pronounced 'cue'), whose proudest boast was apparently that he had never written a line that a child of 12 could not understand.[8] (The *Daily Mail* will have liked that.) He had published his first story based on the hypothesis of a foreign invasion of Britain aided by secret agents in 1893. At that time the anticipated invaders had been the French and the Russians; but by 1908 the likeliest enemy was clearly established as Germany. It was in that year that Le Queux's *Spies of the Kaiser* was first published: a novel that professed to be based on fact. Its plot is worth summarizing, because it is characteristic.

England's green and pleasant land is being undermined by thousands of German agents, most of them disguised as waiters and barbers, and masterminded by the wicked Hermann Hartmann. They are busy spying on defence installations, and preparing sabotage plans for the day – '*der Tag*' – when Germany will invade. They also have 'a dastardly scheme by which, immediately before a dash is made upon our shores, a great railway strike is to be organized, ostensibly by the socialists, in order to further paralyse our trade and render us in various ways unable to resist the triumphant entry of the foe'. (That is where the Wild Wooders come in.) Meanwhile a complacent (and clearly Liberal) government sits back and does nothing. So it is left to a clean-limbed young patriotic upper-middle-class amateur, Ray Raymond, and his plucky English-rose fiancée Vera Vallance (the alliteration is probably to help the 12-year-olds), to foil them on their own. After some madcap adventures, that is what they do; and England is saved. That is *Spies of the Kaiser*. Shortly afterwards P. G. Wodehouse published a splendid spoof on this kind of thing called *The Swoop! or How Clarence Saved England*, in which nine hostile armies land simultaneously – 'England was not merely beneath the heel of the invader. It was beneath the heels of nine invaders. There was barely standing-room' – but are foiled by a Boy Scout. That gives some of the flavour of the 'spy scare' of *circa* 1909.[9]

Le Queux was quite serious about his thousands of German spies. (Wodehouse, of course, was not.) As well as writing about them, he sent files on reported sightings over to the War Office, who then dished them up to the Foreign Espionage subcommittee. Most of them were very insubstantial: like the observation that someone was wearing a wig, or walking in a funny way. Some of them were entries for a competition organized by a popular weekly newspaper offering £10 prizes for the best readers' letters on 'How I Met a Spy'. Colonel James Edmonds, who was the head of army Intelligence and another prime mover behind the setting up of the new agency, admitted that the evidence was flimsy, but maintained that this merely strengthened the case for a bureau to investigate it.[10] The reason it was so thin was that they did not have the means of finding any thicker evidence that there might be. This is a common secret service perception. If you cannot see a menace on the horizon, it might be because there is no menace, or because your binoculars are too weak. The counter-espionage lobby around 1910 assumed the latter, and convinced others, including government ministers, that it was at any rate *safer* to assume the latter, even if it might not be true.

So Edmonds was given his 'contra-espionage' agency; but only a very tiny one, which suggests that ministers were not wholly convinced. It began with nothing but a room in Victoria Street with a desk and a filing cabinet, and of course Kell himself. He was chosen partly because he was junior enough to be expendable if there proved to be nothing for him to do. When he asked for a clerk he was given one, but chided for extravagance. Later he was allowed to recruit a few assistants, including 'a retired police detective' who was almost certainly our old ex-Special Branch friend William Melville. On the eve of the war Kell's department had a staff of eleven, plus the help of Patrick Quinn and his men at Scotland Yard. By then Kell himself had started to be known simply as 'K'. That was coming to be a common secret service device, possibly in order to fool the enemy.[11]

Two other things were done to help him. The first was the compilation of a register of aliens in Britain, which began in 1911 and by July 1913 comprised nearly 29,000 names. Local police chiefs helped with it, except initially in urban areas, where they were considered to be the wrong 'class' of policeman, and 'too much in the hands of their Watch Committees'. It was all kept highly secret, because it was thought that Parliament would make a fuss over it if it ever got to know.[12]

The second helpful measure was the 1911 Official Secrets Act. That *had* to be submitted to Parliament, because its whole purpose was to create new laws and penalties. But it was not done straightforwardly. In a way it was not so much submitted to Parliament, as smuggled past it in disguise. It is not a very edifying tale. In essence, the Act was a blanket measure to enable governments to prevent anyone apart from themselves divulging official information of any kind. (That is contained in 'Section 2'.) The War Office saw it as a weapon to keep in reserve to prevent newspapers publishing stories damaging to national security, if the 'D-Notice' system ever broke down. (The D-Notice system was an agreement reached earlier that year between newspaper proprietors and the War Office, by which the former agreed to censor themselves if the latter told them to.)[13] The Bill was presented to Parliament, however, as a much more modest measure, simply to stop spies communicating military secrets to foreign governments ('Section 1'). That was the disguise. The Attorney-General claimed that there was 'nothing novel in the principle of the Bill': which was either a huge misunderstanding, or just as huge a lie. One or two MPs twigged on to this – 'It upsets Magna Charta altogether,' interjected one – but to no avail. It was a hot Friday afternoon in August, and many MPs had gone home. The Agadir crisis was on. The government insisted that in the 'national interest' the Bill had to pass all its readings then. Members who stood up to question this were roughly pulled down. In the end it was rushed through in about an hour, with only a dozen men (nine Labour and three Liberals) voting against.[14]

All this came about because it soon became clear that there was something, at any rate, in all this talk of German spies. 'Hermann Hartmann', for example, really existed at the time Le Queux was writing; his proper name was Gustav Steinhauer, and he was at the head of a network of German agents in British naval ports. Some of his men were detected and captured before the war. The first one was Siegfried Helm, who was arrested in September 1910 after showing too much interest in the forts overlooking Portsmouth harbour. Others followed, producing a trickle of spy trials which, among other things, helped to keep public interest alive. As well as these, however, a number of spies were spotted, but *not* arrested, until the moment war was declared on 4 August 1914, when nearly all of them (twenty-one out of twenty-two) were rounded up. ('We pounced on them', remembered ex-Detective Inspector Harold Brust later, 'like a leaping tiger.') That was clever, because it meant that Germany was suddenly deprived of intelligence about troop embarkations and so on at a crucial stage.[15] It was undoubtedly a valuable contribution to Britain's initial war effort.

Most of the credit for it was given to Kell's agency, and to the Special Branch of the police, which did the actual arresting. In fact it may not have been quite so creditworthy as it appeared. It is easy to bowl against poor batting, and the German batting in the early 1910s appears to have been atrocious. Most of these early agents were almost ludicrously indiscreet. Siegfried Helm showed his drawings of forts to a ladyfriend, who told the local military. Max Schultz flew a German flag from his houseboat and asked people quite openly for naval secrets. Karl Hentschel gave himself up at two successive police stations, because the desk sergeant at the first one thought he was having him on. Friedrich Schroeder left incriminating maps and letters behind when he moved out of a pub he ran in Rochester. The 'ring' of twenty-two spies rounded up in August 1914 was discovered when a German officer attending King Edward VII's funeral marched straight to the barber's shop in the Caledonian Road which acted as its 'post office', with the Special Branch officer who was routinely shadowing him tagging along behind. The fact that the same post office served all Steinhauer's agents in Britain was an obvious weakness, and suggests a certain lack of guile in German espionage methods. It was a bit like playing repeatedly across the line.

That rather detracts from the quality of the bowling and field placing. It also, to an extent, exonerates government ministers from the charges of apathy directed at them by the likes of Le Queux and Edmonds before 1909. Today it is easy to sneer at the 'naïvity' of men who could not credit that a civilized nation would dishonour itself by spying on an ally: but they may have known their own times better than we think we do. In an 'autobiography' ghosted for him after the war by the sensationalist spy writer Sidney Felstead, Gustav Steinhauer was quoted as saying that even he regarded peacetime espionage as 'a dirty business', basically because it was an abuse of hospitality; which was why (he claimed) he restricted his activities to naval bases.[16] It may also explain why his agents there seem to have been so half-hearted in their deceit. Ministers may have been wrong to dismiss the dangers of German espionage entirely before 1909; but the counter-spy lobby was equally mistaken about its extent.

Of course it is usually better to be safe than sorry; but that may not apply in this case. It is possible that Edmonds's and Kell's exaggerated view of the German spy menace actually impeded them in the task they really had on hand. Most of the genuine spies who were arrested between 1910 and 1914 would probably have been picked up anyway, without any help at all from 'K'. While Steinhauer was deploying his handful of bungling amateurs around the coasts of Britain, and alert policemen and public-spirited young ladies were rumbling them, Kell's outfit was (metaphorically speaking) miles away, busy looking into all that nonsense of Le Queux's about waiters in wigs and hairdressers with funny walks, awaiting the signal for *der Tag*. This will also have spoiled any pleasure they might have derived from the great spy round-up of August 1914. It was only much later on that the full achievement of it was recognized, and MI5 started taking credit for smashing the *whole* German intelligence network at one blow. Before then Kell could not quite believe this. Too few spies had been caught. Where were all the others? The War Office estimated that 75,000 'enemy aliens' (Germans and Austro-Hungarians) were still living in Britain when war broke out.[17] Any of these, or even most of them, could be spies and saboteurs. Kell had no proof of this, but that probably only meant that they were the cleverer ones. That made them all the more dangerous. So he could never let up. According to his wife, Constance, this was the point at which he took to sleeping in his office, 'with many telephones around his bed', so as to be on hand when the star German batsmen appeared at the crease.[18]

MI5 has taken on an important role in modern times, as a general counter-subversive agency concerned with other 'threats' to British security as well as espionage. Its early years, however, gave no hint of this. Even as a counter-espionage agency it was flawed; and so far as we can tell it did not venture beyond counter-espionage – did not have the resources to – before the First World War. It was very specialized, therefore, and relatively insignificant, by comparison with the tried and far more trusted Metropolitan

Police Special Branch, which had the wider role of the two. The Special Branch also had the resources; because when Patrick Quinn asked for more men and money no one accused *him* of extravagance.

In the spring of 1909 he had thirty-four officers under him, excluding the men stationed at ports. In May 1913 the number was seventy-two at least, and may have been slightly more.[19] This rate of growth was unprecedented. Some of it was due to the fact that the branch's traditional responsibilities were becoming more onerous. Foreign refugees are a case in point. Their numbers increased enormously in the early twentieth century, mainly as a result of anti-Jewish pogroms in eastern Europe and Russia. One of Quinn's requests for more men, in July 1909, was made specifically with them in mind. Shortly afterwards there was a little spate of violent crimes involving east European Jewish anarchists living in London, which began with the killing of a policeman near Tottenham marshes by two Letts whom he had surprised robbing a bank clerk, and culminated in the 'Siege of Sidney Street' in Stepney in January 1911, in which three more Letts were burned to death in a house after a gun battle with police.[20] These were probably not 'political crimes' in any generally accepted sense, but they were bound to involve the Special Branch, because foreign anarchists were supposed to be its speciality. They also affected another of its traditional duties, guarding visiting royalty, when the tsar and tsarina – the Jews' persecutors – paid a state visit to Britain in August 1909.

That only accounted, however, for some of the growth. The rest derived from the entirely new duties the Special Branch took on during these years. One of these, as we have seen already, was counter-espionage, in which it did much of the routine leg-work for Kell, and may also have done some of its more cerebral work, though Kell liked to give the impression not.[21] Another was looking after extremist Indian nationalists, especially after the assassination by one of them of Sir William Curzon Wyllie, the Secretary of State for India's political aide-de-camp, at the Imperial Institute in London on 1 July 1909.

The Special Branch started taking an interest in the Indian student community in London from 1907 at the latest, but was hampered by lack of expertise in this field. In June 1908 John Morley, the Secretary of State for India, complained that no one there could tell 'Hindu from Mahomedan, or Verma from Varda', which made the 'ordinary square-toed' English detective, he said, 'wholly useless' against the Indians. After the Wyllie assassination, therefore, a separate section to cover this side was created within the Branch, with help from the government of India in the form of a couple of 'informants' despatched in August 1909, and a Bombay detective superintendent, John Wallinger, who came over early in 1910. Wallinger answered to the India Office in London, and not to Scotland Yard, which was resented at first by the latter, who spent three months in a huff and refused to give him anything to do; but he seems to have broken that down eventually, and they co-operated amicably thereafter both in Britain and on the Continent, where some of the most dangerous Indians lived. (They took some watching. In September 1914 the Punjabi nationalist Ajit Singh escaped from under Wallinger's nose in Paris, chiefly because he had not informed his landlady that he was leaving, which the head of the Indian detective police sympathetically pointed out would have been 'considered a low trick by the agents of the secret service in any country'.)[22] Another thing that was done was to develop and enlarge the practice of intercepting letters and telegrams at the Post Office, with warrants now being couched in far more general terms than had been customary before. Later on this was extended into other areas.[23] All this seemed to work moderately well in the case of the Indians, though latterly the Indian authorities came to feel that Scotland Yard's attention was being distracted away from them by the militant female suffragists, or 'suffragettes'.[24]

They were the third of these new responsibilities that accrued to the Special Branch after 1909. Shortly after the creation of the Branch's Indian section another one, for the suffragettes, was set up in September of that year. The idea came from the Home Secretary, Herbert Gladstone, after his car had been attacked by women. What worried him, he wrote, was the possibility of an assassination attempt by 'a female Dhingra' (Madan Lal Dhingra was Wyllie's killer): not, he hastened to add, because he was afraid for himself, but because of the 'savage reprisals by the crowd' an attack on him or any other minister would undoubtedly provoke against the offending suffragette. Because of the extreme sensitivity of the work only the best officers were chosen for the new section, including Inspector Francis Powell, on the grounds of his unrivalled knowledge of 'these suffragette Maenads' and his *exceptionally good physique* (underlined). Quinn was put in personal charge. One of his surviving reports describes how, after visiting Mrs Pankhurst at her home in the company of a police doctor to see whether she was well enough to be arrested, he was 'subject to abuse' from a group of women waiting on the doorstep. 'The language used', he went on, 'was "Cowards", "Pigs", "Dogs", "Brutes", "Syphilis" and "Gonorrhoea"'; expletives which the doctor in a separate report confirmed, and no doubt helped Quinn with the spelling of.[25]

The suffragettes took the Special Branch not only into new territory, but into a different kind of terrain. The sorts of crime it had been concerned with before had generally been male, foreign, political and violent; militant suffragism was political, certainly, and violent to an extent, but also predominantly female, and entirely home-grown. This could be disconcerting. The Special Branch had never been happy with women. In the 1880s it used to have nightmares about Fenian women walking into the Houses of Parliament pretending to be pregnant but with bombs hidden where their bumps should be: because you could never *search* a female.[26] In the 1910s the problems were different. Ex-Detective Inspector Edwin Woodhall described in his memoirs how when they used to move in to arrest suffragettes after 'some diabolical outrage', they would see 'a pretty little thing shamelessly exploiting the feminine frailty she denied in her speeches as her rightful heritage, utter a pathetic cry for help', and have 'men of all types' rushing in chivalrously to rescue her.[27] That was a new hazard, calling for qualities in Special Branch officers – tact, for example, and gentleness – that had not been especially required before.

Whether it made any *essential* difference to the work and therefore the nature of the Special Branch, however, is open to doubt. All these new duties – suffragettes, spies, Indian seditionists – could be seen as extensions of its customary role. The important point was that they all involved threats of violent crime. In the case of spies, the violent crime was an invasion of Britain by Germany. With the Indians it was assassination. With the suffragettes it was unlikely to go as far as this, whatever Herbert Gladstone may have thought; but it did include damage to a wide range of inanimate targets, from letter boxes and golf courses to famous paintings and churches, and physical attacks on government ministers. All these threats were undoubtedly real, and also undoubtedly – quite apart from their motivation – criminal. It was this that made them legitimate objects of police concern, according to traditional notions of the functions of the British police.

What may be even more telling in this regard than what the Special Branch did, is what it did *not* do. So far as it is possible to tell, it took almost no interest in the British Labour movement at this time. If this is so – and we can never be certain – it is highly significant. Many people on the right of British politics regarded the Labour movement as far more dangerous than any of the other 'threats' that beset Britain in the 1910s, but in a different – more purely 'subversive' – way. The 'great labour unrest' seemed to bear out their fears. Here was Labour 'subversion' in action, eating away at the vitals of the British state. Yet there is no sign of any Special Branch involvement in this area, until very late indeed in the day. Scotland Yard police were quite often sent to help provincial police forces keep order in riotous areas; but no Special Branch men, or detectives of any kind, were ever sent with them. Occasionally a constable would be put into ordinary clothes and told by his superintendent to circulate among the strikers to find out what they were saying or planning. This was to enable the police to deploy their uniformed forces more effectively. There was nothing particularly sinister in that.

Often the police proved inadequate, and the military were called in. They were more systematic with their under-cover work. Edmonds, for example, deployed spies extensively among what he called the 'natives' of Hackney in an industrial dispute there, telling them to buy their plain clothes locally in second-hand clothes shops, no doubt so that they would give off the right smell. During the South Wales coal strike of 1911 General Nevil Macready, the son of a famous actor, also used secret agents widely. One of them, a Captain Wyndham Childs, who will feature in our story later, was 'for a time laid up as a result of exposure' while trying to infiltrate the strikers: possibly because he bought his clothes elsewhere. In these cases the espionage was justified on military rather than political grounds. The first rule for a military commander in any task is to get to know the situation that confronts him properly. Macready complained that he only got prejudiced information from the mineowners, and from the local police, who were in the mineowners' pockets. So he sent out his own scouts, mainly to gather tactical intelligence. It was the natural, sensible, military thing to do.[28]

Throughout this very tense and eventful period just before the outbreak of the war, therefore, a genuine 'political police' agency in Britain seems to be eluding us. A genuine political police is one which is concerned with genuine political crimes: that is, with activities that are defined as criminal *because* they are political, rather than activities which would be defined as criminal anyway, but are also classed as political because they have political motives or aims. Neither the Special Branch nor MI5 was yet a political police force in this sense. Nor was military intelligence, even when it was called in to gather information about political disputes. All of them have convincing defences to put to the charge. Right up to the eve of the war it looks as though Britain had no fully fledged, or even half-fledged, political police.

But that is not quite the end of it. Soon after the beginning of the war, this all changed. Within a very few months Britain *did* have, as we shall see, a proper political police. Part of this can be explained by the war itself, of course; which, because it was so major – so 'total' – created entirely new conditions from the ones that were thought to pertain in peace. Nevertheless, the speed of the transformation suggests that things must have been set up for it. The pieces were all in place. Kell's proto-MI5 was one of those pieces. Others were the Official Secrets Act, and the Aliens Register. The military had experience of domestic espionage during strikes. There were contingency plans to cope with other eventualities, which could be brought down and dusted off in a moment, to be implemented with the least possible delay. One involved a take-over of London by the army in the event of civil strife there, with an intelligence network among the subversives (one intelligence officer suggested using Boy Scouts), and soldiers empowered to shoot on sight.[29] Lastly, so far as subversion was concerned, there was the Special Branch: which if it was not quite a proper counter-subversive police force yet, had all the makings of one.

The reason for this lay in the character of its personnel, and of the man who took over its running just a year before the outbreak of the war. So far as the personnel were concerned, such a development may have been inevitable. Years of trailing anarchists, or Germans, or suffragettes, or whomever, could well have misled them into thinking that they were trailing them because of what they were, rather than because of what some of them might do. Judging by the memoirs many of them penned later on, most of them disapproved thoroughly of the politics of the people they were called upon to watch. The only occasional exceptions were German spies, some of whom – if their motives were 'patriotic' rather than mercenary – they admired. (They were, after all, in a similar line of business to themselves.) One they particularly respected was Karl Lody, a wartime agent who met his eventual death by firing squad with great fortitude. (The story went that as he was about to be shot he turned to the British officer in charge and said, 'I suppose you will not shake hands with a spy?' to which the officer replied, 'No, I will not; but I will shake hands with a brave man.')[30] Anarchists, communists, suffragettes and seditionists, however, were different kettles of fish. 'In my opinion,' wrote John Sweeney, 'there is a law needed which shall deal summarily with such people, and apply a muzzling process preventing them from publicly declaring themselves Anarchists.' Harold Brust got quite worked up about 'these scratching, clawing Suffragettes ... prancing and howling in the streets ... behaving like demented idiots in order to prove to the nation that they were fit and proper persons to have a hand in government affairs'.[31] Men like Sweeney and Brust must have imagined sometimes that they were policing these *opinions*, or felt they ought to be. If they had been called upon to do just that, they would have taken to it naturally. They might not even have noticed the difference.

The person to ask them to do it was Basil Thomson, who succeeded MacNaghten as assistant commissioner in charge of the CID in July 1913. The only (faint) prewar evidence of Special Branch interest in British socialists comes from his time.[32] Thomson came from an interesting background: the son of an archbishop of York, he was educated at Eton, and then went through a succession of jobs before he took on this one, including 'prime minister' of Tonga (there we have the imperial connection again), and governor of Wormwood Scrubs. He had powerful right-wing views – regarding humanitarians, for example, as 'sub-human' – and a strong sense of the potency of subversion, especially among the working classes. One of his most vivid boyhood memories was of pictures of scenes from the Paris Commune that had been pinned up in his schoolroom, and especially of the *pétroleuses*, or female petrol-bombers, who made an awful impression on him. Later, he wrote, those pictures opened his eyes to 'what havoc a tiny destructive minority can work in a civilized community that takes no thought of self-protection'. During the 'great labour unrest' of 1911–13 he regarded the 'Triple Alliance' of trade unions who were threatening concerted strike action as little better than terrorists, and expressed the belief – as we have seen already – that only a European war could save Britain from revolution.[33] The political side of police work clearly interested him more than it did MacNaghten, who may have let Quinn get on with it in his own way. Thomson's 'descent upon Scotland Yard', as a contemporary MI6 man retailed many years later, 'heralded a fresh era' for the Special Branch. It also, apparently, produced friction between him and Quinn, until Thomson wore the latter down and 'took the upper hand'.[34] That probably took until the start of the war, when Thomson's full influence began to be felt.

Wars, of course, are terrible things; but they can also be quite liberating for 'spooks'. When war is declared, the clouds lift. The game is really on. There can be no doubt now that the other side is playing, and in deadly earnest. No one disputes that you should be playing too. Peacetime scruples disappear, as the higher priority of national survival overrides them. Obstacles are cleared from your path, and resources are poured in. The crowd is behind you. And so you can engage, with an easy conscience and a sense of the importance of what you are doing, in what is probably the most intellectually stimulating of all forms of warfare, and also (if you are working at home) the safest.

The First World War had this sort of effect both on the Special Branch and on MI5. Both increased enormously in numbers. By the time of the armistice in November 1918 the Special Branch was 700 strong, compared with 70 in the summer of 1914, and MI5 had 844 officers, compared with around a dozen. Their budgets increased in proportion. To supplement their efforts there was a staff of 1,453 men and women intercepting and censoring letters at the Post Office, and others to do the same with telegrams.[35] The people taken on there were mostly clerks. MI5 and MI6, however, recruited more widely. One man who joined in December 1914 was a medical doctor, taken on because MI6 reasoned that a doctor was 'the last person to be suspected of intrigue'. Together with him in that class of 1914 he later remembered 'ex-policemen, journalists, actors, ex-officers, university dons, bank clerks, several clergy, and to my knowledge at least two titled persons'.

That was at what he described as a 'Spy School', started up then to teach them all what today is called 'tradecraft'. The training included lectures from ex-Detective Superintendent Melville on how to pick locks and burgle houses, followed by practical exercises; others on subjects like 'The Technique of Lying', 'The Technique of Being Innocent', 'The Will to Kill' and 'Sex as a Weapon in Intelligence'; and (finally) 'Dr McWhirter's Butchery Class', which gave advice on how to top yourself if you were caught. They were also given a history lesson, by a cousin of the current Lord Chancellor, who taught them how espionage had a long, continuous and proud tradition in Britain, right back to the time of Walsingham.[36] That will not have done much for their sense of the past, but then history does not matter: only the use that is made of it. Otherwise – if we can credit this account – 'Spy School' clearly gave these new wartime recruits an excellent grounding, especially in practical subjects.

If they were in MI6, they then went off to lie for Britain, dangerously, abroad. The MI5 contingent, together with the Special Branch, mostly stayed behind. They had two main tasks. This was because Britain was fighting two enemies. The first was Germany and her continental allies, which so far as MI5 was concerned meant foreign spies and saboteurs. The second was Germany's allies – witting or not – in Britain itself. They included pacifists, socialists, trade unionists, Irish, malingerers and various other categories who were undermining the war effort in a score of different ways. They had been a worry for years. The problem was thought to be a lack of patriotism, demonstrated, for example, in the prewar wave of strikes. That was uncomfortable, for those who regarded it as a worker's prime patriotic duty to work. Basil Thomson, as we have seen, thought that a war might be the best cure for this; but he was not altogether confident of it, and others were less sanguine. In May 1912 the military commander in South Wales warned that the workers there might even 'utilize' a war 'to enforce their demands for improved wages'; and one of the reasons for all those contingency plans for an army take-over of London was the anticipation that a war might provoke civil unrest among 'the vast numbers of ignorant, underfed, and discontented unemployed' in the Metropolis.[37] The ignorance was a crucial factor. If this kind of thing did happen, it would not really be the fault of the workers themselves, so much as of socialist agitators who preyed on their ignorance and exploited it. Consequently they were a prime target for the counter-subversives.

There may have been something to all this. The years before the First World War had been a period of growing class alienation in Britain. To call one side 'patriotic' and the other not muddies the issue greatly, because there was more than a pinch of class bias in the middle classes' definition of the word; but it is true to say that there was less willingness at this time than at some others for the two (or more) classes to pull together on mutually agreeable terms. This fissure was exacerbated by the fact that the moral issues in this war did not seem quite so clear-cut as, for example, in 1939; and by the unexpectedly bloody and tedious course it took. All these factors – quite apart from socialist subversion and 'German gold' – were bound to arouse discontent during the course of it, and did. The extent of that discontent was kept deliberately hidden at the time, through press and film censorship designed to preserve whatever morale was left; but there can be little doubt of it now.

In France the extremest form it took was mutiny and desertion, which were widespread, especially in the later stages of the war, and might have been more so but for the sheer repression which kept the bulk of the British Expeditionary Force in its place. (More than 300 serving soldiers were executed by firing squad for desertion and other offences.)[38] Even more worrying to the Postal Censor was a sudden fashion among some front-line troops towards the end of 1915 for writing poetry, which he naturally saw as 'an ominous sign of mental disquietude'.[39] At home the alienation took a number of forms. One was resistance to conscription, and movements for a negotiated peace. Another was industrial strikes, of which one of the most serious was probably the engineering stoppage which started in Rochdale in May 1917, and then spread as far as Coventry, Southampton and Ipswich before it was settled eventually. A third was sabotage. This was always difficult to prove, because munitions factories in particular were intrinsically unstable, and apt to blow up quite spontaneously. There was an explosion at a factory in Ardeer in Scotland in July 1915, and a succession of them in 1917, at Silvertown, Arklow and Preston. Scores of workers were killed in them, and at one time they threatened to halt the British offensive in France by depriving it of shells. In February 1917 four brand-new aeroplanes were wrecked by hammer-heads found in their engines, placed there, thought Basil Thomson, either 'by an enemy or a striker or a peace crank'. For other cases of suspected sabotage, especially in Lancashire, Sinn Fein were the more likely culprits.[40] All these incidents gave reasonable cause for concern, and hence work for Kell and Thomson to do.

They divided it up between them on much the same lines as before the war. Kell winkled out the spies; Thomson arrested them, and took charge of the rest. (Wallinger travelled to Switzerland, to deal with German–Indian plots.)[41] The counter-espionage side seems on the whole to have worked well. Kell had a considerable lead in runs at the start of play, of course, due to that great crop of German spy wickets right at the beginning of the war. That was consolidated soon afterwards by the arrest and internment of another 200 enemy aliens whom Kell suspected but could not prove anything against; and eventually by a general policy of internment and repatriation, by which more than 32,000 were locked up in prison camps, 20,000 sent back to their home countries and the rest subjected to restrictions of various kinds. The 'aliens registry' was formalized (the government pretended it was actually started then) by an Order in Council of 5 August 1914, which now put the onus on the aliens themselves to register, within forty-eight hours.[42] Eventually the Aliens Office carried files on 100,000 people, including British nationals who were considered to have 'alien blood'. (Whether the royal family was on the list is not known.) More names were garnered from the postal censors, who compiled a 'Black List' of 13,500 suspicious characters and their addresses.[43] All over the country police officers and others kept a sharp look-out, as never before, for odd-looking people who could be spies. New legislation, especially the cosily named DORA (Defence of the Realm Act), empowered police officers to expel almost anyone they liked from strategically sensitive areas, like coasts, without having to give reasons. Their vigilance is illustrated by the fate of the famous Glaswegian architect and water-colourist Charles Rennie

Mackintosh, who was ordered out of his holiday cottage in Walberswick because the local Suffolk constabulary could not fathom his accent, and suspected that his intricate paintings of wild flowers could really be maps of local estuaries.[44]

All this gave German intelligence really very little chance. It made the effort, but with almost no success. Usually it was the postal censorship which found it out. Spies' letters were intercepted, and traced back. Their contacts abroad were also traced, and Mansfield Cumming's *foreign* intelligence section (MI6) put on to them. In this way Kell could anticipate the arrival of fresh German agents even before they were sent. Dozens were refused admission to Britain on these grounds. Others were apparently 'turned' by Cumming, and when they arrived acted as 'double agents' for Britain. Of those spies who still managed to sneak in despite Kell's and Cumming's vigilance, thirty-seven were captured during the war, of whom twelve were executed (normally in the Tower of London), nine imprisoned, ten interned, five deported and one killed himself.

Most of them were caught in the early months of the war. Sometimes it was done quite cleverly. For example: towards the end of 1915 the postal censors intercepted some suspicious letters to Copenhagen which they knew came from a particular hotel in Bloomsbury, but not from whom. So one of Kell's men had the bright idea of staying in the hotel posing as an artillery expert, and telling each of the other guests a different tale about a (non-existent) new weapon he claimed the War Office was about to deploy. When the story appeared in the next letter to Copenhagen, they would know who had written it. Sure enough, one of the versions of the story turned up. It was about a searchlight ray which had been developed to aid Britain's anti-Zeppelin defences, and which was *invisible*. The agent who had swallowed that unlikely tale was a Swedish woman called Eva de Bournonville, who was subsequently tried and sentenced to death, though in her case the sentence was commuted.[45] If that is true (it comes from a characteristically sensational account by an ex-secret agent), then it was exactly the kind of thing that made counter-espionage such fun.

Usually the opposition was simply no match for this sort of thing, just like before the war. Some spies gave themselves away, by pestering naval ratings in thick German accents with questions about ships and guns. Karl Lody was suicidally careless, not even bothering to turn his reports home into code. It was no contest. So something had to be done to make the game more interesting. One wheeze was to execute spies, but secretly, so that the Germans did not know, and then feed back false information as if it was coming from them. The classic example of this was the case of Karl Friedrich Müller, from whom German intelligence was still receiving reports (as it thought) months after he had been shot in June 1915, and even paying for it. The British secret service used the money to buy a car, which it christened 'Müller' in sentimental memory of him.[46]

By the beginning of 1916 the sightings were declining drastically. The last spy to be executed in Britain, a South American called Zender, met his fate on 11 April 1916. The last arrest of a spy, the Norwegian Hagn, was in May 1917. By then they appeared to be very thin on the ground. At first Kell thought that this was because the Germans were getting cleverer. Late in 1915 he believed he had hit on a subtle form of German sabotage, when he found a suspiciously high proportion of one particular regiment in Dover being invalided from the army. Perhaps the Germans had infiltrated an agent into the Medical Corps; or were paying some quack to advise malingerers on how to fake symptoms. He got Cumming to lend him one of his doctor-spies, and sent him to join the staff of the Western Heights Hospital in Dover to find out: but without unearthing the mole.[47] Soon it became clear that the reason why so few German agents were spotted was that so few of them remained. This was confirmed in April 1916 by a Dutch double agent, who reported that the Germans were 'very short of news from England'.[48]

They tried new methods. They stopped using Germans as agents, because they were too easily spotted, and instead recruited neutrals: North Americans, South Americans, Scandinavians, Dutchmen, Spaniards and even one solitary Serb (a Madame Popovitch). Predictably, they turned out to be unreliable. They also looked for ways around the postal censorship. Pigeons were no good, because they were even more conspicuous than Germans. Anyone hearing cooing from a neighbour's loft immediately alerted the police. In September 1914, according to Basil Thomson, a foreigner walking in a London park was actually arrested and imprisoned because a pigeon had been seen flying away from where he had stopped.[49] Radio transmitters and flashing lights were also easily detected. (You needed a four-horsepower engine to send a radio message then.) So the Germans instructed their agents not to try to communicate at all except by word of mouth. This usually meant sneaking into Britain, taking a quick look round and then rushing back to report. It was not conducive to intelligence in any great depth.

All this success should have pleased Kell; and also Basil Thomson, who had a part in it. He, of course, arrested Kell's suspects, and then interrogated them at Scotland Yard. He was clearly proud of his interrogation techniques, though it is not immediately clear why. When the Irish nationalist Roger Casement was brought to him in April 1916, for example, his first question to him was, 'What is your name?' Casement, obviously puzzled, replied, 'You know it.' 'I have to guard against impersonation,' explained Thomson.[50] A little earlier he had interrogated the famous Dutch spy known as 'Mata Hari', the exotic dancer who was supposed to have seduced military secrets out of elderly Allied generals seeking relief from the tensions of war. She asked him if she could be alone with him, to which Thomson (forgetting all about the *pétroleuses*) agreed. When they were together she spun him a tale that she was a *double* agent, working for the French; whereupon he let her go.[51] That was a misjudgement. But none of it mattered very much. Mata Hari was picked up soon afterwards in France, where she is supposed to have performed her final exotic dance in her cell the night before her execution; and for most of the other spies Thomson interviewed, Kell had easily enough evidence to convict them, or at least to intern them, quite apart from what Thomson might have prised out of them if he had been more skilled. Besides, Thomson had his eyes on bigger and far more dangerous game.

That game, of course, was Britain's other wartime enemy: the one 'within'. This was Thomson's major preoccupation throughout the war, but especially from about the middle onwards. A number of factors made the problem more serious then. One was the introduction of military conscription early in 1916, which, together with natural war-weariness, boosted the various pacifist and quasi-pacifist causes. The main quasi-pacifist organization was the Union of Democratic Control, whose leading light, Edmund Dene Morel, Thomson managed to contrive to get convicted and imprisoned in August 1917. In a report on 'Pacifist and Revolutionary Organizations in the United Kingdom' he prepared for the Cabinet shortly afterwards, Thomson pointed out that Morel had never *denied* being a German agent, which by his reasoning meant he probably was one. He also had 'alien blood' (French, as it happened, but you could never tell with foreigners). Another prominent 'peace crank' was Helena Swanwick, whom Thomson described as 'a woman of German origin' on the grounds that she had been born (of British parents) in Munich.[52] Thomson claimed to have his agents in all these groups. 'Yesterday,' he recorded in his diary for 30 June 1916,

> there was a meeting of the Central 'Stop the War' Committee. The only attendants were two lady police spies, who entered into conversation, neither knowing the other's occupation. At a subsequent election for vacancies on the committee both these ladies were elected, so I shall not be without information![53]

One of his main concerns was to trace their money back to its German source, though by October 1917 he was persuaded that this was a red herring.[54]

A second factor making things more difficult on the home front in these middle years of the war was the Easter Rising of April 1916 in Dublin. That was not really Thomson's pigeon, of course; but he got involved. The Easter

Rising represented – quite apart from anything else – a massive failure for British intelligence in Ireland. Intelligence chiefs in England had been warning for years that the Liberal viceroy, Augustine Birrell, was too lax over these matters, and had run down Ireland's counter-Fenian defences dangerously. The charge was not entirely fair; but the 1916 rebellion was felt to corroborate it. That, of course, suited the critics, who milked it for all it was worth. They may have done more. Two days before the rising the Irish patriot Sir Roger Casement was arrested in Tralee Bay in County Kerry, where he had been landed the night before from a U-boat with German help for the uprising. The agency responsible for his detection was the Naval Intelligence Department (NID) under Captain Reginald 'Blinker' Hall, which intercepted radio messages. Hall had known of the projected rising for some days, but told no one. He was one of those men – we shall come across others later – who never made the mistake of confusing patriotism with loyalty to elected governments, and liked to make his own mind up about what intelligence could be safely entrusted to the latter. Later his second-in-command, Admiral Sir William 'Bubbles' James, described him as 'not at all averse to keeping in his own hands a weapon that would give him enormous power over events'.[55]

In this instance the weapon was Casement. Hall did not trust Birrell one jot, and so he made sure that he did not get his hands on his new prize. Casement was conveyed from the west of Ireland to London without Dublin Castle getting a look in, and was interrogated (as we have seen) by Thomson as well as by Hall. Casement asked them to publicize his capture, so as to abort the rising. Hall refused. The reason he gave was that such an announcement might have the opposite effect. It is highly likely, however, that he wanted the Rising to take place, on the grounds that it would be easier to crush then than later, and possibly also in order to get rid of Birrell (which happened), and shock the government into tightening Ireland's security. At the same time, probably with Thomson's help, he took pages from Casement's 'Black Diaries', with their graphic descriptions of his homosexual encounters (or fantasies) and circulated them around London clubs, parliament and the press. He also sent a copy to the American ambassador. The object of that was to stifle any protest that might prevent his getting his just deserts. It worked, and Casement was hanged on 3 August 1916. That was two birds – the traitor Casement and the Liberal Birrell – disposed of. Another was winged: the pacifist E. D. Morel, who had been a close friend of Casement's ever since they had been associated together in the (anti-imperialist) 'Congo Reform Association' some years before. It was all very gratifying; an object lesson in secret service power which Hall, as we shall see, was never to forget.

Birrell's departure from the Irish viceroyalty was part of a general shift to the authoritarian right in British government circles during the second half of the war. This was another important new factor (our third), because it affected the authorities' *perception* of the 'enemy within'. At the beginning of the war the government had been a Liberal one, despite a couple of defections from the Cabinet in protest. As the war went on, however, the Cabinet became infiltrated by leading imperialists of the day like Lords Curzon and Milner, who were co-opted into the ministry in May 1915 and December 1916 respectively, and then into Lloyd George's five-man 'inner Cabinet'. Others came in at lower levels of the administration. None of them had ever been elected to office (except the South African Prime Minister Jan Smuts, who also joined the Cabinet; but he had not been elected in Britain, and by precious few people in his own country). All of them shared the security services' view of security matters. Kell, Thomson and Hall no longer had to persuade those above them of the reality of the dangers they perceived. Sometimes they even found themselves outflanked on the right. Thomson found, for example, that on the question of 'German gold' ministers were more paranoid than he was. When he reported that he could find no evidence of it, they told him to go away and look harder.[56] Generally, however, the domestic intelligence community found this a far more congenial set of masters than the last. On one thing their hearts beat entirely as one. That was the primacy of the Bolshevik or communist threat, which supplanted all the others, including even Germany, after the Russian revolutions of February and October 1917.

It was then, of course, that what before had been merely a speculative menace took on a real and tangible form. MI6 had an agent in Russia itself, Sidney Reilly, who sent back the most alarming reports. What he saw made him wonder what on earth they were doing fighting the *Germans*. 'Gracious heavens,' he wrote,

> will the people of England never understand? The Germans are human beings; we can afford to be even beaten by them. Here in Moscow there is growing to maturity the arch enemy of the human race ... At any price this foul obscenity which has been born in Russia must be crushed out of existence ... Peace with Germany? Yes, peace with Germany, peace with anybody. There is only one enemy. Mankind must unite in a holy alliance against this midnight terror.[57]

Agents elsewhere described it spreading 'like cancer' across war-torn Europe. On 21 October 1918 Thomson lunched with Sir Samuel Hoare, the man in charge of intelligence in Rome, who told him how Italy was about to become infected.[58] A German general described what happened to his regiment, when it was quartered near one that had just returned from the eastern front. 'This Eastern Division had been infected with Bolshevism. It spread this poison among my men. It was like the breath of Hell. My men withered away.'[59] This was horrible. And it was creeping towards Britain.

There was no mistaking the signs. A Special Branch officer who claimed to have actually read his Marx and Lenin pointed out how close conditions in Britain at that time were – closer, indeed, than in Russia – 'to those laid down by Communist philosophers as being necessary before a Proletarian Dictatorship could be imposed'.[60] There were secret service reports of 'soviets' being formed, clandestinely, in Leeds in June 1917, and a little later in (of all places) Tunbridge Wells. The trade union movement was being subverted by 'cells' planted in individual unions, 'which would grow unseen, as in the incipient stage of cancer, until the heart of the Union was eaten out'.[61] The strike wave which hit Britain in the closing weeks of the war, and then afterwards, testified to the success of this strategy. The most alarming strikes were those which caused large numbers of the Metropolitan Police to down truncheons in August 1918, and then again a year later. Lloyd George thought that the first of these strikes had brought Britain 'nearer to Bolshevism' than at any other time. In October 1918 Lord Burnham, the proprietor of the *Daily Telegraph*, despaired of avoiding 'some sort of revolution', if the police came out again.[62] Another combustible group was soldiers, especially those waiting to be demobbed. (It was they who were responsible for the Tunbridge Wells soviet.) Just after the war there were riots and mutinies in barracks all over Britain, some of them organised by a new 'Sailors', Soldiers' and Airmen's Union' which a disgruntled ex-member, in a letter to the press in March 1919, claimed had been hijacked by 'civilian men and women of extreme Bolshevik principles'.[63] In January that year the red flag was hoisted over Glasgow town hall, and tanks were sent in. To cap it all, Russia had an emissary in Britain, Maxim Litvinoff, who was stumping the country openly inciting revolution, and (Thomson really believed, this time) subsidizing it with 'Moscow gold'.[64]

There may have been a lot in all this: even the Moscow gold. This whole decade, from 1910 to 1920, was probably the most potentially revolutionary period in British history in the whole of the last 150 years. There was no saying what could have happened. Neither the fears of the Right, nor the hopes of the Left, were unreasonable, even though both in the end failed to transpire. The reasons for this need not concern us. The reasons the secret service *gave* for it, however, must. It was this diagnosis that determined most of their counter-subversive activities in these years, and then afterwards.

Basically it was very simple. The 'cancer' metaphor expressed it well. Bolshevism was a disease, which spread by attacking weak cells. As a political doctrine it was both mistaken, and evil. Basil Thomson explained the mistakes by reference to Marx's lack of 'business experience', which meant that he could know nothing of economics. The evil he put down to the fact that Marx, and also (as he believed) most of the leaders of the Russian Revolution, were Jews. This was because revolutions always brought the 'dregs' of society to the top, which made it 'inevitable in a country like Russia' that 'a preponderance of Jews would be found amongst the scum'. The revolution was also part of the international Jewish conspiracy to take over the world, using international socialism as its means. (His position on *The Protocol of the Elders of Zion* was that it was probably a forgery, but substantially true nevertheless.) That was the root of the 'cancer'. The 'weak cells', of course, were the working classes. They were weak because they were apathetic, and poorly taught. He explained the problem in a secret report of 1919.

> Whenever the British working man really understands a question he can be relied upon to show good sense. The difficulty is that he reads very little besides the cheap Sunday papers and the material which is circulated by revolutionary bodies.

That was the cause of the trouble.[65] The treatment followed logically on. It was twofold. First, the disease had to be attacked. Secondly, antibodies had to be injected into the working-class body to help resist it.

The best place to attack a cancer, of course, is at its source. This was one of the British government's strategies. The story of the Allies' military intervention in the Russian civil war in 1918–19, to try to defeat the revolution, is well known, though perhaps not so widely known as it ought to be. Secret agents took part in it too, though they come outside the scope of this book.[66] All their efforts and 'covert operations' failed, partly through lack of support from the politicians. Consequently Britain's front line of defence against Red subversion had to be pulled back much closer to home. If it could not be snuffed out at the centre, then it had to be stopped from spreading.

There was no shortage of volunteers for the task. Communist subversion was not only a political problem, but also an industrial one. Consequently it is highly likely, as the *Daily Herald* claimed in August 1919, that 'Certain of the big firms and associations had spy services of their own to spy upon their employees, and ... that these agencies were closely in touch with the Government espionage system.'[67] In October 1917 an industrial pressure group called the 'British Commonwealth Union' was formed by a man called Patrick Hannon who began as an imperialist and later ended as a fascist, and whose methods included infiltrating secret agents among trade unionists in order to find out about communist subversion. The agents were to report back in code: hence 'Slight influenza but complications feared' was to be read as 'Majority anxious for settlement but Communists exploiting situation'. The

BCU also tried to get its agents (usually ex-servicemen) elected to union posts.[68] Shortly afterwards, in 1919, the 'Economic Study Club' was founded, chiefly as a propaganda agency to replace subversion 'by what, for want of a better term, is known as simple economics'. Its founding father was none other than Admiral Sir Reginald 'Blinker' Hall, the ex-NID man who had taken such an independent line over Casement.[69] Later, as the 'Economic League', it became best known as a secret counter-subversive intelligence agency for industry. There may have been other such semi-covert private enterprise initiatives: rooting out the disease and injecting antibodies at one and the same time.

Government ministries also had their intelligence sections. One was set up by the Ministry of Munitions with help from MI5 in February 1916, to investigate suspicions of subversion and sabotage in factories. Its eventual head was a Major William Melville Lee. It started off as 'MMLI', which stood for 'Ministry of Munitions Labour Intelligence', but then changed its name to 'PMS 2', for 'Parliamentary Military Secretary Department No. 2', so that nobody would be able to guess from that what it did.[70] One of the things it did was to employ *agents provocateurs*, probably knowingly.

One of them achieved some notoriety at the time: though the press censors will have seen to it that it kept within bounds. He went under various aliases, including 'Alex Gordon' and 'Francis Vivian', but his real name was William Rickard. As well as munitions factories, he infiltrated socialist clubs, especially Jewish; and then posed as a member of what was called the 'flying corps', of war resisters on the run. Later he recounted how his 'control' – a man he knew as 'X' – deliberately kept him 'always in a state of chronic hard-upness' so that he would not slip his leash. He also claimed that 'X' got cross if his reports were too tame. He did his best. In munitions factories he suggested that workers put iron filings in the delicate parts of machinery, and water in the petrol. In socialist clubs he tried to persuade the comrades that 'the Government should be physically wiped out and blown up', and that 'capitalists should be kept down by poison and bombs'. In neither case did he meet with much response. His main success was to 'provoke' a case against a socialist called Alice Wheeldon, who also provided safe lodgings for 'flying corps' resisters, which resulted in her conviction and imprisonment in March 1917 for a plot to murder Lloyd George by hammering a poisoned nail through his boot. That case inspired John S. Clarke, the socialist poet, to compose an 'Epitaph' for the man responsible.

> Stop! stranger, thou art near the spot,
>   Marked by this cross metallic,
> Where buried deep doth lie and rot,
>   The corpse of filthy Alex.

> And maggot worms in swarms below,
> Compete with one another,
> In shedding tears of bitter woe,
> To mourn – not eat – a brother.

By then, however, Rickard had been given the traditional free passage to South Africa: which must by now have been bursting at the seams with generations of ex-spies and informers.[71]

This was all highly effective in its way; but very soon the politicians and civil servants got nervous over it. Ramsay MacDonald took Rickard's case up with the government, and attacked the use of spies and *agents provocateurs* in Parliament. That was on the second day of Alice Wheeldon's trial.[72] One of the results of this was that the system began turning counter-productive. The workers resented it, which was unlikely to do much for labour relations in the munitions industry. Consequently the Munitions Ministry turned against it too. They may also have disapproved of Melville Lee's methods. As a result PMS 2 was wound down, during the first few months of 1917. At the same time its records (apart from case files) were destroyed.[73]

The rest of the inheritance was split two ways. Most of PMS 2's personnel went to MI5, whence they had originally come. But Thomson's Special Branch took over its duties (and case files). Thomson had always disapproved of PMS 2, for many good reasons, but also no doubt because it got under his own feet. He was in an expansionary mood. He would have liked to have taken charge of *all* British secret service work: home, foreign and military.[74] He never quite managed that, but he went some way towards it. In November 1916 his Special Branch was formally hived off from the Metropolitan Police CID, with Thomson consequently relinquishing his ordinary police duties in order to concentrate on the Red and other related menaces. The following month he agreed to take over the labour side of intelligence for the whole country. The absorption of PMS 2 was part of that.[75] One result seems to have been that abuses like the antics of 'Alex Gordon' became rarer. The Special Branch was less cavalier, and better disciplined. It kept a watch on all known organizations of the Left, accumulated files on tens of thousands of their members and others Thomson did not like the look of, and sent reports on 'Revolutionary Organizations' to the Cabinet on a regular basis: fortnightly from early 1918, and weekly later. It liaised closely with similar agencies in the Empire. It also raided socialist headquarters and editorial offices. Sometimes the object of that was to make it difficult for left-wing organizations and journals to function, by carrying off membership lists and copy.

By the end of the war Thomson was clearly top dog in a territory he had been disputing with Kell for years. MI5 was now strictly confined to straight counter-espionage, and because the danger of espionage was so much less in peacetime had its grant halved. Thomson in the meantime continued rising.

In April 1919 he took on the title of 'Director of Intelligence', with a new headquarters in a building called Scotland House just across the road from the Yard. (One of the motives behind this move, apparently, was to isolate the Special Branch physically from the trade union virus which had infected the uniformed section of the police.) His brief now covered counter-subversion not only at home, but in the empire. This was the highest he rode, before his fall in 1921.

Even at his apogee, however, he was never entirely on his own. In March 1919, for example, a new agency was formed within the army to combat Bolshevism among the troops, called 'A2 Branch'. Its head was Lieutenant-Colonel Ralph Isham, a virulent anti-communist American who had joined the British Army as a private in 1915, risen quickly from the ranks, and impressed his superiors by dousing a military mutiny at Kempton Park in January–February 1919. A2 had two roles, corresponding with the by now widely accepted dual prescription for curing communist cancer. The first was to attack the disease itself, by means of secret agents. One of Isham's was a Private Gray, who managed to infiltrate the executive committee of the Sailors', Soldiers' and Airmen's Union and 'bring about a rift . . . which largely weakened it and curtailed its activities'. (Later he had less success when he dressed his wife up as 'Gipsy Gray, from Great Yarmouth, The World's Greatest Character Delineator' on Glasgow Green in order to penetrate the 'lower elements' of ex-servicemen there.)[76] Isham's second role was to tour regiments 'Talking to the troops and placing before them the real facts about the devastating effects of bolshevism'. (Thomson suggested he point out to them what the Russian Revolution had done to the value of the rouble.)[77] That was to strengthen the healthy cells.

All this is only part of a much larger and more complicated picture. It must be larger, because of all the evidence we know has been hidden or destroyed. Some of the complications are hinted at in what is still extant, and visible. Ralph Isham, for example, did not only deal with military subversion, but had at least one agent in the innermost councils of Sinn Fein. Michael Collins, who trusted him, knew him as 'Jameson', though his real name may have been Burns; Isham referred to him as 'No. 8' (why *eight*?). He approached the Irish initially as a delegate from the Sailors', Soldiers' and Airmen's Union, which was presumably why he reported to Isham. Later he was uncovered and shot.[78] There are inklings here of all kinds of complexities, possibly confusions, in Britain's domestic espionage underworld: an elaborate warren of secret tunnels, and passages leading off tunnels, going this way and that way beneath the Wild Wood.

The digging of that warren, roughly between 1909 and 1919, constituted one of the most significant events in modern British history. It was not recognized as such at the time, because it was only very dimly perceived by anyone in a position to appreciate its significance. Two groups of people did know about it – or at least, about some of it. They were the tunnelers themselves; and the Wild Wooders themselves. Neither of these groups appreciated its significance, because they were both totally unaware of its novelty. Both were misled, either by their own propaganda or by others', into thinking that this sort of thing had always gone on. Socialists thought it had always gone on because they could not credit capitalism with ever doing without it. For them the line of succession was a continuous one, from Castle and Oliver through Popay to 'filthy Alex'. The tunnellers were taught roughly the same, in their 1915 'Spy School', for example: that espionage was the second oldest profession, and had an uninterrupted history in Britain – a distinguished one, this time – stretching back to Walsingham. Consequently the importance of the revolution they were inaugurating was entirely lost on them.

It was lost on everyone else because they were kept in the dark about it: or as much in the dark as was possible with so much of it about. Even the bits that were revealed rarely got into the respectable, middle-class newspapers of the day, possibly due to the exertions of the D-Notice Committee. The reason it was so carefully hidden was not to surprise the security agencies' prey, who were on the lookout for it anyway, but in order not to risk its being discussed by liberal politicians who might have a blind spot when it came to the Red menace, and hence not be so supportive as they should be of the white knights of Scotland House. 'There are a number of virtuous people', wrote Thomson, who admitted to not fully understanding this himself, 'who think it highly improper for a Government to keep itself quietly informed of what is going on in its own and other countries.'[79] If such people had their way, it could be disastrous. In the glare of any kind of publicity at all, Britain's essential defences could simply wither.

Was this likely in the 1910s? It is hard to say. The anti-espionage tradition was certainly still there. It was found in some unlikely places. One was amongst the government of India, which was more liberal in this regard than one might expect a colonial administration to be; chiefly because its subjects seem to have taken to Victorian values in a big way, and were dangerously sensitive, apparently, on this matter of 'political policing'.[80] (So much for the idea that all those old India hands in Britain's secret services must have learnt their tricks there.) Another anti-spy group was the military. Brigadier-General Wallscourt Hely-Hutchinson Waters, who had been involved in intelligence work for much of his military career, nevertheless wrote in his autobiography in 1926 that in his view 'the results of secret service are usually negligible. Taking it all in all information acquired in this manner may indeed act as a kind of boomerang, and harm the recipients by making them lose their sense of proportion.'[81] That was foreign intelligence. In the case of the domestic kind the prejudice went even deeper. In June 1919 Basil Thomson asked General Sir Douglas Haig if he would pass to him any information about threatened strikes and so on that he picked up in the course of his duties as Commander-in-Chief of the army in Britain. 'I said', Haig recorded in his diary, 'that I would not authorize any men being used as spies. Officers must act straightforwardly & as Englishmen.'[82] The worst thing – the unforgivable sin – was spying on serving soldiers. Even Ralph Isham was sensitive to this. In March 1919 he issued strict instructions to his A2 Branch that this was never to be encouraged.

> Such system of espionage is against all traditions of the British Army and is to be absolutely deprecated. The normal channel for a Commanding Officer to maintain a finger on the pulse of his men is through his subordinate leaders.[83]

That ruling can only be squared with some of Isham's own actions by presuming that it could be bent when soldiers joined trade unions.

There is a strong strain of paternalism there, which – for good or ill – was still characteristic of the British Army. It affected the ordinary middle classes less. They and the working classes were the ones who mattered more, because of their representation in the House of Commons. What did *they* think of all this? It is difficult to know, because they were so seldom called upon to give their opinions. The question rarely came up. Was that because parliamentarians were apathetic, or because the secret service was so clever at hiding? Usually when it did come up, the most impassioned critics of domestic espionage were people who felt themselves to be its targets at the time. In April 1910, for example, the Irish nationalists launched an onslaught in Parliament on British intelligence methods, after Anderson's revelations of the uses he had put them to against Parnell in 1889. T. P. O'Connor, who opened the debate, said that he thought the people of Britain, too, had 'a racial instinct against the spy and the informer': but there was precious little sign of it in the Commons on that day.[84] In March 1917, in a short debate on the Wheeldon case, it was mainly Labour and a handful of Radicals who protested.[85] In August 1919 the *Manchester Guardian* claimed that 'Such methods are peculiarly repulsive to Englishmen, and the fact that our present Ministers have resort to them shows that they are as much out of touch with the feeling of their countrymen as were Sidmouth and Eldon.'[86] Again, the problem with that proposition is that it was never *tested*.

It may be that the middle-class prejudice against domestic espionage which had kept Britain so relatively free from it during the nineteenth century was a good deal weaker by now. Many MPs clearly felt as Thomson did. In March 1917, for example, when the old-fashioned Liberal MP Joseph King began attacking the secret service vote in the Commons – 'this secrecy, this employment of immoral, disreputable, and ungentlemanly means' – he was interrupted by a shout of 'You would rather lose the War!' from another part of the House.[87] Under the threat of war, and then of Bolshevism, most middle-class people may have felt that spylessness, or even relative spylessness, was a dangerous luxury. So it might have been safe to have been a little more open in front of them.

If you were open in front of *them*, however, the Wild Wooders would get to know too. That was the real bugbear. There could be little doubt about *their* hostility to secret service work. Ramsay MacDonald, for example, had always been strong on the subject. 'There are two sections of police officers,' he had pointed out in a debate on aliens in Britain in 1911.

> ... There is the faithful public servant who parades our streets in uniform. We know him afar off – we see him going round the corner – there is no doubt about him ... There is the other gentleman whom you do not know; you find him in the middle of your political refugees, acting as their friend and their prompter.

By 1917 he had not modified his position one whit. He acknowledged that in wartime certain things had to be done which could not 'always be done with clean hands': but only, he said, *abroad*. 'These other things' – spying on workers, the use of informers, *agents provocateurs* and all the rest – 'ought to be stopped'.[88] MacDonald was a worry. He had even voted against the Official Secrets Act. He might become Prime Minister. That posed a problem for the secret service.

Hence the particular sort of secrecy which the British secret service has always tried to maintain, from this time onwards: not just about its activities, which every secret service in the world tries to keep hidden; but also about its very existence, if that is possible. There are two reasons for it. One is Britain's liberal anti-espionage tradition, which continental countries, for example, do not have to the same degree, and which is thought to spell danger for the secret service (and consequently for the security of the nation) if the liberals ever get their hands on it. That is ironic, because it means that it is the country's liberalism (or perceived liberalism) which has forced the secret service into its illiberal (or unaccountable) hole. The second reason is Labour, which was and possibly still is regarded in some secret service circles as a potential incubator of the very danger the secret service exists to protect the country from, and consequently doubly unworthy of being entrusted with control over it. This problem taxed Thomson so much in October 1918, when he looked ahead to what might happen in the postwar years, that he suggested a whole new method of financing the service: from the interest on the gift of a million pounds' worth of War Bonds. The object of that was to free it from its present dependence on parliamentary grants: 'especially if a Labour Government comes into power'.[89] That was an astonishingly radical suggestion; and also, of course, a profoundly undemocratic one.

Chapter 8

Dangers ahead
(1920–40)

For most people the formal end of the Great War in 1920 (when the Versailles treaty came into force) was an unalloyed relief. For the men who ran Britain's counter-subversive agencies, however, it was not. This was because it only marked the end of the war with the *Germans*, who had not been their main antagonists for some time now. Since the middle of 1917, at the latest, most of their energies had been directed not against Germany, but against Russian Bolshevik subversion. And 1920 did not mark the end of the war against that.

If anything it made fighting it more difficult. The British domestic secret service owed nearly everything to the war. Before, both MI5 and the Special Branch had been insignificant and relatively innocuous. The war had metamorphosed them into a full-blown 'political police'. It had done that by persuading people of the reality and seriousness of the German – not the Russian – subversive threat. That was the problem. With Germany defeated, and consequently the subversive threat from that direction defeated too, it removed the public justification for MI5 and the Special Branch in their present forms. It also removed the factor which had suspended people's prejudices against 'political policing' generally while the war was on. Now there was nothing to stop those prejudices returning. Bolshevism ought to have the effect of stopping them, but was not so widely perceived as a threat as Germany had been. The domestic secret service was vulnerable, therefore; from which it followed that Britain's security was vulnerable too.

This was a huge worry. It meant that, after 1920, Britain's domestic secret service had in effect two struggles on its hands. The first was against its real enemies, as it saw them: political criminals and subversives, mostly communist, who endangered the security of the British state. The second was against the obstruction and apathy of some of its political masters: usually Labour, who could be expected to be unhelpful, but also occasionally Conservatives and coalitionists, who should have known better. Sometimes the two struggles could become confused; for if ministers were *very* obstructive, it was always possible that it was because they were covert enemies. That suspicion had far-reaching implications, as we shall see later on.

The period began badly, with two domestic intelligence set-backs, both of which could be – not necessarily fairly – attributed to obstruction and apathy. The first and most disastrous was in Ireland. The weakness of British intelligence there had been clear since the Easter Rising of 1916. That had taken the British authorities very largely by surprise, because its leaders had been careful to keep the secret of it to a very small circle of conspirators indeed. Even Eoin MacNeill, the Chief of Staff of the Irish Volunteers, was kept out of it, with the result that the day before the rising he assumed it had been called off, and told *his* men to go home and put their guns away.[1] That was a mistake, but the general principle was a sound one. Britain had held on to Ireland over the centuries largely because those who had fought to loosen her grasp had always been betrayed. There were two ways of looking at this. Either you could regard it as a tribute to Britain's intelligence system in Ireland, which one nationalist later described as 'the most efficient in the world'.[2] Alternatively, you could see it as a sad comment on the disloyalty and corruptibility of certain Irish. In either case it had to be tackled, if Irish nationalism was to stand a hope of success.

This was Michael Collins's perception. Consequently he resolved to tackle the intelligence problem head-on. His method was ruthlessly effective. First, he penetrated the British intelligence network with his own spies. By the end of 1919 he had about a dozen men placed in the Dublin Metropolitan Police, working for him. Some of them were in the detective or 'G' branch, which included a political section. They found out who the political specialists were, and then Collins sent out a group of Volunteers known as 'The Squad' to kill or maim them. Five were shot during the course of 1919. The following year a new head of the G-branch, W. F. Redmond, was gunned down shortly after his appointment, which had been intended to restore efficiency and morale. When *his* successor was named, he apparently hastily called a press conference to announce that he had not wanted the job, and would on no account have anything to do with political work. He was left alone. As well as the DMP men, nearly a hundred RIC police were killed by 'The Squad' between January 1919 and October 1920.[3] Men resigned; replacements became hard to find; informers kept mum. Both police forces became useless for intelligence purposes. Collins's own intelligence meanwhile went from strength to strength. Dublin Post Office and the Castle administration were riddled with his spies. Irish Boy Scouts were disguised as street urchins, to give warnings of the approach of the police. An organization called Cuman na m'Ban was apparently formed of women posing as prostitutes to lure soldiers and police to their deaths. On 30 March 1920 the IRA issued a proclamation declaring that mere membership of the RIC – not necessarily in a political capacity – marked a man a 'traitor', with predictable consequences.[4] At the beginning of 1920 the Lord Lieutenant of Ireland, Lord French, reported that 'Our Secret Service is simply non-existent. What masquerades for such a service is nothing but a delusion and a snare.'[5] This was something entirely new.

The authorities responded by calling in army Intelligence. The military commander in Ireland, General Macready (whom we last met in South Wales in 1911), suggested that a soldier be appointed to co-ordinate and rejig the whole intelligence system. The man chosen was 'a dapper little fellow with a monocle'[6] called Brigadier-General Sir Ormonde de l'Epée Winter. Like many of these early twentieth-century British intelligence heads, he was an oddity. His background was conventional enough, for his class: public school, army and then India, where his main concern was to get enough money to be able to enjoy himself in moderately dangerous pursuits like pig-sticking and tiger-hunting. He also liked watching surgical operations. Around 1903 he had served in Ireland for a short spell, during which he was acquitted of manslaughter after killing a man by hitting him with an oar. (He claimed the man was attacking him.) In 1911 he did some detective work on the case of a friend of his called Major C. A. Cameron and his wife, who had both been convicted of a crime, with the result that he got Cameron pardoned and the wife released on grounds of her insanity. Later he employed Cameron in covert work for him in connection with Ireland. That seems to have been his only experience of anything approaching intelligence work before 1920. He also had a reputation for amorality, which may have helped.[7]

Winter started as Director of Intelligence in Ireland in May 1920, choosing to be known as 'O'. When he arrived in Dublin he was unimpressed, as he was bound to be, by the state of intelligence there. Like just about every other military man of his time he blamed this on the previous Liberal government's 'parsimony'. In his view the problem was simply one of political will. Lack of it over the past fifteen or twenty years had created a situation in which a minority of conspirators had been able so to 'terrorize the ordinary populace as to render them inarticulate'.[8] If successive governments had taken a firmer line – operated a proper espionage system, found out about the conspiracy and crushed it at its centre – everything would be all right now. The agitators would be locked away, the terrorists hanged, and the people no longer too scared to help the authorities. Violence would have been disarmed, and Ireland would be peaceful, happy and still British. Most of her people wanted to be British, he believed, but were afraid to say.

Winter's task was to help restore Ireland to that condition, if it was not too late. He began by building up an entirely new network of secret intelligence agents, mostly brought over from England because of the difficulty of recruiting Irishmen by this time. This was where Major Cameron came in: as the head of a secret office in London which took on and trained about sixty men to send to Ireland as spies. One of their antagonists later described them as 'crack operators . . . brave men who carried their lives in their hands'.[9] For a few months they succeeded in putting pressure on Collins and his men. Hundreds of raids and arrests were made. One technique was to secrete 'listening sets' in the prison cells of captured IRA suspects, to monitor their conversations. Unfortunately these 'gave poor results, as they were found to be unsuited to the Irish brogue';[10] but they deserve mention as the earliest recorded example of electronic 'bugging' by the British secret service. There was also a plan for agents to assassinate republican leaders covertly, though it is not clear whether or not it was ever implemented;[11] and another to provide the IRA with booby-trapped ammunition. Winter probably regarded these as fair ploys, seeing that his adversaries were doing the same, or worse. 'Was it to be wondered', he asked later, 'that virile men, living in such conditions, should occasionally strike back in retaliation?'[12]

It did not work in the long run, however. Collins had certain advantages. His spies had been in place longer, and were still undisturbed. In 1920 they were given the task of finding out the names of Winter's men, and did. The dirty war between them was effectively won by Collins at nine o'clock on the morning of 'Bloody Sunday', 21 November 1920, when twenty men were targeted for simultaneous assassination by 'The Squad'. One of them escaped unharmed. All the others were woken up and either shot in their rooms or taken into the streets to be butchered. Thirteen died, six were injured. The British government maintained for years afterwards that they were ordinary soldiers, but in fact all of them were leading undercover agents. They had been carefully targeted, in order to undermine Winter's work.

In that they succeeded. 'England', wrote Collins later, 'could always reinforce her army. She could replace every soldier that she lost.' Her spies, however, 'were not so easily replaced'.[13] Men were reluctant to volunteer. If they did, then the authorities may have been too quick to accept them, out of desperation. David Neligan, who had been one of Collins's agents in the DMP before then, described how in the spring of 1921 he went along to the Castle with another man to join the secret service. An official asked them why. They replied that it was because they hated Sinn Fein, and needed the money. That was good enough. 'You are both no friends of the Shinners, clearly!' commented the official; who took them on there and then. Collins was delighted. Among other things the new recruits learned were the secret sign agents made to each other for recognition; how to make invisible ink out of urine; and the British plot to booby-trap IRA ammunition.[14] But by that time the serious intelligence war was already over. 'Bloody Sunday' had been its decisive battle. Thirteen months later the Irish treaty was signed, and southern Ireland was – effectively – lost. Winter left Dublin, no doubt still grumbling about government parsimony, to head a bureau in London where ex-members of the RIC who were scared to stay in Ireland would be assisted to emigrate to the colonies. After that he left Britain. He does not appear in our story again.

It was a bad defeat. What could be learned from it? The trouble was that there were two possible morals, which conflicted. One was that certain situations are intrinsically unconducive to successful espionage: for example, where you have populations who are loyal to your enemies, or can be terrorized by others who are. British intelligence was bound to fail against Collins's tactics in 1919–21, and even if it had been more successful, could not have made any substantial difference to the course of events in the situation of that time. (Britain was critically stretched in other parts of the world besides Ireland.) That was the first moral. It was perfectly plausible. It might also be thought to have been attractive to the intelligence community in one way, because it exonerated them from responsibility for the 1919-21 débâcle. The trouble was, however, that it also undervalued what they did.

So the intelligence community generally plumped for the alternative moral: which was that the débâcle only went to show how vital intelligence was. Britain had held on to Ireland before then through good intelligence, and lost her when that intelligence failed. It followed that intelligence was the crucial factor, and that if it had been better in Ireland around 1920 she would probably be British still. 'I venture to give, as an illustration to show the value of intelligence,' said Sir Reginald 'Blinker' Hall to the House of Commons in November 1921, ' ... our failure to get intelligence about the movements of rebels in Ireland. Had we had a good Intelligence Service such could not have occurred.' That was an early application of the moral. The problem here, of course, was that it seemed to reflect poorly on the intelligence-gatherers themselves. But that could be got over. The trouble in Ireland, claimed Sir Herbert Nield in the same debate, was that 'No officer of the Crown there can depend upon being supported': that is, by ministers. 'That breaks their spirit, breaks their morale, and makes them unfitted to undertake any risks that the situation may require.'[15] The fault, then, as always, lay with a parsimonious and irresolute peacetime government. That was plausible, too.

To compound the problem, Ireland was only one straw – albeit a big one – in the wind. Another came along shortly. At the beginning of November 1921 Sir Basil Thomson was dismissed – or resigned: there were two ways of looking at it – from his post as Director of Intelligence for Britain and the empire. That was the occasion of Hall's remarks about intelligence in Ireland. Hall himself had suffered from government apathy when he had been removed from his own position as Director of Naval Intelligence shortly after the war had ended, with apparently not so much as a word of thanks from anyone who mattered for the patriotic work he had done. (It was after this that he became a Conservative MP.) 'One of the least agreeable traits in the British people', wrote his biographer later, 'is their readiness to drop the pilot as soon as the danger has passed.' Hall's whole point, however, was that the danger was still with them, in a much more menacing form. On the day he left the NID he gathered his staff together and gave them a little homily on this. Of course they were right, he told them, 'to thank God for our victory over the German nation'; but now he wanted to give them 'a word of warning'.

> Hard and bitter as the battle has been, we now have to face a far, far more ruthless foe, a foe that is hydra-headed, and whose evil power will spread over the whole world, and that foe is Russia.

Hence his particular alarm at Thomson's removal, just at the point where, as he put it, 'dangers are ahead'.[16]

Three reasons were given for it. They were distinct, but not incompatible with one another. The first arose out of the Irish troubles, and their extension to Britain in November the year before. This was the third of a series of Fenian and IRA mainland campaigns which had begun in 1867, and is still continuing today. On this occasion it mainly took the form of bombing and incendiary raids on factories and farms, armed hold-ups, attacks on railway signal boxes and telegraph wires, and assassinations of British relatives of the notorious 'Black and Tan' auxiliary police in Ireland. Altogether fifteen people were killed, five of them IRA men, including two who were caught, tried and executed later. One of the others was a police informer in the IRA called Vincent Fovargue, whose body was found on a Middlesex golf course with a note reading 'Let Spies and Traitors beware – IRA' pinned to it, in traditional Irish style. Most of this happened in the first half of 1921. A year later, however, on 22 June 1922, Field Marshal Sir Henry Wilson was also assassinated. He was a committed Ulster Unionist who had recently become security adviser to the new Northern Ireland government. After this there was a respite in Britain from IRA violence until 1938.

Most of this fell on to Basil Thomson's plate. He pulled out all his Special Branch stops: espionage, mail intercepts, raids and the rest, backed up by a new Emergency Powers Act of 1920 (a continuation of DORA), which allowed the deportation and internment of IRA suspects.[17] It is hard to say – as always in these cases, without access to the evidence – how well he did: whether he prevented more outrages than he missed, and whether his efforts had any bearing on the cessation of the campaign. Lloyd George, however, felt that he did not do enough. On 30 October 1921 four young Irishmen were arrested after chalking the slogan 'Up Sinn Fein' in a summer-house on the

Prime Minister's official country estate at Chequers. They were brought to Scotland Yard and interviewed by Thomson, who concluded that 'their act, foolish as it was, was in the nature of a skylark', and let them go. The Prime Minister was livid, and demanded Thomson's head on a charger. The next day he was told to resign.[18] That, at any rate, was one version of the story.

The second is the official one, and recalls the row between Monro and Jenkinson thirty-five years before. A new Metropolitan Police Commissioner, Sir William Horwood, had been appointed in 1920. He resented Thomson's independence, just as Monro had resented Jenkinson's. Like Monro he argued that as he was formally responsible for the whole of the work of the police force, he ought at the very least to be told what Thomson was up to. The latter continued to keep things back from him, and eventually not even to see him for months on end. The Home Secretary decided that this could not go on, and that the best thing consequently would be to bring the Special Branch back under the formal aegis of the CID. Thomson said that if that was done, he would resign. The Home Secretary was adamant, and so Thomson went.[19]

That is the second version. The third may be the most significant: not necessarily because it is closer to the truth, but because of what it says about some contemporary perceptions of the situation. It was hinted at by Horwood in one of his private complaints against Thomson; which was that under him the Special Branch had achieved 'a reputation for espionage on Labour' which had caused 'resentment among a proportion of the working classes'. It also, he told Lloyd George, threatened to offend the common public feeling against 'anything approaching the continental system of domestic espionage'.[20] That last point also recalls Monro and the later Victorians. Thomson's friends in Parliament, who had outgrown Horwood's Victorian prejudices, put it slightly differently. To them it smelled like a plot on the part of the *Daily Herald* and the Labour Party to get rid of Thomson, and probably of the Special Branch too. 'Who says that the Labour Party are unfit to govern?' asked the Conservative MP Sir Frederick Banbury. 'They are governing at the present moment!' Thomson also encouraged the notion that they had 'brought pressure to bear'.[21] The reason, of course, was that he was dangerous to them. He knew all about their Bolshevik tricks. 'He is the only man who has got all the threads in his hand.' Some Labour members scoffed at this. 'I regarded him', said one of them, 'very much as a joke.' His department, far from being a threat, was 'a comic opera, scorned and laughed at by the workers of this country'. But the pro-Thomson brigade was not fooled. 'There will be joy in Moscow over this performance,' claimed Nield. And 'Blinker' Hall immediately moved the adjournment of the House of Commons, in order to discuss what he regarded as 'the grave danger to the public safety" which his removal from office now posed.[22]

That got nowhere. Forty-one MPs supported Hall; 144 voted against. Thomson never returned to public life, and in December 1925 lost all credibility when he was arrested and later tried and convicted, despite a character reference from Hall, for 'fondling' a prostitute in Hyde Park. His story was that he had been there on secret service duty; and that his arrest had been a frame-up by the communists, or by pro-Horwood police.[23] That seems far-fetched, but Hall was willing to credit it. In any case it meant that Thomson was out of commission for good. That was ominous, not only because of the loss of Thomson's own qualities, but because of what it signified more generally.

What it seemed to signify was that the postwar fears of men like Hall and Thomson had been justified. Now that the war was over, the politicians could not be trusted to keep up the country's guard. This was partly through ignorance of the true nature of the Bolshevik threat. Hall and Thomson knew how dangerous that threat was, because they had studied it, and had seen with their own eyes the evidence of the Moscow-backed conspiracy to revolutionize Britain. (There is no room for doubt about this, by the way; it was implicit in the ideology of the Russian Revolution, and it was what the Third Communist International, or 'Comintern', had been specifically set up for in 1919.) They were also aware of the threat because of the way their minds worked. You can acknowledge the existence of a conspiracy without necessarily fearing it, either because you do not accept its potency, or because you sympathize with its aims. Hall and Thomson did fear this conspiracy, first because they believed in the potency of conspiracies generally, and secondly because they loathed socialism in all its forms. In this they were untypical of most of their compatriots, who felt less strongly on these issues than they did.

It was this that lay at the root of many of their difficulties in the 1920s. They were like an exotic species of plant, unsuited to the peacetime climate in Britain, but bred and nurtured in the hothouse environment of the war. When the war ended, and the doors of the hothouse were opened, they would once again be subject to the cooler breezes that prevailed outside. The danger then was that they might wither and die, unless they found some other way to adapt. Ireland and Thomson were symptoms of this process; the first two plants to wither, as the democratic wind suddenly gusted through.

Basil Thomson's eventual successor was Major-General Sir Wyndham Childs, sometimes known as 'Fido', whom we met before as General Macready's secret agent among the strikers in South Wales – the one who was 'exposed' and beaten up. One of Childs's advantages was that he was happy to serve under Horwood, which did not endear him to the Thomson fans. When Sir Henry Wilson was assassinated just a few months after the change-over, and it was discovered that Childs had set no one on to protect him, his stock plummeted even lower. But he was not quite the soft touch his detractors assumed; and on the surface he appears to give the lie to those who thought that by replacing Thomson the government was capitulating to Britain's subversive foes.

He was, for example, sound on communism. 'Sound', in this context, often means uncomprehending. Childs made no bones about this. 'The Communist creed', he wrote later,

> always struck me as peculiar. I will not elaborate upon it, as the subject has been explored time and time again by abler men than myself. Briefly speaking, it seems that the regeneration of England can only come by the elimination of everybody in this country possessing either brains or money. 'Elimination,' I would emphasize, is a term employed in Communist circles as merely a euphemism for assassination.

That was incomprehensible to a rational man. But then the British Communist Party, he went on, did not comprise rational men. Instead it was made up entirely of 'wasters, work-shies, half-wits and professional agitators', most of whom 'had not the slightest idea as to why they were Communists, except that they were generally fed up'. That was the British variety. Abroad it was different: 'for the foreign Communist is merely the Anarchist in a different suit of clothes'. He was the real danger. Communism would never catch on widely in Britain, where the working man was far too solid and sensible; but foreign agitators could cause a lot of incidental damage. They could produce 'untold misery' by fomenting strikes, like the 1926 General Strike, which he insisted was their work; they could corrupt the morals of the young; and they could harm Britain's prestige amongst 'the native population of our great Empire', by giving them the idea that the government was too frightened to turf them out.[24]

So there could be no doubt about Childs's anti-communist credentials. His heart was in the right place. He also managed to achieve a certain amount. This was despite the advent to power of the first (minority) Labour government in Britain in January 1924, which had been expected to be hostile to secret service work of all kinds. He seems to have been quite clever here. On the first occasion he and the new Labour Prime Minister met, Ramsay MacDonald asked to see his own Special Branch file, but was refused.[25] That was a bad start. It was compounded by MacDonald's reaction to the first Special Branch report on subversion in Britain which arrived on his desk, most of which, he claimed, could have been got from the press. That seemed unpromising; but at least MacDonald was not *hostile* to Childs's work. That gave the latter something to work on. He got round MacDonald in two ways. First, he made sure that his reports on left-wing subversion were balanced by others on fascism, to make him seem impartial: which he was, in a way. (He supported the fascists' aims, which he found 'laudable', but disapproved of their methods.)[26] In the second place, he slanted the left-wing side of his reports towards evidence of communist subversion in MacDonald's own Labour Party. This clearly touched a nerve, at a time when the Left was causing the government all kinds of trouble. By the autumn of 1924 the Cabinet was fully persuaded that communists were encouraging strikes, for example, even if it did not go as far as Childs in blaming them entirely; and was ready to ban communists from individual Labour Party membership. In this way Childs, and the Special Branch, managed to stay afloat during this short-lived Labour squall.[27]

At other times the waters were calmer for them anyway. Throughout his whole period as head of the Special Branch Childs kept a close watch on the most obvious sources of communist propaganda and subversion, which were the Communist Party of Great Britain, founded in 1920; and the communist-led National Unemployed Workers' Movement. The communists themselves suspected this, of course, and took counter-measures. Wal Hannington, the leader of the NUWM, proudly recounted in his autobiography how he used to smell out spies and informers – 'a pernicious, toad-like species' – and send them packing. Others he tackled more laterally; like the plain-clothes detective he once spotted on his tail when he was out walking on Hampstead Heath with his small daughter and her friends. The incident is a stark illustration of the lengths to which some communists were prepared to go. Hannington and the children started playing hide-and-seek. 'Sure enough, when I went to hide, he followed; the children did not know who he was and thought he was joining in the game with us.' Hannington then challenged him. He confessed that he was a policeman, that he had been shadowing them since eight o'clock that morning, and that he was 'breaking his neck to "do a piss!"' He could not go behind a bush, in case Hannington gave him the slip. So, wrote Hannington,

> I felt politically and morally justified in increasing his uneasiness, and I knew that in his condition running would not help matters. So I played at long running races with the children, whilst the poor detective, in agony, tried to keep up with us.

That went on for hours, some of them spent in pubs to increase the pressure on the man's bladder.[28] He was one of many police agents Hannington claimed he got the better of.

But he did not spot them all. At least one Special Branch informer appears to have been embedded at the very centre of the NUWM throughout these years, passing reliable intelligence back to Childs.[29] The CPGB was even more riddled. If the police wanted more information on them, they found some excuse to mount a raid, when they went through their correspondence and membership lists. There was a big one, for example, on the headquarters of the CPGB on 14 October 1925. The police also had the resources of the Post Office to help them intercept letters; and of a newer and more hush-hush agency, called GC & CS (for Government Code and Cipher School: later to become GCHQ), to tap into the CPGB's line to Moscow. The communists were pretty well covered. Little went on, at least among the overt membership of these bodies, that was not seen.

It was not always seen clearly or accurately. We know this not from British official sources, which are closed to us, but from elsewhere. The Special Branch spread its net wide. It had close links, for example, with the inter-war 'Investigation Branch' in Australia, which was a kind of equivalent agency there. Sometimes it tried to help by forwarding to the latter reports on suspect Bolsheviks or Irish Nationalists who were thought to be living in Australia, or on their way. Present-day Australia has a far more liberal policy on official historical records than Britain has, which means that those reports can be seen there. Some of them were clearly exaggerated, or even totally wrong.[30] There is no reason to suppose that they were in any way untypical of the rest.

How far beyond this the British Special Branch went is not clear. It certainly kept a watch on trade union and Labour Party branches, in search of communist influence there. Later on – after Childs's time – there is evidence of Special Branch espionage amongst the 1930s hunger marchers, including a report by an informer at a meeting between marchers and MPs at the House of Commons; and on the newly formed National Council for Civil Liberties, on account of the 'well-known … antipathy against the police' of its secretary, Ronald Kidd. This has come to light in documents which were apparently accidentally released by the police to the Public Record Office some time in the 1960s, before being mysteriously withdrawn again.[31] There are likely to be others like them, still considered too sensitive to be revealed to historians after more than fifty years. What they contain can only be guessed at. Contemporary radicals would not have been surprised to find proof in them of police acting as *agents provocateurs*. This was the sort of thing that Hannington suspected, when men came to him with hair-raising schemes for 'making the ruling class sit up'.[32] There are eyewitness accounts during the unemployed marches of men dressed as workers urging their comrades on to violence, and then turning round and arresting them.[33] All this would have been in order to alienate public sympathy from the marchers. But there is no hard evidence that it was ever done.

Childs's greatest coup was the police raid he led on the London offices of 'Arcos', the official Soviet trading company, in May 1927. Arcos was something of an obsession with Childs, who was entirely against any kind of diplomatic or commercial relations with Russia, on the grounds that a communist government was 'incapable of honouring any agreement with a "bourgeois" State'.[34] That was the main point of contention between him and Labour, who were responsible for the resumption of relations; but in the end Childs got his way. The raid was authorized after a tip-off that Arcos was being used as a cover for espionage activities, and had in its possession a secret signals manual that had gone missing from the War Office. It was a dramatic and very public event, involving 150 policemen (fifty from the Special Branch), pneumatic drills and oxyacetylene torches for breaking into strongrooms, and the confiscation of 250,000 documents, all over a period of four days. The missing manual was never found, and the raid caused a great fuss in Parliament; but the government reckoned it had enough evidence of secret *propaganda* activities being carried on behind the Arcos façade to justify a rupture in Anglo-Russian relations again. That was announced later in the month.[35]

Childs was delighted by this; but overall he was frustrated during his time at Scotland House. When he had first taken over there he had been told by an official at the Home Office that smashing communism was to be 'the most important part' of his work.[36] But two things held him back. The first was that he was just not given the necessary official support: even under Conservative ministries. 'I have never been able to comprehend', he later wrote, 'why the successive governments I served always refused to strike one overwhelming and final blow' against communism in Britain. The blow he had in mind was a simple legal ban on the Communist Party and everything associated with it. After 1924 he thought he had an ally in Sir William Joynson Hicks, the Conservative Home Secretary, whose 'enthusiasm', as he wrote, 'almost exceeded my own', and who would undoubtedly have succeeded in wiping out the CPGB entirely 'had he had his way'. 'Jix' was held back, however, by Stanley Baldwin, who Childs believed was the main inter-war obstacle to a resolute anti-socialist offensive in Britain.[37]

This perception was almost certainly correct. Baldwin was a conciliator, a consensus politician, a paternalist who wished to bring peace to the class war, and restore national harmony. That made him both ideologically and temperamentally unfitted to fight the threat from the Left. On clear cases of external subversion he was sound enough: hence the Arcos raid. When it came to more insidious dangers, however, he seemed oblivious. One source of those dangers was thought to be the trade unions. Some right-wingers suspected that they were in Moscow's pay. Even if they were not, they were somehow *intrinsically* alien: foreign to the national character, divisive, undermining Britain's economy and strength; an 'enemy within'. There were constant calls for curbs on them: for legislation to remove their pre-war immunities, for example, and to require strike ballots, protect 'blacklegs', prohibit 'sympathetic' strike action and limit trade unions' political funds. Baldwin resisted them. Worse: on one notorious occasion he gave in to the enemy, cravenly. That was on 'Red Friday', 31 July 1925, when he bought off striking miners with the promise of a £23 million government subsidy to help pay their wages while a Royal Commission looked into their case. Many in his own Cabinet were deeply shocked by this. Joynson Hicks thought it raised the question of who ruled the country: 'The Government or the trade unions?'[38]

Put like this, it made the unions out to be a direct challenge to the state. Yet here was the chief executive of the state, parleying and treating with them. It was just as the Right had long feared. Elected governments could not be trusted to meet the threat of the enemy within.

The second thing holding Childs back was that he would not take matters into his own hands. He was too much of an old soldier, respecting the orders given to him by his formal superiors, and clear about where his duty lay. Others were not. Many intelligence officers, both then and afterwards, saw their loyalties as transcending their political masters, especially if those masters were Labour, and attaching to something – an ideal or a principle or an interpretation of the 'national interest' – which could override their allegiance to mere governments. One man whose actions in 1916 showed quite clearly that he thought in this way was Reginald Hall, who was admonished in the Basil Thomson debate in 1921 for being 'more royalist than the King'.[39] Thomson was like that too. Childs never was. He had strong 'royalist' prejudices, but never pursued them in defiance of his 'King'. He was always, so far as we can tell, strictly correct. He strongly deplored incorrect behaviour in men and organizations, like the fascists, whose ideals he otherwise shared. He was happy to take orders from Horwood, whom he liked anyway, and to work with MacDonald, though he disagreed with him fundamentally on many things. 'My life was one long attempt', he wrote in his memoirs, 'to keep an even balance and judgment';[40] which reads oddly in the light of his political prejudices, but may fairly characterize his practical dealings with those he was politically prejudiced against. Above all, Childs knew where his formal allegiance lay, and would probably never attempt, even in defence of civilization as he knew it against the Red menace, to circumvent or undermine it. This was why, in the last analysis, he was a poor substitute for Basil Thomson, and bound to be a disappointment to the likes of Reginald Hall.

For those who were most alarmed by the Red menace, all this official pusillanimity boded ill. Of course they had other defences. During the course of the 1920s and 1930s a whole range of laws was enacted, some of them continuations of wartime measures, others entirely new, to help the government deal with any revolutionary or subversive threat. They included, for example, a tightening of the Official Secrets Act in 1920; an Emergency Powers Act, passed the same year, which we have come across already; a Trades Disputes Act to curb unions, passed in 1927, just after the General Strike; an Incitement to Disaffection law enacted to stop communist propaganda amongst the armed forces in 1934; a new Public Order Act of 1936; and a number of separate measures for Northern Ireland.[41] As well as these the army devised schemes to help in emergency situations, including plans for intelligence-gathering; and an agency known then as the Supply and

Transport Organization (now the Civil Contingencies Unit) was set up early in 1920 to provide logistical assistance to the authorities in the event of serious disturbances or a general strike. (The Labour government of 1924 was kept in the dark about it.)[42] All this was fine, so far as it went. The problem was that most of it was *contingency* planning only. And contingency planning is only effective, as any good military man will tell you, if you have adequate ongoing intelligence to tell you what the likely contingencies are.

This was where the private and semi-private sectors came in. If governments persisted in neglecting this vital area of internal defence, then it was up to right-minded citizens to take up the burden themselves. Many of them did, enthusiastically. The work clearly appealed to a certain kind of right-wing personality. Childs, with his strictly 'correct' view of these things, found them a constant 'source of trouble'. That was partly because they tended to be 'alarmist', and partly because some of them undertook 'illegal acts which were frequently attributed to me'.[43] That may explain many of the spies and *agents provocateurs* spotted by Hannington and the NCCL, for example, in the 1920s and 1930s: who are just as likely to have been these private enterprise agents as undercover policemen or members of MI5. It makes the full picture of domestic intelligence in Britain in this period a very complicated one, with others besides the official secret services burrowing beneath the communists and their friends.

They had two sorts of sponsors. The first were the industrial, commercial and banking interests which felt financially threatened by (in particular) trade union militancy. The Economic League, which we have met before, is an example, with most of its funds coming from industry and its central council representing large firms.[44] It was one of a number of such organizations, whose main emphasis was on propaganda and parliamentary lobbying, but which sometimes developed intelligence functions too. It was they whom Childs characterised as 'alarmist'. He gave an example.

> I remember on one occasion I met a well-known public man in a state of considerable excitement ... He said that he thought I ought to know that four battalions of Communists were established south of the Thames, all armed with revolvers and capable of mobilization under an hour; that the scheme was to chloroform the guard at Buckingham Palace and blow up the bridges over the Thames.[45]

The source of that hot piece of intelligence was one of these commercially sponsored agencies. We know very little about them apart from glimpses like this. The Economic League seems to have taken up this work around 1925. In that year it announced that it had accumulated 'a considerable body of information on "red" ramifications and methods', which it was circulating to branches confidentially; and that it was arranging to set up 'a permanent clearing house of information in connection with alien organizations and individuals'.[46] How it came by this information we do not know for sure. We do know, however, in the case of a similar agency, the British Empire Union, which not only spied on workers but also engaged in covert operations against the communists. These included stealing papers, setting off stink bombs at Communist Party congresses and on at least one occasion forging a letter to the press, supposedly from the communist leader Harry Pollitt, in order to antagonize the TUC.[47] That happened. But how common this kind of activity was, we cannot tell.

The other main category of private intelligence agencies in the 1920s and 1930s was political. Childs found these 'an intolerable nuisance' too.[48] There is no evidence or indication that either the Liberal or the Labour parties ever got up to this sort of thing, though it is conceivable. That is possibly because they were not clever enough, but more likely because they were more scrupulous, or temperamentally unsuited to it. The main offenders in the 1920s and 1930s were the fascists, and the Conservative Party. The Conservatives set up 'a little intelligence service of our own' in 1927, under an ex-MI5 man called Major Joseph Ball. His main target was the Labour Party, where he apparently managed to place spies at every level.[49] Other private intelligence organizations appear to have been formally independent of both industry and party politics. A man called George McGill, code-named 'G', ran a very shady one until his death (possibly by foul means) in 1926. As well as subversion, it made inquiries into drug-trafficking, the white slave trade and black magic cults. Shortly before his death 'G' recruited – via an undercover agent known as 'H' – a young man called John Baker White to work on the anti-communist side. He came to head 'Section D' of the organization, which carried on after 1926. One of its members was in close touch with the communist Percy Glading; another had a job in Arcos; a third was in the IRA; and a fourth – a naturalist known as 'Max' – could have been Maxwell Knight.[50]

These identifications are important, because they establish what may be some important connections. John Baker White became Director of the Economic League in 1926, and in his later career a member of military intelligence and a Conservative MP. Maxwell Knight joined MI5 in 1925. McGill himself, so White tells us, was a close friend of the Director of MI5, Vernon Kell, and 'could always see the Permanent Secretary to the Cabinet whenever he wished and at short notice'.[51] The Conservatives' intelligence chief after 1927, Joseph Ball, kept in touch (naturally) with his former colleagues in MI5.[52] Another man active in the Conservative Party organization, and in the Economic League, was Admiral Sir Reginald 'Blinker' Hall, the ex-head of NID. Interconnections like this, between political rightists, the Conservative Party, private security organizations and the official secret services, could be multiplied at least a dozenfold. Is there a conspiracy looming here? Or is the paranoia which is an occupational hazard of reading and writing about espionage beginning to creep up on us too?

One undoubted plot which involved most of these elements was the famous Zinoviev affair in October 1924. Briefly, it involved a letter allegedly written by the president of Comintern (Grigori Zinoviev) to the CPGB urging it to press forward the cause of revolution in Britain through its agents in the armed forces and its sympathizers in the Labour Party. It had been intercepted by MI6, though we are not sure how. As soon as he heard of it Ramsay MacDonald drafted a protest to the Russian government; but this could not prevent disaster for his government when the letter was published in the British press just three days before the general election of 29 October 1924. The Conservative-inclined section of the press used the letter as a means of discrediting the Labour government's recent establishment of diplomatic and commercial relations with Soviet Russia, and as evidence of Labour's links with Bolshevism. The sequel was that Labour lost the election, and the Conservatives returned to power.

The Zinoviev letter may have been a forgery, possibly by Russian émigrés in Berlin. If it was, it was a good one. Whether it was or not, it was exploited for partisan ends by a group of men working together secretly (the definition of a 'plot'). Three interests were involved. The first was the press, and in particular the *Daily Mail*. The second was Conservative Central Office, which paid £5,000 for the letter in order to be able to use it in this way. Thirdly, several members and ex-members of the security services were implicated, including Donald im Thurn, ex-MI5, who was at the hub of it all; our old friend 'Blinker' Hall, ex-NID; and Freddie Browning, ex-deputy head of MI6. These were all men who were seized with a burning hatred of Russia and communism, a strong belief in the vital necessity of intelligence work, and a deep distrust of the Labour government. Their action was taken in the best interests of the nation, as they saw it. They also believed that it was effective: that it was this which was responsible for restoring Baldwin to power. That was also Labour's view.[53]

It is easy to see why both sides needed to believe this: the conspirators in order to justify their efforts, and Labour in order to find a scapegoat for its defeat. Whether or not that defeat can be explained as easily as this is questionable. What the letter did was to put the finishing touches to an anti-Red hysteria that was already there, and being exploited by the Conservatives' election managers anyway. It did not create the hysteria. Consequently it cannot be blamed for the full extent of Labour's defeat. In fact it may be wrong to regard it as a 'defeat' at all. Labour actually gained a million votes between 1923 and October 1924. Zinoviev cannot have lost them any votes on balance, therefore, though it may have prevented their winning more. The real victims of the October election were the Liberals, who lost votes and parliamentary seats catastrophically. That may have been partly due to a stiffening of the *anti*-Labour vote, encouraged by Zinoviev. We cannot tell. Overall the Zinoviev affair was probably of marginal importance in practical terms. Which is not to say that it was not highly significant in other ways.

Its significance lies in the fact that it is the first major known instance in modern British history of men associated with the official secret services acting independently of the government of the day, and in collusion with that government's political opponents, with the object of undermining it. We have come across two lesser instances before. One was Robert Anderson's conduct in the *Times*/Parnell controversy of 1889; the other was Reginald Hall's manipulation of Casement's arrest in order to discredit a Liberal Irish viceroy in 1916. In all three of these cases the men concerned acted in obedience to what they saw as a 'higher' allegiance than to their constitutionally elected masters. That, of course, is a development of tremendous import, which entirely overshadows the question of whether or not the Zinoviev letter was a forgery. If it was, and Hall or im Thurn knew or suspected it, then it says something about how compelling their higher allegiance was, to provoke them so far. It is an intriguing mystery. But it is not crucial. The important aspect of the Zinoviev affair is this: that it may indicate a tendency on the part of the secret services, or sections of the secret services, or men connected with sections of the secret services, to slide from being simply the secret agents of the state, which is one thing, into something very different: a 'secret state' in its own right, separate and independent from the overt British state, acting according to different rules and in obedience to different loyalties, and in certain circumstances – when the overt state is not pursuing what the secret service community considers to be the national interest – prepared to use its knowledge, connections and powers to obstruct and even to try to overturn it.

There is no denying the tendency. The question is: how far was it kept under control? There are no signs for the rest of the inter-war period that intelligence or ex-intelligence men ever acted in that sort of way again. Winston Churchill was supplied with secret reports while he was out of office after 1929, which he used to undermine the government's position on disarmament. The man who supplied them to him, however, Major Desmond Morton (who later became his private secretary), had the written permission of three successive prime ministers to do this.[54] There may well have been other cases of the secret services being used for partisan purposes, especially by the Conservatives, with their strong links with the intelligence community; but nothing as important as Zinoviev which has come to light. If this is a true reflection of the real situation, and does not merely indicate some clever concealment, it must be because later on in this period things on the subversive front became more reassuring, so that even the most paranoid of anti-communists did not feel driven to such desperate measures as in 1924.

The official secret service certainly believed the danger had diminished, after about the middle of the 1920s. Its cabinet reports on revolutionary organizations in Britain slowed down considerably, from one a week in 1919 to only four a year by 1933.[55] The failure of the General Strike was a terrible blow for militant Labour, and a boost for right-wing morale. Thereafter growing unemployment – peaking at 2,745,000 in 1932 – cowed the labour force and weakened the trade union movement grievously, as it so often does. Communist efforts to revolutionize the masses did not stop; but now it was more often done covertly – through 'infiltration' – than by open propaganda.[56] That was worrying in its way, but it was also a sign of weakness, and there is no evidence that it went on to any very widespread extent. The number of people who believed in the imminence of Red revolution in the 1930s was minuscule, compared to the previous decade. They really *had* to be paranoiacs.

Those of them who were members of the secret services will have been encouraged by another development too: an important internal change. Among all the different secret service agencies of the 1920s, one was an obvious odd man out. That was the Special Branch under Wyndham Childs; which was different from the other intelligence services in a number of ways. It was more clearly accountable to government and Parliament, through the Metropolitan Police Commissioner and the Home Secretary. It recruited from an entirely different social stratum: from the working and lower-middle classes, who formed the bulk of the uniformed policemen the branch ultimately got its officers from. They were brought up professionally in a policing tradition which emphasized different values and ideals of behaviour from the intelligence services, as we have seen it always had. Very often assistant commissioners, despite being appointed from outside, absorbed some of these values when they joined, and so became distanced from the rest of the intelligence community themselves. We saw this happening in the 1880s to James Monro; it did not happen in the 1910s to Basil Thomson, who resisted the virus, and did his best to counter it with antibodies of his own, which accounted in part for his row with Horwood; but Wyndham Childs, despite his extreme right-wing political views, fell victim to it, as we have seen, very early on. From the point of view of the rest of the intelligence community, he was not really – and his subordinates were even less so – 'one of them'. That may be why he was probably not implicated in the Zinoviev affair (he won a libel case against a journal which claimed otherwise): because he was not invited to take part.[57]

The Special Branch's star, however, was on the wane. In the late 1920s MI5 began retrieving some of the counter-subversive functions Kell had lost to Thomson's new 'Directorate of Intelligence' at the end of the war. In September 1931 the process was apparently completed, with all the Special Branch's responsibilities for investigating 'the Communist and foreign revolutionary movements' being transferred to MI5. The Special Branch then became – what it has remained ever since – MI5's dogsbodies in this field, doing its leg-work for it. The reason given for the change was that when espionage and subversion were as closely related as they seemed to be then (via Moscow), it made little sense to send separate 'packs of hounds' after each.[58] But it had other implications too. One lasting one has been to make it more difficult for historians to find out about covert counter-subversion in Britain after 1931, because MI5 has always been less accountable and consequently *more* covert than the Special Branch. That may have been one of the attractions of the new arrangement to those who, like Austen Chamberlain, believed that it was 'of the essence of a Secret Service that it must be secret'.[59] Another result was to concentrate counter-subversion in Britain from then on almost entirely in the hands of the members of a particular social class: the upper-middles. Hence the 'hounds' metaphor, which came naturally to them.

We are treading on very soft ground indeed here; but this could have had a profound effect on the ethos and behaviour of the British domestic secret service from this time on. Its members were an odd bunch in many ways. All of them were recruited *personally*, from among the friends and acquaintances of men and women already serving in MI5 or MI6. That made them socially extremely exclusive, and close-knit. They all had similar backgrounds and upbringings, and the same narrow range of views. This was reflected in trivial ways, like the silly names they used for each other: Woolly, Buster, Biffy, Bubbles, Blinker, Barmy, Tin-Eye, and so on; which reads rather like a roll-call of Snow White's Seven Dwarfs. This was normal ex-public-school practice, even when the ex-public schoolboys had become fully grown men. They liked 'japes', 'wheezes' and 'mad-cap adventures', which is another characteristic which to an outsider might be mistaken for a sign of arrested development, but was normal for that set. They tended to treat their work as a kind of game: Mansfield Cumming, for example, the first head of MI6, once described it as 'capital sport'.[60] As with other games the rules could be a little complicated, but the object was straightforward, and did not require any great moral or political agonizing to discover or defend it. Like the character 'R' in *Ashenden*, the fictionalized account of his own wartime secret service activities abroad which Somerset Maugham published in 1928, they probably 'regarded intro-spection as unhealthy, un-English and unpatriotic'.[61] Their view of the world tended to be simple and Manichean, with British good being pitted against foreign – usually communist – evil, in an endless struggle to preserve their understanding of the Anglo-Saxon (or Anglo-Norman) way of life. Many of them appear to have modelled themselves on another fictional secret agent, John Buchan's brave, upper-class, resourceful and incorrigibly xenophobic Richard Hannay in *The Thirty-Nine Steps*, which had come out in 1915. Some of them wrote novels themselves, usually sub-Buchan adventure stories full of similar racial and political prejudices, which presumably reflected their own.[62]

Those prejudices also served to break down what had until then been the biggest obstacle to upper-middle-class participation in secret service work in the past, which was the gentlemanly ethic of open and honest behaviour towards one's fellow men. The flaw in that, of course, was that one's fellow men did not necessarily share that ethic, especially if they were not gentlemen themselves. That could give them a dangerous advantage over you. The corollary of this (a new one) was that the gentlemanly ethic need only apply *among* gentlemen; which acted as a release for the amoral energies that may have been particularly strong in the sort of men and women who undertook secret service work. They justified their amorality in two ways. The first was that national survival depended on it: during the First World War, for example, because of the 'total' nature of it; and against the Red menace, which was also 'total', though in a different (ideological) sense. The second was that the enemy was acting even more amorally, which made it necessary to respond in kind. This was sometimes exaggerated: in the case of the Germans during the First World War, for example; but that is not to say that secret service people did not believe it genuinely.

Some of them admitted to feeling uneasy, at least occasionally, about the means they were forced to use. Joan Miller, who worked for MI5 during the Second World War, later claimed that she was always having to struggle against 'an instinctive aversion' to what she was doing, and an 'inescapable sense of guilt'. When another agent bedded a girl working for the CPGB in order to seduce information out of her, and then got her interned, Joan Miller considered it 'shabby', and claimed that the head of his department did too. But they used the information nevertheless, and kept the agent on.[63] There is clearly some ambivalence here. Somerset Maugham's 'R' copes with it, cynically, by employing foreigners to do his dirtiest work for him, so that the department 'could put their clean hands on their hearts and congratulate themselves that they had never done anything that was unbecoming to men of honour'. One such foreign sub-agent is 'the Hairless Mexican', who has been known to shoot a man in a bar for coming between him and his drink, and to slit the throat of a beautiful girl in her sleep after making love to her because he suspected that she was informing on him. He also wears scent. 'He hasn't had the advantages of a public school education. His ideas of playing the game are not quite the same as yours or mine,' explains 'R'.[64] Hence his utility, to men who were still at any rate *half*-shackled to the ancient ideals of their class.

Joan Miller and Somerset Maugham may not be the most reliable of witnesses to this kind of thing. Nevertheless there was a clear contradiction here, a tension between what these people had been taught was right and what seemed necessary, which had to be resolved somehow. That same contradiction may help to explain another characteristic of the inter-war intelligence community: which was the eccentricity of the personal lives and behaviour of many of its members. Either that, or the class from which they were mainly chosen was particularly generously peppered with eccentrics, which is possible. It is this profusion of eccentricity which makes many books about the British secret services such fun to read.[65] It may also be misleading. The adjective most often found qualifying the noun 'eccentric' is 'harmless'; and it must be questionable whether MI5 and MI6 were as ineffective as this implies. Whether anything deeper can be read into these characteristics of the inter-war intelligence community is difficult to say. A psychologist or a sociologist might want to make something of them. For a historian, however, it is probably safest to stick to the most obvious point: which is that they are yet another indication of the growing isolation, and hence potential alienation, of the secret services from the huge majority of the British people and their values.

A good example of this alienation is Maxwell Knight, who became the head of MI5's main counter-subversive section, known as B(5)b, just before the change-over of 1931. His code-name was 'M', for Maxwell, because they already had a 'K'. He had originally been recruited to MI5 in the spring of 1925 at a dinner party by 'K' himself (Vernon Kell), who liked the cut of his jib. In fact (like most jibs) it was cut a little askew. Knight's father had been a scion of an aristocratic Welsh family, but had bankrupted himself, mainly through his generosity to a series of mistresses in the south of France. He died when 'Max' was 13. By that time the young Knight was a withdrawn boy, whose main interest lay in caterpillars. Later he was to become something of an expert on natural history, disconcerting guests with his method of hatching adders' eggs in his pyjama pockets, and having his own nature study programme on children's radio in the 1950s as 'Uncle Max'. At 13, however, he merely seemed difficult. So he was sent to a school for difficult boys, which was also a merchant navy training ship (HMS *Worcester*) anchored in the Thames. Like most public schools of the time, but more so, the regime there was spartan, and the other boys could be cruel. 'New shits', as they were called, had to pass through an initiation ceremony where they crawled along the floor of a deck, being beaten by their seniors with pieces of thick knotted rope as they passed. Homosexual relationships, between senior boys and younger ones known as 'jams', were rife.[66] None of this was unusual at public schools at that time. It may have been possible to survive it and come out at the end of it a normal, balanced young man. Some young men undoubtedly came through this kind of experience *believing* they had survived. Knight may not have been able to fool himself to that extent.

His abnormalities in adult life are by now well known. His most notorious one is his sexual impotence with women, which may have driven his first wife to suicide, and certainly drove the second one to divorce. In the end he did manage a successful marriage, with a woman who had had a bad experience in her own early life which had put her off sex. Joan Miller, who lived with him between his second and third wives, thought he was a homosexual after spotting him one day putting on a 'mincing' gait in front of his good-looking young mechanic, and suspected that he might possibly be being blackmailed on account of it. He also became fascinated by the occult and black magic, partly through his friendship with the fantasy novelist Dennis Wheatley, whom he employed on one or two missions for MI5.[67] He was one of our John Buchan fans, and shared most of his prejudices, against Jews, foreigners, bureaucrats, homosexuals (overtly, at any rate) and socialists. Some of these prejudices are indicated, crudely, in a couple of 'thrillers' he wrote in the mid-1930s.[68] Joan Miller described his views on the communist threat as 'almost an obsession'.[69] All the evidence points to his having been a clever, personable, right-wing extremist, with one or two behavioural eccentricities which together may have added up to a serious personality disorder. That, of course, does not mean that he was not good at his job.

You do not have to be 'normal' in order to be efficient in secret service work, and in some circumstances it probably helps not to be. Maxwell Knight had some great successes with B(5)b before the war, which made him into something of a legend, though of course a highly secret one. (Some of them may have been exaggerated.) His particular skill was for infiltrating agents deep into subversive organizations, for fairly long periods of time. He was very clever about this. He chose his agents carefully, to appeal (politically or on other grounds) to the groups he wanted to infiltrate. In his two most celebrated cases these were women. He took his time: not seeking instant success, but allowing his agents to worm their way in slowly, in order to gain the confidence of the men and women they hoped to betray. His approach was indirect; not to the Communist Party, for example, in the first place, but to a fringe organization, where he would send one of his people to get work as a helper or a clerk, and hope that the approach to join the communists would come from them. That, in fact, was the pattern followed in the most celebrated of his prewar triumphs.

That starred Olga Gray, who when Knight's secretary recruited her in 1931 was the 19-year-old daughter of an impoverished upper-middle-class mother who was active in the Conservative Party. Knight – perceptively – saw that this background fitted her admirably for the role of an intelligent young woman whose circumstances had led her to rebel against her class upbringing and values, and turn to communism; which was not an unusual pattern then. She started attending meetings of the Friends of the Soviet Union in the autumn of 1931, taking on typing work for them, and eventually undertaking a secret mission to India for the CPGB's General Secretary, Harry Pollitt. It was only after this, in 1934 or 1935, that Pollitt asked her to come and work at party headquarters. At every stage the initiatives for Olga Gray's progress from the periphery to the centre of the party had come from the party itself, and not from her. From there she pulled off her greatest coup in January 1938: which was the unmasking of the 'Woolwich Arsenal Spy Ring'. This involved the communist Percy Glading, who Olga Gray discovered was obtaining blueprints of secret weapon parts from a disaffected worker at the Arsenal in order to smuggle them to the Soviets. (Knight may have picked up Glading first through McGill's 'Section D'.)[70] Glading and his collaborators were tried, convicted and imprisoned in March. It was a great triumph. The only drawback was that it meant the end of Olga Gray as an agent, because she was needed to give evidence in court, which blew her cover. Afterwards she claimed that Knight 'dumped' her, to her lasting resentment.[71]

But Knight had other agents. One was Bill Younger, a member of the brewing family, and an Oxford undergraduate in 1933, who was asked to spy on his fellow students. Another was Tom Driberg, who at that time combined membership of the CPGB with authorship of the William Hickey column in the *Daily Express*, and later became a prominent Labour MP. He was eventually rumbled by the communists in 1941 – probably tipped off by Anthony Blunt, who was *their* agent in MI5 – and expelled from the party then.[72] There were dozens more. It seems likely that MI5 had British communism pretty well covered in the 1930s. That was important to the secret service, which for most of this period continued to regard the communists as Britain's main threat.

They may have exaggerated it, and neglected the threat from the political Right as a consequence. This is a charge sometimes levelled against them. It may not be fair, for two reasons. The first is that the communist subversive threat really was more serious than the fascist one. Russia did have designs on Britain. There was an active British Communist Party, tied to Moscow, and with a large reservoir of potential allies for 'popular fronts' on issues like unemployment or the civil war in Spain. By contrast fascism in Britain was risible, except possibly for a brief period between the foundation of Mosley's British Union in October 1932 and the notorious Olympia rally of June 1934, after which it declined. It got little support from Hitler, partly because he, too, was unimpressed by Mosley, and partly because he saw Britain as a potential ally against the Bolsheviks. If there was a subversive danger from this general direction in these years, then it was from people high up in the British establishment who were keen to respond to this. A number of names have been mooted in this connection, with the Duke of Windsor's usually at the top of the list. Whether MI5 had its eyes on developments at this level, or was even – just conceivably – implicated, there is no way of telling. Otherwise, however, the German subversive threat seemed mild. For many years Hitler even refused to send spies to Britain.[73] It was scarcely worth bothering with.

Yet the secret services did bother with it. This is the other reason for suspending judgement on them. Knight's branch, for example, began watching the activities of the Mosley's British Union of Fascists systematically from some time in 1933, which was not so long after their formation. One of its agents there from 1934 to 1938 was the ex-Tory MP Bill Allen. The Special Branch took an interest in the fascists too, mainly to help the uniformed police deal with the street riots their marches were provoking. MI5 also kept a watch on 'fringe' and 'front' German organisations in Britain, like the Anglo-German Information Service in London, which was the fascist equivalent of the Friends of the Soviet Union on the Left.[74] Whether this was as close or as committed a watch as they kept on the communists and their 'cryptos' is hard to say; but it was something. It meant that when the second war against Germany began, in September 1939, they had some sort of foundation on which to build.

Chapter 9

Dazzled and confused
(1940–70)

In 1940 Germany was planning to invade England. In preparation the Gestapo produced a handbook, the *Informationsheft GB*, about the country and its people, for the use of the occupying forces when they arrived. One of its sections dealt with intelligence. This, it averred, was 'a field in which the British, by virtue of their tradition, their experience, and certain facets of their national character – unscrupulousness, self-control, cool deliberateness and ruthless action – have achieved an unquestionable degree of mastery'. The key to this success lay in the English public school system, which was 'calculated to rear men of inflexible will and ruthless energy who regard intellectual problems as a waste of time but know human nature and how to dominate other men in the most unscrupulous fashion'. The Germans greatly envied this. 'What *we* need', said Hitler on another occasion, 'is something like the British Secret Service – an Order, doing its work with passion.'[1] This was quite a tribute, and perceptive in many ways.

It also, however, proved difficult to live up to. On the whole the British secret service is reckoned to have had a good Second World War. It is difficult to be certain, because the documentary evidence is still classified, and most of the informed histories are written by ex-secret service men and officially vetted. One undoubted success was in the field of signals interception and cryptography (today called 'Sigint'), where the achievements of the team which developed the 'Enigma' codebreaking machine at Bletchley Park in Buckinghamshire have become legendary. If that is taken away, however, the record is more patchy. In the older-fashioned field of 'Humint' (or 'human intelligence') all the wartime British secret service agencies had some dire failures, as well as brilliant successes. So far as domestic counter-subversion is concerned, their achievement on balance was probably negative.

They had a difficult task, mainly because it was – initially, at any rate – intangible. Early on in the war the public perception of the subversive threat to Britain far exceeded the reality. This created problems for MI5 and the Special Branch, which were being asked to uncover and take action against dangers which, to a great extent, did not exist. Rumours abounded, just as they had in 1914. Foreign agents were parachuting into England dressed as nuns, and into Scotland dressed as stags. They were flashing messages to the Luftwaffe, poisoning children's sweets, misdirecting convoys, and escaping detection by swallowing 'fog pills' which enveloped them in small clouds. Obviously there was no truth in most of this; but there was just enough to set the government worrying too. Some spies were caught, usually after giving themselves away stupidly (one ordered cider in a pub at breakfast time, for example); but that only gave cause for concern about the non-stupid ones. 'My experience', said the Commander-in-Chief of the Home Forces to a group of Home Guards in June 1940, 'is that the gentlemen who are the best behaved and the most sleek are those who are doing the mischief': in other words, the least suspicious-looking are the ones to be suspected most. That was confusing.[2] In January 1940 a serious explosion at a gunpowder factory at Waltham Abbey started a widespread hunt for German saboteurs, though it was just as likely to have been an accident. There was, of course, a real and significant threat from German 'fifth columnists'; but in the heat of the moment it was almost certainly exaggerated.

Measures taken to counter it included draconian new treason laws, internment without trial and a new crime of 'defeatism'. People were warned in a famous poster campaign that 'careless talk' – with spies around – 'cost lives'. Public-spirited men and women organized themselves into 'Silent Columns' to detect and expose people who were speaking disparagingly about Britain's chances in the war. They came to be known as 'Cooper's Snoopers', after the Minister of Information, Duff Cooper, who had thought up the idea, and should have known better; for the scheme was intensely unpopular (demonstrating that the traditional British distaste for espionage was not yet dead), and soon dropped. Thereafter most of the serious counter-subversive work was left to the professional snoopers, in MI5.

At first they seemed to do very badly. They failed to uncover any significant German fifth-column activity at all during the first few months; probably because there was none to speak of, but Churchill assumed it was because they were incompetent. A few months after the Waltham Abbey explosion, in June 1940, he sacked their head (and founder), Vernon Kell, whom he got on badly with anyway. Maxwell Knight and his B(5)b remained in place. That was just part of a major intelligence reorganization, by which a new 'Security

Executive' was created to oversee all the various agencies, under the ex-Air Minister Lord Swinton and the Conservative Party's chief spymaster, Joseph (now Sir Joseph) Ball. In November 1940 a replacement was finally found for Kell at MI5 in Sir David Petrie, whose previous intelligence experience had been in India.

Under Petrie MI5 had some successes. The biggest one was undoubtedly the 'double-cross system' it managed to operate from the autumn of 1940 onwards, which worked by persuading captured German spies and others to act as double agents on Britain's behalf. (Someone in MI5 may have remembered the old Friedrich Müller trick from the First World War, or Basil Thomson's success in 'turning' an Indian revolutionary called Harish Chandra in 1916.)[3] It was run by a subsection called 'B(1)a', which co-opted a number of new people, mostly academics, for the purpose. One of them, J. C. Masterman, later published a detailed account of the system, which was technically in breach of the Official Secrets Act and (probably) the law of confidentiality; but no one in authority bothered with it then, possibly because it showed what clever boys they all were. One of B(1)a's double agents, Wulf Schmidt, managed to pull the wool over the Germans' eyes for more than five years, relaying false messages by radio to Hamburg, and being rewarded for his efforts with the Iron Cross First Class. Another famous one, a Yugoslav with a playboy life-style called Dusko Popov, is supposed to have been the model for James Bond. B(1)a also used Britons as double agents: an Englishman called Bill Owens, for example, who as a supposed 'traitor' penetrated deep into the Abwehr; and a Welsh Nationalist called Gwilym Williams who posed as a saboteur. In this kind of way, claimed Masterman, *we actively ran and controlled the German espionage system in this country*. That may well be true, though it is also possible that the Abwehr suspected it was being controlled; which will have diluted the achievement somewhat.[4]

That was counter-espionage. On the counter-subversion front the achievement was even less clear-cut. (It may become clearer cut if the volume of Professor F. H. Hinsley's official history of wartime intelligence dealing with MI5, which was delayed by the *Spycatcher* litigation, ever sees the light of day.) Counter-subversion was Maxwell Knight's pigeon. He was under pressure, because of Churchill's insistence that something be done about German 'fifth columnists'. In May 1940 – just before Kell's sacking – he produced the goods. Since February that year he had been keeping a watch on the 'Right Club', which existed to try to purge the Conservative Party of its Jewish element in order to bring to power a government that would come to terms with Hitler. As a means to this one of its members, Anna Wolkoff, was conspiring with a clerk in the American embassy called Tyler Kent to obtain copies of secret correspondence between Churchill and Roosevelt. The idea was that if Roosevelt's secret assurance to Churchill to bring the United States into the war were revealed to the American public, it would lose Roosevelt the next presidential election, thus keeping America neutral, and forcing Britain to deal with Germany in order to avoid inevitable defeat. The plot was discovered by Knight's agents in the Right Club, who included Joan Miller, and Kent and Wolkoff were arrested on 20 May and tried and convicted in October.[5]

That was all very satisfactory. Its sequel, however, had a more controversial side. The Kent–Wolkoff plot was thought to be only part of a wider-ranging one, which included, for example, plans to replace Churchill by Mosley as Prime Minister and bring back the Duke of Windsor – a fascist sympathiser – as king. In case there was anything in this, the Kent–Wolkoff arrests were immediately followed by a great round-up of 750 British fascists (including Mosley) and their supposed sympathizers under clause 18(b) of the 1939 Defence of the Realm Act, and their internment without trial. That was widely criticized at the time, for two reasons. The first was that the trawl was far too wide. Most of the internees – even the fascists – posed no conceivable threat to national security, and some of them only had the most tenuous connections with fascism anyway. That was corrected to a certain extent afterwards, when MI5 personnel (including, again, Joan Miller) went round interviewing the internees to see who could be released. The other complaint was that MI5, and Maxwell Knight in particular, had used dubious methods to incriminate them. This is supposed to be one of the reasons why many of the official files on this whole affair still remain closed.

The most celebrated case of this kind involved a man called Benjamin Greene. It became celebrated largely because he came from an influential family, whose other members included a famous novelist and a future director-general of the BBC. Benjamin Greene was not a Nazi sympathizer, but he was a Quaker and a pacifist, and for some reason Knight had a bee in his bonnet about him. So he set one of his agents on to him: a man called Harald Kurz, nicknamed 'Porpoise' by one of his acquaintances 'because of his antics in the bathroom'.[6] His antics were not confined to there. In his professional life Kurz seems to have been an utter rogue, in the mould of notorious *agents provocateurs* like Castle in the past. First of all he tried to trap Greene into compromising situations with women; then, when that did not work, simply manufactured evidence against him. He probably used similar tricks against others, including the (genuine) British Nazi John Beckett. And Kurz was not the only one. A second agent, calling himself P. G. or P. C. Taylor, gave false evidence against a number of fascist internees. It may have been common practice around this time.[7]

At the very least this indicated poor judgment on Knight's part. It also damaged him. The Greene affair, and the widespread unease that was felt about the internment policy generally, cast him in a poor light, and undermined his authority. In October–November 1940 the Security Executive reviewed the position of the internees. Knight argued strongly for their continued detention, but was overruled. Most of them were released over the next few months, including many whom Knight still regarded as potential threats.[8] It was his credibility that suffered the biggest blow. And that may have had wider repercussions subsequently.

It meant that when he later warned about *communist* subversion in Britain, he was disregarded on that too. This seems to have been where he concentrated his efforts after 1940. In 1942 he helped to uncover 'Dave' Springhall, the CPGB's national organizer, who was channelling military secrets from Soviet sympathizers in sensitive occupations in Britain to Moscow. Springhall was arrested, convicted and sentenced to seven years' imprisonment. Some of the sympathizers were also prosecuted. Douglas Hyde, the news editor of the *Daily Worker*, later claimed that 'A vastly larger number who were guilty of the same activities were never caught.'[9] Knight suspected this. Worse: he apparently cottoned on to the fact that the KGB was penetrating the British civil and secret services. In 1941 he wrote a report on this, headed 'The Comintern is not Dead', and gave it to Roger Hollis, who seems to have been his immediate superior in MI5. Hollis rejected it, on the grounds that Knight's anti-communism was clearly running away with him. Others read it, including Churchill, but ignored it. We do not know what precisely was in the report. It may have been wide of the mark. According to Joan Miller (and also Peter Wright), one of Knight's specific charges was that there was a Soviet agent (unnamed) in MI5.[10] If this is so, and if his other surmises were as well-founded, then this may have been an important opportunity missed.

The Soviet agent in MI5 – or one of them – was Anthony Blunt, who joined in 1940 and served there until the end of the war. He was one of the ring of four notorious 'Cambridge moles' who infiltrated Britain's secret and diplomatic services at this time, and remained undiscovered until 1951, when two of them defected to Moscow. Harold 'Kim' Philby was the most important, by virtue of the highly sensitive positions he managed to achieve within MI6, including heading its Soviet counter-intelligence branch in 1944, and liaising with American intelligence in Washington in 1949. The others were the two 1951 defectors, Guy Burgess, who worked for periods at the War Office and the Foreign Office, and Donald Maclean, who was another and much more highly placed Foreign Office diplomat. They were not the only ones. When Burgess and Maclean defected, inquiries revealed a number of other traitors in subordinate positions, who were duly removed. In the later 1940s two of Britain's atomic scientists, Alan Nunn May and Klaus Fuchs, were also identified as spies, and sent to gaol. Some others were unmasked privately, and their names never revealed. (This was the initial situation with Blunt, too, after 1964 when he agreed to confess in return for immunity, until 1979 when the press caught up with him.) A few were discovered, confronted with the evidence against them, and then 'turned' into double agents for the British or Americans.[11] One or two, or perhaps several, may never have been spotted at all, but continued serving their Soviet masters well into the 1950s and 1960s, and even possibly beyond.

The failure of Britain's security services to prevent and then to detect any of this at the time must be considered to outweigh most of their more positive achievements on the domestic front. It was serious on two counts. First, it indicated some culpable and even ludicrous shortcomings in their selection procedures. Blunt, for example, was accepted by MI5 in the summer of 1940 after being turned down for military intelligence training at Camberley the year before, because of his Marxist past. Presumably the Camberley author-ities had learned of that through MI5.[12] Burgess's case was even odder. He was notorious for outrageous behaviour, foul living and (again) a Marxist past. His various escapades led to his being dismissed from a succession of government and BBC jobs: but always to fall into some other government or BBC job straight afterwards. As late as the spring of 1951 he was working at the British embassy in Washington. The excuse usually given in his case is that no one could be expected to credit that such a depraved creature could possibly be a successful spy. But it is a wonder that his depravity did not count against him more in other ways.

The failure to spot these Soviet 'moles' was also serious in its effects. There can be no doubt that it caused immense damage. How wide that damage went is difficult to tell. A mass of sensitive political and military information was passed to Moscow during and after the war via Philby, Burgess and Maclean. Maclean may also have helped transmit nuclear secrets in 1944–5, with the help of a 'Fifth Man', code-named 'Basil' by Andrew Boyle, who helped him on the technical side.[13] The extent to which any of this can be regarded as undermining Britain's or America's national interests is problematical. The atom secrets conveyed to Russia from every Western source accelerated the Soviets' nuclear bomb programme by a year or two, but no one now doubts that they would have got there eventually on their own. The effects of the other betrayals – of political and strategic secrets – are debatable. Some of them may have reassured the Soviet leaders, at a time when they deeply distrusted (quite reasonably) the good faith of their Western allies in the war. This is a perfectly respectable general argument in favour of espionage, and even treachery: if it chips away at the dangerous suspicions that can be engendered by mutual secrecy. (By the same token, of course, it is an even better argument for not being so secretive.) In this sense the harm Philby and company caused to Britain's security and other interests in the world is a matter for conjecture and interpretation. What is not a matter for conjecture, however, is the harm they did to her secret services, and particularly to MI5.

That harm is obvious. It did not affect the anti-German side of the secret services' wartime work, which the 'moles' were as anxious to prosecute efficiently as any of their more loyalist colleagues: more so than some.

But it clearly undermined their anti-Soviet side, probably to the extent of neutralizing it. Andrew Boyle estimates that at least three dozen British agents abroad 'suffered death, injury or imprisonment through Philby's studied duplicity' between 1945 and 1947.[14] The latter was also responsible for the recapture and presumably execution by the Russians in August 1945 of Konstantin Volkov, who was about to defect and unmask the 'moles'.[15] That gave them another five invaluable years of burrowing. By the end of that time, and possibly for far longer, the Russians will have known everything worth knowing about British espionage in the Eastern bloc, and about counter-espionage in Britain itself. MI5's part in all this will have been betrayed to them by Blunt before 1945, when he ostensibly resigned to become Keeper of the King's Pictures, and possibly afterwards, when he may have kept in touch both with MI5 and with his Soviet 'control'. The implications of this were drastic. It meant that most people in the secret service, so far as their counter-Soviet duties were concerned, had all along been wasting their time.

That, however, was only part of it. With the defection of Burgess and Maclean and the resignation of Philby in 1951–2 the direct harm done to the secret service by Soviet infiltration may have ceased. That depends on whether or not any important 'moles' still remained undiscovered. If any did, then clearly it meant that MI5's and MI6's Russian work thereafter was still pointless. That was the conclusion arrived at by a number of MI5 officers in the early 1960s, when one after another of their cleverest counter-espionage plots went badly wrong. Bugging devices placed in Soviet or Eastern European embassies, for example, proved useless, because they were instantly removed, or people simply stopped talking in the rooms they were placed in. Attempts by MI5 to repeat their old wartime 'double-cross' tricks against the Russians failed abjectly. One such failure was with Sergei Ivanov, who was the Russian spy at the centre of the Profumo scandal of 1963, sharing a prostitute with the then Defence Minister, and consequently elevating the latter's little bit of extra-marital fun into a threat to national security.[16] A more serious failure was the case of George Blake, who when he was first discovered to be spying for the Russians was asked to carry on, as a double agent for Britain, and did so, but *without* changing sides. He was arrested and convicted in 1961, but then 'sprung' from Wormwood Scrubs prison in 1966, apparently by two amateurs, members of the anti-nuclear 'Committee of 100', who took pity on him.[17] 'I just can't believe', said one MI5 man to Peter Wright in the midst of all this, that 'we are as apparently incompetent as we appear to be.' (The clumsy English may be Wright's.)[18] It was this which set the latter on his mission to ferret out the remaining Soviet agent in his own organization, who must – he reasoned – be spilling the beans. His trail led him to Sir Roger Hollis, who was MI5's director, no less, from 1956 to 1965; and eventually to the furore over Wright's book *Spycatcher* in 1987–8.

Hollis may indeed have been a Soviet mole; or his deputy, Graham Mitchell; or even Wright himself. (He was one of the few men who had access to all MI5's 'betrayed' information; has indirectly helped the Russians through *Spycatcher*; and admits that he once shared a flat with the brother of a possible 'Fifth Man', Alister Watson. QED?)[19] Or there may not have been a mole at all. In a sense it scarcely matters, because the main damage was done anyway. That was as a result of the suspicions that the whole Burgess–Maclean–Philby affair aroused thereafter, both within the secret services, and between them.

The very realization that you had been systematically betrayed in the past – that all your most secret moves had been anticipated and countered by the enemy – was demoralizing. So was the thought that the same thing might still be going on. If you tried to close your mind to this, you were reminded of it by those of your colleagues who refused to. Peter Wright's ferretings caused enormous resentment, by his own admission, especially after the Labour MP Bernard Floud, who probably was not a spy, committed suicide the evening after a grilling by him in October 1967. Within MI5, he wrote in *Spycatcher*,

There was talk of the Gestapo. Younger officers began to avoid me in the canteen. Casual conversation with many of my colleagues became a rarity. Those of us involved in the penetration issue were set apart, feared and distrusted in equal measure.[20]

Wright's superiors anticipated this. 'It's a very delicate issue,' Hollis told him in 1959; 'It would have a terrible effect on morale in the Service.' That was the reason he gave for trying to block Wright's inquiries. Wright thought it furnished more evidence of his guilt; but Hollis's successors took much the same line. Even Sir Martin Furnival Jones, who was the next director and shared Wright's concern about Soviet penetration, was against circulating the results of his inquiries on the grounds that it would 'break the heart of the Service. We should never recover ... In my view ... it would be better if no-one knew, ever!'[21] It was clearly bad both for MI5's reputation, and for their *esprit de corps*.

It also damaged *esprit* between *corps*. That did not take much doing so far as MI5 and MI6 were concerned. They had always been rivals. Sometimes their rivalry had been unfriendly in the extreme. It may have been partly a matter of class. MI5, as we have seen, were mainly upper-crust; but MI6 considered themselves to be even upper-cruster, and brighter to boot. One postwar MI6 officer, Anthony Cavendish, afterwards went into merchant banking, where he thought he saw a parallel. 'The merchant banker is generally the intellectual and social superior of the commercial banker,' he wrote in his memoirs. 'Much like the relationship between MI6 and MI5.'[22] MI5 thought they were *too* superior. Over Philby, who was MI6, the mutual hostility was intense. MI5 thought MI6 were treating him with kid gloves: being far too solicitous during his interrogations, and even completing his sentences for him when his customary stammer broke in. Peter Wright, who supplied the hidden microphones and listened in, called it a 'travesty'.[23] MI6 in their turn resented Five's hounding of a man they regarded as decent and innocent, both then and for years afterwards, until 1963 when Philby finally confessed and disappeared.[24] The fact that Five had been proved right all along did not endear them to Six any more. The feud between them continued, stoked (as we shall see) by other events later on. At bottom it sprang from a lack of confidence in each other, which the Burgess–Maclean–Philby affair had done a great deal to exacerbate.

Worst of all was the damage done to Anglo-American co-operation in the intelligence field. This may have been one of the prime targets of the KGB. If they could insert a wedge between MI5 and MI6 on the one hand, and the FBI and the CIA on the other, then they were laughing. This is what in fact happened. Philby, Maclean and Burgess were all at one time or another placed in Washington, where they had access to Anglo-American secrets, including atomic ones. Philby was suspected by the Americans – in particular by James Anderton of the CIA – long before his British chums smelled anything fishy about him. All three of them, together with nearly every other contemporary Soviet agent in Britain, were unmasked eventually not through the efforts of MI5 or MI6, but by the CIA, usually on the basis of testimony from defectors. This made the Americans naturally chary about sharing their secrets with Britain. On the British side that was felt to be serious, in a postwar situation in which Britain needed American help in all kinds of areas to keep her in the 'great power league'. One such area was atomic weaponry, where the Fuchs case in 1950 stopped talks between the two governments about co-operation stone dead. American suspicions of British counter-intelligence took years to recover from that, and from the Burgess and Maclean affair the next year. In 1961 Peter Wright was one of a team sent to Washington to discuss Sigint co-operation with the Americans, one of whom – Angleton – called them 'untrustworthy motherfuckers' for their pains.[25] That was not nice. In 1965 President Lyndon Johnson ordered a secret CIA inquiry into the reliability of the whole British intelligence set-up, which according to Peter Wright resulted in 'a devastating critique of MI5'. Furnival Jones's comment, when he heard about it, was: 'Never can trust the bloody Americans to play it by the rules!'[26] That was probably the lowest point in the relationship between them. At the root of it, again, were Burgess, Maclean, Philby and Blunt, and the suspicion that they might not be the last rotten apples in the barrel.

The suspicion alone was enough. It did not need to be justified. In 1985 Oleg Gordievsky, a British double agent in the KGB, was asked whether Hollis really had been one of theirs. 'Of course not,' he replied. 'But when the KGB saw the chaos caused by the allegations against Hollis, their laughter made Red Square shake.'[27]

That, of course, does not automatically clear Hollis, or anyone else in the post-1951 MI5. That question, though important, is not a proper one for a historian and an outsider to address. One reason is that he has less access to the evidence than the insider does; another is that the whole question seems rather more complex than historians are used to. In other kinds of history they meet this kind of thing occasionally: trickery, deception, bluffs and double bluffs; but not so ubiquitously as in this field. One example will stand for all the rest.

According to Peter Wright, Roger Hollis as a Soviet 'mole' was betraying all Britain's secret service activities to the Russians. That makes it curious that Oleg Penkovsky, the GRU (Russian military intelligence) officer who was 'turned' by MI6 in 1960, and whom Hollis knew about from the beginning, was not unmasked to them before he could reveal Moscow's plans to station nuclear missiles in Cuba to the West in 1962. That revelation led, of course, to the Kennedy–Khruschev confrontation of October–November 1962, when everybody believed they were on the brink of nuclear catastrophe, until Khruschev backed down and withdrew his missiles. Wright's answer to the conundrum is this. Russia *wanted* the Americans to find out about the missiles, but to believe that she was trying to conceal them from them. She wanted that because she was anxious to sow the notion that she had no *intercontinental* missiles, and so needed a shorter-range site. Her humiliation in the resulting crisis was a small price to pay for that disinformation: like sacrificing a queen for a winning position on the board. Penkovsky was a vital pawn in this game: a 'false' defector, planted in order to persuade the Americans that they were learning something his masters wished to remain secret. Later, when his work was done, he was 'arrested' in Moscow (together with his MI6 contact, Greville Wynne), and supposedly executed for treachery: but no one can prove that he is not really living the life of Reilly, still, in a nice little *dacha* in the countryside outside Moscow, under a new name. The trick worked brilliantly, encouraging the Americans to sign a nuclear test-ban treaty the following year, while Russia covertly forged ahead. It also had the effect of diverting suspicion from Russia's MI5 mole, Roger Hollis, which was a bonus; fooling most of Britain's secret servants, apart from Wright. 'We were in the place Angleton called "the wilderness of mirrors",' writes Wright in *Spycatcher*, 'where defectors are false, lies are truth, truth lies, and the reflections leave you dazzled and confused.'[28] For an ordinary historian this is far too clever. But it may be true. Russia, remember, is a nation of chess masters. Consequently it requires another chess master, not a historian, to read their game.

Chess masters, however, sometimes have narrower views of things than historians. This present historian has no pertinent contribution to make to the debate over whether Hollis, or anyone else, was a 'mole'. That debate can be pursued – probably fruitlessly – elsewhere.[29] What the historian can do is to put the debate in perspective, in two ways. The first is by reminding readers of the highly unreliable nature of *all* the evidence that is offered to them, most of which comes ultimately from intelligence personnel – who are not a trustworthy breed at the best of times – with axes to grind. That certainly applies to *Spycatcher*, whose author is clearly obsessed, and also aggrieved, partly over the slightly sordid matter of his pension rights (which incidentally recalls the cases of two other secret service whistle-blowers, Alexander Richmond and Patrick McIntyre, in the distant past). Other authors' accounts are also heavily dependent – though this is not always acknowledged – on insider 'leaks'. This does not necessarily invalidate them, even *Spycatcher*; but it necessitates extreme circumspection on the part of their readers, and a suspension of final judgement, probably for good.

The other caution the historian can enter is against taking any of this too seriously. Intelligence is an intriguing game, but not necessarily a vitally important one, whatever the intelligence people themselves may think. In the field of international relations it is not easy to find irrefutable instances – though there are some – where good intelligence in peacetime has changed things significantly for the better of a nation or of the world, and where poor intelligence has changed things for the worse. (Wartime is different.) The 'moles' in MI5, MI6 and elsewhere from 1940 onwards certainly, as we have seen, damaged those agencies, and the morale and reputation of Britain's secret service generally. Some of its agents died as a result of their activities. The team, therefore, suffered. Whether or not we believe the suffering went any wider than this, and affected, for example, the community more generally, will depend on how important we believe the team is to the community: on our assessment of the extent to which Britain's 'national interest' requires an effective 'secret service'. That is debatable.

One further major question remains. Why did all this happen: the treachery, the penetration, the confusion that followed? So far as the motivations of the leading actors are concerned, the answer seems to lie in the dichotomy that presented itself to them in the 1930s, when they were first drawn to communism, between the world as they saw it – fascism abroad, unemployment at home – and their own indefensible privileges, as members of a highly favoured upper middle class. There are also possible psychological explanations, though they will be different in each individual case. All the four main traitors – Burgess, Maclean, Philby and Blunt – came from public schools, against whose systems of values it was not unnatural for intelligent boys to react, even if they were happy there, and certain aspects of life at which – the secret societies and conspiracies which filled many of their non-working and non-sporting hours, for example – may even, in a perverse way, have encouraged their later duplicities. Cambridge – where they first met together and imbibed their Marxism, at a little nest of colleges on the river between King's and Trinity – can easily appear arrogant, smug and superficial to young men and women who come to it at a rebellious time of their lives, and are unable to penetrate through to the better qualities which may lie beneath. To some people who have had experience of both kinds of educational institution it is not difficult to understand how they could stoke the discontent and even revulsion of many of their products between the wars; most of whom will have grown out of the revulsion subsequently, or found other ways to channel it, but a tiny few of whom were almost bound to turn to deception and treachery, simply because the opportunities for deception and treachery were there.

That really is where the main problem – and the important one, so far as this book is concerned – lies. Why were the opportunities there? How could men like this possibly be admitted into the very occupations in which their treachery was bound to be most effective and dangerous, when signs of their moral instability and political unreliability, in some of the cases at least, must have been obvious from the start?

The obvious place to look for the answer is in the social composition and ethos of the British secret and diplomatic services, which we have touched on before. Socially they were exclusively upper middle class; politically they were predominantly right-wing. They looked for recruits in the same categories, and among people known to them personally. This was their substitute for what today is called 'vetting': an equally dependable way of ensuring loyalty, they would have maintained before 1951, and less insulting to gentlemen. They also tended to lack what most other people would regard as a rounded education and experience of life, and (especially in the case of MI5 before the war) general intelligence.

Consequently for anyone with ulterior motives, and just a mite more brains, but from the right sort of background, it was not hard to fool them. All four Cambridge 'moles' got their jobs – in the secret service, the Foreign Office, the War Office, the BBC and journalism – through personal contacts with people already inside: 'on the old boy net', as Blunt put it in his debriefing in November 1979.[30] They covered over the traces of their early Marxism as well as they could. Blunt and Maclean cultivated the idea that they had grown out of it by then: Maclean very cleverly at his *viva*, by admitting that he still had some residual communist *sympathies*, in a way which apparently impressed his interviewers with his honesty. Philby and Burgess went further, and pretended to have swung over to outright fascism, Philby even earning a medal from Franco for the help he gave to his cause during the civil war in Spain, and Burgess graduating to the War Office via the Anglo-German Fellowship, where he worked for a time as publicity officer. In none of these cases, therefore, could it be said that their new employers were knowingly hiring men with left-wing proclivities. On the contrary, in two they believed that they were taking on sound ultra-rightists, and in the other two cases men whose breeding they were confident would soon prevail over the already wilting fads of adolescence.

Once inside, their loyalty was seldom doubted, even when they started drinking and brawling and sodomizing, and (in Burgess's case) chewing garlic, so long as they seemed decent fellows otherwise. When someone else – a rival intelligence agency, or someone from the CIA – pointed the finger at one of them, his colleagues would rally round him with a loyalty of their own which was touching, and rooted in the deep mutual trust that came of their common origins. If there was a leak or betrayal, but no definite suspect, then 'the conventional view', as Peter Wright puts it, 'was to search for the culprit among the clerks, cleaners and secretaries', who were the class of people who could be expected to be treacherous; not in the upper ranks.[31] It must have been an enormous shock to them to realize, after the defections, that the assumptions that lay behind this could no longer be made. Their own type could be bad eggs too. The Americans were less surprised, because it bore out some of their domestic prejudices against the British upper class. To appease them – if for no other reason – it was clear from 1951 onwards that there would have to be some changes made.

In fact the changes began in 1947, when a secret Cabinet committee ('GEN 183') began trying to weed both communists and fascists out of sensitive government posts. Employees' names were checked against the files of MI5 and the Special Branch, and doubtful people sacked or transferred. Before this they could appeal to a body known as the 'Three Wise Men'. The process worked slowly, so that by January 1949 only seventeen cases had been scrutinized, and eleven of them transferred. After the 1951 defections, and partly at the prompting of the Americans, it was tightened and speeded up. That was when 'positive vetting' came in, which meant initiating inquiries into employees' backgrounds, whether or not the security services had them on their files. It was sanctioned by the Labour government in October 1951, and came into force shortly afterwards. A few dozen suspect civil servants were winkled out as a result. This did not altogether satisfy the Americans, who by this time were well into their 'McCarthyite' phase, and sacking 'leftists' in droves. One obvious initial flaw in Britain was that the procedure was not, apparently, extended to the vetters themselves.[32] Peter Wright's experience (if his account is to be believed) bears on this. He came up for scrutiny for a job in MI5 in 1954. In his case his 'vetting' consisted simply of a masonic handshake, a brief chat about politics, and the embarrassed question, 'Ever been queer, by any chance?' (Wright's response to this was 'Never in my life'; but they let him in anyway.)[33] The lessons of 1951 were clearly taking longer than they should to sink in.

This was despite the new broom which Attlee sent in to run MI5 in May 1946, chosen from outside the secret service deliberately, in order to shake things up. Sir Percy Sillitoe had been a top policeman before his new job, and hated 'Oxbridge types' and excessive secrecy. He told everyone who cared to ask what his new job was, and even put his official address ('Room 055 War Office, S.W.1') in *Who's Who*. He also disliked the idea of 'political police' agencies, which he associated with totalitarianism, and was anxious that MI5 would not slide into. 'I myself', he wrote later, 'would rather see two or three traitors slip through the net of the Security Service, than be party to the taking of measures which could result in such a regime.' MI5 for their part suspected that he had been foisted on them by Labour in revenge for the Zinoviev affair of 1924. They got their own back, apparently, by quoting Latin tags in his presence, in order to show him up. That irritated him. It was not a happy relationship.[34]

Nor was it an unprecedented one. We have seen similar conflicts between secret service and policemanly ethics before, first of all in the 1880s, and then again between the wars. In this case the policeman seems to have lost in the end. 'Dolly, I can't get to grips with a brick wall!' Sillitoe told his wife on one occasion.[35] He left MI5 in May 1953. If he had made any significant changes in the meantime, they do not appear to have endured. Peter Wright's picture of MI5 just after Sillitoe's retirement is of an outfit with an atmosphere rather like that of a minor public school, 'covered with a thick film of dust dating from the wartime years', missing its wartime intellectuals – who had all returned to their universities – dreadfully, and peopled now, as it had been before they arrived, with 'exotic and extravagant personalities' who seemed to spend most of their time larking around.[36] This suggests that the brick wall was still intact. Wright, of course, is a highly partial witness. He always stood outside this circle. Because his father drank, he had never been to public school. He was made to feel this, just as Sillitoe was, and resented it. But his testimony is all we have.

MI5 did change in the post-Sillitoe years; but not in the directions that Sillitoe had marked out for it. Two things that seem not to have changed greatly were the political orientation of its personnel, and its penchant for secrecy. On to this traditional structure were engrafted two new qualities: a certain technological competency, and a freshly professional approach. Later all this was turned on to a widening circle of 'enemies', to create, in effect, the MI5 we know (or rather, do not know) today.

Peter Wright (before he turned to molehunting) was their new technologist: an expert in electronics whose main job was to provide surveillance devices for MI5 initially, and later for other security agencies. The usual euphemism for these devices was 'SFs', for 'special facilities'; today they are more commonly known as 'bugs'. They were developed to overcome the difficulties MI5 were experiencing in 'turning' Russians into British informants, which meant that they would need to find some other way, for example, of discovering what was going on in the Russian embassy. 'SFs' were the answer.

Wright was an enthusiastic champion of these new electronic aids. Soon, he thought, they would entirely supplant older-fashioned ways. In particular he suggested that the newly named Government Communications Headquarters at Cheltenham (formerly 'GC & CS') had already made MI6 redundant: but that was probably just mischief. The serious point was that the future of intelligence clearly lay, in Wright's view, with 'Sigint', and the new technology. That would put his public school detractors ('That's all right, Peter old chap, I don't need to know Ohm's law. I read Greats') firmly in their place.[37]

Within this general field Wright concentrated mainly on bugging embassies, enemy, neutral and friendly; and old favourites like the CPGB headquarters in King Street (which by now must have had more 'bugs' in its walls than wall). Even the government's own Lancaster House in London, where a number of conferences took place in the 1960s to settle independence terms for British colonies, was bugged so that the Colonial Office could know what the natives were saying when their masters were out of the room. When he had finished bugging everywhere in Britain, Wright turned to foreign embassies in Commonwealth capitals: Canberra, for example, and Ottawa. (Colonial intelligence was the responsibility of 'E' branch of MI5.) His skills were exploited in other ways. In January 1959 he was called out to Cyprus to see whether he could find a way of locating the EOKA guerrilla leader Colonel Grivas by tracing his radio messages. That operation was code-named 'Sunshine'. Around 1970 he devised a way of tapping the Irish Republic's telephone system from outside the country, though he was refused permission to put it into practice (he says). He also perfected a means of opening safes by reading the numbers of their combination locks electronically from the inside. That 'gave MI5 potential access to every safe in Britain', which was a useful facility. For most of this, of course, we only have Wright's uncorroborated word.[38] But no one who knows has disputed it.

The 'professionalism' went along with this. The word 'professional' has a strictly literal meaning, and also a number of overtones. It is often used as a euphemism for 'unscrupulous', as in the phrase 'professional foul'. Secret services the world over have probably always been 'professional' to some degree in this sense; but in the 1950s the British may have become more so. The American secret service certainly did, as a matter of deliberate policy formulated around 1948–9.[39] The rationale for this was spelled out in a report by a committee chaired by ex-President Herbert Hoover in 1954, which contains the following pregnant paragraph.

It is now clear that we are facing an implacable enemy whose avowed objective is world domination by whatever means and at whatever cost. There are no rules in such a game. Hitherto acceptable norms of human conduct do not apply. If the U.S. is to survive, long-standing American concepts of 'fair play' must be reconsidered. We must develop effective espionage and counter-espionage services. We must learn to subvert, sabotage and destroy our enemies by more clever, more sophisticated and more effective measures than those used against us.[40]

That, of course, related to the CIA. But the British secret services could use the same kind of excuse. The opposition had no scruples at all. Consequently they could not afford to have any either.

Evidence for this, as one would expect, is thin. Most of it has to do with events in Britain's rapidly dwindling spheres of interest and influence overseas. An early example was an MI6-instigated attempt to subvert the communist Enver Hoxha as leader of Albania in 1949, which failed.[41] Two better-known ones are the coup which toppled the regime of Mohammed Mossadeq and returned the Shah to power in Iran in August 1953, and the abortive plots which Anthony Eden initiated against President Nasser of Egypt in 1956. Both of these were in response to local government seizures of British economic assets. The Iran coup came as the result of 'Operation Boot', a joint MI6–CIA adventure, which according to Chapman Pincher's *Inside Story* also involved the assassination of Mossadeq's chief of police by 'an agent acting on MI6's behalf'.[42] Among the ways considered for bumping off Nasser was a scheme to pump nerve gas into the ventilation system of his Cairo palace ('Operation Salamander'), and giving him an exploding razor which was activated by contact with stubble. (That was sanctioned just as Eden set off for a rest cure at the Jamaican home of the creator of James Bond.) In the formal British colonies this sort of thing was MI5's pigeon. According to Wright, 'Operation Sunshine' was an assassination plot in all but name. 'The plan was simple: to locate Grivas, and bring up a massive concentration of soldiers. We knew he would never surrender, and ... would die in the shoot-out.' Unfortunately for MI5 Britain handed over Cyprus before the finishing touches could be put to this little plan.[43] They were more successful four years later in British Guiana, where they ousted a left-wing Prime Minister, Cheddi Jagan, by provoking a series of strikes.[44] It was around then that Wright claims the British secret service 'got out' of the assassination game;[45] probably through a realization of Britain's declining role in the world after Suez, rather than because of anyone's moral qualms.

This shows what the secret services generally were capable of, at least for a time, and against foreigners. At home the picture was different. No one has ever claimed that MI5 assassinated Hugh Gaitskell, or provoked the 1966 seamen's strike (though according to one school of thought someone's secret service did). It has been suggested that they might have been responsible for the death of Stephen Ward, who was at the centre of the Profumo affair; but the evidence for that is thin.[46] MI5 operatives certainly broke other, lesser rules, without their superiors trying too hard to stop them. Wright (again) recalls how when he first joined full-time in 1954 it was made abundantly clear to him by his MI5 coach, John Cuckfield (later to become a controversial captain of industry) that the only commandment he should have to bother with was the eleventh – 'thou shalt not get caught' – but that if he did ever get caught, then he would be disowned. Hence the bugging and the burgling, which were quite illegal; and one or two other little wheezes they thought up, like pickpocketing suspected KGB officers in the streets, and placing agents in the DHSS headquarters in Newcastle in order to gain access to confidential National Insurance files.[47] That was naughty, of course; but none of it, so far as we can tell, was downright wicked.

Our main first-hand witness, Peter Wright, such as he is, had very little to do with the domestic counter-subversion ('F') branch of MI5. His impression was that that branch was less important than 'D' section (counter-espionage) before around 1970, when the balance shifted the other way. That may have been so. It is consistent with what one would expect of a mainly 'consensual' society, which by and large Britain was in the twenty years or so after the war. That consensus was founded on a bipartisan acceptance of the post-war welfare state and mixed economy, which together constituted a kind of happy compromise between the warring capitalist and socialist tendencies of the past. It was also, incidentally, widely supposed to give the lie to Marxism, whose predictions seemed to leave no room for an accommodation between the classes like this. This was why Britain's remaining Marxists in the 1950s and 1960s were so anti-Labour: because Labour was holding up the natural development of capitalism towards its expected catastrophic end. We now realize that this was only a brief historical diversion, before the engine was hauled back on to the Marxist rails in 1979; but people were not to know that then. In the 1950s and 1960s consensus, or 'Butskellism' as it was sometimes called, seemed set fair for the future; and with it the end of any real threat to the stability and security of Britain against subversives of any political hue.

That should have meant that 'F' branch had little serious work to do; and might have done, if MI5 had been composed of Butskellites itself. But it was not. All the evidence points to its still being to the right of the mainstream of British opinion in political terms, and consequently probably more representative of that minority but still very powerful section of the population which did not regard the welfare state and the mixed economy as shields against subversion at all, but the very opposite. Some even saw them as forms of subversion themselves: sapping the people's self-reliance, and consequently the nation's strength. An example of this is a curious novel published in 1951 by Peter Fleming, the brother of James Bond's creator, called *The Sixth Column*, which was set in a near-future Britain which was well on its way down that slope. A combination of welfareism, full employment and popular broadcasting (especially a proto-Terry Wogan character called 'Paul Osney') has degraded what during the war had been a race of heroes into a 'bureaucratic cage' full of 'mice'. The nadir of the decline comes when the England cricket team is bowled out for nine runs by West Africa [*sic*], and, more obscurely, when a Chinese woman swims the Channel.[48] But that is not the worst of it. Behind all this – and in particular behind Paul Osney – lies a Russian plot, code-named 'Plan D', to soften up Britain in preparation for conquest: which puts an even more sinister complexion on the whole thing. Luckily the secret service – in Fleming's book still staffed by right thinking people – gets wind of this, and foils the plot. This is reminiscent of Constantine Fitzgibbon's best-selling *When the Kissing Had to Stop*, which came out nine years later, on a very similar theme. Not too much, of course, should be made of novels as indicators of opinion; but these two were both born out of real and passionate convictions, on the part of authors who had secret service connections of their own.[49]

Nor was this only the stuff of fiction. Consensus was thought to be pretty widespread, but it did not cover everyone. In certain places – gentlemen's clubs, officers' messes and Oxbridge senior common rooms – hatred of the welfare state was more common than most people outside such haunts would have credited. The idea that the BBC was a vehicle for subversion, for example, was expressed quite seriously and quite often. 'One of the main weapons of Communism is to demoralise the people,' the Conservative MP Sir Waldron Smithers told a committee on broadcasting in 1949. '"Morning Music" and "Bright and Early" are designed to this end.'[50] Another vehicle was believed to be the Labour movement, which some rightists had always suspected was controlled by Soviet puppeteers. These suspicions were given substance in 1951 by the testimony of Douglas Hyde, a communist-turned-Catholic, who revealed among other things how eight or nine MPs elected on the Labour ticket in the 1945 election had in fact been crypto-communists, together with others in the trade unions and elsewhere.[51] In fact if it is read carefully Hyde's book suggests that the scope of this kind of infiltration was fairly limited; but that was beside the point. It had been established for certain that covert infiltration was a communist method. Consequently it had to be guarded against.

Even if MI5 had not been made up of rightists, it would have needed to keep an eye on this. It clearly did. So far as 'cryptos' were concerned it apparently achieved a great coup in the early 1950s by finding out where the CPGB's membership files were kept, burgling the place and photographing 55,000 dossiers, including those on 'covert' communists in the Labour movement and the civil service. The result of 'Operation Party Piece', claims Peter Wright, was that 'the CPGB was never again in a position to seriously threaten the safety of the realm'.[52] But that did not mean that MI5 could relax. Most communists knew, or had a pretty good idea, that they were being watched. If they really wanted to subvert the state, therefore, they would keep well clear of the CPGB. One answer to this was 'positive vetting', which checked for suspects at their point of entry into sensitive government posts. (That was carried out by MI5's section 'C'.) Another was the regular surveillance of other likely targets for subversion, like the Labour Party, the trade unions and the BBC. All these organizations are known to have been under scrutiny by MI5 at this time. When the Labour Prime Minister Harold Wilson made his famous statement about the 'tightly knit group of politically motivated men' he claimed was pushing the Seamen's Union into strike action in 1966, for example, the report on which he based that accusation was an MI5 one.[53] The BBC's vetting system went back to before the War, and involved the files of potential employees being sent secretly to MI5 to check. The result was the effective 'blacklisting' of several left-wingers and brothers and husbands of left-wingers, usually without their realizing it; as well as of some who were mistaken for left-wingers, but were really 'innocent'. (One turned out to be in MI6.)[54] The system seems to have been thorough. How it missed 'Morning Music' and 'Bright and Early' is a mystery.

These procedures had two objects. The first was to watch for traitors, who might betray sensitive information to potential enemies. That was the rationale for the 'positive vetting' system in the government service. The other was to prevent 'extremists' subverting Britain's society directly, either by manipulating people covertly (especially trade unionists), or else by openly airing their views. That last was the purpose of the vetting system at the BBC. It was something relatively new in Britain, which had used to pride itself on the freedom of expression it allowed. Its ultimate justification (though it was never put like this) was that the mass of people were too weak minded to distinguish between safe and dangerous ideas, if they were both equally freely expressed. The same notion lay behind the formation of the 'Information Research Department' in 1947: an anti-communist propaganda agency for areas of British interest abroad in the first place, but soon afterwards extended to the Labour movement at home. Some of its material was intentionally misleading, and the way that material was channelled involved deceit. One channel was the *Daily Mirror* proprietor Cecil King, who Wright claims was also a covert agent for MI5.[55] Hence it counts as a 'covert activity'; part and parcel of what *may* have been quite an extensive operation for these consensual times, aimed at protecting Britons from their own gullibility in the face of a plausible but dangerous set of ideas.

We know that this sort of thing went on, but not the extent. Most contemporaries knew nothing about it at all. This suited the secret services admirably, because they reckoned they worked better in total darkness than in even the dullest of lights. The main reason for this was not that publicity would alert their enemies (though this was part of it), but that it might attract to them ill-informed criticisms which would result in their activities being curbed. That has always been a secret service worry in Britain, where (as we have seen before) liberal hostility to espionage is supposed to run deep.

Whether it ran quite as deep in the 1950s and 1960s as it had at earlier times is a moot point. Popular literature suggests not. Spy novels in the past had always taken a fairly upright stand on the ethical dilemmas associated with secret service work,or at the very least (like *Ashenden*) been ambivalent. After the war they remained ambivalent for a while, but inclining slightly more towards the unscrupulous. The attitude of Geoffrey Household's hero in *A Time to Kill* (1952), for example, is revealing. He finds he has his limits. 'My whole ethical training, my system of taboos and religion and chivalry ... forbade torture even for the sake of my children.' On the other hand he is 'ashamed of this weakness': which is new. He also finds at the end of the book, when it comes to a proper battle-type situation, that he can kill foreigners in *hot* blood.[56] That may mark a turning point. The following year saw the publication of the first of Ian Fleming's James Bond books (*Casino Royale*), where the truly 'professional' (i.e. ruthless) agent comes into his own. Apparently this was with the approval of vast numbers of people, if the sales figures for the Bond books and films are any guide. That should have reassured the real-life Bonds. But they could never tell. After all, *Dixon of Dock Green* was popular too.

So they played safe, and the secret services remained hidden in the deepest shadows of British political life. There were no 'leaks': partly thanks to the D-Notice Committee, which stopped disclosures reaching the newspapers. One or two ex-Special Branch officers published memoirs, but without giving very much away. In most cases they concentrated on the branch's protective duties – acting as bodyguards for 'important personages' – to the exclusion of what ex-Superintendent George Wilkinson, for example, maintained was the much more 'interesting and exciting' side of its work.[57] MI5 men and women were even more discreet. Such self-restraint seems hardly natural. One or two retired secret service men relieved their obvious frustrations by publishing novels under *noms de plume* which were based on real experience. The problem here, for any contemporary who might want to establish the facts from them, was that they were so muddled up with genuine fiction as to make the former impossible to extricate. Officially the very existence of the security services was not acknowledged by ministers, who also refused (on 'national security' grounds) to answer questions on them in Parliament. There were no scandals to bring them into the public light, with the exception of spy cases, which may have distracted attention from the security services' other work. Even ministers knew very little about them, especially if they were Labour. Diaries published subsequently by some of the latter indicate little or no awareness of the secret service's activities, except to wonder occasionally at how little aware of those activities they are.[58] One assumes that Home Secretaries knew what was going on; but even here there is room for doubt.

That doubt arises from the formal relationship between MI5 and the Home Office, which was authoritatively established in a 'directive' issued in 1952 by the then Home Secretary, Sir David Maxwell Fyfe. That directive confirmed that the Director-General of MI5 was 'responsible to the Home Secretary personally'; but did not leave it there. There were three qualifications. The first two were that MI5 was 'not a part of the Home Office', which meant that the Home Secretary did not have full control over it; and that 'on appropriate occasion' the director could appeal over the head of the Home Secretary to the Prime Minister. The third was the most significant. It ran:

> You and your staff will maintain the well-established convention whereby Ministers do not concern themselves with the detailed information which may be obtained by the Security Service in particular cases, but are furnished with such information only as may be necessary for the determination of any issue on which guidance is sought.

That gave MI5 considerable leeway, if it wished to take it. It meant that it could gather intelligence anywhere it liked, and only had to convey that intelligence to its masters if it felt it was necessary for them to know. The effect of this was to establish MI5, in theory at least, as an almost entirely unaccountable body, either to the Home Secretary, or to anyone else. Short of cutting off its money, sacking its Director-General, or asking nicely, there was little a government could do.

That was deliberate, and may even have been well intentioned. The idea was to keep MI5 'absolutely free from any political bias or influence', which it would not be if it was at the beck and call of the dominant party in the state: the government. The same consideration may have lain behind Maxwell Fyfe's definition of MI5's duties, which was similarly non-partisan. It too is worth quoting in full.

> The Security Service is part of the Defence Forces of the country. Its task is the Defence of the Realm as a whole, from external and internal dangers arising from attempts at espionage and sabotage, or from actions of persons and organizations whether directed from within or without the country, which may be judged to be subversive to the State.[59]

That was objective to a fault. It made it clear that the threats MI5 existed to counter were threats to the entire 'realm', and not just to one interest group. It made no attempt to specify them, but left that to the independent judgement of the professionals. The purpose was to prevent the security services' being shackled to any one political viewpoint. But it may not have had this effect.

If not, then it will have been because Maxwell Fyfe's definition left *too* much to the discretion of the professionals. It really was strikingly vague. Almost anything on earth can be 'judged to be subversive to the State' in one way or another, and probably is, by somebody somewhere. Twelve years later Lord Denning attempted a new definition of 'subversion', which at least limited it to attempts to overthrow governments *'by unlawful means'*;[60] but no such qualification appears here. The field was wide open. In effect, MI5 was being given leave to choose its own targets. In view of its social composition, its political tendencies, its virtual unaccountability and the secrecy which shielded all its activities, this could be ominous, from some points of view.

Chapter 10

Dungeons and dragons (1970–88)

Only very rarely in British history has the secret service provoked great public controversy. That is one of the reasons why it does not feature prominently in British history books. Sometimes this is because it has been well hidden. The best way of keeping a secret is by keeping the fact that you are keeping a secret secret too; which is what protected the British secret service for much of its career, especially earlier in the twentieth century. At other times the reason for the lack of serious controversy has been the lack of a serious secret service: as, for example, in Victorian times, when governments deliberately abjured anything of the kind precisely in order to avert such controversy. There have been two major exceptions to this general rule. The first was in the 1810s, when the alleged excesses of Sidmouth's 'spy system' provoked the very controversy that the Victorians thereafter took so much care to avoid. The second came in the 1980s, when similar excesses – or worse – were alleged against the police Special Branches and MI5.

Most of those latter allegations referred back to the 1970s, which were a period of growth for the security services, and possibly of fundamental change. The growth came about in response to a number of new challenges that arose then, or were newly *perceived* then, and which for some contemporaries made these years a uniquely critical time. Richard Clutterbuck, for example, formerly an army major-general and now a lecturer in politics, described the decade up to 1978 as 'amongst the most agonizing in British history', and pervaded by a 'ground swell of fear'.[1] One of the obvious reasons for this was the recent growth of terrorism; whose whole object, of course, was to instil fear.

197

In Britain terrorism was mainly associated with the Irish problem, as it had been for more than a hundred years. That flared up again in 1969, when serious sectarian violence in Belfast and Londonderry led to British troops being sent in, and the formation soon afterwards of the 'Provisional' (or more violent) IRA. In 1974 the Provisionals extended their activities to the British mainland, with a series of bomb outrages presumably designed to frighten the government into conceding a united Ireland against the wishes of the majority in the North. The worst one came on the night of 21 November 1974, when 21 people were killed and 182 injured in explosions in two crowded Birmingham pubs. That was the bloodiest incident, but not the last, in a long if sporadic campaign of terrorism, which had an enormous impact on the evolution of the security services while it was going on.

It did two things. First, it gave rise to a number of measures designed to counter it directly, like new laws and executive orders, new styles of policing and new covert counter-terrorist agencies and methods. Most of these measures eroded civil liberties to some degree. This was most marked in Northern Ireland itself, with 'direct rule' from Westminster being imposed there in 1972, for example; juries abolished for terrorist trials in 1973; and internment of suspects without any trial at all being introduced at various times. In Britain a 'Prevention of Terrorism' Act rushed through Parliament in the wake of the Birmingham bombings in November 1974 gave the police new powers in cases where terrorist activity was suspected, and was followed by other measures, including curbs on television interviews with IRA sympathizers. That was on the surface. Underneath the measures taken are, predictably, more difficult to chart. We do know that intelligence-gathering and covert operations became more extensive and sophisticated. Some of them were adapted from recent British experience elsewhere.

The colonies were a useful laboratory. After the war many of them had taken advantage of Britain's exhaustion to press for self-government, usually by covert rather than open military means: subversion, propaganda, secret organization, infiltration, guerrilla warfare, assassination and terrorism. To meet this the British authorities had been forced to develop new techniques, including better methods of intelligence-gathering, and more subtle and effective propaganda. In Malaya Hugh Carleton Greene, who later went on to become Director General of the BBC, was called in to help.[2] There the British actually succeeded by these means in defeating a major communist subversive threat, which was encouraging. It also implied some general lessons. One of the conduits for those lessons was Frank Kitson, an army officer who served in several of these colonial campaigns against insurgency, and came away from them convinced that he had seen there the shape of wars to come.

His ideas were contained in an influential little treatise published in 1971 under the title *Low Intensity Operations*, which was Kitson's name for this new type of war. He started from the premiss that conventional warfare was on the way out, partly because of the nuclear stalemate, and partly because this covert kind was proving to be so effective. He believed there was a danger of it even in Britain, if for example a grievance ever arose – like 'a significant drop in the standard of living' – which could be exploited by extremists or outside enemies. This had implications for the army, which had to develop a 'low intensity' capability to meet this situation. That would include what by then were coming to be known as 'psychological operations', or 'Psyops'; and the development of an entirely new ethos, in which the traditional military values of strength and courage would be replaced by new ones like brain power and 'deviousness'. That would be sure to upset the old guard; but Kitson believed it was necessary, either to defeat subversion, or else – he intriguingly suggested at one point – to 'foster' it, if the government were in the wrong.[3]

Between 1970 and 1972 Kitson served in Northern Ireland as commander of a brigade in Belfast. He may have been largely responsible for the setting up and development of 'Psyops' units there. If he was not, then somebody else was. By all accounts this side of the army's work expanded enormously over the next ten years, and involved some techniques which could be described as devious. That may be putting it very mildly indeed. Among the 'tricks' attributed to various British intelligence agencies in Northern Ireland in the 1970s – army intelligence, MI5, MI6, British Special Branch, RUC Special Branch – were torture, for which Britain was censured by the European Human Rights Commission in 1976; murder, faked to look like 'sectarian' killings; the planting of bombs in Dublin in 1974 to provoke the Republican Irish government into tougher anti-IRA laws; homosexual seduction and blackmail; 'black' propaganda and disinformation; 'shooting to kill'; fabricating evidence; and 'covering up'. At one stage, because of inter-departmental rivalry, MI5 and MI6 were rumoured to be indulging in covert operations against each other, which will have complicated things.[4] The evidence for this is sketchy and circumstantial, and provides no basis for a final judgement yet. It is possible that we shall never know for sure.

On the British mainland things will not have gone so far. The Metropolitan Police Special Branch expanded to meet the IRA threat, from just over 200 officers in the late 1960s to 379 in 1985. The Home Office claimed that this was not unreasonable, in view of the much greater increase in terrorism over that period.[5] But the Special Branch was not alone. In 1971 a 'Bomb Squad' was set up at Scotland Yard after an explosion (not an IRA one this time) outside the home of Conservative minister Robert Carr in January that year. In 1978 that was absorbed into a new 'Anti-Terrorist Squad'.[6] They will all have liaised with the Northern Irish police authorities, foreign police and intelligence agencies, GCHQ and MI5, whose executive arm the Special Branch was still supposed to be.

These are the bare bones. The task of fleshing them out is hopeless for an outsider, and forbidden, of course, to anyone in the know. Very little has 'leaked' in this area, for very good reasons; far less than in Northern Ireland, for example, or with regard to the security services' other mainland British roles. Occasionally there have been glimpses: a corpse discovered in a Surrey ditch in 1974, for instance, which turned out to be that of a Special Branch informer – and possible *agent provocateur* – among the IRA;[7] and an anonymous MI5 officer ('Mr O') testifying from behind a curtain at a coroner's court in Gibraltar in September 1988, to the effect that MI5 had misled the SAS into believing that three IRA operatives they were shadowing there were more dangerous than they really were, thus justifying the SAS in shooting to kill.[8] But these merely highlighted the problem. The only flashes of publicity concerned blunders, real or apparent. ('Mr O' could have been lying, to get the SAS off the hook.) Presumably they were not typical. That was the point made by Home Secretary Leon Brittan when he defended the Special Branch before a Commons Home Affairs Committee in January 1985. It was always, he said, the mistakes and the wrongdoings that came into the public eye, and were 'dwelt on by some people'. But this was misleading. What was 'less well known' was the Special Branch's record of success.

> It cannot be known, because it cannot be proclaimed. When hundreds of innocent people are saved from a bomb, because of the information that the Special Branch have obtained, which enables them to step in before the bomb actually explodes, that is something that I cannot talk about and which the Special Branch officers cannot talk about. However, it happens, and it happens frequently. There are many people in this country today who are alive but who would be dead if the Special Branch did not exist.[9]

Such enforced silence was frustrating to the security services if he was right. Alternatively it could also have been convenient if he was wrong.

It was convenient in more ways than one. It could cover up counter-terrorist failures by the security services, if any should occur. It could also be used to protect the security services from investigation or criticism for 'mistakes and wrongdoings' in other areas of their activities, entirely unrelated to the terrorist one. This was the second main effect of the IRA bombing campaign of the 1970s in this field: to seem to justify the role of MI5 and the Special Branch and the others *generally*. It did this by allaying doubts. One example is the Conservative MP Peter Rowe, who eloquently described the allaying of his own personal doubts in a Commons debate on official secrecy in the summer of 1988. 'Part of me', he said,

> recoils from the spectacle of a society being permeated by large numbers of anonymous, perpetual schoolchildren, fascinated for life by dungeons

and dragons games played by real people and increasingly persuaded
that everything that happens does so because of a malign, conspiratorial
intent. The idea that my telephone might be tapped . . . , that information
derived from the tap might be entered into records of whose existence
I shall for ever remain ignorant and that it might be seen by people of
whom I am ignorant and who will make what use they may choose of it,
sends a frisson down my spine. I long at such moments for tighter and
more open control . . .

However, when I learn that a 1,700 lb bomb has been placed in
a shopping centre – timed to go off to create the maximum civilian
casualties – and has been reached by brave security men less than five
minutes before it was set to explode, I realize how much we owe to
the security services. I then recoil from measures that might destroy
their effectiveness or diminish their protection against injury from our
country's enemies. In that sense I am schizophrenic as, I am sure, are
many other hon. Members.[10]

That reads like an honest statement of a genuine dilemma. It also illustrates
the advantage to the security services in the 1970s and 1980s of having one
enemy – among all the others – as universally detested as the IRA. That was
why ministers like Leon Brittan, when defending the security services, placed
so much emphasis on this side of their work. It was the easiest one on which
to elicit public sympathy.

How significant it really was compared with the rest of the security services'
activities is difficult to say. Terrorism was clearly a major target, but it was
not the only one. In a way it could be regarded as a good deal less
important than some of the other threats Britain was faced with in the
1970s, for one simple reason. The IRA did not really endanger the British
state. Terrorists only slaughter people; they do not in general subvert them.
States are much more likely to be overthrown by subversion than by isolated
killings. Killings, in fact, usually have the opposite effect: of rallying people
to the forces of order, including covert forces, as we have seen. Few people
were in any doubt about this. Those who talked of a 'crisis' in the 1970s were
certainly not. In Clutterbuck's catalogue of the factors which had contributed
to Britain's 'agony' then, for example, terrorism has a very low place. Far more
important was the industrial situation; as it was also to most of the rest of the
contemporary political Right.

It is important to understand the Right's perception of things at this time,
because it may have been similar to the security services' perception too.
That the 1970s were indeed a 'critical' decade in British history is clear to
everyone today, because of what happened at its end. This was the time
when the Right finally reasserted itself in British politics, after decades in

the wilderness, and began pushing back the 'socialist' tide which had been steadily engulfing Britain for all those years. Before that happened, however, other outcomes seemed feasible. They look unlikely now, because of the way things have turned out, and they looked unlikely to most people then; but they were taken seriously by some on the Right. Clutterbuck is an example. What he feared most, he wrote, was the break-up of 'the complex structure of our industrial society, whereby we earn our livelihood', resulting in economic 'collapse'. The signs he saw of this were price inflation and unemployment, accompanied by demonstrations and strikes in which 'violence was openly advocated, orchestrated and provoked in a way which has been rare in British history'.[11] The prime examples of the last were the miners' strikes of 1972 and 1974, the second of which was supposed to have 'brought down' Edward Heath's government in a way that appeared to strike at the foundations of parliamentary democracy, no less. The main culprits, therefore, were the trade unions, which were widely felt to have grown too powerful – 'over-mighty' was a favourite adjective – in the 1970s.

That was the most common right-wing scenario. There were also some rather more gilded versions of it. Many of them saw sinister influences at work in the background, like communist subversion fomented from abroad. That was supposed to work on two levels. The first was a Soviet Russian campaign to undermine Britain by softening up her 'consensus', preparatory to a more open assault on the West. Already, thought some rightists, this was happening. The 'cold war' was over, and replaced now by 'coexistence' between East and West. That in itself could be seen as a Soviet propaganda success. It lulled the majority of people in Britain into regarding the Russians as non-aggressive. In fact they were not; only their tactics had changed. Instead of relying on military conquest to extend their empire, they had switched to more subtle and sophisticated techniques of 'political warfare, propaganda and subversion ... on a global scale'. Their initial aim was 'not so much to win converts for the Communist cause outright but to weaken the will of the peoples of the Free World to resist the spread of Communism and to confuse Western public opinion as to the true aims of the Communist states'. The next stage would be an attack on 'the morale of non-Communist countries by attempting to bring their values and institutions into disrepute'.[12] The media, of course, were a prime target for this, and also the Church of England ('trendy vicars') and the universities. The right-wing spy writer Donald McCormick particularly singled out late-night satirical programmes on television, and college sociology syllabuses. Then there were the Soviets' 'front' organizations, generally cleverly disguised: sometimes as *anti*-Soviet pressure groups, which was the cleverest disguise of all.[13] It was a broad-fronted, and highly effective, covert attack.

It was complemented by another. That involved the communists' élite subversive corps, and was directed at the highest reaches of British social and political life. Much of the 'evidence' for this came from a Czech defector called Josef Frolik, who had fled to the West in 1969 with the most alarming tales of 'infiltration', generally by means of blackmail and bribery. One target was what he called 'the Princess Margaret circle', which however had managed to resist the virus. Similarly unsuccessful was a 'Czech plot to lay a homosexual trap for the former Conservative leader, Edward Heath', which had to be aborted when the British security service got to hear of it. (The bait in this case was an agent called Jaroslav Reinberger, described by Frolik as an 'organ virtuoso'.)[14]

The communists were supposed to have done better, however, elsewhere. They did best of all with trade union leaders, some of whom were named by the Conservative (and ex-MI6) MP Stephen Hastings under the shelter of parliamentary privilege in December 1977;[15] and with a number – 'around thirty' was the usual estimate – of Labour MPs. One of the chief suspects among the latter was the Prime Minister Harold Wilson himself, who was believed to have been compromised by the Russians during one of his many visits behind the Iron Curtain as President of the Board of Trade in Attlee's government, and then manoeuvred into the leadership of his party when his predecessor, Hugh Gaitskell, died 'mysteriously' in 1963. One of the sources of this idea was the CIA man James Jesus Angleton. Later a defector called Anatoli Golitsin gave more credence to it by recalling rumours he claimed to have picked up that the KGB was about to bump off an opposition leader *somewhere* in the world.[16] That, of course, would explain a great deal.

That was the worst of these right-wing fears in the 1970s, this side of insanity. If it was true, of course, then it posed problems of allegiance. If the government had effectively been taken over, where was a genuine patriot's loyalty due now? The Prime Minister might be an enemy agent. The head of MI5 could be another one. The 'democracy' had been subverted through the media. The royal family was supposed to be apolitical. This was a tough one. One solution is described in a novel by George Shipway published in 1971, *The Chilian Club*, which is probably the best written of what by now had become a well-established little literary sub-genre in Britain. Its heroes are four elderly ex-army super-patriots, helped by the secret service, who take the law into their own hands by assassinating trade union bosses, student agitators, anti-apartheid leaders and lefty bishops, all of whom have mysterious Moscow links, in order to clear the way for the 'bosses' to take over again and 'put the country straight'.[17] The *Daily Express* loved it; and for rightists generally reading *The Chilian Club* must have relieved their frustrations temporarily, like a political wet dream.

So far as is known no one tried to imitate this in real life. But there were plots of other kinds. Some of them involved coups: like two that were rumoured to have been plotted in the 1960s, neither of which came to anything. The first is supposed to have involved a number of high-ranking army officers who approached the Queen Mother in the early 1960s with a plan to topple the first Wilson government in order to spike the unions and get South Africa readmitted to the Commonwealth. The story is that that was scotched when the Queen Mother told them (in effect) not to be silly boys. The second was probably initiated by *Daily Mail* proprietor (and MI5 agent?) Cecil King, who tried to involve Lord Mountbatten and Sir Solly Zuckerman in a similar conspiracy in May 1968. It was Zuckerman who put paid to that, calling it (rightly) 'rank treachery'.[18] Later on, around 1974, a number of 'private armies' sprang up in Britain ostensibly to help the government to combat civil disorder, but with the potential, clearly, to try to stage a coup if the situation seemed to warrant it. The leader of at least one of these armies ('Civil Assistance') believed that Wilson was a communist.[19] But the coup never happened: or so it appears.

These plots – or counter-plots – were the fruits of desperation. But not every rightist in the 1960s and 1970s was as desperate as this. This was not because they regarded the problem as any less serious, but because they realized that it implied its own solution. That followed logically on. If you believe in the potency of a particular subversive plot, then it will be because you believe in the potency of subversion *generally*. You believe, in other words, that people – especially proletarians – are easily led, and hence easily led astray. That is a common rightist attitude, and lay at the root of the rightists' concern about communism in the 1960s and 1970s. But it also had a rider. If people could be easily led astray, they could equally easily – surely – be led back to the right path again. What was needed was an equal effort against communist subversion as was being put into it, and with the same techniques. That should do the trick.

This, of course, was not a new idea. The assumption behind it – that people cannot be trusted – is a fundamental and long-standing conservative one. In the nineteenth century it was a major argument for resisting democracy in Britain, and then in the early twentieth century – when democracy was achieved – a reason for fearing it. That was when conservatives started looking for ways of trying to limit the damage. Propaganda was one, in order to counter the 'manipulation' of the proletariat by the communists. The initiative in this was taken by private enterprises like the Economic League, which was still highly active in the later period. Governments took a hand in it in a crude kind of way during the First World War, and then slightly more subtly during and after the Second: through, for example, the Foreign Office's misleadingly named Information Research Department.[20]

By the 1970s it was plain that these lessons had largely been taken on board. People who mattered – in positions of real authority – knew what was going on. They had the enemy in their sights. The 'once mysterious processes used by the organizers of subversion', wrote Kitson, were now 'exposed for all to see'.[21] That was comforting, especially after Kitson was made deputy commander of Britain's land forces in 1980. Kitson knew his subversives, and how to cope with them. (It is interesting to speculate that if his predecessor in the 1830s had had a copy of *Low Intensity Operations* to hand, there might have been no need for a Great Reform Bill.) Industrialists, politicians and police were becoming just as aware. One highly aware policeman was James Anderton, the Chief Constable of Manchester, who saw the country being threatened by a covert enemy 'more dangerous, insidious, and ruthless than any faced since the second world war', bent on achieving power in order to 'overthrow democracy' and attack 'the most cherished elements of the establishment, including the monarchy'; and thought that *this* was what the police ought to be concentrating their efforts on now, rather than 'basic crime'.[22] That was encouraging too. With such staunch figures in the vanguard of the counter-attack, and sophisticated new techniques of counter-subversion available, the Right – and by extension the country – now stood a chance.

If the police were to take on a more political role in this sense, then it was to their Special Branches that they would look in the first instance. There are indications that this was, indeed, a period when the Special Branches widened their trawl. One indication is the definition of 'subversion' that was coming to be accepted in police circles in the 1970s, and which was a good deal broader, for example, than Lord Denning's had been in 1963. Denning's definition was limited to acts which aimed to 'overthrow' governments, by 'unlawful means'.[23] By 1975, according to a Labour spokesman in the Lords, sedition now embraced 'activities which threaten the safety or well-being of the state, and which are intended to undermine or overthrow Parliamentary democracy by political, industrial or violent means'. Much later a Conservative Home Secretary explained how it was not enough to 'define subversion in terms of those who breach the criminal law. We must be able to know the plans and intentions of those who abuse the freedom that we provide *under* the law'.[24] That added several new criteria, and some ambiguities, which gave the police elbow room if they wanted it.

MI5, being less accountable, probably needed less excuse. Peter Wright claimed that the important development there came around 1972, when 'F' branch – the counter-subversive section – was given a boost, and told to take on board what its director-general called the 'far and wide left', apparently on the orders of Edward Heath. That annoyed Wright, because it diverted attention away from his own 'penetration' inquiry. He also warned that it raised the spectre of a 'Big Brother' society, which was likely to alarm liberals more than it probably genuinely alarmed him. The new targets included extreme left-wing splinter groups that may not have been felt to be worth bothering with before. Potential infiltrators faced problems here, not the least of which, claims Wright, was the leftists' sexual promiscuity; for 'there were some sacrifices even an MI5 officer would not make for his country'.[25] The chastest solution to this was the use of telephone intercepts, which seem to have increased greatly at this time, and with no effective parliamentary – or even ministerial – oversight.[26] Around 1980 a further step is supposed to have been taken in this direction, with the systematic monitoring of a whole range of targets which before then had not been considered either potentially treacherous or subversive, including, for example, trade unions and the Campaign for Nuclear Disarmament. Much of this came out when an MI5 officer called Cathy Massiter started feeling uneasy about it, resigned, and in 1985 told Granada Television. She also claimed that all this new surveillance was being done on the instructions of the government, and for party political – not strictly national – ends.[27]

By then the signs were clear that political espionage in Britain was far more extensive than had used to be thought. A number of particular examples came to light. One notorious one was the case of Mrs Madeleine Haigh, who was subjected to surveillance by her local (West Midlands) Special Branch on the basis of a newspaper letter she had written opposing the siting of cruise missiles in Britain. The police denied it at first, and it was only her persistence which elicited an admission from them in the end. That produced a spate of letters to the press from others who suspected similar Special Branch surveillance on them, but in these cases there was no way of knowing whether or not their suspicions were justified.[28] In 1985 a former chief constable claimed that 40 per cent of his own Special Branch's files were 'totally unnecessary', and concerned 'people who were outspoken rather than ... people engaged in crime'.[29] By then nearly anyone in Britain who was in the slightest degree radical had come to assume, or to suspect, that he or she was on an MI5 or Special Branch list somewhere.

Few of them seemed particularly cross about it. (Some may even have felt flattered.) This, as we shall see, marks a little historical revolution in itself. What did cause some umbrage, however, was the idea that information gathered by this means might be used to damage or even ruin people's careers. This – 'blacklisting' – became an issue in the 1980s, after revelations involving mainly MI5 in the state sector, and the Economic League in the private. 'Blacklisting' offended liberal susceptibilities mainly because it was kept secret from its victims, who in most cases had no inkling of why they were being rejected and consequently no way of defending themselves. That basic natural injustice was compounded by a number of errors that came to light. Some of these were ludicrous. The most notorious concerned the Labour minister Judith Hart, whom MI5 confused at one time with an ex-communist called Mrs *Tudor* Hart, possibly to the permanent detriment of the former's political career.[30] In 1985 the BBC was revealed to have been systematically blacklisting writers and producers on the instructions of an MI5 man who was now – since 1982 – actually physically ensconced there, and on similarly unreliable evidence.[31] This may have been just the tip of an iceberg. 'Blacklisting' pervaded other levels of society. In the private sector much of it was done by the Economic League, whose main activity now was compiling indexes of 'subversives', against which they checked lists of potential employees for client companies. Mistakes were made there, as well.[32] Another security agency – a subsidiary of Securicor – in 1973 advertised among its services to employers 'a man planted among your employees to report on untoward behaviour and to undertake research into the background and antecedents of workers'.[33] So they were into spying, too.

These, of course, were private enterprises, and consequently not strictly part of the official 'secret state'. But the two cannot be separated so easily. In the first place, it is arguable that in an increasingly free enterprise society domestic espionage is likely to take this form, as power is devolved (not dissipated, as is sometimes assumed by free marketists) into private hands. The fact that these particular powers are devolved into private hands does not make them any less powerful, or potentially tyrannical, than if they remained with the state; nor does it mean that the state – which has created the conditions for the devolution – is any the less responsible. But that is a philosophical point. There is also a practical one. The fact is that the two sectors sometimes worked together. The effect of this was to blur the line between them, and to extend the effective aegis of the security services.

There were links, for example, in terms of personnel. The security industry often recruited from the security services, and from the ordinary police. A leading example is Sir Percy Sillitoe, ex-head of MI5, who shortly after he retired in 1953 became involved with a number of private security firms.[34] Ex-policemen will have got current policemen to provide them with information. One regional organizer for the Economic League in 1987 boasted that this happened on a wide scale. There were also hints of a connection between the League and MI5.[35] The traffic in all these cases will have gone in both directions, with the private agencies helping the official security services out with information, and in other ways. In 1988 a former private eye called Gary Murray described how he had been recruited via an 'Institute of Professional Investigators', which he claimed included members of both private and government sectors (which is odd), to work on a freelance basis for the security services, monitoring people with outspoken views, and possibly more than that. He also offered an explanation for the mysterious death of an anti-nuclear campaigner called Hilda Murrell in 1984, which he suggested could have been an operation by another contracted man which went wrong. That was one of the dangers of employing freelances. The advantage, of course, was that if anything did go wrong, they could be disowned.[36]

From a purely historical perspective – looking forward to it from the past – all this looks staggering. Nothing much like it had ever been seen in Britain before. In one way or another, Britons were far more spied upon in the 1970s and 1980s than they had been for 200 years at least, and possibly for the whole of their history. What makes this more remarkable is the strength of their tradition of opposition to this kind of thing before then, which seemed almost to have melted away by the 1980s. Now, if anyone in Britain learned that he was being watched or bugged or phonetapped or docketed, he seemed to take it as a matter of course, with hardly any fuss; as though it were only to be expected in these times. Of course comparisons are odious, and unhistorical; but it is worth noting that if any Victorian (outside Ireland) had suspected this in his or her time, then the outcry, in the press and Parliament, would have been deafening, and probably fatal to any government that could be shown to have sanctioned such practices; on the ground that they offended against the most cherished of the Victorians' civic values, which was their freedom from a political police.

The outcry in Britain in the 1970s and 1980s was rather less deafening than this; but it could be heard, if you listened carefully. It hardly touched the popular press, but that was hardly to be expected from the institution which had probably degenerated more than any other in Britain from the standards set in Victorian times. In a few serious newspapers, the occasional television programme and Parliament, there were some signs of unease. In the ten years from 1979, more time was taken up in Parliament discussing the secret and security services than during the whole of the previous 160 years: since the time of Sidmouth, in fact, with which this later period bore some comparisons. Most of the discussion revolved around two issues, which were usually treated separately.

The first was the counter-espionage one, and concerned the ability of MI5, in particular, to root out communist spies and moles. This was largely a hangover from the Philby–Maclean–Burgess affair of years back, which went on smouldering partly because many people doubted whether it had been entirely cleared up then. Among the doubters were Peter Wright within MI5, and one or two spy writers outside. The whole affair erupted again dramatically in November 1979, when one of those writers induced the new Prime Minister, Margaret Thatcher, to come clean on Blunt, and on the immunity from prosecution which had been granted him in 1964.

That provoked an unusually broadly based protest. Rightists took it as a sign that previous governments and the security services had been soft, or not vigilant enough, on communism. Leftists revelled in the class implications of the affair. Willie Hamilton, the anti-royalist Labour MP, drew an obvious moral.

> Let me give the right hon. Lady some advice ... If she wants to initiate searches for the fifth man, the sixth man and those after him, she does

not need to look for them in the Labour party, in the trade unions, in the comprehensive schools, or even among the British Leyland shop stewards. Let her look for them among the ex-public school boys, those with homosexual propensities, those who voted Tory at the last election and those in social groups 1 and 2.

Others resented what they saw as the special treatment accorded by the upper classes to one of their own. 'The Blunts get their cigars and their smoked trout,' said the *Evening News*, 'while those outside the magic establishment circles, the Blakes and the Vassalls, are locked in jail.' Jonathan Aitken, always a Tory maverick in these matters, saw it as 'a peculiarly British scandal, in which ... the decent chaps decided not to sneak on the old school spy until, unfortunately, those beastly rotters, the journalists, came in and debagged him'.[37] Thatcher insisted that it was not like this at all: that the real reason for granting Blunt immunity was to induce him to spill the beans; but as an 'outsider' herself she may well have shared some of these populist prejudices.

Peter Wright certainly did; and also thought that Blunt was holding some of his beans back – in particular, the name of the real 'Fifth Man'.[38] His suspicions surfaced first of all in 1981, in a book by Chapman Pincher called *Their Trade Is Treachery* for which Wright received half the royalties;[39] and then in *Spycatcher*, which was finally published (abroad) in 1987. Wright attributed much of MI5's continued vulnerability to Soviet penetration to its public school recruitment, and to the close class loyalties which acted as highly effective barriers to the investigations of grammar-school oiks like himself.[40] The next spy scandal involving MI5 undermined that theory a little. Michael Bettaney, who was caught trying to pass papers to the Russians in 1984, was almost as much of an oik as Wright, which showed that you could not over-generalize; though everything else about him fitted, including Oxbridge (after state school), ostensibly far-right political views, and a personality defect: in his case, drink. The Bettaney affair was another serious blow to public confidence in the security services' competence in the field of counter-espionage. By that time, however, the second reason for worry had also loomed into view.

That was to do with the security services' counter-subversive role, which some Labour MPs, in particular, suspected had recently rather got out of hand. At best it was a waste of MI5's and the Special Branch's energies; a point which the Labour leader Neil Kinnock tied in with the other, counter-espionage complaint in 1985.

Does the Prime Minister agree with me that it is wrong that the security services should dissipate time and resources in conducting the surveillance of loyal British people, who have no connection with espionage and pose no threat to the security of this country, when they should be concentrating entirely on real subversives, real spies and real terrorists who do wish us harm?[41]

The idea of that was clearly to emphasize the soundness of the Labour Party on the issue of national security. It may have been for the same reason, or in order to avoid a subject which was so spiky with potential embarrassment in many ways, that Labour took so long to come to the more serious aspect of the charge against MI5, in particular: which was that it was working in a partisan fashion, against the interests of Labour, and in support of right-wing factions within the state.

This charge mainly centred on what became known as the 'Wilson plot', which was an alleged conspiracy by a maverick section of MI5 to undermine the second Labour government of Harold Wilson in 1974–6. There were two versions of it: one had MI5 attempting to blackmail Wilson; the other had them leaking unreliable stories about him to the press, to discredit him publicly. Other leading politicians were also apparently targeted, and other intelligence agencies – including the CIA and South Africa's BOSS – involved. The CIA is likely to have had a hand in it, via James Jesus Angleton and his great MI5 buddy, Peter Wright. The stories against Wilson alleged sexual impropriety with his personal secretary, corrupt land deals and links with the KGB. That was where the Golitsin and Frolik stuff came in. Some of Wilson's ministers were also smeared, including Edward Short, for whom a Swiss bank statement was forged by someone or other, in order to suggest that he was avoiding tax on some ill-gotten gains. It is even possible that the Judith Hart 'mistake' was deliberate. Other targets included the Liberal leader Jeremy Thorpe, and the former Conservative Prime Minister Edward Heath.[42] The campaign seemed to succeed to an extent. Thorpe was ruined as a result of it. Wilson and Heath may also have been casualties. Heath was voted out of the leadership of the Conservative Party and replaced by the right-wing Margaret Thatcher in February 1975. In March 1976 Wilson announced his resignation as Prime Minister, in circumstances which some people considered to be mysterious. Three years later Labour lost power, and then split. This was what the 'plotters' had been after. But of course it does not follow (any more than it had in 1924) that they were responsible for it.

These allegations first saw the light of day in the summer of 1977. They took a while to take hold at first. This was because there was – inevitably – so little proof. Knowledgeable people derided the whole idea, or pretended to. When Harold Wilson himself raised it in the mid-1970s the MP Stephen Hastings called him 'positively paranoic' and urged him to 'see a psychiatrist'. Hastings's own theory was that the story was part of a Russian disinformation plot to undermine the British secret services. They had seen this happen recently in America, during the 'Watergate' scandal, which he claimed was a put-up job by the KGB. 'Now we have the beginning of the same thing in this country.'[43] The historian Christopher Andrew in 1985 did not go that far, but thought the notion of an anti-Wilson plot 'improbable', and suggested that Wilson's suspicions raised doubts about his handling of affairs generally. 'Really!' expostulated the ex-historian Lord Annan in the upper House in February 1988; 'credulity can go no further.'[44] That was the response of many people, which will have daunted others who were nervous of being branded paranoid too.

So the matter went away, for ten years from its first airing in 1977. It came up again chiefly through Peter Wright's *Spycatcher*, which mentioned it in passing. That was important because Wright professed to have first-hand knowledge of the plot: from a group of fellow MI5 officers who he claimed had approached him shortly before the 1974 general election for information about Wilson to use in order to topple him. Wright's version then was that on advice from Lord Rothschild he had refused to play ball. On a later occasion he changed his story to the one that had always been widely suspected: which was that he was the ringleader of the plot himself.[45] At around the same time an ex-army 'black' propagandist from Northern Ireland, Colin Wallace, appeared with more horse's-mouth tales of either the same plot, or a parallel one. He also brought documentary evidence with him: mainly his notes, made at the time.[46] Both these sources were tainted. Wright had his grievance over his pension, and a general air of 'flakiness'; and Wallace had just completed a gaol sentence for a manslaughter charge, which he claimed was a put-up job.[47] That hardly inspired confidence. But then secret agents – practised deceivers that they are – seldom do.

Three separate issues, or sets of issues, are involved here. The first is the question of whether there was a plot against Wilson and his government, and possibly Heath, and on what scale. The evidence for some kind of plot is convincing: the Edward Short Swiss bank statement, for example, and examples that have come to light of 'black' propaganda from the 1970s associating Labour ministers with extremist and terrorist causes.[48] Of course it is feasible that these were all part of a cunningly contrived *counter*-plot: forgeries of forgeries by MI5's enemies (the KGB, MI6) in order to discredit it, perhaps; or even by MI5's friends, in order to discredit – eventually – the people who were doing the discrediting. In this field no possibility, however apparently bizarre, should ever be entirely ruled out. The likeliest explanation, however, is the straightforward one. There were plots afoot. They may not have *worked*. They seemed to, because of the way things turned out; but in fact there are other and better ways of explaining the falls of Wilson and Heath and the rise of 'Thatcherism' in this period, than these conspiratorial ones. That again depends largely on one's view of the efficacy of conspiracy generally. But something was going on. Wilson was not imagining it. Plots (probably more than one) were hatching on the

Right of British politics and society, designed to bring him down by foul – or foul-ish – means. That seems definite, albeit somewhat vague.

The second issue concerns the involvement of the security services in all this. The hard evidence here is patchier. A *Daily Express* journalist called William Massie has claimed that he was briefed with anti-Wilson material by MI5: but he could not know of that for sure. Maurice Oldfield, the head of MI6 at the time, thought that a section of MI5 was plotting against Wilson, and told this to Chapman Pincher, who believed it: until he learned, he says, that Oldfield's sources were simply Pincher's own 'lunch table gossip', and Wilson himself.[49] Peter Wright's testimony is more direct, but disconcertingly fluid. Colin Wallace's is better. His contemporary notes have been forensically tested, and shown to be genuine – that is, genuinely contemporary.[50] The problems here are that there is no irrefutable evidence of what was done *with* them; and no clear indication of the link between Wallace's Northern Irish 'Psyops' outfit, and other security agencies. These difficulties are real. But they are exactly what we would expect to find in this situation. This is an added complication. The most sensitive secret service operations are always devised in such a way as to make them 'deniable'. Secret services work deviously, through covert agents, hidden networks and 'fronts'. If there *was* any MI5 involvement in a Wilson plot, we would be bound to find it hard to trace it. If it were any easier, then we might begin to suspect that it really was a 'counter-plot'.

The more innocent they seem, the more guilty they are likely to be. That, of course, is a typically secret service way of thinking, and a warning to any spy writer who values his sanity that perhaps he should get out before the disease finally gets him too. But there is one more issue arising from the 'Wilson plot' allegations which has to be examined first. It has the advantage of short-circuiting these problems surrounding the question of their veracity, yet it is more important in a way. The issue is this: irrespective of whether there *was* an MI5 plot against Wilson, *could* there have been? Was it feasible, in view of what we know about MI5, its management and the political situation of the time? Was MI5 capable of it? The fact that the possibility was seriously discussed suggests that it may have been. That would be an important conclusion in itself: equivalent, for example, to finding out that a man who cannot be proved to have been guilty of a particular crime nevertheless has criminal proclivities.

The main medium-term significance of the 'Wilson plot' affair, in fact, was to raise this very point about MI5. The allegations could not be proved, but neither could they be dismissed out of hand. They seemed in many ways to *fit*. For example: MI5 certainly had opportunities to plot, even under the strict terms of the Maxwell Fyfe directive, which were nothing like as constrictive as was often assumed.[51] It also had motives galore. 'Patriotism' was one, if an MI5 man were convinced that Wilson really was a KGB mole. The interest of the agency was another. The secret services had always distrusted Labour, partly because Labour distrusted them. Before the war the relationship between them had been awkward, to say the least; and it was exacerbated by Attlee's foisting of an outsider on MI5 as director-general in 1947. In 1965 Wilson apparently tried to do the same again, and appoint the Lancashire Chief Constable, Eric St Johnston, to replace Hollis, but was persuaded out of it by his intelligence adviser, George Wigg.[52] Labour also tried to clip the security services' wings. In 1964, for example, Wilson stopped MI5 from tapping MPs' telephones. In 1969 he pruned the Information Research Department, and in 1977 Callaghan closed it. Merlyn Rees claimed he curbed Northern Ireland's 'Information Policy' (or Psyops) unit in 1976. At the same time they put pressure on MI5 to recruit ex-state schoolboys, and appointed an outsider from the Foreign Office to head it in 1978.[53] Even if one accepted that these measures were not treacherously intended, they could be regarded as detrimental to the security of the state. That tied in with the 'patriotic' motive again. And 'patriotism' was something MI5 had a great deal of.

It was, however, a very particular kind of patriotism, defined to a great extent by the prejudices of the people who made up MI5. They had always been an odd bunch, as we have seen: socially and politically entirely untypical of the nation as a whole, eccentric and often not very bright. This does not seem to have changed appreciably by the 1970s. The best evidence for that is probably the testimony of a number of 'establishment' figures who were close to MI5 in this period, and who could occasionally be found voicing concern about the type of person it took on. One example is Lord Carver: a former top soldier who had been a customer of MI5's in the past, and was not at all happy about the quality of the service he had received. He criticized in particular its recruitment procedures, which seemed to him to operate 'on the basis that, provided the man or woman is a friend of a friend of a friend, he or she must be all right'; and also its 'obsession with secrecy'. The result, he said, was that 'the people concerned seemed to live in a completely closed world whereby what really went on and what people actually thought and did, they just did not understand'. Another critic was Lord Beloff, a Tory academic, who gained the impression from the references he was asked to write on students being considered for MI5 posts that it was 'employing people whose degree of political sensitivity was rather low'. Lord Dacre, a historian who in the past had worked for both MI6 and MI5, described the 'occupational danger of enclosed societies' like the latter as 'a tendency to live in a private world' and so lose 'balance and a sense of proportion': sometimes to the extent of fantasy and paranoia. Former Conservative Prime Minister Edward Heath also had his doubts. Some MI5 men, he insisted, were 'admirable'. But others were not.

I also met people in the security services who talked the most ridiculous nonsense and whose whole philosophy was ridiculous nonsense. If some of them were on a tube and saw someone reading the *Daily Mirror*, they would say 'Get after him, that is dangerous. We must find out where he bought it.'[54]

(If Heath ever told MI5 that to their faces, they probably inferred that the Czechs had got him after all.) None of these critics was a notable left-winger. Yet the impression they all gave was that MI5 was to the right even of them, and paranoid to boot.

All this together might be thought to amount to a fair measure of circumstantial evidence in support of the hypothesis of a security service anti-Wilson plot. That is less important, however, than what it says about the security services in any case. To many liberals in all political parties in the 1980s it raised doubts about their impartiality, their competence and their integrity which were reasonable in the circumstances, and had a bearing on broader issues of principle, like the problem of 'accountability', and the place of secret services in democracies generally. These were big questions, which seemed to many to deserve proper investigation and scrutiny from the outside. The response of the government of the day, however, was quite different.

Its main response was to try to suppress any informed discussion of the security services at all. Uninformed discussion was something else. Outsiders could still write their books about them if they wanted: like (presumably) this one. They could always be dismissed as mere speculation. Insiders might be allowed to 'leak' in certain circumstances: if it were done anonymously, and in a way that emphasized the importance of their work. One or two spy writers made quite good livings by processing and publishing such leaks, which sometimes amounted almost to whole books, under their own names or *noms de plume*. There were also some parliamentary exceptions. On three occasions the Prime Minister actually initiated discussions in the House of Commons herself: over Blunt in 1979, the Hollis allegations in 1981 and Bettaney in 1985.[55] The Home Secretary, Douglas Hurd, claimed that this made her government more 'open' in these matters than any other in history.[56] But that was disingenuous. All these cases related to the efficiency of the security services, not their role. They had to do with Soviet infiltration, and the means taken to prevent it. Though they might reflect badly on MI5 at the time, they also confirmed the need to strengthen it. They only opened the doors that MI5, and the government, wanted opening. All other doors had to remain tight shut. That meant blocking parliamentary questions; refusing inquiries; muzzling current or former security service personnel; and chasing them through the courts if they ever slipped their muzzles off.

That was the policy. It was not always entirely successful. In 1977, for example, under a Labour government, three men were prosecuted under the Official Secrets Act for publishing information about GCHQ. It became known as the 'ABC' trial, after the defendants' initials, and achieved notoriety from the outset when it was revealed that the jury for it had been 'vetted' by the Special Branch. Despite this it ended with a whimper, with one of the defendants – a serving soldier – being sentenced to a term of imprisonment, but the others, who were journalists, being conditionally discharged on the grounds that nearly all the 'secrets' they had revealed had been culled from public sources like *Flight International* and the *Civil Service Yearbook*. Soon afterwards two American whistle-blowers were summarily deported for their part in the affair. The government had a more complete success with Sarah Tisdall, who was given a six months sentence for leaking documents connected with the deployment of cruise missiles in Britain in March 1984; but possibly only because she pleaded guilty from the start. Then came a disaster. Clive Ponting, another civil servant in the Ministry of Defence, was charged under the Official Secrets Act for revealing that his minister, Michael Heseltine, had deliberately lied to Parliament over an incident during the Falklands War. In this case the defence pleaded that the 'public interest' justified Ponting; the judge ruled that the public interest was identical to the government's interest (which certainly simplified things), and summed up for a conviction: but the jury disregarded him, and acquitted. 'Ministers Aghast', was the *Daily Telegraph*'s headline the next day.[57] The result was that they never trusted the old Official Secrets Act again.

More specifically: they did not trust *juries*. This was not often spelled out openly, but when it was it was in terms that could not be faulted on grounds of logic. 'I don't personally believe so much in the value and the judgments of any jury of twelve persons, picked at random for their ignorance and lack of qualifications, in making judgments of that kind,' the Conservative MP Ivor Stanbrook told a television interviewer in November 1988. 'You must have this thing clearly defined, and not hazarded upon the opinion of a jury which may be swayed one way or another.'[58] This was in connection with a white paper on the reform of the Official Secrets Act published by the government in June that year, which had proposed that in cases like this (and some others) a 'public interest' defence, or indeed any other kind of defence, should simply not be admissible. If it could be shown that the defendant had leaked official information, for whatever reason and in whatever circumstances, then he or she would be automatically guilty, and the jury *instructed* to convict.[59] That would plug that particular hole.

In the meantime the government proceeded against further leakages and revelations in ways which avoided the need for juries altogether. This did not always work perfectly either. With broadcasting companies the usual methods were to appeal to their directors, or issue D-Notices, or slap injunctions on. In one notorious instance in January 1987 the Special Branch was sent in to raid the BBC's Glasgow headquarters in order to stop the showing of a television programme about a projected spy satellite called 'Zircon'. It succeeded for a while; but eventually the Special Branch had to send back all the material it had seized in the raid, and the programme went out the following year. A similar (albeit less heavy-footed) process delayed the transmission of a BBC radio series on the secret services for a few months in 1987–8. In the case of books and articles by ex-secret agents, ministers hit on another method: which was to appeal to the law of 'confidentiality', which because it was a *civil* law, not a criminal one, could be decided by judges alone. They even took this weapon with them abroad, though to very little effect. In December 1986, for example, the Dublin High Court decided against them over the posthumous memoirs of the wartime MI5 agent Joan Miller, *One Girl's War*, which was consequently released for publication there. Much the same happened with Peter Wright's *Spycatcher*; though only after an interminable progress through the courts of half a dozen countries, starting in December 1986 with Australia, where Wright was living and the book was first published, and ending in October 1988 in the British House of Lords.

The *Spycatcher* case was widely considered to be humiliating to the government, not only because it lost nearly everywhere, but also because of the expense of the whole action, the harm it did to the reputation of certain government witnesses, especially the Cabinet secretary, and what appeared to be its counter-productive effect. By the end of it *Spycatcher* had sold more than a million copies worldwide, most of them because of the notoriety given to it by the government, and many of them smuggled into Britain from other countries. Many of the government's own supporters found it hard to understand what exactly they were at. Julian Amery thought the affair revealed 'a singular lack of a sense of humour', at best.[60] Yet after it all ministers did not seem unduly depressed. When they were quizzed on it they insisted that it had been 'money well spent'.[61] Sometimes they behaved almost as if they had actually won.

The reason for this was that, from their point of view, they had. Of course the battle had been lost: but they must have seen that coming for some time. So far as the larger campaign was concerned, it was not a bad defeat at all. What they were mainly interested in was securing their hold over a particular little piece of territory, which they believed to be strategically vital: the new principle of 'confidentiality', which they took to be the obligation on the part of all public servants never unofficially to disclose anything they learned in the course of their duties, right up to their deaths (and maybe beyond). The Law Lords supported that principle. Their judgement in favour of the publication of *Spycatcher* was clearly reluctant. They still thought Wright was a rotter (or, in the words of the usually highly urbane Lord Annan, 'a shit').[62] Nothing could excuse his 'treachery', which according to one of the Law Lords was just as 'heinous' as anyone's who had betrayed his *country*: not even the submission that it was in the public interest to know that MI5 was up to no good. The only pro-*Spycatcher* argument that impressed them was that because it was so widely available anyway, it would look stupid to close the stable door now.[63] That did not affect the main principle, which presumably future 'leakers' could still be got on; especially after 1989, when it was due to be enshrined in the new Official Secrets Act.

Insiders could not speak out, and outsiders could not look in. That was the other side of the coin. Outsiders quite often tried to look in, but were always rebuffed. In Parliament there was a 'long-standing and well-established convention that these matters are not discussed across the floor of the House', which was supposed to justify ministers in refusing to answer questions on any issue connected with the security services, however serious.[64] On one occasion, in 1984, the House of Commons Home Affairs Committee undertook an inquiry into the work of the police Special Branch, against the government's wishes; but it was a feeble affair, chiefly because the committee was never let within sniffing distance of any proper evidence, or of anyone who actually worked for the Branch.[65] This sort of thing was not approved of. Parliamentary scrutiny was discouraged. Ministers were solely responsible. If there was anything to be done, then they were the ones to do it.

There clearly were things to be done. The 'Wilson plot' allegations, for example, really had to be checked. In May 1987 the Prime Minister announced that she had checked them, by asking the current Director General of MI5 to conduct an internal investigation. His conclusion, which she accepted because he was a man of 'integrity', was that MI5 was as pure as the driven snow.[66] She also told of certain reforms she had instituted in MI5. All of them related to its 'management', and were designed to make it stronger, in two ways. The first was by improving recruitment procedures to prevent future Soviet penetration: though the government could not say exactly how, in case it gave hints to the KGB as to where it might target its new generation of moles. The second reform was to institute new 'grievance procedures', in particular the appointment of a 'staff counsellor' (Sir Philip Woodfield), to hear complaints from disaffected officers who might otherwise be tempted, like Cathy Massiter and Peter Wright, to blow the gaff.[67] That should help prevent MI5 stumbling into the public light again on future occasions; and in that way protect it in its main, counter-subversive role.

None of these 'reforms' made the security services any more 'accountable'. Indeed, their purpose was the very opposite. The government made no bones about this. It did not believe in accountability. It was too dangerous. It meant spreading secrets, which carried the danger of their spreading into the wrong hands. Who could be trusted? One possibility was judges. Most of the 'penetration' inquiries in the past had been headed by them. They were reliable; certainly, on past showing, by comparison with juries. One government spokesman thought they might be considered for a more general kind of oversight role, on the grounds of what he called, somewhat curiously, their superior 'knowledge and wisdom of the world'.[68] Other candidates were less likely. A committee of the House of Commons was clearly out of the question, because it would need to be broadly representative. So were Privy Councillors, who sounded very grand and responsible, but included some pretty fishy characters nevertheless. 'I amused myself in the bath this morning,' revealed Julian Amery in December 1986, 'thinking of Privy Councillors who might be selected . . . Some of them are rather old, and some have dubious pasts.' An example was the shadow Foreign Secretary, Dennis Healey, who had been a communist many years before.[69] That would never do.

That was one argument against bringing in others besides ministers to keep a check on the security services. Another was that it would be bound to act as a check in other senses too: holding them back, and possibly giving rise to pressures for curbs on their powers. Such pressures were bound to be ill informed, because there were certain aspects of the secret services' work – which might contain the best arguments for not curbing them – that could not be revealed to anyone. This apparently had been the CIA's recent experience since Watergate, when its accountability to Congress had been tightened up, to the detriment of both itself and (it was claimed) America's national security.[70] It was generally at this point in the argument that terrorism was brought in, in order to point the danger of an over-accountable, over-curbed security service. It was a 'dangerous world', as the Home Secretary pointed out to the House of Commons in December 1986. (A few days later his under secretary said the same thing in the same words in a virtually identical speech; which must have been boring for those who sat through both.) In these conditions it was essential, in the national interest, to preserve both 'the integrity and the necessary confidentiality of that service', above every other consideration.[71]

That meant no accountability, beyond the ministers properly concerned. New legislative changes mooted in November 1988 made no essential difference to that. 'Confidentiality' was tightened up, by incorporating it into a new Official Secrets bill, as we have seen. The Home Secretary, Douglas Hurd, claimed that this Bill was a 'liberalising' one, on the ground that it no longer protected trivial information, as section 2 of the old Act technically had. As the old Act had never been used in trivial cases in the past, however, that was a meaningless concession, as he must have known. In all other ways the new Bill was the reverse of liberal. So was the Security Service Bill which complemented it, and proposed a major change by officially acknowledging the existence of MI5 for the first time, but only in order to regularize some of its shadier activities. By the terms of it the Home Office had to issue warrants for bugging and burglaring, which would be 'monitored' by a 'commissioner', appointed by the government and sworn to secrecy; and a tribunal of lawyers would field complaints from those members of the public who ever managed (in the face of the Official Secrets Act) to find out enough to know that they *had* complaints to make against MI5.[72] At first sight that looked pretty meaningless, too.

The basic position, therefore, was unchanged. The security services' 'integrity', or completeness, was preserved. They remained responsible to the Home Secretary, but were not obliged to tell him everything, and so were not *completely* responsible to him. So far as Parliament was concerned, or the Privy Council, the security services were not allowed to tell them anything, and the Home Secretary not obliged to; which left them as much in the dark as before. It was a closed system, which probably had a lot to be said for it, but depended on people's trusting the minister if a lot was not also going to be said against it, and suspicions and resentments not aroused. That might have been possible in some periods of British history: the 'consensual' times, when there had been broad public agreement about political and social values, and a belief in the integrity (in the other sense) of people in public life. During the 1980s, however, there was neither. Consequently for much of that decade it was difficult to reassure many people that the security services were not corrupt and tyrannical, even though it was possible that they were not: or at least, not *very*.

The policy of suppression obviously encouraged this suspicion, especially the hounding of *Spycatcher*, which could be explained innocently, as we have seen, but made it *appear* as though a skeleton or two might be dangling behind some of those doors. One possible skeleton was the 'Wilson plot'. If there really was nothing in that, the government must have been sorely tempted to break its own rule of secrecy in order to show it, for it clearly cast suspicion on ministers, its main beneficiaries, as well as on MI5. One or two of the trails even seemed to approach No. 10; via the large number of right-wing Conservative MPs who had secret service connections, and especially the late Airey Neave, who had masterminded Thatcher's succession to Heath in 1975, and had had links with some very shady intelligence people indeed. That really would make this, as one Labour MP put it in December 1986, 'the biggest political scandal of the century'.[73] It was a nasty slur for a government to carry around with it, especially if it was undeserved; a high price to pay for what might have been in reality a highly principled defence of MI5's 'integrity'.

There were better reasons, however, for mistrust in the 1980s, arising from the nature of what came to be called 'Thatcherism' – the ideology – itself. Thatcherism was essentially an amalgam of two broad ideas. The first was an absolute and dogmatic faith in economic individualism as the only right and natural choice for free people. It shared this by and large with the Victorians, whose 'values' Thatcher made a great play in the early 1980s of wanting to revive. The second idea, however, was very un–Victorian; or at least, not often associated in Victorian times with the first idea, whose adherents would have baulked at it. That was a deep lack of confidence in the capacity of free people to make that right and natural choice, because of their vulnerability to subversion by evil forces from the outside. This made a huge difference. The ultimate justification of the Victorians' liberalism had been popular consent. Now that was devalued. Popular opinion was untrustworthy, because it could so easily be subverted. Economic individualism had taken its place as the ultimate justification for any government policy or act. That had wide-ranging implications, most of which were in some senses anti-democratic. And anti-democrats were the last people, surely, to be entrusted with the management of a covert political police.

The dangers could be seen in the nature and the 'style' of government which took hold of Britain from 1979–on. Nothing like it had ever been seen there before. Early on in her premiership Margaret Thatcher boasted of being a 'conviction' politician, which essentially meant a dogmatic one. She made a virtue of intolerance, especially with regard to socialism, which she persisted in branding as an 'alien' and hence unpatriotic creed. She clearly had no feeling for 'civil liberties' as they were generally understood; no instinctive objection to people's bring watched, recorded, filed or indexed, by the proper authorities. She had no great esteem for democracy, or even for freedom, except of the individualistic kind. The idea that people should band together to pursue their interests collectively seemed to her to be the purest tyranny. It was also, she felt, potentially dangerous in circumstances where national security was involved, which was one of the reasons (American pressure was suspected to be another) for her government's ban on trade unions at GCHQ in 1984. In that same year, in connexion with the miners' strike, she referred to trade unions – or she may have meant certain individual trade unionists: it was never made entirely clear – as an 'enemy within'. All this indicated a somewhat restricted view of what constituted tolerable or loyal political activities, whose corollary must have been a correspondingly broader definition than most people would have given of *in*tolerable political activities on the other side.

It was not just a question of attitudes. Other prime ministers (though not many) have also held strong opinions, which however have been tempered in practice in response to pressure and advice. In Britain it is called compromise, or consensus politics; in the United States of America it is institutionalized in the doctrine of 'checks and balances'. That was not Thatcher's way. Opposition was not something to be listened and trimmed to, but to be removed. In her cabinet it was stigmatized as 'wetness' and eventually wrung right out of the system, leaving it bone dry. Other previously relatively independent bodies, like the civil service and the broadcasting authorities, were brought to heel. In the case of the civil service the process was called 'politicization'. The BBC came under furious political pressure over a number of issues in the 1980s, and by the end of that decade was widely assumed to have caved in. New appointments to its top posts were blatantly political, and all pretence at 'balance' in its management was ditched. The commercial sector seemed to be going the same way early in 1989, when its governing authority was reconstituted, and an extreme right-winger (Lord Chalfont) chosen as its deputy chairman who was one of the keenest spotters of 'socialist subversion' in the media, and had links with the security services to boot. Some people believed – though they may have exaggerated the danger – that the government's campaign to make schools and universities more 'accountable' was part of the same trend. Other sources of obstruction, like local government and trade unions, were emasculated more overtly. For those who believed in a pluralistic kind of democracy, it was an unhappy time.

Complementing these developments was the assertion of a new 'right to manage' in industry and in the public sector – that is, to manage people – whose anti-democratic undertones are obvious. 'Management', in fact, was one of the 'buzz-words' of the day. ('Buzz-word' was another.) Its techniques could be subtle. Enormous efforts were put into manipulating public opinion, through sophisticated advertising and public relations methods, using deceit and misrepresentation in a deliberate effort to distort the pure democratic process, if there can be said to be such a thing. Both political sides were involved in this, but the Right far more whole-heartedly than the broad Left, for reasons – chiefly its belief in subversion – which have already been spelled out. The Right always had accepted the need to manipulate the public to some degree, if only to prevent its being manipulated by somebody worse. There was no reason why that should exclude the use of the security services to this end, apart from the risk – which secrecy would minimize – of being found out.

Indeed, it was far easier to imagine a government like this misusing its security services than any other British government of any political complexion for the past 150 years. Others might have misused them – and undoubtedly did – *despite* their principles; this government would not even have had to contravene its principles to any great extent. It is also easy to imagine its being *able* to misuse the security services, because of the ideological affinities between them, which were – again – closer than between any other peacetime British government and its security service since Luddite times. MI5 will have loved Thatcher: especially her rousing talk of 'enemies within', which was, of course, exactly what paid their rent; and the way in which – in public at least – she defended them against every sort of critic, including the rightist Wright. She may have owed her position to them, which would have bound them very close indeed; but even if not her heart, and more importantly her guts, were clearly in the right places. Only one thing may have jarred. Socially they were not quite so snug a fit. In origin Thatcher was at the *petit* end of the *bourgeois* scale, which was a little lower than most MI5 personnel; she was also grammar school educated, and a woman. All this will have taken a little getting used to.

That problem, however, was not insuperable. If MI5 were posher than Thatcher, they were still not as posh as MI6, who will have had greater difficulties relating to her, especially after their failures over the Falklands in 1982. There are also signs that the gap with MI5 had already narrowed considerably by the time she came to power, and probably narrowed more subsequently. In November 1979 the former Labour Home Secretary Merlyn Rees averred that 'the type of person who has been recruited [to MI5] in the past 10 or 15 years' was 'completely different' from previously: at which James Callaghan interjected, 'Thank God'; and Lord Birdwood a few years later claimed that they now strove positively for a broader social mix.[74] What that meant in practice was unclear. MI5's recruitment policy was one of the secrets it clung on to most tenaciously.[75] It probably became more meritocratic. Peter Wright recalls Michael Hanley, the director general from 1972 to 1979, boasting of having achieved his job 'on his merits, not through the old boy network', which led Wright to suspect him of 'socialism'; but the latter's viewpoint, of course, was extreme.[76] In 1984 an ex-MI5 officer acknowledged that the intake by then had become 'broader than in the old days', but claimed that it made no difference to the 'overall tone' of MI5, which was still 'right-wing'.[77] Some people from working-class backgrounds may have been let in. (Michael Bettaney is an example.) In general, however, most of the new sorts of recruits must have been middle class as always, but of a different type. If they were recruited from state grammar schools there will have been fewer landed gentry among them, and more ideological capitalists. The public schools were shifting their emphasis towards the latter too: taking in more *nouveaux riches*, and concentrating on turning them into what one contemporary headmaster called 'pirates' rather than the 'prefects' of old.[78] That will have affected the social and political composition of MI5, but not necessarily 'democratized' it significantly. The overall effect will have been to identify it even more closely than previously with the 'Thatcherites'; which was unlikely to produce a situation in which the latter could be depended upon to check and balance it.

On the other hand, this may have been what people had come to expect by then. The pressures for checks and balances in the 1970s and 1980s were not as great as they would have been a few years before. Liberals were against the government on these issues, but there were fewer liberals (in all political parties) than there had been in the past. This was another factor giving rise to anxiety on the part of the few older-fashioned liberals who still remained. There were simply not enough of them to exert any kind of effective constraint from the outside.

The signs of this were plain. Scandals galore about secret service activities came to light in the 1980s, and yet almost no one seemed scandalized. Some of the scandals involved counter-terrorism, which was a damper on liberalism for most folk. That will explain, for example, the lack of any significant public protest over the cases of the 1974 Birmingham and Guildford bombers, who were strongly suspected of having been wrongly convicted; and over several shootings of unarmed IRA agents in Northern Ireland and elsewhere, which were felt to have been unnecessary and possibly intended deliberately as a means of 'executing' suspects whom it might be difficult to convict in a court of law. Most of the latter were followed by blatant 'cover-up' operations, one of which involved 'smearing' and then removing the senior British policeman appointed to inquire into it, when it looked as though he might be nosing out the truth.[79] That gave rise to considerable publicity, but to none of the strong *feeling* which is always necessary to fuel a really effective protest over anything. That was because no one felt any sympathy for the victims of these injustices, who were after all IRA members and supporters, and consequently unentitled to any more scrupulous consideration by the representatives of the people they sought to kill and maim. That was understandable, if dangerous. But it does not explain everything. Other excesses had nothing to do with terrorism. They too failed to strike any loud liberal chords.

The two main responses to these excesses in the 1980s were resignation, and disbelief. The resignation is mirrored in much of the spy fiction of the period, which may also have done something to reinforce it. Spy stories were still immensely popular in Britain, more so than anywhere else in the world, which must be significant.[80] From the mid-1960s onwards their ethos changed considerably, chiefly under the influence of 'John le Carré' (John Cornwell), who had once been in the business himself. Their heroes were no longer romanticized, but the very reverse. They were less principled, more sordid, sometimes vicious; yet they were still, it seems, regarded sympathetically. One of le Carré's characters describes the intelligence community as 'a squalid procession of vain fools, traitors too, yes; pansies, sadists and drunkards, people who play cowboys and Indians to brighten their rotten lives';[81] but his readers did not appear to mind. They stayed with him, accepting all this as admirable in some cases, no doubt, but more often as simply necessary, in a world which the spy novelists increasingly depicted as a place of corruption and deception, in which ordinary moral values did not and should not (for safety's sake) apply. Whether people took this to be a faithful reflection of reality is hard to say. What they did seem to do was to extend the amorality implicit in it to their perception of real events outside. For this, of course, spy fiction was not wholly or even significantly responsible. There are deeper reasons for the growth of disenchantment and cynicism in Britain in the 1970s and 1980s, which cannot be fully explored here. The decline of religion may have had something to do with it; or the loss of empire; or a knock-on effect of terrorism; or the influence of American culture; or the degeneration of the popular press; or moral subversion (from somewhere); or the crisis of capitalism in the West. Whatever the cause, the effect was that people's expectations were lowered. In a word, they had become more cynical.

The other common response was the reverse of this. Many people were simply reluctant to credit that this sort of thing – the excesses – could go on. Some of this reluctance was rooted in a faith in British traditions of parliamentary government, legal accountability, decent behaviour on the part of the nation's leaders and the like which had always been a little wishful, and may by this time have become almost entirely delusory, but were nonetheless necessary both for governments to sustain, and for people to believe. They were powerful myths, which it can be argued had been instrumental in maintaining social cohesion and order in Britain for years. Wright's and Wallace's testimonies conflicted with them directly, and carried the most unsettling implications, if they were true. For example: if there was anything in the most serious charge made, and MI5 had indeed been partly responsible for replacing one British government by another in the 1970s, then it raised doubts about the whole nature of the British political system – about 'democracy' and the way it might be being manipulated, and about the 'rule of law', or the lack of it, in certain important areas of public life – which could be shattering. For liberal intellectuals it raised the even more disturbing notion that the order and rationality they generally preferred to see behind most historical developments were chimerical, and that in reality the course of events was determined almost arbitrarily, by 'conspiracies'. It was almost as though they were being asked to believe that the course of the planets had suddenly been discovered to be a put-up job, to make it *look* as if they were logically circling the sun. It was simply too much to stomach, without the most solid and credible evidence imaginable; which of course none of it – least of all Peter Wright's – was.

The security services had a significant advantage here. Many people, possibly most of them, were predisposed to give them the benefit of the doubt. Either they believed the stories that were told about the security services, or some of them, and did not mind; or they *would* have minded the stories if they had believed them, but either did not believe them, or did not consider them significant. To a great extent it depended – again – on their views of the potency of conspiracy generally. If you believed in conspiracy generally you would be inclined to credit MI5's conspiracies, but you would also be inclined to believe in the conspiracies MI5 claimed to be conspiring *against*, which could be taken to justify them; if you did not believe in conspiracies generally, then you would be sceptical about both. The second category embraced most liberal-minded people, which was why there was not more liberal protest than there was. People like this – the potential critics – would need an awful lot of convincing before they would accept that things were as wrong as the 'paranoiacs' painted them. The only people who could *know* whether things were as wrong as that, however, were men and women whose testimony was intrinsically *un*convincing, because they were professional liars, and inclined to paranoia themselves. There was almost no way of escaping from that.

The security services had another defence. That was the image they acquired, and may possibly have cultivated, of absurdity. When there *was* criticism of them in the 1980s it very often took the form of mild ridicule, which was far easier for them to weather than other kinds of censure would have been. The *Spycatcher* saga, for example, was treated largely as a great national joke, with Peter Wright in his funny broad-brimmed Australian hat as the main comic character. A rather good spoof version of it by William Rushton called *Spy Thatcher* came out in 1987, emphasizing the ridiculous side of Wright and his MI5 world. Christopher Andrew's pioneering 1985 history of British intelligence, *Secret Service*, reinforced this impression by making great play of his spies' eccentricities. It was a brilliant disguise. People tend not to take eccentrics seriously. The assumption is that silliness renders the sillies ineffective, and consequently harmless. That may even have been the idea. It had occurred to people before. As far back as the fifth century BC the Chinese writer Sun Tzü had maintained that the ideal spy was 'a man of keen intellect, though in outward appearance a fool'.[82] The effect was certainly disarming. In January 1988 the shadow Home Secretary, Roy Hattersley, pointed out quite reasonably that 'it is possible to be ridiculous and tyrannical simultaneously'; but the point may not have struck home.[83] The same mistake was often made at this time about the upper classes more generally.

That was how MI5 survived. But it was at a price. The price to itself was probably more management efficiency, of the kind that was being forced on other institutions and agencies too during the Thatcher years, sometimes quite inappropriately. The price to the people was incalculable. Management reforms are not necessarily a boon to everyone, if they produce a better-managed tyranny. It is possible – though we cannot know for sure – that this is what happened to MI5. If so another result, of course, will have been to make it less of a joking matter all round.

The price to the *government* of all this controversy surrounding the security services in the 1980s was a change in the public's perception both of those services, and of the political system of which they were a part. At its simplest level the change was that the public *started* perceiving them, far more widely than they ever had before. In 1988 the government of the day formally acknowledged MI5's existence for the first time ever, in announcing a parliamentary Bill which would incorporate its conventions into statute law.[84] That was a recognition of the fact that it was no longer possible to protect the security services by pretending they were not there, which had been the strategy, and a generally successful one, before then. In the past people had known about them, of course, but only in the back of their minds. Now the floodlights were on them, or at least on the screens behind which they sheltered, which meant that they could no longer bank on being ignored. It also brought other problems. Because only the screens showed up in the floodlights, people grew suspicious about what might be going on behind. That was bound to happen, quite irrespective of whether anything untoward was going on there or not.

This had always been seen as the danger. Sir Robert Armstrong, the cabinet secretary who came out of the Australian *Spycatcher* trial with a reputation for dissimulation but could be refreshingly candid at times, admitted this during his cross-examination in November 1987. He was asked what harm could be done by allowing *Spycatcher* to be formally published, when it had already been widely circulated and was clearly known to the Russians in any case. His answer was that 'the mere fact of publication in this country will undoubtedly promote discussion of, and articles about, the topics here, and thus lead to a heightened sensitivity and awareness of the methodology, philosophy, and organization of the service'.[85] It was this that had to be avoided: not potential enemies' 'awareness' of MI5, but the people's, in case they did not like what they became aware of.

There were two reasons for this. One was that it might lead them to try to clip MI5's wings, as we have seen. The other was that it might disillusion them. For years it had been widely assumed in Britain that her secret services simply did not behave as *Spycatcher*, for example, now suggested they had. People had no idea that they burgled and bugged on so wide a scale, plotted to assassinate foreign presidents, and acted against democratically elected British governments in the way *Spycatcher* alleged. 'Awareness' of all this, whether it was true or not, might undermine their trust. People would become cynical towards the secret services, and by extension towards the politicians responsible for them. They might also stop believing what they were told. An example of this came during the course of 1988, after the shooting of the three IRA agents in Gibraltar by the SAS, when there was widespread scepticism about the official version of events. When later it was suspected that MI5 had been the source of anonymous smears in the popular press against one of the witnesses who testified against the official version, that was widely credited too.[86] This was clearly admirable in a way: uncritical acceptance of authority is not generally considered to be an admirable quality in any animal higher than a sheep; but it could also be unhelpful, from a government's point of view. A government which is not believed is not respected. That was likely to be one of the effects of the spy controversy of the 1980s, if the authorities were not successful with their new security service and official secrets bills in sweeping it all under the carpet again.

It might even do more than that. The 'Wilson plot' allegations in particular were dangerous in a much more radical way. They raised doubts not only about the security services and the credibility of the government, but about Britain's entire democratic processes more generally. The mere suspicion that Thatcher *might* have been cheated into power by a secret service plot did that. If this was the way things were done, then why bother to vote? Alternatively, anti-Thatcherites could use it as a convenient excuse. It is always a comfort for a loser to believe he has been defeated fraudulently; it also justifies *him* in breaking the rules. In other words, the suspicions undermined – if only marginally – Thatcher's *legitimacy*, which is a serious matter in any kind of state. Even without the suspicions, however, the knowledge that governments policed their people so very thoroughly – distrusted them, therefore – will have chipped away at many people's sense of identity with the state. This could be dangerous. Alienation could lead to dissent, which in its turn might be a fertile breeding ground for new forms of subversion. This meant that the security services might now in effect be provoking some of the very threats they were supposed to exist to prevent. And that, of course, was precisely what most British critics of domestic espionage had long held against it, for at least the past 200 years.

Epilogue

Secret service history may be a health hazard. It attacks the mind. After long periods immersed in it everything looks different. Apparently solid objects start quivering and crumbling; fixed points move; spaces appear where there used to be shapes; and shapes start materializing out of nothing at all. There is no firm ground anywhere: no certainties, no reference points. People turn out to be not what they seemed; institutions do not function as they were supposed to; accepted truths may be deliberate disinformation; spies and moles are everywhere; and the cleverest and most dangerous of them are those who appear most unlikely and innocent. It is a bewildering world, even for historians, who are used to regarding things sceptically, but not quite as sceptically as this.

The way of coping with it, if you adopt the secret service approach, is quite simple. You cannot measure the evidence against any external criteria, because they are all unreliable. What you can do, however, is to try to fit it all together, to see if it *holds* together, irrespective of anything outside. That will produce likely hypotheses, which are the closest you can get to certain truth. The likeliest hypothesis is the one in which all the fits are closest, and there are fewest loose ends hanging over at the end.

This method produces some interesting results. One was MI5's case against Harold Wilson in the 1960s and 1970s, which was put together in precisely this way. Another is Peter Wright's case against Roger Hollis. But it can be taken further than this. In the hands of a historian with a rather broader perspective than most secret service people seem to have, and consequently a wider range of evidence, some fascinating possibilities emerge. One of them in particular is far likelier – because a far snugger fit – than MI5's 'Wilson' theory was.

It runs like this. There were in fact two main Russian (or they may have been Czech, or Chinese, or Militant Tendency) moles. The first one was Peter Wright, some of the evidence against whom we have reviewed already.[1] The other was none other than Margaret Thatcher herself. That may seem implausible, but mere implausibility has never deterred dedicated mole-hunters in the past. It could even be seen as a clinching point in the theory's favour, if the communists are as cunning as we take them to be. In reality it is not as implausible as it appears. It fits every one of the known facts, without a single loose end left dangling outside. It solves the nagging problem of why Wright published *Spycatcher*, for example, and why Thatcher publicized it, in spite of the damage to Britain's covert defences they must have known these actions would cause. It explains the 'Wilson plot' (that is, the *anti*-Wilson plot), which now turns out to be merely a sub-plot of this much wider conspiracy. Lastly, it fits all the major recent developments in British political life perfectly.

It goes back – as all the best Marxist plots should – to Marx. Marx, of course, did not describe himself as a Marxist, but as a scientific socialist, by which he meant that he believed the path to socialism followed natural laws. One of those laws was that capitalism had to pass through certain predetermined stages of development, before the conditions for a socialist revolution could arise. During the course of the later of these stages capitalism's own inherent contradictions would result in the growth of mergers, lower wages, high unemployment and reaction in the political sphere. These were necessary in order to arouse the proletariat to throw off its capitalist chains.

After the Second World War, however, this did not seem to be happening in Britain. Capitalism was reaching an accommodation with the workers, via the welfare state and the mixed economy ('Keynesianism'), which was wholly unanticipated by the communists. The result could be to stave off the socialist revolution there indefinitely. That was what worried the KGB, who had of course (unlike MI5, perhaps) read their Marx. It was at this point that they must have activated Thatcher, and infiltrated her into power in Britain, with the help possibly of Hollis, and certainly of Wright. Wright's part in the plot was to remove Wilson and Heath, who as political 'moderates' (relatively) were the chief obstacles to the ambitions of the Soviets. This would have the effect of returning British capitalism to the orthodox Marxist rails. That is how it turned out. Britain is far more Marxist now, in this sense, than she was under Wilson and Heath. It only remains for MI5 to start looking for a week or two that cannot be accounted for in Thatcher's early life, which will be the time when she was spirited away to Moscow to be brainwashed and briefed. (The intellectual quality of the arguments she was fed with suggests that she could have been as young as 13 at the time.) Of course they may not try; or they may simply go through the motions, and pretend to draw a blank. That however will merely go to show how far MI5 is still penetrated, or even riddled, by KGB moles.

That is where this kind of logic gets us, if we pursue it all the way. Historians do not usually go in for this sort of thing, partly because they are not bothered so much by 'loose ends', which are, after all, a part of real life; and partly because they do not take so easily to 'conspiracy' explanations of events. This is the crucial difference between the two approaches. Historians shy away

229

from conspiracy theories because their broader outlook makes them aware of the large number of circumstances that would need to be manipulated in order for a significant conspiracy to succeed. Secret service people think it is simpler than that. People are malleable, and can very easily be turned into paths they might not otherwise choose to travel by clever minorities working covertly. That, of course, has profound implications for democracy, because it means that majorities cannot be trusted; which is another factor discouraging democrats and liberals, as well as historians, from adopting conspiratorial interpretations of significant political developments. What divides the two sides on this is a profound disagreement over the whole nature of politics, and of humanity in its political aspect.

For this reason it is impossible to get to the bottom of these questions – and consequently to reach a final judgement on the real significance of the counter-conspiratorial agencies which have been the subjects of this book – on the basis of the evidence alone. That evidence is fundamentally ambivalent. It is also unreliable, because our source for much of it is those counter-conspiratorial agencies themselves. The reason *they* are not to be relied on arises from their role. In order to counter subversion, you have to believe in it. If you believe in it, you are likely to indulge in it. You may call it something else: probably 'counter-subversion'; but it comes to the same thing. Counter-conspirators are nearly always – curiously – conspirators too. This may, in fact, be how most political conspiracies arise: as responses to other conspiracies perceived, or imagined, by people whose propensity to perceive conspiracies also indicates a likely propensity to combat them by conspiratorial means. That will have been the genesis of the 'Wilson plot', for example, if there ever was such a thing.

One of the results of all this counter-conspiring has almost certainly been the falsification of the historical record in this area. Usually it has not been done deliberately: with future historians, that is, specifically in mind. (Sometimes it may have been. Important people are more often concerned for their posthumous reputations than we less important ones might think.) Generally the purpose of any deception was to fool contemporaries: contemporary enemies of the state, obviously, and also – perhaps a little less obviously – contemporary enemies of the counter-conspirators, who might not be the same people at all. A common deception was to try to pretend that a particular counter-subversive agency simply did not exist, or was less extensive in its role or its powers than it really was. The best way of doing that was by maintaining an absolute official secrecy: imposing oaths of confidentiality on counter-subversive agents for life, censoring the media, declining to reply to questions in Parliament, and refusing outsiders – and this is where the historian *is* directly and deliberately affected – access to any government documents relating to the secret services, sometimes as many as seventy or a hundred years after the events they referred to had taken place. This last ploy was often obscured by the fiction that the government operated what was called a 'thirty-year rule' in these matters, by which it was commonly understood that sensitive documents were released after that time, whereas in truth only the most innocuous ones were. Scarcely any official records directly relating to Britain's peacetime security services over the past century have ever been released. Some have been destroyed, or lost; others are marked simply 'Closed'. There are a number of possible reasons for this, like incompetence, 'national security', protecting reputations and covering up villainy. A fifth may be to preserve as low a profile as possible for the present-day security services. That is entirely consistent with the approach of most British governments, and of the secret services.

Another trick was to acknowledge one particular secret service agency, supposedly reluctantly, as a means of diverting attention and criticism from other more secretive and possibly more potent ones underneath. Some of those could have been foreign: such as, in recent times, the CIA. The Metropolitan Police Special Branch performed this sort of function for some years, for example, keeping the liberal heat away from Jenkinson's and Gosselin's even more covert agencies early on, and then from MI5. An ex-Deputy Director General of MI5, Sir Eric Holt-Wilson, once indicated that this was also part of MI5's own role later. MI5, he told the Americans confidentially in 1941, was the 'only counter-espionage agency which is ever mentioned in the newspapers'. Nevertheless it was in fact 'only one cog' in a 'super machine' which covered the whole empire (as it then was), and was centred around a Registry of no fewer than four and a half *million* names of 'suspicious persons', which was its pride and joy. Nobody outside the secret services had 'any inkling' of this.[2] MI5, in other words, was merely the relatively acceptable face of what was widely considered to be an unacceptable phenomenon, which helped to obscure the fact that less acceptable things were going on underneath.

This could have been deliberate. It was certainly not beyond the wits of some security people to think of it. Lord Kennet, for example, did. In 1988 he described how as 'a very junior officer in one of the secret services' forty years before he had started to get worried about the names of the heads of those services becoming known. So he suggested

that it might be a good idea if each service was divided into two parts, one which was visible to the public consisting of two or three people with good manners and a nice bottle of sherry in the front office who were accessible only on confidential terms; the rest being the operational side which remained totally unknown to everybody. It seemed to me that that was the safest way to save the bacon of those services from undue publicity.

Unfortunately, Kennet went on,

The proposal was turned down for the very interesting reason that the senior officers did not think that they could find anybody to undertake the very boring job of being in the front office with the sherry![3]

Nevertheless, the idea of having tunnels beneath tunnels was an obvious one, and may be another factor putting historians as well as contemporaries off the scent.

Deception to this degree is probably unique. No other field of history, not even diplomatic, is so bedevilled with it. It creates certain problems. The temptation is to assume that an awful lot of secret service activity and wrongdoing is being covered up, but that is not necessarily so. Secret service people have sometimes – as we have seen – tended to exaggerate their role, either to impress their paymasters, or to deter their enemies. Those enemies have often exaggerated it too. This is another inevitable result of secrecy: to give rise to suspicions which may be undeserved.

That was possibly the case in the early years, in French revolutionary and Luddite and Chartist times. Thereafter such suspicions evaporated for a while, except among some *very* paranoid (usually foreign) people on the political Left; and there is no good reason to suppose that the confidence which prevailed then about mainland Britain's essential 'spylessness' was at all misplaced. It is the example of the mid-Victorians, in fact, which gives the lie to the prevalent belief in most intelligence circles today that espionage is a natural, unavoidable and essential tool of any human society: because they do appear genuinely to have renounced it, and not to have suffered markedly – if at all – as a result. It is possible of course to explain that, in ways which leave the general point about the necessity of secret intelligence still fairly intact. The mid-Victorians were merely lucky; as they were also, it could be said, with the success of their free enterprise capitalism. This still forms, however, an awkward historical lacuna, for those unfortunates who find it difficult to imagine any sort of life without spies.

The cover-ups began later, as Britain started to deviate more and more sharply from the standards and values she had maintained in this area in Victorian times. The fact that she had once lived by those values compounded the tendency to cover up. Britons had got used to the idea that they were not spied on by their own governments, which itself performed a useful governmental function by helping to keep them content. Disillusionment on this score might undermine that. Hence the unusual degree of secrecy that surrounded the growth from around 1910 onwards of a proper system of covert political policing in Britain, which embraced not only that system's methods but also, where possible, its very existence, as we have just seen. It is difficult, still, to delve beneath that secrecy. For that reason it is likely that the narrative account of the development of Britain's modern security services which is offered in the last three or four chapters of this book is a *minimal* one, giving only a very partial impression of a phenomenon whose ramifications are almost certainly considerably more extensive than is indicated here. In this connection, it is worth considering a parallel case. Australia had a domestic secret service from the First World War onwards, whose activities are far better known because historians there *are* allowed to examine the historical record. The picture that emerges from that record is of a consistently more extreme and intrusive system of political surveillance than is known about in Britain, exploited for partisan purposes (especially against Labour) by unscrupulous prime ministers, and indulging in widespread scaremongering and 'dirty tricks'.[4] The question naturally arises from this: were Australian intelligence agencies *worse* than Britain's in this regard? That is one possibility. The other is that Britain's were just as badly behaved, but that we know less about it, because of what has been, in effect, a great historical cover-up.

Secrecy also has other implications. In so far as it limits accountability, it is also likely to encourage corruption of various kinds, and what is usually called 'excessive zeal', on the part of the agencies protected in this way. The late nineteenth-century historian Lord Acton put it best, as he did with so many 'Victorian values', when he wrote that 'every thing secret degenrates'.[5] That could serve as a salutary warning from his time to ours. In the particular case of MI5 this inherent danger was aggravated by another, related factor. One way of ensuring secrecy is through loyalty. MI5 sought *that* by recruiting very narrowly, from among the acquaintances and consequently the social class of its existing officers. It did not always work, as Blunt's case shows. But it may have had other effects. One was to limit the loyalty of MI5's members to their own class. This was not necessarily deliberate, or even a matter of which MI5 was aware. Its agents may have tried hard to be objective, and by their own lights 'apolitical'. They genuinely believed they were guarding the nation's interests: but it was *their* conception of those interests, which was unlikely to have been a broadly based one, simply because their own social and ideological base was so circumscribed. That was replete with potential perils from a democratic point of view, some of which may actually have materialized.

The particular class MI5 recruited from may also be significant. Generally they were upper-middles. Nearly all of them were public school educated; and in one way or another they mostly had strongly individualistic streaks. Middle-class individualists have always furnished the most and best domestic spies in Britain, probably because they lack other classes' social sense. The individualist ethic encourages this, or at least does not discourage it as much as do other class moralities, according to which spying on one's fellow men and women is almost the lowest thing one can do. It would be interesting to know whether foreign domestic espionage agencies also recruit predominantly from this same class, or (in communist countries) from the relicts of it. If so, there might be a fascinating general theory waiting to be formulated here. In the meantime, and so far as Britain alone is concerned, there can be no doubt at all that domestic secret service work has always appealed to the middle rather than to the upper or working classes, and to the political Right more than the political Left; which clearly gives the middle classes and the Right an enormous advantage, *if* domestic secret service work is as effective as its closest friends and its sharpest critics maintain.

Among other classes until recently, and among the middle classes at one time, domestic espionage has generally had a poor press. Those involved in it have been accused of lying, cheating, manufacturing evidence, provoking or inventing outrages, and latterly of plotting to oust an elected government. Some of the accusations may have been false; or the domestic secret services may, in fact, have done much worse. In any case such abuses are clearly an innate tendency of any domestic espionage system, which it may in some circumstances be difficult to control. It is rational, and probably wise, to be suspicious of secret political policemen and women, if for no better reason than that they are highly suspicious people themselves. It is a fundamental rule of life – though it may not have been expressed so clearly before – that the last people on earth you should trust, in any situation, are those who are distrustful of you.

These dangers and tendencies have always existed in connection with domestic espionage in Britain. They were the reasons the Victorians spurned it: spurned the treatment for subversion not only because they felt it was unnecessary, but because they feared its side-effects. A secret political police, they believed, was not only the mark of a sick society, but also one of the things that *made* it sick. They anticipated that in the hands of unscrupulous governments it might be used for partisan ends. They also predicted that it would bring its own nemesis, by alienating people from their rulers and hence provoking irresistible pressure for change. The situation, of course, has changed enormously since their time. Terrorism, in particular, renders some form of covert domestic intelligence-gathering agency necessary in a way it was not when terrorists usually only succeeded in blowing up themselves. That is what sustains the security services today. It may also justify them. But it does not dispose of the danger which is inherent in them, and has manifested itself countless times in history: that the medicine can, if it is not administered under the very strictest and widest supervision, have effects which are as damaging as the disease.

Notes

Preface

1. Quoted in Bruce Merry, *Anatomy of the Spy Thriller* (London: 1977), p. 113.
2. Herbert T. Fitch, *Traitors Within* (London: 1933), p. 19.
3. *Guardian*, 29 September 1988.
4. Below, page 18.

1 Sly and subtil fellowes (4000 BC to AD 1790)

1. Phillip Knightley, *The Second Oldest Profession: The Spy as Bureaucrat, Patriot, Fantasist and Whore* (London: 1986).
2. Genesis 42; Numbers 13; Joshua 2.
3. Francis Dvornik, *Origins of Intelligence Services* (New Brunswick, NJ: 1974), pp. 6, 11.
4. Ibid., ch. 1 *passim*; Sun Tzü, ed. James Clavell, *The Art of War* (London: 1981), pp. 8–10, ch. 13.
5. Homer, *The Odyssey*, trans. E. V. Rieu (London: 1946), pp. 69, 160–1; Virgil, *The Aeneid*, trans. W. F. Jackson Knight (London: 1956), pp. 51–9.
6. Luis A. Losada, *The Fifth Column in the Peloponnesian War* (Leiden: 1972); Andre Gerolymatos, *Espionage and Treason: A Study of the Proxenia in Political and Military Intelligence Gathering in Classical Greece* (Amsterdam: 1986).
7. H. Michell, *Sparta* (Cambridge: 1952), pp. 162–4; Chester G. Starr, *Political Intelligence in Classical Greece* (Leiden: 1974), p. 11; Donald Engels, 'Alexander's intelligence system', *Classical Quarterly*, n.s., vol. 30 (1980), p. 336.
8. Dvornik, op. cit., pp. 52–3.
9. See, for example, John Cam Hobhouse's maiden speech in the House of Commons, 9 May 1820, in *Hansard*, 2nd series, vol. 1, cols 258–9.
10. Jock Haswell, *Spies and Spymasters* (1977), p. 12; Dvornik, op. cit., p. 76.
11. E.g. ibid., pp. 15, 24, 26, 46.
12. Ibid., p. 93.
13. Chester G. Starr, *Civilization and the Caesars* (Ithaca, NY: 1954), p. 141.
14. Dvornik, op. cit., pp. 101–9; W. G. Sinnigen, 'The Roman secret service', *Classical Journal*, vol. 57 (1961–2), pp. 66–70; Starr, *Civilization and the Caesars*, p. 206.
15. Ibid., p. 363; Dvornik, op. cit., pp. 109, 131; W. G. Sinnigen, 'Two branches of the late Roman secret service', *American Journal of Philology*, vol. 80 (1959), pp. 238–54.

16   Dvornik, op. cit., p. 217; Richard W. Rowan, *Spy and Counter-Spy* (London: 1929), pp. 194–7.
17   Dvornik, op. cit., p. 224.
18   Starr, *Political Intelligence in Classical Greece*, pp. 40, 5; *Civilization and the Caesars*, p. 221.
19   E.g. Starr, *Political Intelligence in Classical Greece*, pp. 5, 40; Losada, op. cit., p. 111.
20   Dvornik, op. cit., pp. xv-xvi.
21   Starr, *Civilization and the Caesars*, p. 158.
22   Starr, *Political Intelligence in Ancient Greece*, p. 44.
23   Dvornik, op. cit., p. 142.
24   Ibid., chs III–V.
25   J. R. Alban and C. T. Allmand, 'Spies and spying in the fourteenth century', in C. T. Allmand (ed.), *War, Literature, and Politics in the Late Middle Ages* (Liverpool: 1976), pp. 73–101.
26   Niccolo Machiavelli, *The Prince* (1513), ch. 19; *Discourses* (1512–17), bk II, chs. 1, 13; bk III, ch. 6; *The Art of War*, ed. Neal Wood (Indianapolis, Ind.: 1965), pp. 170, 142.
27   Dvornik, op. cit., pp. 313–14.
28   Brian Chapman, *Police State* (London: 1970), p. 14.
29   Ibid., p. 15; Yves Levy, 'Police and policy', *Government and Opposition*, Vol. I (1966–7), pp. 488–9.
30   Chapman, op. cit., pp. 15–27.
31   Haswell, op. cit., pp. 22–3.
32   Printed in *Report from the Secret Committee on the Post-Office* (PP 1844 xiv), Appendix, p. 95.
33   William Shakespeare, *King Henry V*, Act II, scene II.
34   Alban and Allmand, op. cit., pp. 74, 89, 90–100.
35   Felix Raab, *The English Face of Machiavelli* (London: 1964), pp. 30–2.
36   G. R. Elton, *Policy and Police* (London: 1972), pp. 327–9.
37   Lacey Baldwin Smith, *Treason in Tudor England* (London: 1986), p. 158.
38   Ibid., p. 163; Elton, op. cit., p. 331.
39   F. S. Boas, 'Richard Baines, informer', *The Nineteenth Century*, vol. 112 (1932), pp. 742–51; Leslie Hotson, *The Death of Christopher Marlowe* (London: 1925); F. S. Boas, 'Robert Poley: an associate of Marlowe', *The Nineteenth Century*, vol. 104 (1928), pp. 543–52; Eugenie de Kalb, 'Robert Poley's movements as a messenger of the court', *Review of English Studies*, Vol. IX (1933), pp. 13–18; A. D. Wraight, *In Search of Christopher Marlowe* (London: 1965).
40   Conyers Read, *Mr Secretary Walsingham and the Policy of Queen Elizabeth* (London: 1925), Vol. II, pp. 225, 320, 370–1, and Vol. III, p. 287 fn.
41   Elton, op. cit., p. 331.
42   Conyers Read, op. cit., Vol. I, p. 436.
43   Anthony Munday, *The English Romayne Life . . .* (1582), pp. 20–1, 66.
44   Conyers Read, op. cit., Vol. III, ch. 12.
45   Ibid., Vol. II, pp. 420, 400–5; Leo Hicks, 'The strange case of Dr William Parry', *Studies* (Dublin), September 1948, pp. 343–62; Baldwin Smith, op. cit., pp. 11–19.
46   Conyers Read, op. cit., Vol. I, p. 436.
47   C. H. Firth, 'Thomas Scot's account of his actions as intelligencer during the Commonwealth', *English Historical Review*, Vol. 12 (1897), pp. 116–26; 'Thurloe and the Post Office', *English Historical Review*, Vol. 13 (1898), p. 528.
48   Ibid., pp. 530, 532.
49   James Walker, 'The secret service under Charles II and James II', *Transactions of the Royal Historical Society*, 4th series, vol. XV (1932), pp. 211–35; Henry Gee, 'The

Derwentdale plot, 1663', *Transactions of the Royal Historical Society*, 3rd series, vol. XI (1917), pp. 125–42; J. Y. Akerman, *Secret Service Expenditure of Charles II and James II* (London: 1851).
50 William Beaumont (ed.), *The Jacobite Trials at Manchester in 1694* (Manchester: 1853), introduction, and p. lxxxix.
51 James Sutherland, *Defoe* (London: 1937), pp. 158, 161.
52 Paul S. Fritz, 'The anti-Jacobite intelligence system of the English ministers, 1715–1745', *Historical Journal*, Vol. XVI (1973), pp. 281–3, 288; G. V. Bennett, *The Tory Crisis in Church and State 1688–1730* (Oxford, 1975), pp. 249, 227; Spring Macky (ed.), *Memoirs of the Secret Service of John Macky, Esq. . . .* (1733), p. lvi.
53 *Report from the Secret Committee on the Post-Office*, pp. 3–4, 8; C. H. Firth, 'Thurloe and the Post Office', pp. 530–1; E. R. Turner, 'The secrecy of the post', *English Historical Review*, Vol. 33 (1918), pp. 320–2; Kenneth Ellis, *The Post Office in the Eighteenth Century* (London: 1958), ch. 6.
54 Ellis, op. cit., Appendix I; Fritz, op. cit., p. 268.
55 Ellis, op. cit., p. 76; J. Necker (1784), quoted in Levy, op. cit., p. 488.
56 Firth, 'Thomas Scot's account . . . ', p. 122.
57 Quoted in Peter Fleming, *Invasion 1940* (London: 1957), p. 53.
58 Firth, 'Thomas Scot's account . . . ', p. 121.
59 Bennett, op. cit., p. 226; Turner, op. cit., p. 321.
60 *Report from the Select Committee on the Post-Office*, pp. 9–10; Ellis, op. cit., pp. 63–4.
61 Fritz, op. cit., p. 270.
62 Hicks, op. cit., pp. 345–6; Conyers Read, op. cit., Vol. III, p. 19 and Vol. II, p. 420.
63 Walker, op. cit., p. 223; Beaumont, op. cit., introduction; G. V. Bennett, 'Jacobitism and the rise of Walpole', in Neil McKendrick (ed.), *Historical Perspectives: Studies in English Thought and Society* (London: 1974), pp. 86–7.
64 Conyers Read, op. cit., Vol. II, pp. 321, 376–7, 419.
65 Beaumont, op. cit., introduction.
66 Conyers Read, op. cit., Vol. II, pp. 316–17, 333–5.
67 Ibid., Vol. II, pp. 327, 331, 415.
68 Eveline Cruickshanks, *Political Untouchables: The Tories and the '45* (London: 1979), p. 47.
69 Conyers Read, op. cit., Vol. III, pp. 19, 24 and Vol. II, pp. 382–3.
70 Walker, op. cit., p. 221.
71 Bennett, *The Tory Crisis*, p. 248; Fritz, op. cit., p. 282.
72 William Shakespeare, *Venus and Adonis*, line 655.
73 A. O. Meyer, *England and the Catholic Church* (London: 1967 edn), p. 170.
74 Randle Cotgrave's French–English Dictionary (1611), quoted in *Oxford English Dictionary*, under 'Spy'; *Oxford English Dictionary*, loc. cit.; Samuel Johnson, *A Dictionary of the English Language* (new edn, 1799).
75 Meyer, op. cit., p. 105.
76 Above, pages 16–17; *Report from the Secret Committee on the Post-Office*, p. 8; Ellis, op. cit., p. 76.
77 Walker, op. cit., p. 212.
78 Leon Radzinowicz, *A History of English Criminal Law and its Administration from 1780*, Vol. II (London: 1956), pp. 5–16.
79 Ibid., Vol. II, pp. 327–32, 338.
80 Ibid., Vol. II, p. 147.
81 Adam Smith, *Lectures on Justice, Police, Revenue and Arms* (1763), quoted in Radzinowicz, op. cit., Vol. III (London: 1956), pp. 420–3.

82   Radzinowicz, op. cit., Vol. III, p. 91 and Vol. I (London: 1948), pp. 318–19.

2   The most powerful means of observation (1790–1805)

1   *Parliamentary History*, Vol. XXXII, cols 364–7, HC, 16 November 1795.
2   Ibid., col. 376.
3   Marianne Elliott, *Partners in Revolution. The United Irishmen and France* (New Haven, Conn.: 1982), p. 57.
4   Sidney Hook, *From Hegel to Marx* (1950; new edition, London, 1962), pp. 269–71.
5   E. H. Stuart Jones, *The Last Invasion of Britain* (Cardiff: 1950).
6   E. P. Thompson, *The Making of the English Working Class*, 2nd edn. (Harmondsworth, 1968), p. 183; Roger Wells, *Insurrection. The British Experience 1795–1803* (Gloucester: 1983), pp. 81–2.
7   Thompson, op. cit., p. 146; Wells, op. cit., pp. 70–1.
8   Marianne Elliott, 'Irish republicanism in England: the first phase, 1797–9', in Thomas Bartlett and D. W. Hayton (eds), *Penal Era and Golden Age. Essays in Irish History, 1690–1800* (Belfast: 1979), pp. 204–21; and 'The "Despard conspiracy" reconsidered', *Past and Present*, no. 75 (1977), pp. 46–61.
9   Leon Radzinowicz, *A History of English Criminal Law and its Administration from 1780*, Vol. IV (London: 1968), p. v.
10   Ibid., Vol. I, (London: 1948), pp. 220–3.
11   Alfred Cobban, 'British secret service in France, 1784–1792', in *English Historical Review*, Vol. LXIX (1954), pp. 226–61.
12   Harvey Mitchell, *The Underground War against Revolutionary France* (Oxford: 1965); W. R. Fryer, *Republic or Restoration in France? 1794–7* (Manchester: 1965).
13   Richard Cobb, *A Second Identity: Essays on France and French History* (London: 1969), pp. 184–91.
14   Wells, op. cit., p. 30; J. Ann Hone, *For the Cause of Truth: Radicalism in London 1796–1821* (Oxford: 1982), pp. 72–9.
15   Wells, op. cit., p. 32.
16   Ibid., pp. 34–5; Clive Emsley, 'The Home Office and its sources of information and investigation 1791–1801', *English Historical Review*, Vol. XCIV (1979), p. 538.
17   Kenneth Ellis, *The Post Office in the Eighteenth Century* (London: 1958), pp. 68–9.
18   Emsley, op. cit., p. 532.
19   Hone, op. cit., p. 68; Albert Goodwin, *The Friends of Liberty* (London: 1979), pp. 320–1.
20   Wells, op. cit., p. 34.
21   Hone, op. cit., pp. 69–70.
22   Emsley, op. cit., pp. 542, 545, 554; and Wells, op. cit., p. 39.
23   Wells, op. cit., pp. 39, 41; Emsley, op. cit., pp. 558, 541.
24   Goodwin, op. cit., pp. 457–61; Emsley, op. cit., pp. 555–6.
25   Wells, op. cit., p. 42.
26   Emsley, op. cit., pp. 548–9.
27   John T. Gilbert (ed.), *Documents Relating to Ireland 1795–1804* (Shannon: 1970), preface, pp. xi–xii.
28   R. B. McDowell, *Ireland in the Age of Imperialism and Revolution 1760–1801* (Oxford: 1979), pp. 529–30.
29   J. A. Froude, *The English in Ireland in the Eighteenth Century*, Vol. II (London: 1874), p. 413.
30   W. J. Fitzpatrick, *Secret Service under Pitt* (London: 1892), p. 163.

Notes

31 W. E. H. Lecky, *A History of Ireland in the Eighteenth Century*, Vol. III, new edn (London: 1892), p. 372.

32 Fitzpatrick, op. cit., ch. 1, p. 93, ch. 14; Froude, op. cit., Vol. III (1874), pp. 278–84; *Dictionary of National Biography* (London: 1921–2 edn), vol. XII, p. 688.

33 Fitzpatrick, op. cit., p. 302; Thomas Reynolds[son], *The Life of Thomas Reynolds, Esq., Formerly of Kilkea Castle in the County of Kildare*, 2 vols (London: 1839), Vol. I pp. 262–6.

34 E.g. Fitzpatrick, op. cit., p. 163.

35 Reynolds, op. cit., Vol. II p. 497.

36 *Dictionary of National Biography*, Vol. XIV, p. 333.

37 Fitzpatrick, op. cit., pp. 104, 173.

38 Froude, op. cit., Vol. III, pp. 271–2; Charles Hamilton Teeling, *History of the Irish Rebellion of 1798* (London: 1828; new edn, Shannon: 1972), p. 44.

39 Emsley, op. cit., p. 547.

40 Frank O'Connor, *The Big Fellow: A Life of Michael Collins* (London: 1937), pp. 89–90.

41 Froude, op. cit., Vol. III p. 237; W. J. Fitzpatrick, *'The Sham Squire', and the Informers of 1798* (London: 1866), pp. 322–3.

42 Elliott, *Partners in Revolution*, pp. 165, 205–7; Fitzpatrick, *Secret Service under Pitt*, p. 69; Reynolds, op. cit., Vol. I, ch. 4.

43 Elliott, *Partners in Revolution*, pp. 248, 252, 256, 282, 316.

44 Wells, op. cit., p. 31.

45 Fitzpatrick, *Secret Service under Pitt*, pp. 98–9.

46 *Dictionary of National Biography*, Vol. XXI, p. 178.

47 Teeling, op. cit., pp. 43–4.

48 Emsley, op. cit., pp. 541, 543.

49 Fitzpatrick, *'The Sham Squire'*, p. 136.

50 Anon., *The Mercenary Informers of '98: Containing the History of Edward Newell, Major Sirr, Jemmy O'Brien, & Thomas Reynolds . . .* (Dublin: n.d. [1846]), pp. viii, 36, 50, 73, 77; Gilbert, op. cit., pp. ix, xv–xvi.

51 Emsley, op. cit., pp. 553–4.

52 F. W. Chandler, *Political Spies and Provocative Agents* (Sheffield: 1933), pp. 3–6; Emsley, op. cit., pp. 551–2.

53 Elliott, 'Irish republicanism in England', p. 219.

54 Chandler, op. cit., pp. 7–25.

55 Contemporary account quoted in Hone, op. cit., p. 59 (my emphasis).

56 Emsley, op. cit., p. 561.

57 Reynolds, op. cit., Vol. I, p. 360 *et passim*.

58 Froude, op. cit., Vol. III, pp. 289, 315.

59 Hone, op. cit., p. 55; Elliott, 'Irish republicanism in England', p. 215; John Binns, *Recollections of the Life of John Binns* (Philadelphia, Pa: 1854), pp. 80–154, *passim*.

60 Ibid., p. 131.

61 Hone, op. cit., p. 50; Reynolds, op. cit., Vol. I, p. 358 (original emphasis).

62 A. J. Eagleston, 'Wordsworth, Coleridge, and the spy', in Edmund Blunden and Earl Leslie Griggs (eds), *Coleridge: Studies by Several Hands on the Hundredth Anniversary of his Death* (London: 1934), pp. 73–87.

3 Spies and bloodites! (1805–25)

1 J. Ann Hone, *For the Cause of Truth: Radicalism in London 1796–1821* (Oxford: 1982), p. 137.

2   *Hansard*, 1st series, vol. 36, col. 996, HL, 16 June 1817.

3   Ibid., col. 1000.

4   *Report of the Committee of Secrecy*, (1817), printed in *The Annual Register, or a View of the History, Politics and Literature for the Year 1817* (London: 1818), 'General history' section, pp. 12–19.

5   See Hone, op. cit., ch. 4, *passim*.

6   G. Lathom Browne, *Narratives of State Trials in the Nineteenth Century: First Period* (London: 1882), Vol. II, p. 68.

7   *Report of the Secret Committee of the House of Lords on the Disturbed State of Certain Counties* (1812), printed in *Annual Register for 1812*, (London: 1813) 'State papers', p. 391.

8   Malcolm I. Thomis, *The Luddites* (London: 1970), p. 42.

9   *Report of the Secret Committee*, pp. 388, 392.

10 F. O. Darvall, *Popular Disturbances and Public Order in Regency England* (London: 1934), pp. 282–3.

11 Samuel Bamford, *Passages in the Life of a Radical* (Heywood: 1841–3; new edn, Oxford: 1984), pp. 39–40.

12 Darvall, op. cit., p. 126.

13 *Report of the Secret Committee*, p. 391 (my emphasis).

14 *Hansard*, 1st series, vol. 23, cols. 970–6, HC, 10 July 1812.

15 J. L. and Barbara Hammond, *The Skilled Labourer*, new impression (London: 1927), pp. 279–84; Darvall, op. cit., pp. 288–9; E. P. Thompson, *The Making of the English Working Class*, 2nd edn (Harmondsworth: 1968), p. 621; Thomis, op. cit., p. 130.

16 Darvall, op. cit., pp. 193–5.

17 Hammond, op. cit., pp. 274–5; Thomis, op. cit., p. 91.

18 Darvall, op. cit., p. 191.

19 Bamford, op. cit., p. 36.

20 Ibid., p. 16.

21 Thomis, op. cit., p. 43.

22 Cf. Thompson, op. cit., p. 647.

23 *State Trials*, vol. 32 (London: 1824), cols 1–674. Shorter accounts of the trial appear in Lathom Browne, op. cit., ch. 5; and in John Stanhope, *The Cato Street Conspiracy* (London: 1962), ch. 2.

24 His name was Lord Ellenborough. See *Dictionary of National Biography*, vol XI (London: 1921–2), p. 661.

25 Anon., *Spies and Bloodites! The Lives and Political History of those Arch-Fiends Oliver, Reynolds, & Co. . . .* [London: 1817], p. 29; Hammond, op. cit., p. 353.

26 The *Leeds Mercury* account was read out to the House of Commons by the reformist MP Sir Francis Burdett on 16 June 1817, and so is reproduced in *Hansard*, 1st series, Vol. 36, cols 1016–19.

27 *Hansard*, 1st series, vol. 37, col. 343, HC, 11 February 1818.

28 A. F. Fremantle, 'The truth about Oliver the spy', *English Historical Review*, vol. 47 (1932) pp. 601–16; R. J. White, *Waterloo to Peterloo* (London: 1957), chs. 13–14.

29 Thompson, op. cit., pp. 728–31; Fremantle, op. cit., pp. 612–13.

30 *News of Sunday*, 6 July 1817, quoted in Anon., *Spies and Bloodites!*, p. 29; *Hansard*, 1st series, vol. 37, cols. 352, 849, HC, 11 February, 5 March 1818.

31 Hammond, op. cit., p. 367.

32 Fremantle, op. cit., p. 616.

33 Anon., *Spies and Bloodites!*, p. 36.

34 Bamford, op. cit., pp. 117–18.

Notes

35 P. Berresford Ellis and Seamus Mac A'Ghobhainn, *The Scottish Insurrection of 1820* (London: 1970), p. 218.
36 Anon., *Spies and Bloodites!*, p. 36.
37 *Hansard*, 1st series, vol. 36, cols 988, 1001, 1003, 1016–23, (HL and HC, 16 June 1817).
38 Ibid., 1st series, vol. 36, cols 1044 ff., HL, 19 June 1817; 1208 ff., HC, 27 June 1817; 1408 ff., HC, 11 July 1817; vol. 37, cols 338 ff., HC, 11 February 1818; 539 ff., HL, 19 February 1818; 791ff, HL, 5 March 1818; and 820 ff., HC, 5 March 1818.
39 *Examiner*, no. 497 (6 July 1817), p. 417; William Hazlitt, 'On the spy-system', *Morning Chronicle*, 30 June, 15 July 1817, reprinted in *Complete Works* (London: 1932), Vol. 7, pp. 208–14; *Fairburn's Edition of the Whole Proceedings on the Trial of James Watson, Senior ...* (London, 1817).
40 Above, page 22.
41 *Hansard*, 1st series, vol. 36, col. 1221, HC, 27 June 1817 (Lord Nugent); vol. 37, col. 351, HC, 11 February 1818 (Bennet); 1st series, vol. 36, cols. 1019, 1245, HC, 16 and 27 June 1817 (Burdett) (my emphasis).
42 Anon., *Spies and Bloodites!*, p. 2.
43 *Hansard*, 1st series, vol. 36, col. 1046, HL, 19 June 1817.
44 Anon., *Spies and Bloodites!*, p. 2.
45 *Hansard*, 1st series, vol. 36, col. 1224, HC, 27 June 1817.
46 Ibid., vol. 37, col. 272, HC, 10 February 1818 (Hamilton); vol. 37, col. 834 HC, 5 March 1818 (Lascelles); vol. 37, cols. 361, 845–6, HC, 5 and 11 March 1818 (Bennet).
47 Ibid., 1st series, vol. 36, col. 1214, HC, 27 June 1817 (Glenelg); vol. 36, col. 1007, HL, 16 June 1817 (Liverpool).
48 Ibid., 1st series, vol. 37, cols. 383–5, HC, 11 February 1818.
49 Lathom Browne, op. cit., Vol. II, pp. 278–9; Bamford, op. cit., p. 145.
50 Ellis and Mac A'Ghobhainn, op. cit., pp. 137–8.
51 Alexander B. Richmond, *Narrative of the Condition of the Manufacturing Population and of the Proceedings of Government Which Led to the State Trials in Scotland ...* (London: 1824), pp. 124, 162.
52 Bamford, op. cit., p. 118.
53 Ibid., p. 93.
54 Lathom Browne, op. cit., Vol. II, p. 310.
55 *Hansard*, 2nd series, vol. 1, cols. 244–5, HC, 9 May 1820.
56 Stanhope, op. cit., *passim*; Thompson, op. cit., pp. 769–74; *State Trials*, vol. 33 (London: 1826), cols. 681–1566.
57 *Hansard*, 2nd series, vol. 1, cols. 54–63, HC, 2 May 1820.
58 Ellis and Mac A'Ghobhainn, op. cit., p. 140.
59 Ibid., *passim*; and [Peter MacKenzie], *An Exposure of the Spy System Pursued in Glasgow ...* (Glasgow: 1833), *passim*.
60 *Annual Register*, 1820, pp. 456–8, 462–3.
61 Ellis and Mac A'Ghobhainn, op. cit., pp. 271–80; Stanhope, op. cit., ch. 5; *Annual Register, 1820* (London: 1821), pp. 394, 405–6, 950–2.
62 *Hansard*, 2nd series, vol. 1, col. 260, HC, 9 May 1820.
63 Ibid., 1st series, vol. 36, col. 1056, HL, 19 June 1817.
64 Ibid., 1st series, vol. 37, col. 856, HC, 5 March 1818 (Tierney); 2nd series, vol. 1, cols. 249–50 HC, 9 May 1820 (Wilson).
65 *Examiner*, no. 497 (6 July 1817), p. 417.
66 E.g. Donald Read, *Peterloo* (Manchester: 1958), Appendix B.
67 Richmond, op. cit., pp. 124–5, *et passim*.
68 See [Peter Mackenzie], op. cit., p. 8 *et passim*; and Ellis and Mac A'Ghobhainn, op.

cit., ch. 6.
69 *Hansard*, 1st series, vol. 37, col. 368, HC, 11 February 1818.

4 Mild and paternal government (1825–50)

1 *Hansard*, 3rd series, vol. 11, cols. 258–9, HC, 15 March 1832.
2 [Peter Mackenzie], *An Exposure of the Spy System Pursued in Glasgow . . .* (Glasgow: 1833), p. 3.
3 Alexander B. Richmond, *Narrative of the Condition of the Manufacturing Population and of the Proceedings of Government Which Led to the State Trials in Scotland . . .* (London: 1824), pp. 11 ff.
4 Macaulay, speech in House of Commons, 2 March 1831, reprinted in *Speeches, Parliamentary and Miscellaneous* (London: 1853), Vol. I, pp. 11–26.
5 *Report of the Committee of Secrecy* (1817), printed in *Annual Register* for 1817 (London: 1818), 'General history' section, p. 18.
6 Richmond, op. cit., p. 174.
7 Leon Radzinowicz, *A History of English Criminal Law and its Administration from 1780*, Vol. I (London: 1948), p. 28 n.
8 Anon., 'The local government of the metropolis, and other populous places', *Blackwood's Edinburgh Magazine*, vol. 29 (1831), pp. 83–5.
9 Charles Reith, *British Police and the Democratic Ideal* (London: 1943), p. 17.
10 Radzinowicz, op. cit., Vol. IV, (London: 1968), ch. 8.
11 Ibid., Vol. IV, pp. 181–2, 192.
12 Ibid., Vol. IV, p. 163.
13 Bernard Porter, *The Refugee Question in Mid-Victorian Politics* (Cambridge: 1979) pp. 114–15.
14 *Hansard*, 3rd series, vol. 11, col. 283, HC, 15 March 1832.
15 *Report from the Select Committee on the Petition of Frederick Young and Others* (PP 1833 xiii), pp. 409–10.
16 *Hansard*, 3rd series, vol. 20, col. 838, HC, 22 August 1833.
17 *Report from the Select Committee on the Petition of Frederick Young*, p. 411.
18 Radzinowicz, op. cit., Vol. IV, pp. 187, 282.
19 F. C. Mather, *Public Order in the Age of the Chartists* (Manchester: 1959), pp. 199–204.
20 *State Trials*, vol. 7 (London: 1896), cols 421–2 (trial of Dowling, September 1848).
21 Mather, op. cit., pp. 194–6.
22 Kevin B. Nowlan, *The Politics of Repeal* (London: 1965), p. 210.
23 *State Trials*, vol. 7, cols 304–14 (trial of Smith O'Brien, High Court, Dublin, September 1848).
24 Mather, op. cit., pp. 185, 208.
25 *Reynolds's Political Instructor*, vol. I, no. 13 (2 February 1850), p. 100.
26 See David Goodway, *London Chartism 1838–1848* (Cambridge: 1982), pp. 87–96; John Saville, *1848: The British State and the Chartist Movement* (Cambridge: 1987), ch. 5.
27 Mather, op. cit., p. 196.
28 Ibid., pp. 182–92; Radzinowicz, op. cit., vol. IV, pp. 239–42.
29 *Report from the Secret Committee on the Post-Office*, 1844 (PP 1844 xiv), pp. 11–14.
30 *Hansard*, 3rd series, vol. 24, cols 139–42, 340–1, HC, 3 and 9 June 1834.
31 7 Geo. IV cap. 54: *An Act for the Registration of Aliens*; 7 & 8 Vict. cap. 66: *An Act to Amend the Laws Relating to Aliens*.

32   *Hansard*, 1st series, vol. 34, col. 1060, HL, 11 June 1816.
33   Harry W. Rudman, *Italian Nationalism and English Letters* (London: 1940), ch. 4;
     F. B. Smith, 'British Post Office espionage, 1844', *Historical Studies* (Melbourne), vol.
     14, no. 54 (1970) pp. 189–203; F. B. Smith, *Radical Artisan: William James Linton
     1812–97* (London: 1973), pp. 53–8.
34   *Hansard*, 3rd series, vol. 75, cols. 1274–6, HC, 24 June 1844.
35   Mather, op. cit., p. 203.
36   K. Ellis, *The Post Office in the Eighteenth Century* (London: 1958), p. 139.
37   *Report from the Secret Committee on the Post-Office, 1844*, pp. 13–19.
38   *Hansard*, 3rd series, vol. 79, cols. 307–30, HC, 8 April 1845.
39   Ellis, op. cit., p. 141; *Hansard*, 3rd series, vol. 77, col. 703, HC, 18 February 1845.
40   Sir Rowland Hill and George Birkbeck Hill, *The Life of Sir Rowland Hill and the
     History of Penny Postage* (London, 1880), Vol. 2, p. 29.
41   Mather, op. cit., p. 198.
42   Belton Cobb, *The First Detectives and the Early Career of Richard Mayne* (London:
     1957), p. 96.
43   *State Trials*, vol. 7, col. 1110 (trial of Mullins, October 1848).
44   *Hansard*, 3rd series, vol. 11, col. 253, HC, 15 March 1832.
45   [Mackenzie], op. cit., frontispiece (original emphasis).
46   *The Times*, 15 April 1848, p. 4.

5   No police over opinion (1850–80)

 1   *Scottish Trade Protection Society Monthly Report*, no. 156 (February 1965), p. 3;
     Scottish Record Office: L4.09.
 2   Christopher Andrew, *Secret Service: The Making of the British Intelligence Commu-
     nity* (London: 1985), p. 5.
 3   G. B. Henderson, *Crimean War Diplomacy and Other Historical Essays* (Glasgow:
     1947), pp. 238–41.
 4   Andrew, op. cit., pp. 7–9; Jock Haswell, *Spies and Spymasters* (London: 1977),
     p. 81.
 5   Richard Popplewell, 'British intelligence and Indian "subversion": the surveillance
     of Indian revolutionaries in India and abroad, 1904–1920', PhD thesis, University
     of Cambridge, 1988, pp. 5–8, 18.
 6   Mark Girouard, *The Return to Camelot: Chivalry and the English Gentleman*
     (London: 1981); Martin J. Wiener, *English Culture and the Decline of the Industrial
     Spirit 1850–1980* (London: 1981).
 7   Haswell, op. cit., p. 83.
 8   See Bernard Porter, *Britain, Europe and the World 1850–1982: Delusions of Gran-
     deur* (London: 1983), ch. 1.
 9   See Donald C. Richter, *Riotous Victorians* (London: 1981).
10   *Annual Register 1855* (London: 1856), 'Chronicle', p. 107.
11   Bernard Porter, *The Refugee Question in Mid-Victorian Politics* (Cambridge: 1979),
     pp. 86–8.
12   E.g. ibid., pp. 114, 135–6.
13   *The Times*, 27 December 1859, pp. 6, 9.
14   *Household Words*, vol. 1, no. 26 (21 September 1850), p. 613.
15   *Daily News*, 25 April 1853, p. 5.
16   Thomas Erskine May, *Constitutional History of England since the Accession of
     George III*, Vol. 2 (London: 1863), p. 275.

17 *Household Words*, vol. 1, no. 26, p. 611.
18 *Report of Home Office Departmental Committee into Metropolitan Police* (6 May 1868), pp. 14–15: copy in Public Record Office (PRO), HO45/10002/A49463/2; Belton Cobb, *The First Detectives and the Early Career of Richard Mayne* (London: 1957), *passim*.
19 Anthea Trodd, 'The policeman and the lady: significant encounters in mid-Victorian fiction', *Victorian Studies*, vol. 27, no. 4 (1984), p. 452.
20 Bernard Porter, *The Origins of the Vigilant State: The London Metropolitan Police Special Branch before the First World War* (London: 1987), p. 7.
21 Police report on George Graham, 'Aeronaut', 15 April 1851, in PRO MEPOL 2/43.
22 Porter, *Refugee Question*, pp. 202, 208.
23 Ibid., p. 16.
24 Robert Payne, *Marx* (London: 1968), p. 235.
25 Michael St J. Packe, *The Bombs of Orsini* (London: 1957), *passim*; Porter, *Refugee Question*, chs 3, 6.
26 Lord John Russell to Prince Albert, 25 May 1850, in Royal Archive, RA I20/43.
27 Porter, *Refugee Question*, pp. 151–7, 189; Phillip Thurmond Smith, *Policing Victorian London: Political Policing, Public Order, and the London Metropolitan Police* (Westport, Conn.: 1985), pp. 87–9.
28 *Reynolds's Newspaper*, 31 January 1858, p. 1; *Morning Advertiser*, 19 February 1858, p. 4.
29 Porter, *Refugee Question*, pp. 152–3.
30 *State Trials*, new series, vol. VIII (London: 1898), cols 887–1064.
31 Porter, *Refugee Question*, pp. 133–4.
32 Ibid., pp. 175–83.
33 Ibid., pp. 154–7.
34 Ibid., pp. 163–8.
35 Ibid., pp. 156–7.
36 Ibid., pp. 209–10.
37 P. K. Martinez, 'Paris communard refugees in Britain, 1871–1880', PhD thesis, University of Sussex, 1982, p. 54.
38 Ibid., Appendix I, pp. 421–8.
39 Royden Harrison, 'A British police report on Karl Marx', *Bulletin of the Society for the Study of Labour History*, no. 4 (1962), p. 54. The correspondence is in PRO HO/45/9366/36228.
40 Porter, *Refugee Question*, p. 214.
41 Justin McCarthy, *A History of Our Own Times*, Vol. 4 (London: 1880), pp. 137–8.
42 Leon O'Broin, *Fenian Fever: An Anglo-American Dilemma* (London: 1971), chs 1–2, *passim*.
43 Thurmond Smith, op. cit., p. 186.
44 O'Broin, op. cit., p. 198.
45 Ibid., pp. 211–12; Thurmond Smith, op. cit., pp. 193–5.
46 O'Broin, op. cit., p. 213.
47 Below, page 109.
48 Thurmond Smith, op. cit., p. 194.
49 'Henri le Caron', *Twenty-Five Years in the Secret Service: The Recollections of a Spy* (London: 1892), pp. 29–30, 36–8. See also J. A. Cole, *Prince of Spies: Henri Le Caron* (London: 1984); Charles Curran, 'The spy behind the Speaker's chair', *History Today*, vol. 18 (1968), pp. 745–54.
50 Below, page 118.
51 They are in two boxes at the Public Record Office, HO144/1536–7.

52 'Alfred Aylmer', 'The detective in real life', *Windsor Magazine*, vol. 1 (1895), p. 505.

6 A permanent organization to detect and control (1880–1910)

1 K. R. M. Short, *The Dynamite War: Irish-American Bombers in Victorian Britain* (London: 1979).
2 Bernard Porter, 'The *Freiheit* prosecutions, 1881–1882', *Historical Journal*, vol. 23, no. 4 (1980), pp. 833–56.
3 S. H. Jeyes and F. D. How, *The Life of Sir Howard Vincent* (London: 1912), ch. 5.
4 Bernard Porter, *The Origins of the Vigilant State: The London Metropolitan Police Special Branch before the First World War* (London: 1987), pp. 41–5.
5 Ibid., pp. 45–6.
6 Ibid., pp. 46–7, 50, 56.
7 Ibid., pp. 47–8.
8 Ibid., pp. 51–3.
9 Bernard Porter, 'The historiography of the early Special Branch', *Intelligence and National Security*, vol. 1 (1986), p. 382.
10 Porter, *Vigilant State*, pp. 53–5.
11 Ibid., pp. 52, 57–8.
12 Ibid., pp. 73–7.
13 Ibid., pp. 88–9.
14 Paper headed 'Secret Service', in Public Record Office, T1/11689/25138, p. 6.
15 Porter, *Vigilant State*, pp. 48, 54–5, 75.
16 Ibid., pp. 56–8.
17 Millicent Garrett Fawcett, *What I Remember* (London: 1924), p. 114.
18 Algernon West, *Recollections 1832–1886* (London: 1899), Vol. 2, p. 194.
19 *Pall Mall Gazette*, 26 January 1885, p. 1.
20 Porter, *Vigilant State*, pp. 63–4.
21 Harcourt to Gladstone, 16 May 1883, in Gladstone Papers, British Museum, BM Add Ms 44198, ff. 68–71.
22 Short, op cit., p. 266.
23 Porter, *Vigilant State*, pp. 85–6.
24 John Littlechild, *The Reminiscences of Chief-Inspector Littlechild* (London: 1894).
25 Porter, *Vigilant State*, p. 82.
26 Ibid., p. 92.
27 T. W. Moody, '*The Times* versus Parnell and Co., 1887–90', *Historical Studies* (Dublin), vol. 6 (1968), pp. 147–82.
28 *Hansard*, 5th series, vol. 16, cols 2421–2, HC, 21 April 1910.
29 Leon O'Broin, *The Prime Informer: A Suppressed Scandal* (London: 1971), pp. 108–9.
30 Ibid., p. 65.
31 Ibid., pp. 63, 73–4, 86, 95.
32 J. A. Cole, *Prince of Spies: Henri Le Caron* (London: 1984), chs 23–30; *Reynolds's Newspaper*, 8 April 1894, p. 1, and 23 June 1895, p. 1.
33 *Hansard*, 5th series, vol. 16, cols. 2335–432, HC, 21 April 1910.
34 Porter, *Vigilant State*, p. 118; Monro to Home under secretary, 24 December 1891, in PRO MEPO1/54.
35 Porter, *Vigilant State*, pp. 102, 116, 141.
36 Bernard Porter, 'Secrecy and the Special Branch, 1880–1914', *Bulletin of the Society for the Study of Labour History*, vol. 52, no. 1 (1987), pp. 11–12; *Vigilant State*, pp. 136–42.

37 Porter, *Vigilant State*, pp. 101–3.
38 Ibid., pp. 114–15; Richard Bach Jenson, 'The international anti-anarchist conference of 1898 and the origins of Interpol', *Journal of Contemporary History*, vol. 16 (1981), pp. 323–47.
39 Porter, *Vigilant State*, pp. 83, 147–8; Sir Melville MacNaghten, *Days of My Years* (London: 1914), p. 65.
40 Memoirs of Dr Jack Dancy, in the possession of Professor John Dancy, p. 1923; and see below, page 135. These recollections were penned many years afterward, but with regard to Melville correspond with what we know from other sources.
41 *Who's Who* (London: 1914), p. 1435.
42 Porter, *Vigilant State*, pp. 125–6.
43 Ibid., pp. 122–3.
44 Ibid., p. 125; 'Isabel Meredith', *A Girl among the Anarchists* (London: 1903), ch. 4.
45 Porter, *Vigilant State*, pp. 115–16; Alan Kimball, 'The harassment of Russian revolutionaries abroad: the London trial of Vladimir Burtsev in 1898', *Oxford Slavonic Papers*, vol. 6 (1973), pp. 48–65.
46 Bernard Porter, 'The origins of Britain's political police', *Warwick Working Papers in Social History*, no. 3 (1985), pp. 12–13.
47 Anderson memorandum, 13 December 1898, in PRO HO45/10254/X36450.
48 Porter, *Vigilant State*, pp. 71, 135–6.
49 Littlechild, op. cit., p. 96.
50 John Sweeney, *At Scotland Yard* (London: 1904), ch. 8.
51 Herbert Fitch, *Traitors Within* (London: 1933), pp. 19, 23–5; *Memoirs of a Royal Detective* (London: 1935), p. 234.
52 *Hansard*, 5th series, vol. 16, col. 2359, HC, 21 April 1910.
53 Porter, *Vigilant State*, pp. 128–9.
54 Leon O'Broin, *Revolutionary Underground: The Story of the IRB, 1858–1924* (Dublin: 1976), p. 127.

7 A holy alliance against this midnight terror (1910–20)

1 The Methodist minister is quoted in R. W. Perks to Winston Churchill, 6 February 1911, in the Churchill Papers (Churchill College, Cambridge), 12/6/52; Baron von Horst is the subject of an undated and unsigned report in the Ralph Isham Papers (University of Yale), and is mentioned in Sidney Felstead, *German Spies at Bay* (London: 1920), pp. 201–2.
2 Herbert Fitch, *Traitors Within* (London: 1933), p. 47.
3 William Barry, 'Forecasts of to-morrow', *Quarterly Review*, no. 416 (1908), p. 6; W. C. D. Whetham, 'Inheritance and sociology', *The Nineteenth Century*, vol. 65 (1909), p. 79.
4 Bernard Porter, *The Origins of the Vigilant State: The London Metropolitan Police Special Branch before the First World War* (London: 1987), pp. 44–5.
5 Above, page 83.
6 W. S. Adams, *Edwardian Portraits* (London: 1957), p. 129.
7 Basil Thomson, *Queer People* (London: 1922), p. 265.
8 David Stafford, 'Conspiracy and xenophobia: the popular spy novels of William Le Queux, 1893–1914', *Europe* (Montreal), vol. 4 (1981), p. 169.
9 William Le Queux, *Spies of the Kaiser: Plotting the Downfall of England* (London: 1909); P. G. Wodehouse, *The Swoop! or How Clarence Saved England: A Tale of the Great Invasion* (London: 1909); David French, 'Spy fever in Britain, 1900–1915',

Historical Journal, vol. 21 (1978), pp. 355–70.

10   *Proceedings* of the Sub-Committee on Foreign Espionage, first meeting, 30 March 1909, pp. 3–4; in PRO CAB16/8.

11   Nicholas Hiley, 'The failure of British counter-espionage against Germany, 1907–1914', *Historical Journal*, vol. 28 (1985), pp. 867–89; Constance Kell, 'A secret well kept', MS biography of her husband in the Kell Papers, microfilm copy in Imperial War Museum; James Edmonds, 'Memoirs', in Edmonds Papers III/5/1, Liddell Hart Centre, King's College, London; Memoirs of Dr Jack Dancy, in the possession of Professor John Dancy, p. 1924.

12   Porter, *Vigilant State*, p. 168.

13   Alasdair Palmer, 'The history of the D-Notice committee', in Christopher Andrew and David Dilks (eds), *The Missing Dimension* (London: 1984), p. 235.

14   *Hansard*, 5th series, vol. 29, cols. 2251–60, HC, 18 August 1911.

15   There are dozens of accounts of these events in memoirs, like Harold Brust, '*I Guarded Kings': Memoirs of a Political Police Officer* (London: n.d.), from whom the quotation comes (p. 97), and in popular spy histories. The best modern ones are Christopher Andrew, *Secret Service: The Making of the British Intelligence Community* (London: 1985), pp. 61–73; and Hiley, op. cit.

16   S. T. Felstead (ed.), *Steinhauer: The Kaiser's Master Spy. The Story as Told by Himself* (London: 1930), pp. 10–11, 30, 47.

17   David Saunders, 'Aliens in Britain and the empire during the First World War', *Immigrants and Minorities*, vol. 4 (1985), p. 24 fn. 28.

18   Kell, op. cit., p. 140.

19   Porter, *Vigilant State*, p. 166.

20   The best recent book on these events is Colin Rogers, *The Battle of Stepney. The Sidney Street Siege: Its Causes and Consequences* (London: 1981).

21   Porter, *Vigilant State*, pp. 170–1.

22   Richard Popplewell, 'British intelligence and Indian "subversion": the surveillance of Indian revolutionaries in India and abroad, 1904–1920', PhD thesis, University of Cambridge, 1988, p. 193.

23   Porter, *Vigilant State*, p. 176.

24   All this is from Richard Popplewell, 'The surveillance of Indian revolutionaries in Great Britain and on the Continent, 1903–14', *Intelligence and National Security*, vol. 3 (1988), pp. 56–76.

25   Porter, *Vigilant State*, pp. 164–5.

26   Ibid., p. 32.

27   Edwin Woodhall, *Detective and Secret Service Days* (London: n.d.), p. 43.

28   Porter, *Vigilant State*, pp. 173–5.

29   Ibid., p. 169.

30   There are many sources for this story; one is Edwin Woodhall, *Spies of the Great War* (London: 1932), p. 106.

31   John Sweeney, *At Scotland Yard* (London: 1904), pp. 223–4; Harold Brust, *In Plain Clothes* (London: 1937), p. 60.

32   Porter, *Vigilant State*, pp. 175–6.

33   Basil Thomson, *The Scene Changes* (London: 1939), pp. 10–11, 225; *Queer People* (London: 1922), p. 263; above, page 125.

34   Dancy Memoirs, pp. 1260, 1262.

35   Nicholas Hiley, 'Counter-espionage and security in Great Britain during the First World War', *English Historical Review*, vol. 101 (1986), pp. 100–26.

36   Dancy Memoirs, pp. 1132, 1460, 1481 ff., 1690 ff., 1912, 1937 ff.

37   Home Ports Defence Committee memorandum, 4 May 1912, in PRO ADM1/8264;

memorandum by Major-General [illegible], 11 December 1908, in PRO WO32/5270.

38 Gloden Dallas and Douglas Gill, *The Unknown Army* (London: 1985), p. 40.
39 Popplewell, 'British intelligence and Indian "subversion"', p. 190.
40 Thomson, *The Scene Changes*, pp. 328, 356.
41 Popplewell, 'British intelligence and Indian "subversion"', p. 184.
42 John Clement Bird, 'Control of enemy civilians in Great Britain 1914–1918', PhD thesis, University of London, 1981; Saunders, op. cit..
43 Hiley, 'Counter-espionage and security in Great Britain during the First World War', p. 105.
44 'Charles Rennie Mackintosh: Dreams and Recollections', broadcast on Scottish Television, 30 August 1987.
45 Woodhall, *Spies of the Great War*, p. 118.
46 Thomson, *The Scene Changes*, p. 329.
47 Dancy Memoirs, pp. 1875–2061, *passim*.
48 Thomson, *The Scene Changes*, p. 274.
49 Thomson, *Queer People*, p. 38.
50 Thomson, *The Scene Changes*, p. 274.
51 Thomson's own version of this is retailed in *Queer People*, pp. 182–3.
52 Andrew, op. cit., pp. 199–201; Thomson Report on 'Pacifist and revolutionary organizations', November 1917, in PRO CAB24/4 paper G173, pp. 3–6.
53 Thomson, *The Scene Changes*, p. 297.
54 Ibid., p. 359; Andrew, op. cit., pp. 200–1.
55 William James, *The Eyes of the Navy: A Biographical Study of Admiral Sir Reginald Hall* (London: 1955), p. 71. On the Casement episode generally, see ibid., pp. 112–14; Andrew, op. cit., pp. 247–9; and Eunan O'Halpin, 'British intelligence in Ireland, 1914–21', in Andrew and Dilks, op. cit., pp. 59–60.
56 Andrew, op. cit., pp. 200–1.
57 Phillip Knightley, *The Second Oldest Profession: The Spy as Bureaucrat, Patriot, Fantasist and Whore* (London: 1986), p. 60.
58 Thomson, *The Scene Changes*, p. 376.
59 Ralph Isham to General C. C. Lucas, 24 March 1919, in Isham Papers.
60 W. H. Thompson, *Guard from the Yard* (London: 1938), p. 91.
61 Thomson, *Queer People*, pp. 282–3, 302; report on 'Bolshevism in England', n.d., in Isham Papers.
62 Andrew, op. cit., p. 228; Thomson, *The Scene Changes*, p. 375.
63 'Secret' report on the SSAU, 29 April 1919, in Isham Papers.
64 Thomson, *Queer People*, p. 299.
65 Ibid., pp. 273, 280, 283–5; report on 'Bolshevism in England', ?May 1919, p. 10, in Isham Papers.
66 On this see Andrew, op. cit., ch. 6.
67 Nicholas Hiley, 'British internal security in wartime: the rise and fall of P.M.S.2, 1915–17', *Intelligence and National Security*, vol. 1 (1986), p. 396.
68 Barbara Lee Farr, 'The development and impact of right-wing politics in Great Britain 1903–1932', PhD thesis, University of Illinois, 1976, pp. 150–78.
69 *Fifty Fighting Years*, privately published by the Economic League (London: 1969), p. 4.
70 Hiley, 'British internal security in wartime', pp. 402–3.
71 Ibid., pp. 406–9; Nicholas Hiley and Julian Putkowski, 'A postscript on P.M.S.2', *Intelligence and National Security*, vol. 3 (1988), pp. 326–31; Andrew, op. cit., pp. 195–6; F. W. Chandler, *Political Spies and Provocative Agents* (Sheffield: 1933), pp. 100–12; Raymond Challinor, *The Origins of British Bolshevism* (London: 1977),

pp. 144–7, and *John S. Clarke, Parliamentarian, Poet, Lion-Tamer* (London: 1977), p. 44; *Daily Herald*, 27 December 1919, p. 8.

72 *Hansard*, 5th series, vol. 91, cols. 648–58, HC, 8 March 1917.
73 Hiley, 'British internal security in wartime', pp. 409–10.
74 Thomson, *The Scene Changes*, pp. 358, 377.
75 Andrew, op. cit., pp. 195–6.
76 Unsigned report to Field Marshal C-in-C Forces in Great Britain, 22 May 1919, p. 3; L/Cpl J. Swinburn to Assistant provost marshal, Glasgow, 29 September 1919: in Isham Papers. For the context of alll this, see Stephen R. Ward, 'Intelligence surveillance of British ex-servicemen, 1918–1920', *Historical Journal*, vol. 16 (1973), pp. 179–88.
77 Brigadier-General C. C. Lucas circular to Commanders-in-Chief, 4 March 1919; Thomson report on 'Bolshevism in Britain', ?May 1919: in Isham Papers.
78 Reports on interviews with 'No. 8', from the winter of 1919–20, are in the Isham Papers; his identity is revealed in David Neligan, *Spy in the Castle* (London: 1968), pp. 55–6, 65–6.
79 Thomson, *Queer People*, p. 275.
80 Popplewell, 'British intelligence and Indian "subversion"', chs. 2–3, 6.
81 W. H.-H. Waters, *'Secret and Confidential': The Experiences of a Military Attaché* (London: 1926), p. 36.
82 28 June 1919; quoted in Keith Jeffery, 'The British army and internal security 1919–1939', *Historical Journal*, vol. 24 (1981), p. 378.
83 Circular of 21 May 1919, in Isham Papers.
84 *Hansard*, 5th series, vol. 16, col. 2354, HC, 21 April 1910.
85 Ibid., 5th series, vol. 91, cols. 648–58, HC, 8 March 1917.
86 *Manchester Guardian*, 6 August 1919, p. 6.
87 *Hansard*, 5th series, vol. 91, col. 653, HC, 8 March 1917.
88 Ibid., 5th series, vol. 24, col. 2145, HC, 28 April 1911; vol. 91, col. 658, HC, 8 March 1917.
89 Hiley, 'Counter-espionage and security in Great Britain during the First World War', p. 124; Andrew, op. cit., p. 231.

8 Dangers ahead (1920–40)

1 Eunan O'Halpin, 'British intelligence in Ireland, 1914–1921', in Christopher Andrew and David Dilks (eds), *The Missing Dimension* (London: 1984), p. 60.
2 David Neligan, *Spy in the Castle* (London: 1968), p. 44.
3 O'Halpin, op cit., pp. 70–3; Tom Bowden, *The Breakdown of Public Security: The Case of Ireland 1916–1921 and Palestine 1936–1939* (London: 1977), pp. 96–103; Neligan, op. cit., p. 92.
4 Sir Nevil Macready, *Annals of an Active Life*, Vol. II (London: n.d.), pp. 443, 463.
5 Christopher Andrew, *Secret Service: The Making of the British Intelligence Community* (London: 1985), p. 253.
6 Neligan, op. cit., p. 101.
7 Sir Ormonde Winter, *Winter's Tale* (London: 1955), *passim*; Andrew, op. cit., p. 255.
8 Winter, op. cit., p. 293.
9 Neligan, op. cit., p. 100.
10 Winter, op. cit., p. 298.
11 Bowden, op. cit., pp. 119–20.
12 Winter, op. cit., pp. 310–1.
13 Bowden, op. cit., p. 135.

14 Neligan, op. cit., pp. 133–8.
15 *Hansard*, 5th series, vol. 147, cols 2041–2, 2050–1, HC, 3 November 1921.
16 William James, *The Eyes of the Navy: A Biographical Study of Admiral Sir Reginald Hall* (London: 1955), p. 177; *Hansard*, 5th series, vol. 147, col. 2043, HC, 3 November 1921.
17 Peter Hart, '"Operations abroad": the IRA in Britain, 1920–1923', unpublished article, *passim*. I am grateful to Dr Hart for a sight of this paper.
18 Basil Thomson, *The Scene Changes* (London: 1939), p. 392.
19 *Hansard*, 5th series, vol. 147, cols 2051–60, HC, 3 November 1921 (Edward Shortt, Home Secretary).
20 Andrew, op. cit., p. 282.
21 *Hansard*, 5th series, vol. 147, col. 2064, HC, 3 November 1921; Thomson, op. cit., p. 393.
22 *Hansard*, 5th series, vol. 147, cols. 2068, 2077–8, 2050, 1931, HC, 3 November 1921.
23 Rupert Allason, *The Branch: A History of the Metropolitan Police Special Branch 1883–1983* (London: 1983), pp. 86–7.
24 Sir Wyndham Childs, *Episodes and Reflections* (London: 1930), ch. 23; Barbara Weinberger, 'Communism and the General Strike', *Bulletin of the Society for the Study of Labour History*, no. 48 (1984), pp. 31–57.
25 Andrew, op. cit., p. 300.
26 Childs, op. cit., pp. 217, 223.
27 Trevor Barnes, 'Special Branch and the first Labour government', *Historical Journal*, vol. 22 (1979), pp. 941–51.
28 Wal Hannington, *Unemployed Struggles, 1919–1936* (London: 1936), pp. 145–6.
29 Ralph Hayburn, 'The police and the hunger marchers', *International Review of Social History*, vol. 17 (1972), p. 627.
30 Frank Cain, *The Origins of Political Surveillance in Australia* (Sydney: 1983), pp. 239–40, 242.
31 Hayburn, op. cit., p. 630; Royden Harrison, 'New light on the police and the hunger marchers', *Bulletin of the Society for the Study of Labour History*, no. 37 (1978), pp. 17–23.
32 Hannington, op. cit., pp. 142–3.
33 Hayburn, op. cit., pp. 631–2.
34 Childs, op. cit., p. 239.
35 Harriette Flory, 'The Arcos raid and the rupture of Anglo-Soviet relations, 1927', *Journal of Contemporary History*, vol. 12 (1977), pp. 707–23.
36 Childs, op. cit., p. 209.
37 Ibid., pp. 209–10.
38 Patrick Renshaw, 'Anti-Labour politics in Britain, 1918–27', *Journal of Contemporary History*, vol. 12 (1977), pp. 693–705.
39 *Hansard*, 5th series, vol. 147, col. 2086, HC, 3 November 1921.
40 Childs, op. cit., p. 217.
41 Gerald D. Anderson, *Fascists, Communists, and the National Government: Civil Liberties in Great Britain, 1931–1937* (Columbia, Mo.: 1983), *passim*.
42 Keith Jeffery and Peter Hennessy, *States of Emergency: British Governments and Strikebreaking since 1919* (London: 1983), chs 3–5; Keith Jeffery, 'The British army and internal security 1919–1939', *Historical Journal*, vol. 24 (1981) pp. 377–97; Barnes, op. cit., pp. 946–7.
43 Childs, op. cit., p. 216.
44 Economic League, *Fifty Fighting Years* (London: 1969), p. 4; Labour Research Department, *What Is the Economic League?* (London: 1937), pp. 7–11.

45 Childs, op. cit., pp. 216–17.
46 Economic League, *5th General Report* (London: 1925), quoted in *State Research Bulletin*, no. 7 (August–September 1978), p. 138.
47 Ron Bean, 'Liverpool shipping employers and the anti-communist activities of J. M. Hughes, 1920–25', *Bulletin of the Society for the Study of Labour History*, no. 34 (1977), pp. 22–6.
48 Childs, op. cit., p. 215.
49 Andrew, op. cit., p. 339.
50 John Baker White, *True Blue. An Autobiography: 1902–1939* (London: 1970), pp. 129–30, 142.
51 Ibid., p. 129.
52 Andrew, op. cit., p. 340.
53 L. Chester, S. Fay and H. Young, *The Zinoviev Letter* (London: 1967); Sibyl Crowe, 'The Zinoviev letter: a reappraisal', *Journal of Contemporary History*, vol. 10 (1975) pp. 407–32; Andrew, op. cit., ch. 10.
54 Andrew, op. cit., p. 355.
55 Jeffery and Hennessy, op. cit., p. 6.
56 Douglas Hyde, *I Believed: The Autobiography of a Former British Communist* (London: 1951), *passim*.
57 Childs, op. cit., p. 246.
58 Andrew, op. cit., p. 362.
59 *Hansard*, 5th series, vol. 174, col. 674, HC, 15 December 1924.
60 Phillip Knightley, *The Second Oldest Profession: The Spy as Bureaucrat, Patriot, Fantasist and Whore* (London: 1986), p. 30.
61 W. Somerset Maugham, *Ashenden, or The British Agent* (London: 1928; new edn 1952), p. 120.
62 Eric Homberger, '"Uncle Max" and his thrillers', *Intelligence and National Security*, vol. 3 (1988), pp. 312–21.
63 Joan Miller, *One Girl's War* (Dingle, Ireland: 1986), pp. 37, 51, 83–4.
64 Somerset Maugham, op. cit., pp. 45, 62–3, 180.
65 Especially Christopher Andrew's *Secret Service*, op. cit.
66 Anthony Masters, *The Man Who Was M: The Life of Maxwell Knight* (London: 1984; paperback edn 1986), ch. 1.
67 Ibid., pp. 55–6, 87–9, 163–4, 222; Miller, op. cit., pp. 111–12, 154.
68 Homberger, op. cit.
69 Miller, op. cit., p. 66.
70 Above, page 165.
71 Masters, op. cit., ch. 4.
72 Ibid., pp. 80, 213–14.
73 Enno Stephan, *Spies in Ireland* (London: 1963), p. 34.
74 Richard Thurlow, *Fascism in Britain: A History, 1918–1985* (London: 1987), *passim*; and 'British fascism and state surveillance, 1934–45', *Intelligence and National Security*, vol. 3 (1988), pp. 77–99; Paul Cohen, 'The police, the Home Office and surveillance of the British Union of Fascists', *Intelligence and National Security*, vol. 1 (1986), pp. 416–34.

9 Dazzled and confused (1940–70)

1 Peter Fleming, *Invasion 1940: An Account of the German Preparations and the British Counter-Measures* (London: 1957), pp. 177, 192, 194 fn.

2   Ibid., p. 58fn.
3   Above, page 138; Basil Thomson, *The Scene Changes* (London: 1939), pp. 260–1.
4   J. C. Masterman, *The Double-Cross System in the War of 1939 to 1945* (New Haven, Conn.: 1972), p. 3 (original emphasis); Phillip Knightley, *The Second Oldest Profession* (London: 1986), pp. 144–53.
5   Anthony Masters, *The Man Who Was M: The Life of Maxwell Knight* (London: 1984; paperback edn 1986), ch. 6; Joan Miller, *One Girl's War* (Dingle, Ireland: 1986), ch. 2.
6   Masters, op. cit., p. 140.
7   Richard Thurlow, *Fascism in Britain: A History, 1918–1985* (London: 1987), pp. 200–7; and 'British fascism and state surveillance, 1934–45', *Intelligence and National Security*, vol. 3 (1988), pp. 88–93; Masters, op. cit., pp. 174–205; Miller, op. cit., pp. 91–4.
8   Thurlow, 'British fascism and state surveillance', pp. 93–5.
9   Douglas Hyde, *I Believed: The Autobiography of a Former British Communist* (London: 1951), p. 144.
10 Masters, op. cit., ch. 9; Peter Wright, *Spycatcher: The Candid Autobiography of a Senior Intelligence Officer* (New York: 1987), p. 188.
11 On all this see Andrew Boyle, *The Climate of Treason*, revised paperback edn (London: 1980), *passim*.
12 Ibid., p. 195.
13 Ibid., pp. 317 ff.
14 Ibid., p. 308.
15 Bruce Page, David Leitch, Phillip Knightley, *The Philby Conspiracy* (London, 1981), ch. 12.
16 Anthony Summers and Stephen Dorril, *Honeytrap: The Secret Worlds of Stephen Ward* (London: 1987), ch. 7.
17 'Richard Deacon', *The British Connection: Russia's Manipulation of British Individuals and Institutions* (London: 1979), pp. 221–2; Michael Randle and Pat Pottle, *The Blake Escape* (London: 1989).
18 Wright, op. cit., p. 175.
19 Ibid., p. 251.
20 Ibid., p. 324.
21 Ibid., pp. 127, 331.
22 Anthony Cavendish, *Inside Intelligence* (privately printed, 1987), p. 134.
23 Wright, op. cit., pp. 44–5.
24 Boyle, op. cit., pp. 421–2.
25 Wright, op. cit., p. 151.
26 Ibid., pp. 273–5.
27 Quoted in Anthony Glees, *The Secrets of the Service: British Intelligence and Communist Subversion 1939–51* (London: 1987), p. 399.
28 Wright, op. cit., pp. 205–10, 305.
29 For example, in Chapman Pincher, *Too Secret Too Long* (London: 1984); and 'Nigel West', *Molehunt* (London: 1987).
30 Boyle, op. cit., p. 195.
31 Wright, op. cit., p. 122.
32 Peter Hennessy and Gail Brownfeld, 'Britain's cold war security purge: the origins of positive vetting', *Historical Journal*, vol. 25 (1982) pp. 965–73; E. H. Cookridge, *Shadow of a Spy* (London: 1967), p. 252.
33 Wright, op. cit., pp. 29–31.
34 'Nigel West', *A Matter of Trust: MI5 1945–72* (London: 1982; paperback edn 1983),

p. 29; 'Richard Deacon', *A History of British Secret Service* (London: 1980 edn), pp. 442–3; Christopher Andrew, *Secret Service: The Making of the British Intelligence Community* (London: 1985), pp. 489–90; Wright, op. cit., p. 36.
35 Andrew, op. cit., p. 490.
36 Wright, op. cit., pp. 32, 36–7.
37 Ibid., pp. 75, 120.
38 Ibid., pp. 58, 155–6, 358, 119.
39 Anthony Verrier, *Through the Looking Glass: British Foreign Policy in the Age of Illusions* (London: 1983), p. 66.
40 Edward F. Sayle, 'The historical underpinnings of the U.S. intelligence community', *International Journal of Intelligence and Counterintelligence*, vol. 1 (1986), p. 2.
41 Verrier, op. cit., ch. 3; Cavendish, op. cit., p. 53.
42 Jonathan Bloch and Patrick Fitzgerald, *British Intelligence and Covert Action* (Dingle, Ireland: 1983), p. 112; Verrier, op. cit., pp. 107–8; Chapman Pincher, *Inside Story* (London: 1978, paperback edn 1979), p. 90; Cavendish, op. cit., pp. 129–32.
43 Wright, op. cit., p. 155.
44 Bloch and Fitzgerald, op. cit., p. 31.
45 Ibid., pp. 121, 125–6; Verrier, op. cit., p. 158; Pincher, *Inside Story*, p. 90; Wright, op. cit., pp. 160–1.
46 Summers and Dorril, op. cit., paperback edn (London: 1988), 'Postscript'.
47 Wright, op. cit., pp. 31, 124, 360.
48 Peter Fleming, *The Sixth Column: A Singular Tale of our Times* (London: 1951), pp. 27–8, 164.
49 Duff Hart-Davis, *Peter Fleming* (London: 1974; paperback edn 1987), pp. 214–15, 327–9, 383–5.
50 Hennessy and Brownfeld, op. cit., p. 974.
51 Hyde, op. cit., p. 212.
52 Wright, op. cit., pp. 55–6.
53 *Hansard*, 5th series, vol. 730, cols 42, 1603–27, HC, 20 and 28 June 1966.
54 Mark Hollingsworth and Richard Norton-Taylor, *Blacklist: The Inside Story of Political Vetting* (London: 1988), pp. 97–103; *Observer*, 18 August 1985.
55 Bloch and Fitzgerald, op. cit., pp. 90–1; Wright, op. cit., p. 369.
56 Geoffrey Household, *A Time to Kill* (London: 1952; paperback edn 1971), p. 77.
57 George Wilkinson, *Special Branch Officer* (London: 1956), p. 12.
58 E.g. Tony Benn, *Office without Power*, Vol. II (London: 1988), p. 181.
59 Printed in *Lord Denning's Report*, Cmnd 2152 (London: 1963), p. 180.
60 Ibid., p. 80 (my emphasis).

10   Dungeons and dragons (1970–88)

1 Richard Clutterbuck, *Britain in Agony: The Growth of Political Violence* (London: 1978), p. 19.
2 Anthony Short, *The Communist Insurrection in Malaya 1948–1960* (London: 1975), p. 416.
3 Frank Kitson, *Low Intensity Operations: Subversion, Insurgency, Peace-Keeping* (London: 1971), pp. 7–8, 25, 71, 199–200.
4 *Lobster* (Hull), no. 11 [1986], pp. 41–2; Kennedy Lindsay, *The British Intelligence Services in Action* (Dundalk, Ireland: 1980); John Stalker, *Stalker* (London: 1988); Anthony Cavendish, *Inside Intelligence* (privately printed, 1987), pp. 153–6.

5   Home Office memorandum, 9 July 1984, printed in *House of Commons, Fourth Report from the Home Affairs Committee, Session 1984–5: Special Branch* (London: 1985), pp. 95–6.
6   Rupert Allason, *The Branch: A History of the Metropolitan Police Special Branch 1883–1983* (London: 1983), pp. 150, 162.
7   Geoff Robertson, *Reluctant Judas* (London: 1976).
8   *The Times*, 8 September 1988.
9   *Report from the Home Affairs Committee . . . Special Branch*, p. 118.
10 *Hansard*, 6th series, vol. 137, cols 1460–1, HC, 22 July 1988.
11 Clutterbuck, op. cit., p. 19.
12 Ian Greig, *The Assault on the West* (Petersham, Surrey: 1968), pp. 1–2.
13 'Richard Deacon', *The British Connection: Russia's Manipulation of British Individuals and Institutions* (London: 1979), chs 18, 19.
14 'Deacon', op. cit., p. 228; Josef Frolik, *The Frolik Defection* (London: 1975; paperback edn 1976), pp. 58–9.
15 *Hansard*, 5th series, vol. 941, cols 505–15, HC, 14 December 1977.
16 Chapman Pincher, *Inside Story* (London: 1978; paperback edn 1979), p. 70; *Their Trade Is Treachery* (London: 1981; paperback edn 1982), pp. 77–8.
17 George Shipway, *The Chilian Club* (London: 1971; paperback edn 1972), p. 190.
18 Barrie Penrose and Roger Courtiour, *The Pencourt File* (London: 1978), pp. 297–9, 315–17; Pincher, *Inside Story*, p. 135.
19 Penrose and Courtiour, op. cit., pp. 243–6.
20 Above, page 193.
21 Kitson, op. cit., p. 199.
22 Anderton speaking on BBC TV on 16 October 1979, and reported in the *Guardian*, 22 September 1980; and an undelivered speech reported in ibid., 17 March 1982.
23 Above, page 196.
24 *Report from the Home Affairs Committee . . . Special Branch*, p. 97; Douglas Hurd, quoted in the *Guardian*, 16 January 1989 (my emphasis).
25 Peter Wright, *Spycatcher: The Candid Autobiography of a Senior Intelligence Officer* (New York: 1987), pp. 359–61.
26 *Observer*, 30 October 1988.
27 Ibid., 24 February 1985; 'MI5's official secrets', *Twenty-Twenty Vision*, Granada TV, 8 March 1985.
28 *Guardian*, 20, 22 and 24 September 1983.
29 John Alderson, quoted in *Report from the Home Affairs Committee . . . Special Branch*, p. 55.
30 Penrose and Courtiour, op. cit., pp. 237–9.
31 *Observer*, 18 August 1985; *Hansard*, 6th series, vol. 102, cols 695–701, HC, 24 July 1986; Mark Hollingsworth and Richard Norton-Taylor, *Blacklist: The Inside Story of Political Vetting* (London: 1988), p. 100.
32 'The boys on the blacklist', 'The secret life of Ned Walsh' and 'Secrets of Wine Office Court', *World in Action*, Granada TV, 18 February 1987, 1 and 8 February 1988; *State Research Bulletin*, no. 7 (1978), pp. 135–43; Hollingsworth and Norton-Taylor, op. cit., ch. 7.
33 Tom Bowden, *Beyond the Limits of the Law* (Harmondsworth: 1978), p. 257; Hollingsworth and Norton-Taylor, op. cit., p. 212; 'The secret life of Ned Walsh', Granada TV, 1 February 1988.
34 Tom Clayton, *The Protectors* (London: 1967), p. 22; Bowden, op. cit., p. 256.
35 'The boys on the blacklist', Granada TV, 18 February 1987; *Labour Research*, vol. 74, no. 2 (February 1985), p. 34.

36 'After dark', Channel 4 TV, 16 July 1988; *Hansard*, 6th series, vol. 137, col. 1453, HC, 22 July 1988 (Merlyn Rees); *Lobster*, no. 16 (1988), pp. 25–9.

37 *Hansard*, 5th series, vol. 974, cols 437, 447, 449, HC, 21 November 1979.

38 Wright, op. cit., pp. 213–24.

39 Chapman Pincher, *A Web of Deception* (London: 1987; paperback edn 1988), p. 44.

40 Wright, op. cit., pp. 243–5.

41 *Hansard*, 6th series, vol. 78, cols 896–7, HC, 9 May 1985.

42 Penrose and Courtiour, op. cit., *passim*; *Lobster*, no. 11 [1986], *passim*; David Leigh, *The Wilson Plot* (London: 1988), *passim*.

43 *Hansard*, 5th series, vol. 936, col. 1216, HC, 28 July 1977; and cf. 'Deacon', op. cit., p. 258.

44 Christopher Andrew, *Secret Service: The Making of the British Intelligence Community* (London: 1985), p. 502; *Hansard*, 5th series, vol. 493, col. 226, HL, 10 February 1988.

45 'The spy who never was', *World in Action*, Granada TV, 16 July 1984; Wright, op. cit., pp. 368–72; 'The Wilson Plot', *Panorama*, BBC TV, 13 October 1988.

46 *Lobster*, nos. 11 [1986], 13 [n.d], 14 [n.d.]; *Channel 4 News*, Channel 4 TV, 26 June 1987.

47 *Lobster*, no. 11 [1986], pp. 45–51; 'A convenient conviction', Channel 4 TV, 8 July 1987; *Independent*, 2 September 1987.

48 E.g. Labour Campaign for Reform in the Security and Intelligence Services, *Forgery*, Occasional Publications No. 1 (Hull: 1988).

49 'The Wilson Plot', *Panorama*, BBC Television, 13 October 1988; *Sunday Express*, 15 November 1987.

50 *Channel 4 News*, 26 June 1987.

51 Above, page 195.

52 'Deacon', op. cit., p. 238.

53 *Lobster*, no. 11 [1986], pp. 2, 28, 33; *Hansard*, 6th series, vol. 125, col. 580, HC, 15 January 1988; Miranda Ingram, 'Trouble with security', *New Society*, 31 May 1984; Leigh, op. cit., p. 90.

54 *Hansard*, 5th series, vol. 494 cols 1149–50, HL, 16 March 1988; vol. 483, cols 178, 188, HL, 12 December 1986; 6th series, vol. 125 col. 612, HC, 15 January 1988.

55 Ibid., 5th series, vol. 974, cols 402–10, HC, 21 November 1979; 6th series, vol. 1, cols 1079–81, HC, 26 March 1981; 6th series, vol. 78, cols 895–96, HC, 9 May 1985.

56 Ibid., 5th series, vol. 974, cols 402–10, HC, 21 November 1979; 6th series, vol. 1, cols 1079–81, HC, 26 March 1981; 6th series, vol. 78, cols 895–96, HC, 9 May 1985; 6th series, vol. 106, col. 942, HC, 3 December 1986.

57 David Hooper, *Official Secrets: The Use and Abuse of the Act* (London: 1987), chs 10–12; *Daily Telegraph*, 12 February 1985.

58 'Wouldn't you like to know?', *World in Action*, Granada TV, 21 November 1988.

59 *Reform of Section 2 of the Official Secrets Act 1911*, Cmd 408 (London: 1988).

60 *Hansard*, 6th series, vol. 125, col. 631, HC, 15 January 1988.

61 Ibid., 6th series, vol. 139, col. 16, HC, 24 October 1988.

62 Noel Annan, 'Betrayal', *New York Review of Books*, 24 September 1987, p. 53.

63 *The Times*, Law report, 14 October 1988.

64 *Hansard*, 5th series, vol. 936, col. 1223, HC, 28 July 1977 (Dr Shirley Summerskill).

65 *Report from the Home Affairs Committee . . . Special Branch*, p. v.

66 *Hansard*, 6th series, vol. 115, col. 724, HC, 6 May 1987.

67 Ibid., 6th series, vol. 106, col. 943, HC, 3 December 1986 (Douglas Hurd); 5th series, vol. 494, col. 1164, HL, 16 March 1988 (Earl Ferrers).

68 Ibid., 5th series, vol. 493, col. 215, HL, 10 February 1988 (Lord Campbell of Croy).

69   Ibid., 6th series, vol. 106, col. 954, HL, 3 December 1986.
70   Ibid., 5th series, vol. 493, col. 229, HL, 10 February 1988 (Lord Kennet).
71   Ibid., 6th series, vol. 106, col. 145, HC, 3 December 1986; vol. 107, col. 800, HC, 15 December 1986.
72   *The Times*, 24 November 1988.
73   *City Limits*, 27 October 1988, p. 6; *Hansard*, 6th series, vol. 107, col. 784, 15 December 1986 (D. N. Campbell-Savours).
74   *Hansard*, 5th series, vol. 974, col. 413, HC, 21 November 1979; 5th series, vol. 494, col. 1152, HL, 16 March 1988.
75   Above, page 217.
76   Wright, op. cit., p. 350.
77   Ingram, op. cit.
78   John Rae in *Observer*, 6 April 1980.
79   Stalker, op. cit., *passim*.
80   Lars Olé Sauerberg, *Secret Agents in Fiction* (London: 1984), p. 5.
81   'John le Carré', *The Spy Who Came In from the Cold* (London: 1963; paperback edn 1964), p. 321.
82   Sun Tzü, ed. James Clavell, *The Art of War* (London: 1981), p. 92.
83   *Hansard*, 6th series, vol. 125, col. 590, HC, 15 January 1988.
84   Ibid., 6th series, vol. 142 cols 121–3, HC, 23 November 1988 (Douglas Hurd).
85   *Guardian*, 25 November 1987.
86   *Private Eye*, 23 December 1988; *Observer*, 29 January 1989.

Epilogue

1   Above, page 182.
2   John Costelloe, *Mask of Treachery* (London: 1988), pp. 353–4.
3   *Hansard*, 5th series, vol. 493, col. 229, HL, 10 February 1988.
4   See Frank Cain, *The Origins of Political Surveillance in Australia* (Sydney: 1983).
5   Quoted in Sissela Bok, *Secrets. On the Ethics of Concealment and Revelation* (Oxford: 1984), p. 25.

Further reading

The two best general histories of British intelligence are Christopher Andrew, *Secret Service: The Making of the British Intelligence Community* (London: Heinemann, 1985), and Phillip Knightley, *The Second Oldest Profession: The Spy as Bureaucrat, Patriot, Fantasist and Whore* (London: Deutsch, 1986). Neither goes back much before 1909, though Andrew has a 33-page 'Victorian prologue'. 'Richard Deacon', *A History of British Secret Service* (London: Muller, 1969; revised edn, Granada, 1980), is much fuller on the earlier periods, and the best of the more popular histories. All these books cover foreign as well as domestic intelligence.

There are special studies of a number of events and incidents involving domestic secret service activities in Britain over the past 200 years. Most of them are cited in the Notes. Here we shall confine ourselves to modern secondary works which treat these matters at some length, and not merely incidentally.

For the 1790s the best modern accounts of covert government counter-subversive measures in Britain and Ireland can be found in J. Ann Hone, *For the Cause of Truth: Radicalism in London 1796–1821* (Oxford: Clarendon Press, 1982); Roger Wells, *Insurrection: The British Experience, 1795–1803* (Gloucester: Alan Sutton, 1983); Marianne Elliott, *Partners in Revolution. The United Irishmen and France* (New Haven, Conn.: Yale University Press, 1982); and the same author's 'Irish republicanism in England: the first phase, 1797–9', in Thomas Bartlett and D. W. Hayton (eds), *Penal Era and Golden Age* (Belfast: Ulster Historical Foundation, 1979). These can be supplemented on the British side by the early chapters of E. P. Thompson, *The Making of the English Working Class* (London: Gollancz, 1963); and by Clive Emsley, 'The Home Office and its sources of information and investigation 1791–1801', *English Historical Review* (hereafter *EHR*), vol. 94 (1979) pp. 532–61. W. J. Fitzpatrick, *Secret Service under Pitt* (London: Longman, 1892), covers Irish espionage, whose funding is discussed in John F. McEldowney, 'Legal aspects of the Irish secret service fund, 1793–1833', *Irish Historical Studies* (hereafter *IHS*), vol. 25 (1986), pp. 129–37.

The part played by the Post Office in domestic intelligence is described in E. R. Turner, 'The secrecy of the Post', *EHR*, vol. 33 (1918) pp. 320–7; Kenneth Ellis, *The Post Office in the Eighteenth Century* (London: Oxford University Press, 1958), ch. 6 and appendices; the parliamentary *Report from the Secret Committee on the Post Office of 1844* (PP 1844 xiv); and in works on the Mazzini letter-opening affair (below).

The classic accounts of the turbulent 1810s are J. L. and Barbara Hammond, *The Skilled Labourer* (London: Longman, 1927), and E. P. Thompson, *The Making of the English Working Class*. A more recent contribution is Stanley H. Palmer, *Police and*

Plots and Paranoia

Protest in England and Ireland 1780–1850 (Cambridge: Cambridge University Press, 1988). Hammond and Thompson both devote a great deal of attention to the career of the notorious spy 'Oliver' in 1817. Another interpretation, defending Oliver, can be found in A. F. Fremantle, 'The truth about Oliver the Spy', *EHR*, vol. 47 (1932), pp. 601–16. Good general modern accounts of unrest and subversion and measures to counter them in this period are Malcolm I. Thomis, *The Luddites* (Newton Abbot: David & Charles, 1970); F. O. Darvall, *Popular Disturbances and Public Order in Regency England* (London: Oxford University Press, 1934); and R. J. White, *Waterloo to Peterloo* (London: Heinemann, 1957). All deal with the government's use of spies and informers. On specific plots and incidents, see John Stanhope, *The Cato Street Conspiracy* (London: Cape, 1962), which also covers an earlier incident involving the spy Castle; and P. B. Ellis and S. Mac A'Ghobhainn, *The Scottish Insurrection of 1820* (London: Gollancz, 1970).

The 1820s saw the formation of the earliest proper police forces, first in Ireland and then in Britain. Stanley H. Palmer (above) is good on this. Another sound account of the evolution of the Irish constabulary is Galen Broeker, *Rural Discontent and Police Reform in Ireland, 1812–36* (London: Routledge & Kegan Paul, 1970). For the London Metropolitan Police, the best book is Leon Radzinowicz, *A History of English Criminal Law and its Administration from 1750*, Vol. IV (London: Stevens, 1968), especially ch. 5. There is also a lot in the same volume on attitudes to 'espionage'; and (on pp. 184–9) an account of the Popay affair of 1833.

For the 1840s, domestic secret service activities against the Chartists are analysed in F. C. Mather, *Public Order in the Age of the Chartists* (Manchester: Manchester University Press, 1959), especially ch. 6. The Mazzini letter-opening affair is covered in Harry Rudman, *Italian Nationalism and English Letters* (London: Allen & Unwin, 1940), ch. 4; F. B. Smith, 'British Post Office espionage, 1844', *Historical Studies* (Melbourne), vol. 4 (1970) pp. 189–203; and in the works on Post Office history mentioned above. That last incident involved the surveillance of foreign refugees, which is treated more generally for the 1850s and 1860s in Bernard Porter, *The Refugee Question in Mid-Victorian Politics* (Cambridge: Cambridge University Press, 1979); and in Philip Thurmond Smith, *Policing Victorian London: Political Policing, Public Order, and the London Metropolitan Police* (Westport, Conn.: Greenwood Press, 1985).

Government measures to counter Irish-American Fenian plots in the 1860s are described in that last book, and in Leon O'Broin, *Fenian Fever: An Anglo-American Dilemma* (London: Chatto & Windus, 1971). The British government also employed a famous agent among the Fenians in America, whose story is recounted in J. A. Cole, *Prince of Spies: Henri Le Caron* (London: Faber, 1984), and in Charles Curran, 'The spy behind the Speaker's chair', *History Today*, vol. 18 (1968), pp. 745–54.

The 1880s saw renewed covert government activity against both Fenians and continental revolutionaries. Bernard Porter, 'The *Freiheit* prosecutions, 1881–1882', *Historical Journal* (hereafter *HJ*), vol. 23 (1980) pp. 833–56, deals with measures taken against German anarchists at the beginning of that decade. New counter-Fenian measures are described in K. R. M. Short, *The Dynamite War* (Atlantic Highlands, NJ: Humanities Press, 1979); Richard Hawkins, 'Government versus secret societies: the Parnell era', in T. Desmond Williams (ed.), *Secret Societies in Ireland* (Dublin: Gill & Macmillan, 1973); Charles Townshend, *Political Violence in Ireland* (Oxford: Clarendon Press, 1983); Leon O'Broin, *The Prime Informer: A Suppressed Scandal* (London: Sidgwick & Jackson, 1971); and Bernard Porter, *The Origins of the Vigilant State* (London: Weidenfeld & Nicolson, 1987), chs 3–5.

The bulk of *The Origins of the Vigilant State* traces the early history of the Metropolitan Police 'Special Branch' from the 1880s through to 1914. It can be supplemented by the same author's 'The historiography of the early Special Branch', *Intelligence and National Security* (hereafter *INS*), vol. 1 (1986), pp. 381–94; and 'Secrecy and the early Special Branch', *Bulletin of the Society for the Study of Labour History* (hereafter *BSSLH*), vol. 52 (1987), pp. 8–16. Rupert Allason, *The Branch: A History of the Metropolitan Police Special Branch 1883–1983* (London: Secker & Warburg, 1983) is more general, and not always reliable. Tony Bunyan, *The History and Practice of the Political Police in Britain* (London: Julian Friedmann, 1976), ch. 3, is better; and some general histories of the Metropolitan Police Force and the CID deal with the Special Branch briefly. An important new aspect of the Branch's work in the later 1900s is described in Richard Popplewell, 'The surveillance of Indian revolutionaries in Great Britain and on the Continent, 1908–14', *INS*, vol. 3 (1988), pp. 56–76.

Counter-espionage comes into the reckoning around 1910. The background to this is dealt with in David French, 'Spy fever in Britain, 1900–1915', *HJ*, vol. 21 (1978), pp. 355–70; A. J. A. Morris, The *Scaremongers* (London: Routledge, 1984); and two books by David A. Stafford on early spy novels: 'Spies and gentlemen', *Victorian Studies*, vol. 24 (1981), pp. 489–509, and 'Conspiracy and xenophobia: the popular spy novels of William Le Queux, 1893–1914', *Europe* (Montreal), vol. 4 (1981), pp. 163–85. The best accounts of the origins of MI5 are the general histories by Andrew and Knightley, and Nicholas Hiley, 'The failure of British counter-espionage against Germany, 1907–1914', *HJ*, vol. 28 (1985), pp. 835–62. Other more general histories of MI5 are John Bulloch, *MI5: The Origin and History of the British Counter-Espionage Service* (London: Barker, 1963); Tony Bunyan, *The History and Practice of the Political Police in Britain*; and 'Nigel West', *MI5: British Security Service Operations 1909–45* (London: Grafton Books, 1981).

Another product of the spy scare of the 1910s was the Official Secrets Act of 1911. Its history is dealt with in David Williams, *Not in the Public Interest: The Problem of Security in Britain* (London: Hutchinson, 1965); David Hooper, *Official Secrets: The Use and Abuse of the Act* (London: Secker & Warburg, 1987); David Leigh, *The Frontiers of Secrecy* (London: Junction Books, 1980), pp. 35–9; K. G. Robertson, *Public Secrets: A Study in the Development of Government Secrecy* (London: Macmillan, 1982), ch. 5; Patrick Birkinshaw, *Freedom of Information. The Law, the Practice and the Ideal* (London: Weidenfeld & Nicolson, 1988); and ch. 4 of the *Report of the Departmental Committee on Section 2 of the Official Secrets Act*, the 'Franks Report', Cmnd 5102, (London: HMSO, 1972). Alasdair Palmer, 'The history of the D-Notice committee', in C. Andrew and D. Dilks (eds), *The Missing Dimension* (London: Macmillan, 1984), pp. 227–49 relates to self-censorship by the press.

For the period of the First World War and just after, the best secondary accounts are Andrew, *Secret Service*, chs 5–9; Knightley, *The Second Oldest Profession*, ch. 3; and three important articles by Nicholas Hiley: 'Counter-espionage and security in Great Britain during the First World War', *EHR*, vol. 101 (1986), pp. 100–26; 'British internal security in wartime: the rise and fall of P.M.S.2, 1915–1917', *INS*, vol. 1 (1986), pp. 395–415; and (with Julian Putkowski), 'A postscript on P.M.S.2', *INS*, vol. 3 (1988), pp. 326–31. Raymond Challinor, *The Origins of British Bolshevism* (London: Croom Helm, 1977), pp. 144–7, describes secret service operations among opponents of the war in Britain. The army's postwar domestic intelligence function is described in Stephen R. Ward, 'Intelligence surveillance of British ex-servicemen, 1918–20', *HJ*, vol. 16 (1973), pp. 179–88; and in Keith Jeffrey, 'The British army and internal security 1919–1939', *HJ*, vol. 24 (1981), pp. 377–97. It is also worth looking at 'Richard Deacon', *A History of British Secret Service*, chs 15–20, and John Bulloch, *MI5*, chs 9–12.

After the war Ireland became, briefly, a prime focus for secret service activity. Events connected with intelligence leading up to that are treated in W. F. Mandle, 'Sir Antony

Plots and Paranoia

MacDonnell and Crime Branch Special', in Oliver MacDonagh and W. F. Mandle (eds), *Ireland and Irish Australia* (London: Croom Helm, 1986), pp. 175–94; Leon O'Broin, *Dublin Castle and the 1916 Rising* (Dublin: Helicon, 1966); and Eunan O'Halpin, 'The secret service vote and Ireland, 1868–1922', *IHS*, vol. 23 (1983), pp. 348–53. The best accounts of the 1920–21 crisis are Andrew, *Secret Service*, ch. 8; Charles Townshend, *The British Campaign in Ireland 1919–21* (London: Oxford University Press, 1975) and *Political Violence in Ireland*, especially ch. 7; Tom Bowden, *The Breakdown of Public Security: The Case of Ireland 1919–21 and Palestine 1936–39* (London: Sage, 1977), and the same author's *Beyond the Limits of the Law* (Harmondsworth: Penguin, 1978), ch. 7; and Eunan O'Halpin, 'British intelligence in Ireland, 1914–1921', in C. Andrew and D. Dilks (eds.), *The Missing Dimension*, pp. 54–77.

Special Branch and MI5 activities amongst mainland dissident groups in the later 1920s and 1930s are dealt with in Andrew, *Secret Service*, chs 9–11. Knightley, *The Second Oldest Profession*, ch. 3, and Bunyan, *Political Police in Britain*, chs 3–4, also touch on them. These can be supplemented by the following articles about the surveillance of left-wing political groups: Ralph Hayburn, 'The police and the hunger marchers', *International Review of Social History*, vol. 17 (1972), pp. 625–44; Harriette Flory, 'The Arcos raid and the rupture of Anglo-Soviet relations, 1927', *Journal of Contemporary History*, vol. 12 (1977), pp. 707–23; Royden Harrison, 'New light on the police and the hunger marches', *BSSLH*, no. 37 (1978), pp. 17–49; John Stevenson, 'The police and the 1932 hunger march', *BSSLH*, no. 38 (1979), pp. 24–7; Trevor Barnes, 'Special Branch and the first Labour government', *HJ*, vol. 22 (1979), pp. 941–51; Colin Holmes, 'The raid on the headquarters of the CPGB', *BSSLH*, no. 40 (1980), pp. 23–8; and Barbara Weinberger, 'Communism and the General Strike', *BSSLH*, no. 48 (1984), pp. 31–57. The episode of the Zinoviev letter is treated in L. Chester, S. Fay and H. Young, *The Zinoviev Letter* (London: Heinemann, 1967); and in Sibyl Crowe, 'The Zinoviev letter: a reappraisal', *Journal of Contemporary History*, vol. 10 (1975), pp. 407–32. The best account of the career of Olga Gray, who spied on the CPGB for MI5, is in Anthony Masters, *The Man Who Was M* (London: Blackwell, 1984), ch. 3.

Private enterprise activities in this field are described in Ron Bean, 'Liverpool shipping employers and the anti-communist activities of J. M. Hughes, 1920–1925', *BSSLH*, no. 34 (1977), pp. 22–6; Arthur McIvor, 'Political blacklisting and anti-socialist activity between the wars', *BSSLH*, vol. 53 (1988), pp. 18–26, and the same author's '"Crusade for capitalism": the Economic League, 1919–1939', *Journal of Contemporary History*, vol. 23 (1988), pp. 631–55. The Economic League's career can be followed through to the present day in *State Research Bulletin*, no. 7 (1978), pp. 135–43; Tony Bunyan, *Political Police in Britain*, ch. 6; Tom Bowden, *Beyond the Limits of the Law*, pp. 241–60; and Mark Hollingsworth and Richard Norton-Taylor, *Blacklist: The Inside Story of Political Vetting* (London: Hogarth Press, 1988), ch. 7.

For MI5 and Special Branch surveillance of the far Right between the wars, see Paul Cohen, 'The police, the Home Office and surveillance of the British Union of Fascists', *INS*, vol. 1 (1986), pp. 416–34; Richard Thurlow, *Fascism in Britain: A History, 1918–1985* (Oxford: Blackwell, 1987); and the latter's article 'British fascism and state surveillance, 1934–45', *INS*, vol. 3 (1988), pp. 77–99.

The Second World War brings us back to counter-espionage, which is treated generally for this period in Andrew, *Secret Service*, chs 12–14; Knightley, *The Second Oldest Profession*, chs 22–4; and 'Nigel West', *MI5*, part III. On Maxwell Knight of MI5, see Anthony Masters, *The Man Who Was M*; Joan Miller, *One Girl's War* (Dingle, Ireland: Brandon, 1986); and Eric Homberger, '"Uncle Max" and his thrillers', *INS*, vol. 3 (1988), pp. 312–21. Thurlow's *Fascism in Britain*, ch. 9, his article 'British fascism and state surveillance' (above), and Peter and Leni Gillman, *'Collar the Lot!' How Britain Interned and Expelled its Wartime Refugees* (London: Quartet, 1980), all have a great deal on MI5's contribution to the policy of internment. The libertarian implications of government efforts to counter subversion are dealt with in Neil Stammers, *Civil Liberties in Britain during the Second World War* (London: Croom Helm, 1983). Finally, MI5's 'double-cross' system, for using Germany's own spies against her, is described in detail in J. C. Masterman, *The Double Cross System in the War of 1939–1945* (New Haven, Conn.: Yale University Press, 1972).

After 1945 we are treading on very soft ground indeed. 'Nigel West' has published characteristic histories of all the main security services in this period. Those relevant to us are: *A Matter of Trust: MI5 1945–72* (London: Weidenfeld & Nicolson, 1982); *GCHQ: The Secret Wireless War 1900–86* (London: Weidenfeld & Nicolson, 1986), chs 7–10; and (under his real name, Rupert Allason) *The Branch*, chs 9–12. Geoff Robertson, *Reluctant Judas* (London: Temple Smith, 1976), is about the life and violent death in 1974 of an alleged Special Branch informer, Kenneth Lennon. It is also worth looking at the *Fourth Report from the Home Affairs Committee of the House of Commons, Session 1984–5, on the Special Branch* (London: HMSO, 1985); and at Tony Bunyan's book (above).

Critiques of the security services started appearing in the later 1970s, and have proliferated since. Examples are: Carol Ackroyd, Karen Margolis, Jonathan Rosenhead and Tim Shallice, *The Technology of Political Control* (London: Pluto, 1977); Tom Bowden, *Beyond the Limits of the Law*; E. P. Thompson, 'The secret state', in *Writing by Candlelight* (London: Merlin, 1980), pp. 149–80; 'News Line', *Britain's State within the State* (London: New Park Publications, n.d.); Kennedy Lindsay, *The British Intelligence Services in Action* (Dundalk, Ireland: Dunrod Press, 1980); the series of articles on 'Security' by Duncan Campbell published in the *New Statesman* between 1 February and 11 April 1980; Crispin Aubrey, *'Who's Watching You?'* (Harmondsworth: Penguin, 1981); Jonathan Bloch and Patrick Fitzgerald, *British Intelligence and Covert Action* (Dingle, Ireland: Brandon, 1983), which also has a great deal on MI5 and MI6 'covert operations' abroad; the Labour Party, *Freedom and the Security Services* (London: Labour Party, 1983); and Mark Hollingsworth and Richard Norton-Taylor, *Blacklist*. Two journals dedicated to uncovering and monitoring this kind of thing are *State Research* (London; begun in 1977, now defunct), and *Lobster* (Hull; 1983–present).

There is no shortage of literature on the Russian 'moles' who infiltrated the security services and other areas of government before and during the war. Some of the better-known books are: B. Page, D. Leitch and P. Knightley, *The Philby Conspiracy* (New York: Doubleday, 1968); Andrew Boyle, *The Climate of Treason* (London: Hutchinson, 1979); H. Montgomery Hyde, *The Atom Bomb Spies* (London: Hamish Hamilton, 1980); Chapman Pincher, *Their Trade Is Treachery* (London: Sidgwick & Jackson, 1981), *Too Secret Too Long* (London: Sidgwick & Jackson, 1984) and *A Web of Deception* (London: Sidgwick & Jackson, 1987); Barry Penrose and Simon Freeman, *Conspiracy of Silence: The Secret Life of Anthony Blunt* (London: Grafton, 1986); 'Nigel West', *Molehunt* (London: Weidenfeld & Nicolson, 1987); Peter Wright, *Spycatcher* (New York: Viking Penguin, 1987); Anthony Glees, *The Secrets of the Service: British Intelligence and Communist Subversion 1939–51* (London: Cape, 1987); Phillip Knightley, *Kim Philby: KGB Masterspy* (London: Deutsch, 1988); Robert Cecil, *A Divided Life: A Biography of Donald Maclean* (London: Bodley Head, 1988); and John Costello, *Mask of Treachery* (London: Collins, 1988). One of the outcomes of the controversy about 'moles' in the civil and security services was 'positive vetting': on which see P. Hennessy and G. Brownfield, 'Britain's cold war security purge; the origins of positive vetting', *HJ*, vol. 25 (1982), pp. 965–73.

On the scope of the domestic activities of the British security services since the war the most revealing account - if it is reliable - is Peter Wright's *Spycatcher*. His allegations of an MI5 plot against the Wilson government of 1974–6 were first published by Chapman Pincher in *Inside Story* (London: Sidgwick & Jackson, 1978), and by Barrie Penrose and Roger Courtiour in *The Pencourt File* (London: Secker & Warburg, 1978). More recently *Lobster* – especially issue nos 11, 13 and 14 – and David Leigh, *The Wilson Plot: The Intelligence Services and the Discrediting of a Prime Minister 1945-1976* (London: Heinemann, 1988) have elaborated them. Paul Foot, *Who Framed Colin Wallace?* (London: Macmillan, 1988), may be the most important of these exposés, but appeared too late for its evidence and conclusions to be considered here. Since the 'Wilson plot' allegations, other people have been discovering similar plots agaist *them*. Two very different ones are described in Peter Hain, *A Putney Plot?* (London: Spokesman, 1987), and in John Stalker, *Stalker* (London: Harrap, 1988).

Index

Index

Index

Index

God, first spymaster 2; threatened abolition 44
Golitsin, Anatoli 203, 210
Gordievsky, Oleg 183
'Gordon, Alex', *see* Rickard, William
Gosselin, Nicholas 104, 107, 110, 113, 119, 124, 231
Government Code and Cipher School (GC & CS) 161, 189
Government Communications Headquarters (GCHQ) 17, 78, 189, 199, 215; trade union ban (1984) 220
Graham, Sir James 73, 77–8
Grahame, Kenneth 125
Gray, Olga 172–3
Gray, Private 147
Great Exhibition (1851) 87, 91
Great War, *see* First World War
Greece, ancient 3
Greene, Benjamin 178
Greene, Hugh Carleton 198
Greenwich Park bomb (1894) 114, 116–17
Grey, second Earl 42, 44, 50, 53, 70, 73
Grivas, Colonel 189–90
Grosvenor, second Earl 53
Guildford bomb (1974) 223
Gwynn, Nell 15

habeas corpus, suspensions of (1790–1820) 38, 43, 53, 58
Hagn, Karl 139
Haig, Sir Douglas 148–9
Haigh, Madeleine 206
Hall, Sir Reginald, and Casement 141–2, 167; removal from NID 155–6; founder of Economic League 145; on Irish failures 155; supports Thomson 157–8, 163; involved in Zinoviev affair 166
Hamilton, Willie 208
Hampden Clubs 43–4
Hanley, Michael 222
Hannington, Wal 160–1, 164
Hannon, Patrick 144
Harcourt, William Vernon 102–9 *passim*
Hardie, Andrew 59–60, 79
Hardy, Thomas 33, 37
Harley, Robert 16
Harold, King 10
Hart, Judith 206, 210
Hastings, battle of 10
Hastings, Stephen 203, 210
Hattersley, Roy 225
Hazlitt, William 53
Healey, Dennis 218
Heath, Edward, and miners' strike 202; Czech trap for? 203; orders surveillance of broad left? 205; secret service plot against?

210–11, 219, 229; on security services 213–14
Helm, Siegfried 128
Henry V, King 10
Henry, Edward 116, 124
Hentschel, Karl 128
Heseltine, Michael 215
Hicks, Sir William Joynson 162
Hill, Sir Rowland 78
Hinsley, Sir F.H. 177
historical records, access xii, 161, 230–1, 233; *see also* evidence
Hittites 2
Hitler, Adolf 173, 175, 177
Hoare, Sir Samuel 142
hoax bombs 115
Hobhouse, John Cam 61
Hoche, Lazare 27
Holden, Robert 35
Holland, third Baron and Lady 76
Hollis, Sir Roger 179, 181–14, 213–14, 228–9
Holt-Wilson, Sir Eric 231
Home Affairs Committee report on Special Branch (1985) 200, 217
Home Office 28; employment of spies in 1790s 29–31, 35, 39; in 1810s 62; reduced in 1840s 73, 75–6; ignorant of Sanders's methods (1850s) 92; ban on public meetings in Hyde Park (1866) 86; survey of socialism (1871) 96; and Fenians (1866–7, 1880s) 97–9, 103–5, 108; on MacIntyre's revelations 114; relationship with MI5 195, 218
Home Office Intelligence Bureau (1867–8) 98
home rule, *see* Irish home rule
homosexuality 171–2, 187, 203, 209
Hoover, Herbert 189
Horst, Baron von 121
Horwood, Sir William 157–8, 163, 168
Household, Geoffrey 194
Household Words 88–9
Hoxha, Enver 190
Hughes (Bishop of New York) 87
Humbert, King of Italy 114
Humbert, Jean 27
'Humint' 82, 175
hunger marches, surveillance of (1930s) 161
Hunt, Henry 49, 65, 79
Hunt, Leigh 53
Hurd, Douglas 205, 214, 218
Hyde, Douglas 179, 192
Hyde Park, Great Exhibition (1851) 87; riots (1855 and 1866) 85–6; Thomson arrested in (1925) 158

imperialism 84, 121, 142, 144; *see also* Empire
Incitement to Disaffection Act (1934) 163

Index

Index

Lee, William Melville 145
Leeds soviet (1917) 143
Leeds Mercury 50, 53
Lees, Robert 59
Lefebure, John 20
Legitimation League 117, 119
Lenin, Vladimir 118, 143
Letts 130
Leving, William 19
liberal capitalism, *see* free marketism
Liberal Party 123, 142, 166
liberalism, *see* liberty; whiggism
liberty, early notions of 9–10, 54–5, 60, 68–9
Littlechild, John 110–11, 115, 117
Litvinoff, Maxim 143
Liverpool 74, 85, 97
Liverpool, Lord 44, 49, 55–6, 60, 65
Lloyd George, David 122, 142, 145, 156–7
Local Government Board bomb (1883) 101
Lody, Karl 134, 138
London Bridge bomb (1884) 101
London Corresponding Society 31–2, 36
London Metropolitan Police, *see* Metropolitan Police
Louis, King of Portugal 118
Louis Napoleon, *see* Napoleon III
Louis XIV 9
Low Intensity Operations 198–9, 205
loyalties of MI5, transcending governments 141, 163, 167, 203
Luddism 42–3, 45–9, 61, 221, 232
Lunt (spy) 15, 19
Lynam, George 31, 33–5, 38

McCarthy, Justin 97
Macaulay, Thomas Babington 67, 77
McCarthyism 187
McCormick, Donald 202
McCullen, J. 52, 56
MacDermott, 'Red Jim' 107–8
MacDonald (informer) 47
MacDonald, James Ramsay 146, 150, 159–60, 163, 166
McGill, George 165, 173
Machiavelli, Nicolo 8, 11, 23, 26
McIntyre, Patrick 113–14, 117, 185
Mackenzie, Peter 65
McKinley, William 114
Mackintosh, Charles Rennie 137–8
Macky, John 16
Maclean, Donald 179–83 *passim*, 185–7, 208
MacNaghten, Melville 115, 118, 134–5
McNally, Leonard 32–3
MacNeill, Eoin 152
Macready, Nevil 133, 153, 158
mail interception 10; *see also* Post Office
Maitland, General 45

Malaya 198
'management' 221; of MI5 217, 225
Manchester 42–3, 56, 96, 205
Manchester Guardian 149
Manners, Societies for the Reformation of 21
Mansion House London bomb (1881) 101
Manteuffel, Baron 88, 91
Mar, eleventh Earl 20
Margaret, Princess 203
Marlowe, Christopher 12, 15
Marx, Karl 91, 95, 98, 143–4, 229
Marxism 191, 239; *see also* communist threat
Mary, Queen of Scots 14
Massie, William 212
Massiter, Cathy 206, 217
Masterman, J.C. 177
'Mata Hari' 139–40
Maude (spy) 19–20
Maugham, Somerset 169–70
Maule, Sir William 79
May, Alan Nunn 179
May, Erskine 89
Mayne, Sir Richard 79, 87, 91
Mayo, sixth Earl 83
Mazzini, Giuseppe 77
Melville, William 113–7, 119, 127, 135
Metropolitan Police, early history 69–73; political work (1850–80) 89–98 *passim*; political work after 1880, *see* Special Branch *and* Special Irish Branch; strikes (1918–19) 143; foreign recruitment in Britain 118; *see also* Criminal Investigation Department; detective branch; police
Meunier, Théodule 116
MI5, founded (1909) 120, 125, 127; recruits Melville 115–16; counter-espionage (1909–14) 128–9; First World War growth 133, 135, 137–40 *passim*, 145–6, 151; loses out to Special Branch after War 146; connexions with private agencies 165–6; recovers counter-subversive role in 1930s 168–74 *passim*; Second World War 176–80; Soviet penetration 180–5 *passim*; rivalry with MI6 182–3, 199, 211; post-War reforms 187–9; covert operations in colonies 190; shift to counter-subversion (*c.*1970) 191–6 *passim*, 205; alleged excesses (1970s) 190, 197, 199–201, 206–7, 219–21; controversy over continued Soviet penetration 208–10; 'Wilson plot' allegations 211–14, 217, 219 *et passim*, 229; reforms (1989) 218–19; character and ethos 169–72, 221–2, 231, 233
MI6, founded 120; First World War 'spy school' 135; assists MI5 138; report from Russia 142; intercepts Zinoviev letter 166; personnel 169, 171, 182, 222; Soviet

270

Index

penetration 179, 181, 185; rivalry with MI5 182–3, 199, 211; and Penkovsky 184; covert operations (1949–56) 190; redundant? 189
middle ages 7, 10–11, 16
military, *see* army
military conscription, *see* conscription
military intelligence, mediaeval 10; C19th neglect 82; *see also* Army intelligence
Millen, F.F. 97, 107
Miller, Joan 170, 172, 178–9, 216
miners' strikes (1911) 133; (1972, 1974) 202; (1984) 220
Ministry of Defence 215
Ministry of Munitions 145–6
Mitchell, Graham 182
Mitchell, James 59
mixed economy 191, 229
'moles', *see* Soviet penetration
Monro, James 105–7, 109–10, 112, 115, 124, 157, 168
Morel, Edmund Dene 141
Morley, John 130
Morton, Desmond 167
Moscow gold 143, 162
Moses 2
Mosley, Oswald 173–4, 178
Mossadeq, Mohammed 190
Most, Johann 102
Mountbatten, first Earl 204
Müller, Karl Friedrich 138–9, 177
Mullins, (Chartist) 79
Munday, Anthony 13
Murphy, Patrick 85–6
Murray, Gary 207
Murrell, Hilda 207
Murrey, James 56–7, 62
mutinies (1797) 27; (1914–18) 136; (1918–19) 143, 147

Nally, Patrick 112
Napier, Sir Charles 74
Naples plot (1855) 82
Napoleon Bonaparte 41, 54
Napoleon III 91, 93
Nasser, Gamal Abdel 189–90
National Council for Civil Liberties, surveillance of (1930s) 161, 164
National Political Union 71
'national security' argument for secrecy 19, 194, 220, 231
National Unemployed Workers' Movement 160
naturalization investigations 95, 98; Act (1844) 77
Naval intelligence 141, 145, 156, 166
Naval mutinies, *see* mutinies
Nazis, *see* fascists

Neave, Airey 219
Neligan, David 154
Nero 4
Newell, Edward 33, 36, 40
Nield, Sir Herbert 155, 157
Nizam al-Mulk 5, 8–9
'No.8', *see* Burns
Normanby, first Marquis 73
Northern Ireland 156, 163, 198–9, 211–13, 223
Nottingham riots (1831) 66
Nugent, Baron 54–5
Numbers, Book of 2

O'Brien, Smith 74
O'Connor, Arthur 30
O'Connor, Feargus 78, 87
O'Connor, T.P. 149
Odysseus 2
Official Secrets Act (1911/20) 120, 127–8, 133, 150, 163, 177, 215, 218
Official Secrets Bill (1989) 200, 215, 217–18, 226
Okhrana 8
'old boy net' 186; *see also* public schools
Oldfield, Maurice 212
Oliphant, Laurence 82
'Oliver the Spy' (William Richards) 50–2, 55–7, 60–1, 63, 79, 148
Orsini Plot (1858) 91–2, 94, 110
Owens, Bill 177
Oxbridge 188; *see also* Cambridge moles

pacifists 136–7, 140, 178; *see also* Campaign for Nuclear Disarmament
Pall Mall Gazette 108
Palmerston, third Viscount 91, 93
Panizzi, Antonio 82
Pankhurst, Emmeline 131
paranoia 11, 18, 111, 166–7, 210, 213–14, 224, 232
Paris 9, 131; Commune (1871) 95, 134
Parliamentary reform, *see* Reform
Parnell, Charles Stewart 111–12, 149
Parnell Commission (1888–9) 111–13, 167
Parry, William 14, 19–20, 37
partisan use of secret service 113, 163, 167, 206, 210, 233–4
'Party Piece, Operation' 192
paternalism 9, 149
patriotism, early C19th radical 54, 62; 20th right-wing 113, 121–2, 136, 141, 203, 213, 220; German 134; *see also* loyalties of MI5
Peel, Sir Robert 69–71, 79
Pembrokeshire invasion (1797) 27, 40
penetration, *see* Soviet penetration
Penkovsky, Oleg 184
Pentrich rebellion (1817) 43, 50–1, 53

271

Index

Index

Index

Index